THE MAKING OF A LEADER

Michael + Lara
Rasmussen
09/07

THE MAKING OF A LEADER

Frank Damazio

Foreword By
C. Peter Wagner

DEDICATION

I dedicate this book to three spiritual fathers who have had significant influence upon my life and ministry. First, I acknowledge Pastor Leonard Fox, from San Bernardino, California, who laid the first Christian foundations in my life. Next, I recognize Pastor Dick Iverson, of Portland, Oregon, for his words of wisdom that have continually given me godly direction. Finally, I show my appreciation to Kevin Conner, from Melbourne, Australia, who has given me many keys to the Word of God, countless hours of personal, fatherly instruction, and a beautiful wife, his daughter, who has encouraged me over the last five years of the writing of this book.

Published by City Bible Publishing
9200 NE Fremont
Portland, Oregon 97220

Printed in U.S.A.

City Bible Publishing is a ministry of City Bible Church and is dedicated to serving the local church and its leaders through the production and distribution of quality materials.

It is our prayer that these materials, proven in the context of the local church, will equip leaders in exalting the Lord and extending His kingdom.

For a free catalog of additional resources from City Bible Publishing, please call 1-800-777-6057 or visit our web site at www.citybiblepublishing.com.

The Making of a Leader
© Copyright 1988 by Frank Damazio

ISBN 0-914936-84-0

Table of Contents
THE MAKING OF A LEADER

FOREWORD

In the life of today's church there is no issue more crucial than leadership. We live in a time of great worldwide harvest with tens of thousands coming to Christ each day. But, unfortunately, many of those who express a desire to follow Jesus end up in the world once again because there has been no church to fold them into Christian fellowship. The major reason for this is the lack of church leadership. Evangelism speeds along in high gear while leadership training has barely shifted into first.

Frank Damazio, and many others like him, see this issue clearly and they have set out to do something about it. One of the principal reasons the Pentecostal and charismatic movements are decidedly outpacing the traditional churches in their growth rates is that they have recognized the fact that traditional forms of selecting and training people for pastoral ministry are woefully outmoded.

Many independent charismatic leaders are bypassing the established seminary system in preparing people for ordination. While they are teachers, they are also doers of the Word. Frank Damazio stands out among them because he is a doer who also has an enviable capacity to analyze what he is doing, to write it in clear, understandable prose, and thereby to pass valuable insights on to others.

I regard *The Making of a Christian Leader* as a highly important document in contemporary Christianity. In it Frank Damazio explains in fascinating detail the cutting edge philosophy of church leadership representing what I consider a wave of the future as we move into the third millenium.

I hope this book is widely circulated and taken to heart not only by those Pentecostals and charismatics already congenial to its approach, but even more importantly by those responsible for training the future leadership in mainline and evangelical traditions. Only as they do so will it be possible to shift gears and allow leadership training to keep pace with what God is doing in our world.

C. Peter Wagner
Fuller Theological Seminary
Pasadena, California

INTRODUCTION

Human history gives lengthy endorsement to the fact that no generation can rise above the level of its leadership. Nations rise and fall according to the effectiveness of their governments. These truths are also applied to businesses, organizations, churches, families and individuals. It's a fact that when leadership falters, followers are hurt, scattered and become easy prey for predators. And when leaders are destroyed, lawlessness prevails. It is imperative therefore, that men and women, young and old, dare respond to the Call of God and choose to become strong and reliable Christian leaders of integrity. The miracle of godly leadership is possible because God Himself promises to inject His Presence, character, wisdom and ability upon surrendered followers who will be subject to His guidance. The task is not always easy for His ways are higher than our ways. The path of righteousness is endowed with both trials and blessings. God gave His Best . . . and He expects *your best* in return. Are you willing to do whatever is necessary to maximize your leadership potential for His glory? This is what this book is all about . . . **The Making of a Leader.**

I wrote the original text while I was teaching this subject at the Portland Bible College. Because the content is born out of a classroom educational setting, you will consequently be challenged to study and wrestle with deep biblical mandates, parables and principles. You will be drawn into marvelous learning cycles in which your mind will be awakened to envision new truths, grasp spiritual insights, and thereby grow into that special calling and destiny God has empowered you to fulfill. I desire that you be a champion in Christ! It is my single-minded goal as an author and teacher/pastor to excell in every gift I possess to enable and equip you to *see* and become all God has for you. I believe the roots of biblical study and training is the vigorous tradition that has extended the Gospel to every generation. Leaders are born as well as prepared and guided into maximizing their potentials as servants and pillars in the house of God. The mark of a dynamic leader is clearly manifested in whatever he puts his hand to. It is therefore my hope that Christian leaders will devote their priorities to again place the church in the focal point of society.

We need to raise up modern day Daniels who will boldly speak the uncompromising Word of God amidst the crushing pressures and temptations of this modern day Babylon society. The Goliaths are taunting our Christ-less society which flounders without Biblical roots. The jeering giants of the enemy are taking control by misguiding a confused and troubled nation through humanism, secularism, new age thinking and cults of every description. The Goliaths of drugs, alcohol, pornography, violence and sexual permissiveness are evidenced in every neighborhood as well as on the screens of television and movies. These seemingly insurmountable obstacles need to be attacked by a new breed of Christian leadership. We need anointed leaders like David who said to his men, "Pursue . . . overtake the enemy . . . recover all!"

Are you anointed to serve and lead? Only the true anointing of God can equip a Christian leader with power from on high. God can do what man cannot . . . and He will do it through you if you are dedicated to penetrate this hard-hearted generation with the Word of God. I challenge you to immerse yourself in His Word, in this book, and view my seven hour video teaching sessions on *Maximizing Your Leadership Potential*. If you do these things, I have faith that God will indeed bless you with vision and holy determination to change our world for the cause of Christ.

Keep moving forward!

Sincerely,

Pastor Frank Damazio

CHAPTER 1
THE NATURE
OF LEADERSHIP

Every century the Church struggles through leadership failures. Sometimes these come in a pattern that follows the rise and fall of economic growth. Times of prosperity seem to foreshadow a rise in carnality and spiritual disease in the Church.

The Church in America has certainly experienced this in the 1980s. A number of very prominent Christian leaders underwent dramatic, highly publicized moral failures. The very mass media that enlarged some of these ministries have amplified the impact of their fall. Have leadership failures in the Church ever been so shocking or morally repugnant? Unfortunately, a look through history shows us they have been this bad and worse. Perhaps it only seems worse in our time because the whole world knows.

Can anyone doubt that God is allowing the Church to be shaken? The Church needs more than "damage control" to try to survive this dismal period. The Church must rebuild its leadership on the solid, biblical foundation of anointed servanthood.

One of the keys to helping the Church move forward is the person reading this book. You. If you answer God's call to genuine service, God will use you. But you need to know that your ability to relate successfully to leadership will determine the fruitfulness of your service. And that's true whether you serve in a governmental leadership role in the Church, or in a supportive congregational ministry.

What is the nature of true Christian leadership? What's wrong with current popular notions on the subject, and how can we reach a godly understanding? Chapters One and Two of The Making of a Leader will help us recover a scriptural definition of Christian leadership.

The Twisted Image
Changing Definitions of Leadership
Mention the word "leadership" and many concepts appear in people's minds. Some of these

popular concepts are too vague and general, and others are more worldly than biblical. Many popular concepts focus on what a leader does:

Goes ahead or in advance of, acts as a guiding force
Motivates people toward a certain purpose or goal
Draws people into a certain course of action through persuasion or example
Gives direction and structure to others' work and efforts
Advises and coordinates others' ideas
Leads others into a life of holiness by example
Holds the authority to lead others by instruction or correction

These definitions of leadership are good, but they are too general. Today the Church needs concepts of leadership that are both biblical and specific. One of the purposes of this book is to provide more specific and biblical definitions of leadership.

Some concepts of Church leadership are merely carry-overs from non-Christian contexts. Such popular concepts owe more to business principles than to Scripture. Granted, Church leadership needs to know how to balance its books, manage its time, delegate responsibilities, and cut back its less useful programs. However, the Church is not just a spiritual equivalent to a General Motors or a Georgia Pacific.

God has given certain principles in His Word by which His leadership and Church are to function. If the practices of business executives take priority over the specific guidelines of the Word of God, the Church will be a large but lifeless organization (as many churches are today), instead of a growing and lively spiritual organism. If administrative methods replace the spiritual principles of God's Word, then the Church will be like a wineskin without the wine (Mark 2:21,22).

Many Church leaders who have been taught business practices by our seminaries and universities have too often viewed the Body of Christ as a worldly business. Leaders who view the Church as a corporation, instead of a New Covenant community, also tend to see the Church's programs as marketing tools. They tend to see services as business meetings, instead of anticipations of God's voice. They see Church government as a democracy or a dictatorship, rather than a servanthood. These leaders view themselves as presidents and CEOs, instead of God-ordained servants. They see Church members as individual stockholders, instead of Christians with vital ministries.

These business-based attitudes have robbed the Church of her spiritual life and vitality. They have increased the scaffolding but decreased the lively stones of God's building (I Peter 2:1-9). They have emphasized scholarship over sainthood, professionalism over Holy Spirit unction, and the external over the internal. Such professionalism tends to replace God's ways with man's ways, presenting the constant danger of hypocrisy and spiritual destitution.

Jesus Himself criticized the professional externalism of the religious leaders of His day, because they had become hypocrites (Matthew 23:1-39). They had worked hard to accumulate intellectual knowledge, but weren't accountable to practice what they had learned. These Scribes and Pharisees found it far easier to study Scripture than to live it.

So it is with many of our leadership-training institutions. They emphasise knowledge above action; degrees rather than the decrease that John the Baptist described when he said, *"He must increase but I must decrease"* (John 3:30).

Tragically, today's over-emphasis on academic degrees has contributed to the pride, hypocrisy, and spiritual lifelessness in many of the Church's leaders. As we shall see in the Bible, God does not emphasise the academic development of His leaders as much as their development in character, wisdom and piety. God does not put any premium on ignorance, but that does not mean that He puts His priority on academic training.

Why has so much of the Church twisted God's biblical standards into a total opposite of their original image? One reason is the change in our understanding of true biblical leadership. The introduction of the terms "clergy" and "laity" have contributed to this misunderstanding. Before dealing with the principles of leadership preparation, we must first examine these leadership concepts. We will examine the definition, background and influence of these two words before dealing biblically with the concepts which they attempt to describe.

"Clergy" vs. "Laity"

In their application to the Church of Jesus Christ, the terms "clergy" and "laity" contain seeds both of truth and falsehood. It is true that the New Testament presents two general distinctions of ministry. But in doing so, the New Testament never uses the words "clergy" and "laity," or their root meanings.

The New Testament presents all Christians as ministers in the sense that all have definite ministries to perform in the Body of Christ. The New Testament does designate two different general functions in the Church, which we refer to as governmental and congregational. But this general distinction is never made in an attitude of complete superiority of one over the other, as has been the general understanding of clergy being superior to laity.

The relationship between the governmental and congregational ministries is similar to the biblical relationship of a husband to his wife. The husband and wife are equal as persons, but do differ in their specific function or role. Similarly, the governmental and the congregational ministries in the Body are equal as persons, but different and unique in the functions that they perform. The terms "clergy" and "laity" are misleading, because they have come to suggest unbiblical distinctions between Christians in the Church.

Today we generally understand the word "clergy" to apply to the group of ordained persons in a religion, as distinguished from the "laity," or common people. It is interesting, however, to note the source of the distinction. The word "clergy" derives from an Old English word meaning "clerk," which is derived from the ecclesiastical Latin word, "clericus," which means "priest." Thus the concept of a clergy is historically equivalent to the concept of a priesthood. Note what the Oxford English Dictionary states about the cultural background of the word "clerk":

"The original sense [of a clerk] was a man in a religious order . . . as the scholarship of the Middle Ages was practically limited to the clergy, and these performed all the writing, notarial and secretarial work of the time; the name "clerk" came to be equivalent to "scholar" and specially applicable to a notary, secretary, recorder, accountant or penman. The last [i.e., penman] has come to be the ordinary sense, all the others being either archaic, historical, formal, or contextual."

The Middle Ages concept of clergy as scholars has carried over to the religious thinking of our day. This association has made people think that clergy are scholars, and in order to be a member of the clergy, one must be a scholar. But the New Testament does not put scholarship before the condition of sainthood or having a shepherd's heart as necessary qualifications for those in the ministry.

Some important examples from the New Testament will verify this. Even Paul (a favorite example of those who support scholarly emphases in the Church, because of his training under the scholar Gamaliel) puts greater emphasis on shepherding, character and preaching the cross of Jesus Christ than on scholarship in his epistles. (For examples, see I Corinthians 1:3,13; I Timothy 3; Titus 1.) It is interesting to note that Paul, a trained and noted scholar of his day, was sent primarily to the Gentiles, an ignorant and unlearned people. On the other hand, Peter, the ignorant, unlearned fisherman, was sent to the Jewish people, the theologians of their day. God's ways are different from our ways.

Today the Church has managed to think that scholars are the best prepared ministers, and that the best preparation for the ministry is an academic one. Such an over-emphasis has helped to cause several problems. Many take pride in their position as ministers ("knowledge puffs up"). A theological vocabulary has developed, which is totally inaccessible to the average person. An intellectualism has developed which renders many unable to meet the practical needs of the people of God, and which has even led many to deny the divine authority of Jesus Christ and His Word. It is sometimes true that "Theologians have a gentle habit of playing by themselves in a walled garden shut off from the public view and using a language which nobody else understands."

Historically, as the Church of Jesus Christ became politically identified with the non-Christian world around her, she also became educationally and professionally identified with the world. The question of how much and what kind of education was necessary to prepare people for the Christian ministry has been a subject of controversy in American seminary education since the founding of America's first theological college, Harvard.

The original purpose of Harvard College was to train men to preach the Gospel of Jesus Christ. Students were required to read the Bible devotionally twice a day, and had to obtain permission from their teachers to travel out of town on visits. Today, however, Harvard has greatly strayed from its original purpose. It stands as a representative example of what has happened in many of our seminaries and divinity schools. Simply stated, academic requirements have replaced biblical requirements for the ministry.

To demonstrate that men's intellectual requirements have at times outweighed God's spiritual requirements for ordination and ministry, let us note excerpts from the 1977-1978 catalogues of three of the most well-known divinity schools in America today. In the decade since these catalogues were issued, the basic requirements for graduation at these institutions have changed little. Language in the catalogs, however, has improved in some cases to show increased attention to the Church herself, at least in use of general terminology.

Yale Divinity School

"Presbyterian students should remember that in most instances knowledge of the Greek and Hebrew languages is required for ordination. Since students expecting to be ordained by the UPUSA must take the Standard Ordination Examinations in the spring of their senior year, they should be prepared to take a Bible content examination in the winter of their second year and should take Church Polity the fall semester of their senior year." (p. 57)

"The minimum requirement for the Master of Divinity degree is the successful completion of three academic years of study with a total schedule of not less than seventy-two semester hours." (p. 59)

"The Master of Arts in Religion degree offers the opportunity for preparation for new and special forms of the ministry that do not require ordination. The minimum requirement for the Master of Arts in Religion degree is the successful completion of two academic years of study with a total schedule of not less than forty-eight semester hours. [But] ordinarily the Divinity School will not recommend any student for ordination on the basis of the Master of Arts in Religion degree." (p. 65)

Harvard Divinity School

Harvard has a coat of arms on the cover of its catalogue, with the Latin word "veritas," which means truth.

"An important part of the Divinity School is the Center for the study of World Religions. The center was established in 1958 to encourage the pursuit of a coordinated study and understanding of different religions and historical traditions. It is particularly concerned with the relationships between various religious communities in both practice and theory, past and present, and with the religiousness of man in its varieties. Its small residence center provides a unique experience in community for people of different faiths. The total program of the Center is developed in collaboration with the various departments of the University." (p. 24)

"Evaluation at the Divinity School is made using letter grades . . . on a Satisfactory/Unsatisfactory system. For the successful completion of the Masters in Theological Studies program, a minimum of twelve of the sixteen half-courses must be completed with honor grades, (B — or above) . . ." (p. 29)

"The Master of Divinity student must demonstrate a reading knowledge of one of the languages of theological scholarship (Hebrew, Greek, Latin, German, French) . . ." (p. 31)

"Special instruction in the polity and procedures of specific denominations is offered for candidates whose ordination requirements include such training." (p. 33)

"Candidates for the degrees of Master of Divinity and Master of Theological Studies must have received a Bachelor's degree in Arts, Science or Philosophy from an accredited college or university. It is possible for students without such a degree to be admitted if satisfactory evidence of equivalent educational preparation can be provided. Each applicant is asked to submit:
— a college record transcript;
— recommendations of academic ability; professional promise and statements of character;
— a one thousand word statement, describing the student's general background, previous academic work, and reasons for desiring admission to the degree program at Harvard Divinity School.

"Recognizing the wide diversity of undergraduate programs available to students today, the Admissions Committee is aware that no single set of criteria of preparation for seminary studies is possible. It is preferable for the students to have a strong background in history, philosophy, literature and the social sciences. Previous work in the field of religion is certainly appropriate but not to the exclusion of other humanistic studies. Some familiarity with the natural sciences, fine arts and music is most desirable, but an undergraduate concentration in the natural sciences, engineering, or the performing arts may make it necessary for the applicant to supplement college preparation with work in the humanities and social sciences. Applicants are expected to have at least an elementary knowledge, preferably a good reading knowledge, of one of the following languages: Hebrew, Greek, Latin, German or French." (p. 34, 35)

"Every Doctor of Theology candidate, before receiving the degree, must have satisfied the Committee with regard to certain general requirements of:
(a) demonstrating the appropriate linguistic qualifications;
(b) passing a General Examination on his field;
(c) writing an acceptable thesis; and
(d) defending it satisfactorily in a final examination" (p. 41)

Princeton Theological Seminary

On the back cover of the Princeton catalogue is the seal of the trustees of their theological seminary, a picture of rays of light coming out of an eye which is positioned above an opened Holy Bible.

"It is recommended that the candidate's baccalaureate preparation include at least sixty semester hours...in such liberal arts studies as English, philosophy, literature, history, and ancient and modern languages, together with some work in the natural and human sciences, especially psychology and sociology."

"(The) Religion and Society (Program) aims to develop theologically reflective participation in the worldwide struggle for justice and peace. Work is directed both as primarily theological inquiry and as creative contribution to human action in the transformation of economic and political realities. The program attempts to hold thought and action together in pedagogy (teaching), communal dialogue of faculty and students, and in fashioning opportunities for participation in religious, associational and academic settings."

"Secular" Seminaries?

These seminary catalogue excerpts show us several unfortunate "twists" that have worked their way into many seminaries, and thus many of our churches. The twists are:

1 — That the study of the different religions of the world in the name of "broadening one's understanding" has led into such a religious mixture that some "ministers" today deny the existence of the personal God of the Bible, the Bible's inspiration, and the unique and universal message of salvation through the cross of Jesus Christ;

2 — That academic requirements have almost totally replaced biblical requirements (i.e., of anointing, wisdom, integrity, etc., N.B. I Timothy 3 and Titus 1 for the ministry ordination);

3 — That scholarship is nearly equated with ministry;

4 — That intellectual knowledge has become the criterion for ordination over spiritual knowledge of Jesus Christ and His ways;

5 — Invention of a special term, "ministerial candidates," implies that only some Christians are called to a ministry in the Lord;

6 — That only an academic system of grading should be used to evaluate "ministerial candidates," rather than the standards of God's Word;

— The implication that a man lacking knowledge of Hebrew, Greek, German, French or Latin is unable to function as a competent Bible teacher in the Body of Christ;

— That a broad liberal arts education is necessary to effectively minister the Gospel of Jesus Christ to society.

What is the outcome of all these twists in the education of religious leaders? General studies in areas of Religion and Society and other related programs compromise clear biblical positions and conclude in a cloud of humanistic, non-Christian verbage spreading a gospel of world unity on purely human terms.

Whenever the Church does not maintain the Word of God as its only final standard, she finds herself compromising God's truth in many areas. In the name of "higher education," the Church tends to lower her spiritual life in Jesus Christ--a sacrifice she cannot afford to make. Because the Church has allowed higher education to dominate her preparation of leadership, we find the Church equating education with ministry. In substantiating this, it is interesting to note that one of the words for learned men as a group (the literarily skilled intelligentsia) is the word "clerisy," equivalent to the Middle Latin word "clericus," meaning priest or clergy.

The Church has lost much of her spiritual power in winning souls for Christ, because she has substituted worldly academic standards for biblical ministry standards in her leaders. The Church must return to the Word of God for her emphasis in education and ministry preparation. As the Church does return to the Word of God as her source, she will experience the confirmations and blessings that God promised in His Word.

"Priest" vs. "Elder"

To further explore how the Church developed a twisted view of leadership, let us now look at the relationship between the concepts of "priest" and "elder." A priest is generally defined as a person who performs religious ceremonies, and/or functions in the pastoral or ministerial office. It is understood that an ordaining body of a higher religious authority must invest the priest with authority to perform these functions. At this point, it's useful to make several observations concerning the Church's traditional and modern use of the word "priest."

Mediator. The concept of the priest being the mediator between God and man is a totally Old Testament concept. It was necessary only until the life and sacrifice of Jesus Christ, who is now the Church's great high priest (Hebrews 2:17; 3:1; 4:14,15; 5:1,5,10; 6:20; 7:1,26-28; 8:1-3; 9:7,11,25; 10:21; 13:11), and the only mediator between God and man (I Timothy 2:5; Hebrews 8:6; 9:15; 12:24).

Inclusion. The concept of a priesthood that does not include all believers is a carry-over from the Old Testament. It was abolished on the cross of Christ. The New Testament teaches that all Christians are priests (I Peter 2:5,9) and are to offer spiritual (not sacramental) sacrifices of thanksgiving to God for what He has accomplished through His Son for them on the cross (I Peter 2:5; Hebrews 13:15,16).

Leadership. The concept of a separate priesthood as being the leadership of the Church is a perversion of the governmental ministries of apostle, prophet, evangelist, pastor and teacher that God has given to lead the Church (Ephesians 4:10-12).

Holiness. The root of the Greek word for priest means "sacred" or "holy." ("Hieros" is the Greek root word; "hierus" is the Greek word for priest.) This meaning has caused many people to assume that the priesthood is to be holy, but that the people at large do not need to be as holy or cannot be as holy. In the Old Testament this was true, but it does not extend to the New Testament, where all Christians are described as members of a *"holy priesthood"* (I Peter 2:5,9).

The preservation of the idea of a separate priesthood has been essential to the preservation of the hierarchical structure of many churches. Indeed, the word "hierarchy" is derived from the Greek word for priest, "hierus." To destroy the concept of a separate priesthood would be to alter the present hierarchical structures of some churches, which are based strictly on earthly authority. Some churches state that they believe in the existence of the priesthood of all believers, in addition to a separate priesthood. Because the two concepts are in conflict, this kind of statement can only exist in theory, not in practice.

Status. Certain religious societies and orders distinguish between "priests," "brothers," and "sisters." The distinctions show an unbiblical delineation of position in the Church, and an attitude of priestly superiority. The New Testament, on the other hand, teaches that all Christians are brothers and sisters in Christ (Romans 1:13; 7:1,4; 8:12; I Corinthians 1:10,11,26; 2:1; 3:1; II Corinthians 1:8; Galatians 1:11; Ephesians 6:10; Phillippians 1:12).

Authority. The word "priest" is derived from an Old English word "preost." This word is an unexplained alteration for the word "presbuteros," which is translated as "elder" in the New Testament. This unexplained alteration in words and meanings parallels the unexplained way that some churches have evolved unbiblical priestly hierarchical authority structures. The New Testament delineates many different congregational ministries. But it has always taught that the

governmental and ruling ministry of the Church lies in the hands of the elders ("presbuteros")
or the bishops ("episkopos") and not in the hands of priests. (See Acts 14:23; 15:2,4,6,22,23; 16:4;
20:17,28; Ephesians 4:11,12; I Timothy 5:17; Titus 1:5; Philippians 1:1; I Timothy 3:1,2; Titus 1:7;
I Peter 2:25. Also see "priest" in The Random House Dictionary of the English Language.)

The Clergy as the Professionals

Another major cause of the Church's unbiblical division between the "clergy" and the "laity"
is the professional status the Church accords to clergy. The process of elevating clergy to the
status of "professional Christian" follows a chain of logic that looks like this:

Since the:	clergy =	priesthood
and the:	priesthood =	profession
and:	profession =	professional
THEREFORE:	clergy =	professional

Let us now explain this logical progression of how the clergy were equated with professionalism.

As we have already seen, the concept of "clergy" is equivalent to the concept of a separate
priesthood. The word "clergy" is derived from a Latin word which is a variant of the word "clerk."
This word, in turn, comes from the ecclesiastical Latin word "clericus," which means priest. Both
by shared linguistic background and by tradition, clergy and priesthood are equated. Thus, we
have the first part of our logical progression: "clergy = priesthood."

Next, we see that the word "profession" in general defines a group of people engaged in a
particular occupation or calling. The word "profession" is derived from a Middle Latin word,
"profession" or "professio." Originally, "profession" referred to the taking of vows to a religious
order. Many separate religious orders were formed around certain disciplined, holy or charismatic
leaders who "professed" with their lives a walk with God. Particularly during the Middle Ages,
but also throughout Church history, the men who took the vows of a religious order were called
priests (after their training and ordination). These vows began to be understood as constituting
the making of a "profession" for God.

Generally speaking, each of these religious orders had its own religious emphasis (although
these have expanded over the course of time). The Jesuits emphasize education; the Dominicans,
preaching; the Franciscans, poverty. People who desired to escape the societal corruptions of the
Middle Ages generally removed themselves from society to join a particular religious order.
People who did not join a religious order were generally criticized by the religious, and denigrated
as "common people" who had no real desire to sacrifice their all for God. This same attitude of
superiority has prevailed throughout Church history. The man who wanted to make a serious
"profession of Christ" became a "priest," and the woman who wanted to make a serious "profession
of Christ" became a "sister" or nun. Thus we observe the second general statement of our logical
progression: "priesthood = profession."   Those who made professions of Christ in religious orders
made certain vows or commitments to God and to their particular religious groups. The three
most common vows were: poverty (living in the religious community with no personal belongings),
chastity (living celibately, with no marriage partner) and obedience (total obedience to God
through the leaders of the religious order).

Although most of the religious orders began with pure motives, their perversions of New
Testament truth are obvious. Some of these perversions:

1. Becoming religious-order centered, rather than local church centered, which includes all

those who believe in Jesus Christ.

2. Requiring celibacy which Paul the apostle predicted would come to the Church and who categorized such a teaching as a doctrine of demons (I Timothy 4:1-5).

3. De-emphasizing the Word of God by putting the constitutions of the particular religious orders on an equal or superior basis.

4. Withdrawing from the very part of society which most needed the preaching and life of the Gospel of Jesus Christ to help them also come to know the Lord (Matthew 5:13,14).

5. Dismissing the common man as unable to live a perfectly good Christian life in his own occupation.

Let us now look at the last part of our logical progression. Today we generally define the word "professional" as a person who follows a specific occupation or renders a specific kind of service as his means of financial support. A professional person makes a regular routine or business practice out of something which amateurs do only for amusement or recreation.

In this sense, the members of the religious societies became professionals. They were professional receivers, preachers, tradesmen, religious society men, or teachers. All of this was done in the name of their underlying religious profession to Jesus Christ.

Eventually, "profession" and "professional" were also applied to people fully engaged in any specific business activity for profit. Business and trade guilds were organized, with some patterns of organization similar to the religious orders. There was an understanding that they were "professing" the ideals for which their occupation stood, even as priests or sisters "professed" Christ. The medical field, for example, became the medical "profession" in the sense of its original desire to live up to the high ideals and duties of physicians contained in the oath of Hippocrates, the Greek "Father of Medicine" (c.460-360 B.C.). Thus, we have the third and fourth parts of our logical progression: "profession = professional" and, therefore, "clergy = professional." To restate our logical progression:

	clergy =	priesthood
	priesthood =	profession
	profession =	professional
THEREFORE	clergy =	professional

Those considered to be in the clergy, therefore, were looked upon as "professionals." Those who received a theological and "professional" education were considered to be part of the clergy, or at least, well prepared for a particular denominational ordination. Neither of these ideas, however, are biblical.

To expand this idea of a professional "clergy" being the main or only people involved in spiritual activity and ministry, we will look at five key words. We will see how the terms "Business," "Office," "Authorization," "Ordination," and "Laity" have been commonly but erroneously applied to Christian service and leadership.

"Business" of the Ministry

The word "business" is generally understood as the activity of someone who is consistently engaged in an effort to generate profit. Today, the word "business" more often refers to a person's official or professional duty, function or occupation, as contrasted with recreation or pleasure. The word "business" is simply derived from the word "busy."

Two common misconceptions have become attached to the concept of the "business of the ministry." First, people have thought that those involved in ministry must be financially supported by the Church or charitable donations, and should maintain the same level of organizational prestige as non-Christian businesses or professions. That is not and should not always be true. Even though Paul (as a chosen vessel of the Lord) had the power to require financial support from churches, he rejected such support many times, to prevent people from accusing him of preaching the gospel for monetary advantage (I Corinthians 9:1-27; II Thessalonians 3:6-12).

Moreover, Paul wrote that one basic qualification of an ordained elder was that he be free of the love of money or covetousness (I Timothy 3:3). Many who think of the ministry as totally similar to any worldly profession think of ministers as receiving financial support, as working for hire. This unfortunate attitude has helped lead many people into the ministry for financial gain. Many ministers, in the name of the Lord, have literally robbed the flock of God.

One of the tests of God's ordaining on a ministry: to preach the gospel and teach the Word naturally, eagerly and in one's own free time, regardless of any financial support. It is good for local church pastors to test their young men in training for the ministry by observing how spontaneously they minister the Word of God, with no expectation of money or position. This brings to light their motives for ministry.

A second major misconception regarding "the business of the ministry" is this: only those in a full-time, financially supported ministry of the Church are doing the work of the Lord on a full-time, totally committed basis. This has led to the "ordained" (paid ministers) doing all the work of the Church. To repeat what we have already said, all Christians are called by God to His work. Each Christian has a special and important function to fulfill in the Body of Christ (I Corinthians 12). Many Protestant churches have fallen into the same false delineation of Christian service that is part of the Catholic tradition.

"Office" of the Ministry

The word "office" generally refers either to a position of professional responsibility, or to a room where the business of a professional person is transacted. The word comes from the Latin word "officium" which means service, duty or ceremony. "Officium" is related to the Latin "opus," for "work."

Several erroneous concepts appear when the term "office" is applied to the ministry:

Many feel that as long as a person performs a certain prescribed ceremony, he is correctly functioning in his ministerial office. On the contrary, ceremonies can easily become stagnant and lifeless. To really function in one's office of ministry, one must be working in a flexible way with the anointing of the Holy Spirit.

Many think that to function in an office of ministry is to sit in a room doing paperwork, writing and waiting for people to come in for help. Ministering to people's spiritual needs will sometimes take place in an office. Really fulfilling one's office of ministry, however, means meeting people's spiritual needs wherever they are. Jesus and the apostles did this when they went out to minister to the lost and dying.

Many feel that any person with a name or title on the door of an "office" is likely to meet the spiritual needs of the people. On the contrary, to really function in one's "office" of ministry, one does the work of saving and healing lives, and does not depend on titles, positions, certificates or official rooms for that kind of service. Paul's commendation of ministry, for example, was not his man-given title, position or temple office. His commendation was the spiritual fruit that God enabled him to produce in other people's lives. Paul stated, *"Are we beginning to commend ourselves again? Or, do we need, as some, letters of commendation to you or from you? You are our letter, written in our hearts, known and read by all men; being manifested that you are a letter of Christ, cared for by us, written not with*

ink, but with the Spirit of the living God, not on tablets of stone, but on tablets of human hearts"
(II Corinthians 3:1-3).

"Authorization" of the Ministry

The word "authorization" commonly refers to the state or quality of being given official authority or power to perform a duly sanctioned function. The word "authorization" is derived from a Middle Latin word, "auctorizare," which means to increase or to grow.

Many in the Church today misunderstand what constitutes an "authorized" ministry. This stems from the belief that a Church system confers authority, directly resulting in a position of privilege which increases a person's personal reputation and prestige. This does not constitute ministry authorization.

It is God who anoints a person to minister, and at best, organizations of men can only agree with His anointing. The goal of ministry is spiritual increase and growth in other people's lives, not personal prestige for the minister. The goal of spiritual increase comes not from receiving a title, but from earnest service by the person who trusts God to yield the increase.

The word "authorization" is derived from the Latin word "auctor." When interpreted spiritually, "auctor" carries a host of meanings which in themselves make a fascinating study in leadership. By extension, "auctor" has the spiritual meanings of:

A progenitor of spiritual families
A builder of spiritual buildings
An author of spiritual writings
A doer of spiritual deeds
A teacher of spiritual knowledge
A messenger of spiritual good news
A spiritual advisor of actions
A promoter of spiritual measures
A supporter of spiritual laws
A spiritual leader in public life
A model of spiritual conduct
A witness to spiritual promises
A spiritual guardian of women and minors
A champion of others' spiritual welfare

The person who actually performs some or all of the above functions is the one who is truly authorized to serve the Lord on a "full-time" basis.

"Ordination" of the Ministry

"Ordination" is commonly defined as the act of officially investing a person with ministerial functions and holy orders. The word is derived from the Latin word, "ordinare," which means to set in order, to arrange, appoint or regulate. To officially "ordain" someone to the ministry is to formally appoint someone to this work, and to regulate the ministry activities of that person.

In the Church, however, true ordination does not precede ministry; it follows it. Only after obviously functioning in certain areas of spiritual influence and ministry, by the enablement of the Holy Spirit, is a person truly ordained by God to do the work of a ministry. A man is not ordained by man so that he can function. Instead, he is recognized by man because he has already been spiritually ordained by God, and has already been functioning in the ministry that God has given to him!

"Laity" and Ministry

The extreme gap between the superior status of clergy and the low status of laity is changing in many churches. The change sometimes seems more in theory than in reality, however. Let us look for a moment at the word "laity."

It has a diverse, interesting background. "Laity" is generally defined as the body of people outside a particular profession, and most often refers to those not in the clergy. The word "lay" still affects our thoughts about the "laity," though it is less commonly used in this context today. "Lay" means uninstructed and unlearned. In 1535, the Coverdale translation of the Bible translated Acts 4:13 this way: "They saw the boldness of Peter and John and marvelled for they were sure they were unlearned and lay people."

Is it not interesting that the Jewish leaders considered Peter and John, two of the greatest ministers of the gospel of Jesus Christ, to be mere "lay" people?! Has not the Church held this same attitude throughout her history, toward ministers of the simple gospel of Jesus Christ?

The word "lay" also had the connotation of "unholy." Thus, in 1609 the Douay Bible translated I Samuel 21:4 in this way: "I have no lay breads at hand, but only holy bread."

Whether we like it or not, through the years the Church has considered lay people as uneducated and unholy compared to the clergy. The terms "lay brother" and "lay deacon" exemplify this misunderstanding about true ministry. The Catholic Church defines a "lay brother" as "a man who has taken the habit of a religious order, but is employed mostly in manual labour and is exempt from the studies or choir-duties required of the other members." It defines a "lay deacon" as "a man in deacon's orders who devotes only part of his time to religious ministrations, while following a secular employment."

Thus the term "lay people" implies those who work in manual labor, who seldom do religious studies, and work for the Lord on a strictly part-time basis. This concept has its roots in Greek philosophy, which considered man's spirit holy, but his body evil.

The word "laity" is also directly related to the late Latin word "laicus," which is a different form of the word "lake." One of the main senses of "lake" is play, sport, fun, glee, tricks and "goings-on." The Church has created a striking contrast in using the word "laity" to refer to those who are involved with the less important or "playful" things of life, while using the word "clergy" to refer to those tho are involved in the more important or "spiritual" things of life. Has this not been the Church's prevalent attitude?

It is even more interesting to note that the word "lake" is an old form of the word "lac," meaning a defect, failing, moral delinquency, fault, offense, absence of something, or the condition of being censored. When the word "lac" referred to a limb of the body, it meant a crippled limb; when it referred to a geographical district, it meant a destitute area. The Church has also held the attitude that the common, lay people have so many faults and moral weaknesses that what they have to say need only be censored. The attitude has existed that the laity are a crippled limb of the Body of Christ, who live their lives in a spiritually destitute district. Though many churches are attempting to escape this thinking, it still underlies the attitudes in many churches.

The Lord is moving His people to break down all of the walls of error that have been built to separate clergy from laity. He is restoring our ability to see ministries in a scriptural way. The New Testament never uses the concept of clergy as opposed to laity. Instead, it emphasizes the importance of all Christians finding and functioning in their ministries.

It is in this context that you will discover your own unique ministry to the Body of Christ, your own role in rebuilding the Church.

CHAPTER 2
CHURCH LEADERSHIP: BACKGROUND AND CONFLICTS

In Chapter One, we studied the definitions and concepts that will help you begin to understand Christian leadership.

Sometimes, however, a little information begets many questions. How did we reach today's confusion over Christian leadership? How can we lay a sound biblical foundation that will let us rebuild Church leadership--without repeating the errors of the past?

To re-establish God's design for the Church today, it is crucial to understand biblical leadership, and the history of Church leadership.

Where the Conflict Began — Religious Hierarchies

What produced such anti-biblical ministry concepts as the separation of clergy and laity? We have to go back to the early Church to find the roots of today's conflict over leadership roles.

The early Church was organized in a way that let all members of each congregation play an active role in the Church's life. Within her membership, the early Church had a variety of people with different spiritual gifts that were profitable to the entire local body of believers. The two main areas of gift-function were those Christians who guided and labored in the Word of God, and those who participated in the various congregational ministries of I Corinthians 12:4-11 and Romans 12:3-8. These portions of Scripture enumerated the various congregational ministries in the Church. Though these verses do not provide the complete list of ministries, they give us a good idea of the diversity of the gifted congregational ministries:

the word of wisdom	the interpretation of tongues
the word of knowledge	serving
the gift of faith	teaching
gifts of healing	exhorting
the working of miracles	giving

prophecy	governing
the discernment of spirits	showing mercy
various kinds of tongues	

Many members of the early Church operated in these different ministries of the Spirit, but they did not necessarily have names or titles. The early Church apparently considered the actual work of ministry to be much more important than an office. Prophesying to the edification of the Church, or showing mercy to the weak members of the congregation, must have produced more true growth than the creation of titled positions for every ministry function. The same is true today.

Today, unfortunately, the Church has lost much of the spontaneous, God-given power of the Holy Spirit in her daily walk. She depends more on the strength and power that goes with a titled position, rather than experiencing the obvious power of God's Spirit, who needs no long introductions or apologies for His work. The work was more important than the rank, and the early Church put her emphasis on the function of the saints of God, rather than on their official position.

When it was necessary to create a position, the early Church chose out from among her members those who already manifested the wisdom, character and anointing of the Lord upon their lives. Selection of deacons in Acts 6:3 is one such example. In this way, the early apostles underscored the principle that it is the man who sanctifies the office, not the office that sanctifies the man. The Church today would do well to choose out from among her members those who are already functioning in the area of their calling. When she does not, she may be "laying hands on empty heads," and expecting "the dove that has no wings to fly."

The writing of the Church fathers was clear on the subject of ruling and governing. They held that the ability to function was always founded upon present service and ability, rather than mere rank or position. The early Church Fathers did not desire to "fill positions" in the Church just for its own sake. Today, the Church needs to restore this same attitude.

Within the first three centuries, the early Church experienced a drastic change in its governmental structure. She has never yet entirely retrieved herself from its dregs. The first century Church had basically two offices: bishops (elders, pastors, overseers or shepherds) and deacons. Oversight of each local congregation was totally in the hands of the local Church eldership, while deacons ministered to the practical needs of the people.

However, the heart of a deacon (a servant) was required in each bishop. Polycarp of Smyrna (who wrote c. 110-117) held that the first duty of the bishops was compassion and mercy, visiting all of those with infirmities. The next two chapters of The Making of a Leader will expand on the necessity of having a servant's heart.

In the second century, a third office began to emerge in the Church. Elders were added to deacons and bishops (the local pastors). In this structure, unfortunately, the group of local elders had total power over the one man in the bishop's office. This did have an advantage, however. The bishop (the senior pastor) was still the one man who received the mantle of leadership, and his other elders recognized this, but he could not use this position to domineer his fellow elders.

It was James, the bishop/pastor of the local church at Jerusalem, who rose up and applied the Old Testament to the issue of circumcising Gentiles, during the Apostolic Conference in Acts 15. In practical terms, James was the one man who "steered the bus," but he consulted with his fellow team leaders on how to reach their goal. This illustrates how God appoints one man among the local church elders to be "first among equals," not to dominate, but to receive a specific mantle of anointed direction.

By the third century, however, the office of the bishop or senior elder in the local congregation was taken to an extreme. Bishops of various local churches began to exercise total authority over local elders and deacons. This domination by one man resulted in spiritually suppressing the functions of the deacons in serving the local church. Gradually, certain bishops received extended power over many other local congregations. And finally, the office of the local bishop was taken to an unbiblical extreme in its authority over many elders and their local churches. Almost total power resided with the bishop, and not with the local elders as it had originally.

Why did the early Church allow such a magnification of the office of the local bishop? The reasons were many.

The Church felt that she could more easily stem the tide of immorality and intellectualism by giving more power to one man.

The Church believed that she could accomplish a greater unity against divisive heresies if she exalted certain strong teachers.

The Church began to use one man from each local assembly to represent them to the bishops of other local assemblies, which gradually led to the exaltation of this one man over the other local elders as the "episcopus par excellence."

The Church began to desire to financially support certain local bishops so that they could give all of their time to ministering to the people, which began to politically separate certain men who desired position and prestige.

The Church began to desire local bishops to perform most of the work of the ministry, because they had the most education, which led to a governmental corps of mostly bishops overseeing education, doctrine, marriages, baptisms, the communion table, the elders, the deacons, and even Church property and monies.

The Church began to look mainly to the bishop's office for all major teaching, and thus the local elders were considered only "teachers," while the bishop was considered as the joint apostle/prophet (the true traveling ministries of separate apostles and prophets having receded into the background.)

The culmination of this move to give supreme authority to the bishops is illustrated in the way that Ignatius of Antioch referred to the bishop. "We ought to regard the Bishop as the Lord Himself," wrote Ignatius. Consequently, the Church fell away from the New Testament pattern. Now, bishops were considered as apostles, prophets and evangelists; local elders became pastors and teachers; deacons mainly served the bishops and elders; congregational members were simply "not in the ministry" of the Lord.

We can thank God, however, that since the Reformation He has been continually restoring the New Testament pattern of the local Church, and freeing His people from bondages of non-scriptural authority.

The Change of the Concept of a Minister

In the Church today, leaders are called "ministers" more often than they are called "shepherds." The word "shepherd," however, is a more accurate term to describe a man of God serving Christ's flock, especially as it is contrasted with the way that the word "minister" is used today. Today, the word "minister" refers to an ordained pastor, elder or reverend who does the work of the Lord on a full-time basis. We need to ask ourselves , however, if this is the New Testament concept of the word "minister." Are only some members of the Body of Christ "ministers," or are all members of the Body of Christ "ministers" in the New Testament sense of the word, which is "servant?"

The word "minister" (or servant) has undergone a drastic and very unfortunate change, both grammatically and theologically, since its original use in the New Testament Church.

Grammatically. In the early Church (c. 33 A.D.) "minister" was used as a verb, an action word. The word "minister," of course, is intimately connected in meaning with that of the word "ministry." Thus, all Christians in the early Church had a ministry of actively, dutifully, functionally and effectively working for the Lord and His people. This was true for fishermen and doctors, regardless of occupation or level of education.

The concept of a "minister" (a Christian servant) with a "ministry" (a specific service in the Body) applied to anyone who performed normal Christian functions. Leading someone to Christ, helping widows, praying for the sick, exhorting other saints were functions all Christians performed. The work load of the Church was not in name, title, position or salary. It was in action, commitment, spontaneity and individual service. All Christians acted to perform "ministry" that extended the kingdom of Jesus Christ.

Unfortunately, the concepts of "minister" and "ministry" gradually changed from their original grammatical meaning and usage. Gradually, the word "minister" was used to refer to the name, title, position or salary of those few who performed certain sacred New Testament activities. Preaching, water baptizing, serving communion, anointing the sick and counseling came to be functions of the "minister." Today the transition is complete. "Minister" is no longer used as an action word, but as a noun, to name a person, place or thing.

Today, "minister" refers to the title of a special person who has been ordained by a certain denomination. This person functions out of a place (a special office or study), and fills a hierarchical position (a thing, not an action). In this, the Church has lost the New Testament emphasis that "minister" should describe Christian activity and function, and not merely name a position, title or salary-holder. This represents a major reversal of Bible teaching.

Theologically. In the early Church (33 A.D.), "minister" referred to all members of the Body of Christ who had a part in serving. The theological meaning of the word did not apply to a small elite, but to active Christians in general. Nor did "minister" make any distinction between clergy and laity as we use it today. All believers in the early Church were understood to be "ministers" (servants) of the Lord Jesus Christ, in fulfilling different roles in the kingdom.

Today, on the other hand, the word "minister" refers to one man doing the work of the Lord. The contemporary Church confers this title only on a small number of men whom God has called to serve Christ and the Church as a "pastor," a "reverend," a "bishop" or a "doctor." In this framework, the "unordained," common people are not considered an essential and valid part of the ministry.

As the builder of the Church, the Lord will not leave His people in a destitute state in which only part of His Body functions properly. In these last days, God is pouring out His Spirit upon the Church to restore to her the truth that all Christians are called to a ministry.

The false concept of an extreme division between the clergy and the laity has given rise to many problems:

Positionally-minded people pursue ministry positions without aspiring to true service in the Church.

Professionally-oriented people may attain a Church title, yet miss the anointing of God.

Authoritarian people may domineer the flock of God, thinking that ministry is exercising power over people's lives. Hypocrites, like Pharisees, lay onto others the heavy burdens that they would not touch with one of their own fingers.

The division between clergy and laity produces a lazy majority of Christians in the Church who do not realize their callings in God.

Deacon boards rule over local elders and congregations.

Politically-oriented leaders put professionalism, money and man-pleasing before serving the flock and pleasing God.

An overworked minority does most if not all of the true "ministering" in the Body of Christ.

Original New Testament Definition. The above definition is a far cry from the Body of Christ as the New Testament defined it. To Christians in the early Church, "minister" was a verb, an act of service, and it was understood to be an inseparable part of their Christian faith. In the 20th Century, "minister" is a noun, the name given to one special individual who has attained a position of high religious status. The following simple diagram illustrates both the grammatical and theological change in the understanding of "minister" that has occurred in Church history.

A.D. 33   **20th CENTURY**

CHURCH HISTORY

"Minister"	"Minister"
Grammatically: a verb, an action word.	Grammatically: a noun, the name of a person.
Theologically: a function and service of all Christians.	Theologically: a position for one high-status individual.

God wants to overthrow the false division between clergy and laity, along with its pitiful results, and restore the New Testament truth to ministry. In The Making of a Leader, we will not refer to Church leaders as "ministers." Because God intends "minister" to be an action, rather than the name of a title, we will refer to a Church leader as "a ministry," and to leadership in general as "ministries." In light of the Bible's own directives on the subject, this seems the most appropriate title for a position. This overturns today's confusion over function versus title, and it restores the understanding that God alone can establish ministry.

Leading by Service in the Old Testament

"The king's favour is toward a wise servant . . ." (Proverbs 14:35)

"A wise servant shall have rule over a son that causeth shame and shall have part of the inheritance among the brethren" (Proverbs 17:2).

In the Old Testament, a leader of God's people was, first of all, a servant of God and of His people. Servanthood went before leadership, and was a vital part of leadership. All of the Old

Testament leaders named below were described as servants, of God and of others:

> **Abraham:** God's servant (Genesis 26:24)
> **Moses:** God's servant (Exodus 14:31; Numbers 12:7,8; Deuteronomy 34:5; Joshua 1:1,2,7)
> **Joshua:** Moses' servant (Exodus 33:11)
> **Caleb:** God's servant (Numbers 14:24)
> **Samuel:** God's servant (I Samuel 3:9)
> **David:** Saul's servant (I Samuel 29:3; God's servant, I Chronicles 17:4)
> **Elijah:** God's servant (II Kings 9:36)
> **Isaiah:** God's servant (Isaiah 20:2)

These are just a few of the many leaders in the Old Testament whose leadership was founded on servanthood to God and others. Please note that in this list, both Joshua and David were servants to the leaders over them, whose positions they were later to fill. (We will examine more carefully the area of servanthood in Chapter Five, "The Heart Qualifications of Leadership.")

From Serving to Leading

The Hebrew word for "leader" is "nagiyd." It has servanthood as a base element, and developing out of that base, setting forth an example to the people.

The meaning to this Hebrew word for "leader" stands in interesting contrast to the Hebrew word for "king." Though the Hebrew word for king, "melech," was fairly neutral in meaning, it allowed the possibility of despotism. This is what Samuel warned the Israelites against, in I Samuel 8:9-18, when they asked for a king. And that is what Saul's kingship degraded into.

By contrast, a "nagiyd" leader has at its root the picture of a man under authority, one who is subject to a higher power, and who fulfills the wishes of that power. That was the kind of ruler God wanted to give the people: a man who would listen to His will, and execute it faithfully with divinely appointed authority. David, a man after God's own heart, was God's "nagiyd" for Israel.

"*Nagiyd*" is translated in the following ways:

"*Captain*"	Isaiah 9:16 and 10:1 and 13-14; II Samuel 5:2; II Kings 20:5; II Chronicles 11:11
"*Ruler*"	I Samuel 25:30; II Samuel 6:21; I Chronicles 5:2; II Chronicles 6:5 and 11:22
"*Prince*"	I Kings 14:7; Job 3:15 and 12:19,21 and 29:9 and 34:18; Psalms 76:12; Proverbs 28:16; Ezekiel 28:2; Daniel 9:25,26 and 11:22
"*Governor*"	I Chronicles 29:22; II Chronicles 28:7; Jeremiah 20:1
"*Nobles*"	Job 29:10

Consequently, to be a captain, ruler, prince, governor or noble of the people of God, a person must first come squarely under the authority of almighty God.

The root meaning of "nagiyd" contains another important element: to stand out boldly, to announce, to manifest. This is a natural complement to the action of receiving commands from almighty God. God's "nagiyd" both receives the commands of the King of Kings, and then boldly stands forward to announce and manifest them. By extension, this carries the meaning of being an example to the people on how to follow the command of God. God's "nagiyd" leader is the first to model the will of God for others to follow. He takes the forefront and leads by example, whether in battle with God's enemies or in establishing truth and justice in God's kingdom.

The Shepherd-Leader

The shepherd is a beautiful illustration of the leader who goes before his people to prepare the way for them. He must go before God's people, in his own experience and lifestyle, so that he can lead them safely past dangers into good, green pasture.

The shepherd in Psalm 23, who is a type of Christ and a picture of every leader of God's people, must have advance knowledge of the lands ahead, and must actively take steps to lead the flock into the safe paths of the Lord. (For a complete study on the spiritual application of Psalm 23 to the life of the Christian leader, read A Shepherd Looks at Psalm 23, by Phillip Keller, Zondervan, 1970.)

Governmental Ministries in the New Testament

Ephesians 4:11 lists the governmental ministries of the Body of Christ: apostle, prophet, evangelist, pastor and teacher. In the past, many Christians have viewed these gifted ministries as the only people in the Church who have a specific work to do for the Lord. As we have already seen, all Christians have a work to do for the Lord. The governmental ministries oversee and develop these ministries in the rest of the Body of Christ. Ephesians 4:12 tells us that these five governmental ministries prepare the saints for their various ministries--but do NOT do all the ministering for the saints.

A survey of various translations is very helpful in exploring the full meaning of Ephesians 4:12, which shows us the function of the governmental ministries:

King James Version: *"For the perfecting of the saints, for the work of the ministry, for the edifying of the Body of Christ."*

Amplified Bible: *"His intention was the perfecting and the full equipping of the saints (His consecrated people), that they should do the work of ministering toward building up Christ's Body (the Church)."*

Living Bible: *"Why is it that he gives us special abilities to do certain things best? It is that God's people will be equipped to do work for Him, building up the Church, the Body of Christ, to a position of strength and maturity."*

Knox Bible: *"He has given the apostle, prophet, evangelist, pastor and teacher, thus organizing the saints for the work of the ministry."*

New American Standard: *"for the equipping of the saints for the work of service, to the building up of the Body of Christ."*

Jerusalem Bible: *"So that the saints together might make unity in the work of service."*

The New Testament in Modern English by J.B. Phillips: *"His gifts were made that Christians might be properly equipped for their service, that the whole Body might be built up"*

From this overview, it is clear that all Christians have a function in the Body of Christ, which they perform with oversight and equipping from the governmental ministries in Ephesians 4:11. We can further illustrate the proper function of the governmental ministries with the following diagram:

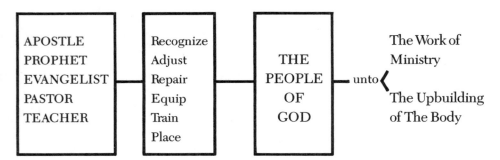

These governmental ministries are given to the Body of Christ to place and adjust members of the Body, so that the Body itself can do the work of the ministry. Governmental ministries furnish, provide, dress, array and gird the Body so that the Body may function properly.

There is an obvious distinction between governmental and congregational ministries which we must not overlook. The two ministry groups do have a difference in function and a difference in authority. But the terms "clergy" and "laity" have no legitimate application here. Both governmental and congregational ministries have an important function in the house of the Lord. They differ in regard to function, but have equal importance in regard to their necessity and significance in the Church.

In Ephesians 4:12, use of the verb "to perfect" helps us picture the function of the governmental ministries. This word "perfect" is the Greek word "katartismos," which means to complete thoroughly, to repair or to adjust. From this word we derive the English words craftsman and artisan, with the idea of someone who works with his hands to make or to build something.

The Greek word "katartismos" is a compound word, comprised of "kata" and "artismos." When compounded in a Greek verb, "kata" has the meaning of a standard by which judgment may be passed. The governmental ministries are thus the standard by which judgment is passed. They are, by extension, the measuring rod for all ministries coming up in the Body. Their ability to perform this function depends on aligning themselves with the perfect measuring rod, the Lord Jesus Christ.

"Artismos" means to repair or to adjust as a craftsman. This Greek word is translated several ways, each of which gives a different aspect of truth concerning the function of the governmental ministries. "Artismos" is translated as mended, fitted, perfectly joined together, restored, prepared and framed. Let us take a closer look at several of these key words in the New Testament.

Mending. "*And going on from thence he saw other two brethren, James the son of Zebedee and John his brother, in a ship with Zebedee their father, mending their nets*" (Matthew 4:21).

James and John were bringing the broken strands of their nets together with the solid strands, to repair the nets. They were mending, adjusting and equipping the net to do the work of fishing. These strands, that had been broken under the pressure of their work, had to be mended. What they were doing in the natural was prophetic of what they were destined to do in the spiritual, to mend the Church, for Jesus had called them to be "fishers of men."

Mending broken lives is the work of the governmental ministries of the Body of Christ. They bring broken and battered strands together with whole strands to make a strong net which will catch fish (souls) for Jesus.

When the net broke, James and John did not dive into the water and try to do the work of the net in catching the fish. Rather, they restored the broken part, so the net itself could function in its work. Many pastors in the Church today try to do the work of the whole

Body, instead of fulfilling their ministry of equipping the Body to do its work.

Fitted. "*The vessels of wrath fitted to destruction*" (Romans 9:22).

Here the Greek word "artismos" is used to describe the fitting or forming of clay into vessels by a potter. God is the potter Who makes vessels of honor or vessels of wrath. A person can respond to the Lord as pliable clay, or he can reject the hand of God's shapings. The Lord is the source of all adjustment and correction. The governmental ministries are instruments in His hand, which He uses to bring correction.

Perfectly Joined Together. "*Now I beseech you brethren...that there be no divisions among you; but that ye be perfectly joined together in the same mind and in the same judgment*" (I Corinthians 1:10).

The Corinthian Church had been torn from within by the spirit of schism and division. The apostle Paul desired all the joints and parts of the Body which were out of place to come into adjustment. Paul wanted a mending to take place in the Body so that it could function with complete coordination.

The Church greatly needs the five-fold office ministries to be released to their proper function of healing wounds and building again that which was broken down. The Body of Christ will be "*perfectly joined together*" only when these ministries can fulfill this work in the Body.

Prepared. "*Wherefore when he cometh into the world he saith, 'Sacrifice and offering thou wouldest not, but a body thou hast prepared for me'*" (Hebrews 10:5).

This passage quotes a Messianic prophecy found in Psalms 46:6. The body prepared for Jesus was a human body of flesh and bones, prepared by the Holy Spirit in Mary's womb. When Jesus came into the world, He came into a "prepared" body for the single purpose of doing the Father's will.

As a sinless and perfect body was prepared for the Lord Jesus, so God is preparing a many-membered Body through which His Son continues His spiritual ministry on the earth. The Father uses the governmental ministries to prepare and perfect that Body (the Church) so that it can accomplish His eternal purpose of subjugating all things under the feet of Jesus Christ.

Framed. "*Through faith we understand that the worlds were framed by the Word of God* (Hebrews 11:3).

Here the writer is not talking about the original act of creating the worlds, but rather of putting into order, arranging and fitting for use that which already existed. The already-created worlds were set into order by the Word of God. The universe was adjusted or arranged by God's Word. Similarly, the power of the spoken Word of God will be seen through the governmental ministries as they help to bring the Body of Christ into order.

In the classical Greek, the compound word "katartismos" had three interesting meanings and uses. The first meaning was that of setting in order a city which had been torn apart by factions and schisms. The process of restoring that city to its original beauty would be called "katartismos."

The second meaning of this beautiful word in classical Greek conveyed the idea of responsibility to thoroughly prepare someone or something for any given task or purpose. The word referred to outfitting a ship for sailing. If any ship encountered a storm at sea, or if there was a malfunction in any part of the ship, the seamen would be in great trouble. The Church is like a ship, and the governmental ministries are responsible to outfit and equip her for her mission of safely carrying the saints across the sea of wicked humanity. If the Church ever finds herself sinking from storms or raging winds, it is often the fault of the ministries who did not equip her properly for her voyage.

The third meaning of "katartismos" in classical Greek was that of preparing an army for battle. If an army encounters defeat in battle, lack of preparation may be the fault. The governmental ministries of the Church must carefully equip the army of the Lord with the right spiritual equipment so it will be prepared to win its battles.

Discernment — A Crucial Governmental Function

One of the most important functions of the governmental ministries in the Church is to have spiritual eyes that can discern those who are called to a particular work in the Body, and to be able to release them to that work. To show the importance of this necessary function of leadership, we need only look to the Lord Jesus, who also performed this ministry while on earth. Jesus had the spiritual eyes to see, in a marred vessel, the potential that could be developed for use in the kingdom of God. He had the wisdom to look past the many defects in the vessel and to discern the treasure buried beneath its surface.

To release the numerous ministries in the Body of Christ that are now lying dormant, Church leadership must function with a spiritual discernment like Christ's. It will happen no other way. Ministry must learn to look past the natural deficiencies and see the spiritual potential that others have in the Lord. Isaiah 11:3-4 contains a prophetic word which was fulfilled in Christ's ministry. It states, "...He shall not judge after the sight of His eyes, neither reprove after the hearing of his ears." Jesus did not judge after the wisdom and insight of men, but after the knowledge and discernment of God. This can be illustrated in His choosing of Levi, the tax collector.

Levi the Tax Collector. Tax collectors were very unpopular in New Testament times. Taxes wre not paid by mail, as today, but were collected by an imperial officer as a daily routine. This imperial officer was usually a part of the customs authority of the land. Hatred of paying duty to the Roman government was, as it were, engraven in the very human nature of the people who were subject to Rome. In Judea, the tax collector was a representative object of the hatred of the Roman Empire. The tax itself was viewed as sinful. If the tax collector was a Jew (as was Levi), he was considered to be a rebel and a renegade in the eyes of his countrymen.

In spite of all this, the wisdom of God was at work against the wisdom of men. Jesus saw Levi's potential for apostleship, and for the authorship of one of the Gospel accounts, Matthew's Gospel. Jesus had the spiritual insight to release the ministry of those who were unloved and those who had the least external promise of a successful ministry. Jesus was not bound by human discernment or approval. He was not judging after the sight of His natural eyes, nor the hearing of His natural ears.

Similarly, the leaders of the New Testament Church today must be set free from the externalities of worldly judgments. They must begin to choose potential leaders acording to spiritual discernment.

James and John. Jesus also had the spiritual eyes to call James and John out of their trade as natural fishermen, into the ministry of spiritual fishermen. James and John did not have theological training or worldly recognition, but Jesus had the spiritual eyes to call them into fruitful ministries in the kingdom of Heaven.

Paul. Jesus also called and changed Saul--the persecutor of the early Church--into Paul, the apostle to the needy Gentiles.

Timothy. Likewise, Paul had spiritual eyes to release ministry in others. Paul worked with a timid, frail young man named Timothy because he saw a potential of God in him. Paul eventually released Timothy to be a great warrior in the kingdom of God. Church ministries today must pray and believe God for the same ability. The life of the Church depends upon it.

Releasing Ministries

The process of recognizing and releasing ministries in the Body of Christ takes time and consistent, watchful care. The steps of this process are:

Recognize the ability and potential in the person
Focus on the positive areas in the person
Challenge this person to fulfill his potential and develop his gifts
Be willing to spend time with him
Be willing to be frustrated with him, without giving up on him
Encourage him through the times of his mistakes
Plant a vision in his heart of true shepherding
Give him opportunities for development
Put confidence in his ministry
Pray his ministry into existence

A full description of the proper and necessary functions of the governmental ministries of the Church would require a volume of its own. But this list of biblical descriptions gives an idea of their tremendous variety and importance. In exercising their leadership functions, governmental ministries are called:

Trainers of the soldiers in the army of the Lord
Restorers of the broken bones of the Body of Christ
Framers of the boards of God's House
Exercisers of the muscles in Christ's Body
Shapers of the stones in the Temple of the Lord
Healers of the breeches in the hedge of God's garden
Liberators of the bound
Adjusters of the out-of-joint
Menders of the torn
Equippers of the Body of Christ
Placers of God's people
Organizers of the Lord's kingdom
Molders of God's clay vessels
Seers of potential for God's service

New Testament Eldership

In the overall framework of Church leadership, the governmental ministries operate within the context of Church eldership. In the New Testament, Church government is entrusted to the eldership, which includes the five-fold governmental ministries of Ephesians 4:11-12. Governmental ministries operate within the support, strengthening and accountability of the eldership.

Elders are called and recognized by character qualifications as well as ministry and functional duties. True biblical eldership, therefore, is not only what a person is, but what a person does.

Important Eldership Terms

Elder. Greek: "Presbuteros." The eldest, or a person advanced in life, or senior. Of rank or position of responsibility, either among the Gentiles or in the Jewish nation. In the Church, the same word applies to those who are appointed to exercise spiritual oversight and care for a local church.

Bishop. Greek: "Episkopee." Office of overseership, for the purpose of watching over and inspecting. As a ministry office, a "bishop" is one of the governmental ministries.

Deacon. Greek: "Diaconia." A servant, one who serves another in any task or job; to support, to minister, to wait upon. All Christians function as deacons, though not all hold an office as such.

Scriptures Concerning Eldership

The book of Acts makes eighteen references to elders, ten relating directly to the ministry of an elder in the New Testament Church. Other writers also refer to eldership.

"They . . . sent (a gift) to the elders by the hands of Barnabas and Saul" (Acts 11:30).

"And when they had ordained them elders in every church, and had prayed with fasting, they commended them to the Lord, on whom they believed" (Acts 14:23).

"They determined that Paul and Barnabas, and certain other of them, should go up to Jerusalem unto the apostles and elders about this question" (Acts 15:2).

"Then pleased it the apostles and elders with the whole church, to send chosen men of their own company to Antioch with Paul and Barnabas...and they wrote letters by them after this manner; 'The apostles and elders and brethren send greetings . . .'" (Acts 15:22,23).

"And as they went through the cities, they delivered them the decrees for to keep, that were ordained of the apostles and elders which were at Jerusalem" (Acts 16:4).

"And from Miletus (Paul) sent to Ephesus, and called the elders of the church" (Acts 20:17).

"Take heed therefore unto yourselves, and to all the flock, over which the Holy Ghost hath made you overseers" (Acts 20:28).

"And the day following Paul went in with us unto James; and all the elders were present" (Acts 21:18).

"Paul . . . to all the saints in Christ Jesus . . . with the bishops and deacons" (Philippians 1:1).

"This is a true saying, If a man desire the office of a bishop, he desireth a good work." This passage, in I Timothy 3:1-7, goes on to establish the behavior and character qualifications for an overseer, then vs. 8-13 do the same for a deacon. Titus 1:6-9 also establishes qualifications for an elder.

"Against an elder receive not an accusation, but before two or three witnesses" (I Timothy 5:19).

"For this cause left I thee in Crete, that thou shouldest set in order the things that are wanting, and ordain elders in every city" (Titus 1:5).

"Is any sick among you? Let him call for the elders of the church; and let them pray over him, anointing him with oil in the name of the Lord" (James 5:14).

"For ye were as sheep going astray; but are now returned unto the Shepherd and Bishop of your souls" (I Peter 2:25).

"The elders which are among you I exhort, who am also an elder" (I Peter 5:1).

Appointing of Elders

Operation of The Eldership. The argument for a plural, co-equal leadership as the highest authority in the local church does not stand up to the test of careful scriptural examination. Elders were ordained by the apostles. Elders were instructed and directed at times by the apostles, and elders worked in a supportive role to the God-appointed leaders.

The eldership is definitely a local church ruling body. It operates, however, under the direction of the senior ministry, who must himself be one of the five governmental ministries. Nothing in

Scripture appears to support the eldership's co-equality in decision-making and governance of a local church. Elders are responsible to work with the senior ministry, and to govern and feed the sheep. Though elders have many active duties, only one man can "drive the bus," as James did in the apostolic conference in Acts 15.

The man who leads is the senior ministry, who should work with the elders, and wisely lead with their full support and unity. Scripture requires the senior ministry to receive open counsel and even rebuke from the eldership. Scripture does not allow controversy over secondary issues such as methods or style. But Scripture does teach specifically that in failure of ethics, morality or doctrine, elders must actively confront senior ministries. The Bible does not teach mutual agreement at any price, nor stagnation until agreement is reached. God makes many important spiritual provisions for His Church through the vision, anointing and talents of His chosen leaders. At the same time, these gifts must function through the support and strength of a unified eldership. Both forms of leadership are crucial to the Church.

Ordination and Appointment of Elders. In the first century Church, elders were not appointed on the basis of their executive abilities, their career or social success, or their public relations skills. They were chosen and appointed because of their spiritual qualifications.

In establishing elders, the act of appointment precedes the act of ordination. Appointment entails the institutional elements of naming a person to an office: to name or select a person for a position; to set a time and place for an act or meeting of appointment; to outfit, equip or furnish a person for a set of prescribed duties. In some cases, a probationary or trial period may pass between appointment and full ordination. The New Testament in many cases describes the trying and proving of a servant's ministry.

The act of ordination involves ordering, establishing and investing with authority. This act confirms what the Spirit has already made obvious in a person's life--that he or she is called and gifted to perform certain ministry functions.

Scriptural Ministry Functions of Eldership

All elders are to rule in the local church. All are called to teach. Christ gives some elders to the Church to be teachers and preachers of the Word to a degree which requires extra time, skill and effort on their part. These, especially, are worthy of "double honor" (I Timothy 5:17). Some elders provide their own financial support and still make adequate time to function as elders; these are sometimes called "lay" elders. A church staff elder is released to give his time to eldering on a full-time basis.

Ministry Function of Elders

Function	Description/Scriptures
Overseer, guardian	Greek *"Episkopos"* Acts 20:28; I Peter 2:25
Ruler	Greek *"Proistemi"* To stand before, to preside, to practice. Romans 12:8; I Timothy 3:4,5,12 and 5:17; I Thessalonians 5:12; Titus 3:8,14. The New Testament defines no higher earthly authority than the elders of a local assembly. Elders are to glorify Christ by making decisions based on sound biblical principles of love and equity.
Feeder	Greek *"Poimano"* To tend as a shepherd. Acts 20:28; John 21:16; Jude 12.
Prayer warrior	To make powerful intercessions and spiritual warfare for special needs in the church. James 5:15-16; Revelation 5:8 and 8:3,4.

Watchman	Greek *"Gregoreo"* To keep awake spiritually. Acts 20:28-30; I Thessalonians 5:6,10; Luke 12:37, 39; Ezekiel 3:17-21.
Student of the Word	To maintain correct doctrine. I Timothy 3:2; II Timothy 2:24; Titus 1:17.
Teacher/Defender of Sound Doctrine	Such an elder is *"apt* (adept) *to teach"* I Timothy 3:2; II Timothy 2:24; Titus 1:7. *"He must hold fast to the sure and trustworthy Word of God as he was taught it, so that he may be able both to give stimulating instruction and encouragement in sound (wholesome) doctrine, and to refute and convict those who contradict and oppose it--showing the wayward their error"* (Titus 1:9, Amplified Bible).
Compassionate	I Timothy 3:5; Ezekiel 34.
Example to Believers	He is to be exemplary in all he is, says and does. This includes character, lifestyle, work, family life and marriage. Philippians 3:17; Thessalonians 3:9; I Timothy 4:12 and I Peter 5:3.
Leader	Hebrews 13:7,17,24; Luke 22:26.
Sacrificial Servant	II Samuel 24:24; Luke 14:25-33; Romans 12:1,2; John 10:11.
Wise Counselor	Mark 15:43; Luke 23:50; Psalm 16:7; Proverbs 1:25, 30; Proverbs 20:18; Isaiah 9:16; Proverbs 11:14.
Hard Worker	I Timothy 3:1; I Thessalonians 5:13; Philippians 2:30; I Corinthians 3:13-15; Ephesians 4:12; Proverbs 24:30-34.
Bearer of Burdens	*"And Moses said unto the Lord, 'Wherefore hast thou afflicted thy servant . . . that thou layest the burden of all this people upon me?' . . . . And the Lord said unto Moses . . . 'I will take of the spirit which is upon thee, and will put it upon them; and they shall bear the burden of the people with thee, that thou bear it not thyself alone'"* (Numbers 11:11,16,17). Exodus 18:22; Deuteronomy 1:12; Galatians 6:5.
Loyal Team Man	Philippians 2:19-22.
Encourager of the Brethren	Like Barnabas, the "son of consolation," who first discipled Paul, and then supported his ministry.
Sharer of the Vision	Like Jonathan's armor-bearer, who said to his master, *"Do all that is in thine heart; turn thee; behold, I am with thee according to thy heart"* I Samuel 14:7.
Transparent	A quality of life, resulting from having no sins or secret motivations to hide, in which his own plans and intentions are open for all to see.
Submissive	The root of all sin is self-will, *"for whatever is not of faith is sin"* (Romans 14:23). The elder must be so submissive to the will of God that he actively seeks it, and does not resist change or new decisions in pursuit of his own comfort.
Liberal Giver	In sacrificial giving, it isn't the size of the gift that matters, it's the cost to the giver, and the love and faith in which the gift is offered. II Corinthians 8:2,5 and 9:5,6.
Positive in Faith	As a shepherd-ruler, an elder must maintain an active, positive faith to help others do the same. An elder must lead the people in rising to the challenges of spiritual warfare or hard circumstances, and responding in faith. A negative attitude, cynicism, or lack of faith

	will harm everyone he is called to help.
Disciplined	A disciplined lifestyle captures the blessings of the Lord and releases them to their full purpose.
Keeper of Unity	Unity and harmony in the Church begins with the elders! Their own unity and harmony, in turn, depends upon their knowledge of the Word and its important principles. If each elder is guided by the Holy Spirit, the Word, and active prayer, the eldership will be unanimous in all decisions. Ephesians 4:1,2; Isaiah 65:8; I Corinthians 1:10.
Worshipper	A lifestyle of worship releases the moving of the Holy Spirit. Revelation 4:4-11.
Protector of the Flock	Satanic attacks come both from outside the flock, and from inside. As shepherds, elders play an important role in protecting the flock of God.
Filled with the Holy Spirit	His life must be open and receptive to the influence of the Holy Spirit.
Properly Motivated	A weakly motivated elder will be indifferent to the needs and sufferings of God's flock. An improperly motivated elder will be driven by personal need, rather than the moving of the Holy Spirit.

In this study on Church eldership, we have intentionally excluded certain issues in eldership where the Bible does not develop a complete definition. Two such undeveloped areas in the ministry of eldership and Church structures are: co-equality of eldership, and the relationship of eldership to the senior elder, or senior pastor.

We believe God has allowed a diversity of views and successful church structures to develop in the New Testament Church. The Bible clearly requires churches to have elders. Beyond that, it does not define how many elders a church should have, who should be the senior elder, and whether calling as one of the five-fold Ephesians 4:11 governmental ministries should be a requirement for all elders.

Let each church be wise and sensitive to God in this area of leadership.

Contrast: True vs. Domineering Leadership

God is restoring true Biblical leadership to the house of the Lord. A healthy, united eldership does a great deal to bring harmony to the Church, and maintain balanced leadership that does not domineer God's flock. Governmental leaders must also take great pains to "maintain the unity of the Spirit in the bond of peace." This section will address one of the key issues in doing this: maintaining the balance between exercise of authority and showing of mercy.

A true leader of God is firm and strong, but nevertheless does not domineer the people of God. It is the false leader who is so insecure in his relationship with God and with others that he must compensate by unscriptural domination and dictatorship over God's people. Let us look at some strong New Testament warnings against tyrannizing, overbearing, bullying, and totally controlling or possessing the flock of God.

Example of the Nicolaitans. In the book of Revelation, the apostle John wrote under a prophetic spirit to the Churches of Pergamum and Ephesus. Through John, the Lord rebuked the Church in Pergamum for tolerating some people who taught the doctrine of the Nicolaitans. The Lord commended the Church in Ephesus for rejecting the Nicolaitans: *"Yet this you do have, that you* *hate the deeds of the Nicolaitans, which I also hate"* (Revelation 2:6). The Lord also spoke to those at Pergamum in a related matter:

> *"But I have a few things against you, because you have there some who hold the teaching of Balaam who kept teaching Balak to put a stumbling block before the sons of Israel, to eat things sacrificed to idols, and to commit acts of immorality. Thus, you also have some who in the same way hold the teaching of the Nicolaitans"* (Revelation 2:14,15).

The Church at Thyatira also had some Nicolaitans, since it also had the same teaching of immorality and idolatry (Revelation 2:20-25). Here the name "Jezebel" describes not only a woman who was like the wicked Phoenician queen and wife of Ahab, but also any leadership that was like her.

The Nicolaitans were condemned for fornication and idolatry. By studying the meaning of the name "Nicolaitan," it is possible to observe another reason for their condemnation. This heretical sect followed a man named Nicolaus. Although we do not know very much about Nicolaus or his leadership of this sect, "Nicolaitan" itself means "victorious or triumphant over the people." In addition to causing fornication and idolatry, the Nicolaitans may well have raised domineering leadership (like Jezebel) over the Churches in Ephesus, Pergamum and Thyatira. In these days of restoration, God is causing His leaders to be gentle, loving and protective of the inheritance for whom He shed His own blood.

Example of Diotrephes. A second example of domineering leadership in the New Testament is that of Diotrephes. The apostle John, the beloved of Jesus, wrote:

> *"I wrote something to the Church, but Diotrephes, who loves to be first among them, does not accept what we say. For this reason, if I come, I will call attention to his deeds which he does, unjustly accusing us with wicked words; and not satisfied with this, neither does he himself receive the brethren, and he forbids those who desire to do so, and puts them out of the church. Beloved, do not imitate what is evil, but what is good"* (III John 9-11a).

Diotrephes is an excellent example of domineering leadership, one who pridefully desires to be exalted above the brethren. It is interesting to see how other translations present parts of III John 9-11a:

"But Diotrephes, who loveth to have the preeminence among them" (King James Version)

"Who loves to have the foremost place among them" (Weymouth)

"Who likes to take the lead" (Moffatt)

Who *"loves to push him forward"* (Living Bible)

"Who is eager to be a leader" (Norlie)

Who is *"their would-be leader"* (New English Bible)

And *"He does not take the brothers into his house"* (Basic English)

"He neither maketh the brethren welcome" (Rotherham)

"He refuses to receive our friends" (New English)

And he *"tries to expel them from the congregation"* (New English)

III John 6-9a presents some characteristics of leaders who are proud and domineering.

They love self-exaltation and pride: *". . . but Diotrephes . . . loves to be first among them"* (III John 9).

They reject apostolic doctrine and counsel: *". . . but Diotrephes . . . does not accept what we say"* (III John 9).

They unjustly and unreasonably make open accusations against leadership: *". . . I will call attention to his deeds which he does, unjustly accusing us with wicked words . . ."* (III John 10a).

They are unable to receive all Christian brothers: *". . . and not satisfied with this, neither does he himself receive the brethren"* (III John 10b).

They publicly reject and attempt to dominate Christians who do receive all Christian brethren: *". . . and he forbids those who desire to do so, and puts them out of the Church"* (III John 10c).

What began as a seed of pride and self exaltation in Diotrephes ended in a public spirit of exclusivism and unteachableness. All Christian leaders are warned by his example to remain humble before the Lord and their brethren, to avoid the same sin.

Peter's Warning. A third example of a New Testament warning against domineering leadership is in I Peter 5:1-5, which states:

"The Elders which are among you I exhort, who am also an elder, and a witness of the sufferings of Christ, and also a partaker of the glory that shall be revealed: Feed the flock of God which is among you, taking the oversight thereof, not by constraint, but willingly, not for filthy lucre, but of a ready mind; neither as being lords over God's heritage, but being examples to the flock."

Here Peter puts leadership by example in contrast to lording one's authority over the flock. A Christian shepherd should never lord his authority over God's flock unless he wants them, in turn, to lord their authority over their families and those under them. It is also true that those who dictate imposition of their position upon others usually find it very difficult to submit to anyone themselves. The Amplified Bible puts these verses this way:

"I warn and counsel the elders among you--the pastors and spiritual guides of the Church--as a fellow-elder and as an eye-witness (called to testify) of the sufferings of Christ, as well as a sharer in the glory (the honor and splendor) that is to be revealed (disclosed, unfolded):

Tend--nurture, guard, guide and fold--the flock of God that is (your responsibility), not by coercion or constraint but willingly; not dishonorably motivated by the advantages and profits (belonging to the office) but eagerly and cheerfully.

Not as (arrogant, dictatorial and overbearing) domineering over those in your charge, but being examples--patterns and models of Christian living--to the flock (the congregation).

And (then) when the Chief Shepherd is revealed, you will win the conqueror's crown of glory.

Likewise, you that are younger and of lesser rank be subject to the elders--the ministers and spiritual guides of the church, giving them due respect and yielding to their counsel. Clothe (apron) yourselves, all of you, with humility--as the garb of a servant, so that its covering cannot possibly be stripped from you, with freedom from price and arrogance--toward one another. For God set Himself against the proud--the insolent, the over-bearing, the disdainful, the presumptuous, the boastful, and opposes, frustrates and defeats them--but gives grace (favor, blessing) to the humble."

Paul was in agreement with Peter when he wrote to the Corinthians:

"But I call God as witness to my soul, that to spare you I came no more to Corinth. Not that we Lord it over your faith, but are workers with you for your joy; for in your faith you

are standing firm" (II Corinthians 1:23,24)

Teaching of Christ. Jesus Christ, who had more reason to Lord His authority over people than any of His undershepherds, was the example of a Good Shepherd to the flock of God. He firmly taught His position-minded apostles that leadership in the kingdom of God was different than leadership in the world.

> *"Then came to him the mother of Zebedee's children with her sons, worshipping him, and desiring a certain thing of him.*
>
> *And he said unto her, 'What wilt thou?' She saith unto him, 'Grant that these my two sons may sit, the one on thy right hand, and the other on the left, in thy kingdom.'*
>
> *But Jesus answered and said, 'Ye know not what ye ask. Are ye able to drink of that cup that I shall drink of, and to be baptized with the baptism that I am baptized with?' They say unto him, 'We are able.'*
>
> *And he saith unto them, 'Ye shall drink indeed of my cup, and be baptized with the baptism that I am baptized with: but to sit on my right hand, and on my left, is not mine to give, but it shall be given to them for whom it is prepared of my Father.'*
>
> *And when the ten heard it, they were moved with indignation against the two brethren.*
>
> *But Jesus called them over unto him, and said, 'Ye know that the princes of the Gentiles exercise dominion over them, and they that are great exercise authority upon them.*
>
> *But it shall not be so among you: but whosoever will be great among you, let him be your minister;*
>
> *And whosoever will be chief among you, let him be your servant:*
>
> *Even as the son of man came not to be ministered unto, but to minister, and to give his life a ransom for many'"* (Matthew 20:20-28).

Christian leaders must not think of having great positions or of being served. On the contrary, they must meekly guide the flock by being themselves everything they want the flock to be. Loving, not lording, is the standard in God's Kingdom.

Ezekiel's Word. The prophet Ezekiel gave a most appropriate word to all of the shepherds of natural Israel, which can be applied to all of the shepherds of spiritual Israel, the Church. Ezekiel stated:

> *"And the word of the Lord came unto me, saying, Son of man, prophesy against the shepherds of Israel, prophesy, and say unto them, Thus saith the Lord God unto the shepherds; Woe be to the shepherds of Israel that do feed themselves! Should not the shepherds feed the flocks?*
>
> *Ye eat the fat, and ye clothe you with the wool, ye kill them that are fed: but ye feed not the flock.*
>
> *The diseased have ye not strengthened, neither have ye healed that which was sick, neither have ye bound up that which was broken, neither have ye brought again that which was driven away, neither have ye sought that which was lost; but with force and with cruelty have ye ruled them.*
>
> *And they were scattered, because there is no shepherd: and they became meat to all the beasts of the field, when they were scattered.*
>
> *My sheep wandered through all the mountains, and upon every high hill: yea, my flock was scattered upon all the face of the earth, and none did search or seek after them.*
>
> *Therefore, ye shepherds, hear the word of the Lord;*
>
> *As I live, saith the Lord God, surely because my flock became meat to every beast of the*

field because there was no shepherd, neither did my shepherds search for my flock, but the shepherds fed themselves, and fed not my flock;

Therefore, O ye shepherds, hear the word of the Lord;

Thus saith the Lord God; Behold, I am against the shepherds; and I will require my flock at their hand, and cause them to cease from feeding the flock; neither shall the shepherds feed themselves any more; for I will deliver my flock from their mouth, that they may not be meat for them.

For thus saith the Lord God; Behold, I, even I, will both search for my sheep, and seek them out.

As a shepherd seeketh out his flock in the day that he is among his sheep that are scattered; so will I seek out my sheep, and will deliver them out of all places where they have been scattered in the cloudy and dark day.

And I will bring them out from the people, and gather them from the countries, and will bring them to their own land, and feed them upon the mountains of Israel by the rivers, and in all the inhabited places of the country.

I will feed them in a good pasture, and upon the high mountains of Israel shall their fold be: there shall they lie in a good fold, and in a fat pasture shall they feed upon the mountains of Israel.

I will feed my flock, and I will cause them to lie down, saith the Lord God.

I will seek that which was lost, and bring again that which was driven away, and will bind up that which was broken, and will strengthen that which was sick: but I will destroy the fat and the strong; I will feed them with judgment" (Ezekiel 34:1-16).

Indeed, this passage to the shepherds of natural Israel should speak very meaningfully to 20th century shepherds, also. We must not neglect the desperate needs of the sheep whom God has put under our care.

The following columns show in general terms the contrast between true and false leadership. True leaders love the people of the Lord, while false leaders lord their authority over the people.

True Leadership

Concentrates on influence from WITHIN by encouraging, inspiring and motivating.

Enjoys a good relationship with co-workers, showing respect for the individual.

Works with co-workers toward long-range goals, with concern for the workers' development.

Aims to make himself unnecessary.

Values individual workers; encourages and praises rather than condemns them.

Desires power WITH co-workers, encourages input and feedback, shares credit for the results.

Always willing to discuss decisions and reasons for the decisions, unless circumstances do not allow.

Liberates the individual, encourages ideas and

Domineering Leadership

Depends on external controls from WITHOUT, using restrictions, rules, regulations.

Relates to co-workers from an "I'm superior--you're inferior" standpoint.

Demands immediate results, even if it damages the potential in the co-worker.

Creates an atmosphere where the subordinate is permanently dependent on him.

Has a low opinion of workers; very critical of others' mistakes.

Desires power OVER co-workers, takes credit for all accomplishments, wants no constructive criticism.

Interprets questions as personal criticism or disloyalty.

Limits individual freedoms, prefers to make all

participation, equips people to produce definite results.	decisions, does not train anyone else to function effectively.
Is a "heart" man, portraying a genuine concern for others.	Is a "head" man, showing little or no human compassion.
Is considerate and concerned for others.	Is concerned only with himself.

Leadership Motives. In surveying the characteristics of a godly leader, we cannot avoid seeing that pure and spiritual motives in the heart give rise to growth. By contrast, if a leader seeks high position sheerly for exaltation, he will only use people to his own ends, rather than serving their needs.

Furthermore, if a leader wants primarily to make people dependent upon his presence (thus giving him a sense of power), he will never properly train those under him who desire to be used of the Lord. God sets tremendous importance on a leader's reasons and motives. The wrong motives will poison a leader's work, while the right motives will overcome a host of difficulties.

In the gospels, we often see examples of improper motivations from the scribes, Pharisees and lawyers. When these religious leaders came to Jesus with a question, or even just as they pursued their daily activities, they always had ulterior motives. Note how the Holy Spirit constantly exposes their wrong motives for our admonition in the gospel of Matthew:

"But they do all their deeds to be noticed by men" (Matthew 23:5a)

"Woe unto you, scribes and Pharisees, hypocrites, because you devour widows' houses, even while for a pretense you make long prayers" (23:14)

"And behold, there was a man with a withered hand. And they questioned him (Jesus), *saying, 'Is it lawful to heal on the Sabbath?'--in order that they might accuse him"* (12:10)

"And the Pharisees and Sadducees came up, and testing him asked him to show them a sign from heaven" (16:1)

"And when he left there, the scribes and the Pharisees began to be very hostile and to question him closely on many subjects, plotting against him, to catch him in something he might say" (Luke 11:53,54)

It is obvious from these scriptures that the scribes and Pharisees and lawyers did not have pure motives concerning the Lord Jesus. In contrast, God's leaders must have pure motives toward God and His people. God's leaders must not feel that their status as servants is just a form of "paying their dues" that will get them "up the ladder" later on. A leader is a servant all of his life.

Carnal Motives. What are some of the improper motives a person could have in aspiring to leadership? What motives could affect you? It is a difficult exercise, but test your own motives. Ask yourself the questions that follow.

Would you like the glory of a fulfilled ministry more than the process of meeting people's spiritual needs?

Do you want power, position, the increased authority that goes with an office and a title of respect?

Just once, would you like to be the top dog, a teacher over students, the guy in the front of the room giving orders?

Why shouldn't you get your chance to shine, to prove you're better, to be enjoyed and praised for your own abilities and traits?

And if you got your chance, would it be so wrong if you were held up for public approval, and served by others?

There are many seducing spirits in the world. The man or the woman who wants to serve God knows that we must resist the temptation to harbor improper motives.

Godly Motives. On the other hand, the motivations that God wants to see in the lives of His leaders are the motivations that will impel us upward.

A desire to serve others and meet their needs, to make them successful in their callings and ministries, as Jonathan did for David.

A hunger to show the love and mercy of God to those that so desperately need it.

A deep, stubborn commitment to be faithful to the will of God in our lives.

An urgency to lead others to Christ.

A need to unite family members under Christ's headship.

A drive to help the spiritually sick, poor and oppressed.

Example of Christ. Jesus Christ Himself showed us the proper motives in desiring to be a minister of the Gospel when He told the Jews in the synagogue the purpose of the Spirit of the Lord in being upon Him:

"And he came to Nazareth, where he had been brought up: and, as his custom was, he went into the synagogue on the sabbath day, and stood up to read.

And there was delivered unto him the book of the prophet Esaias. And when he had opened the book, he found the place where it was written,

'The Spirit of the Lord is upon me, because he hath anointed me to preach the gospel to the poor; he hath sent me to heal the broken-hearted, to preach deliverance to the captives, and recovering of sight to the blind, to set at liberty them that are bruised,

To preach the acceptable year of the Lord'" (Luke 4:16-19).

May Christ's motives be ours.

Conclusion

The following fable about frogs, taken from Aesop's Fables, summarizes well the need of being servants to God's people, rather than dominating them.

"The frogs wanted a leader. They bothered Jupiter so much with their requests that he finally tossed them a log into the pond, and, for a while, the frogs were happy with their new leader.

Soon, however, they found out they could jump up and down on their new leader and run all over him. He offered no resistance nor even a response. The log did not have any direction or purpose in his behavior, but just floated back and forth in the pond. This practice exasperated the frogs, who were really sincere about wanting 'strong leadership.'

They went back to Jupiter and complained about their log-leader and appealed for much stronger administration and oversight. Because Jupiter was weary of the complaining frogs, he gave them a stork who stood tall above the members of the group and certainly had the appearance of a leader.

The frogs were quite happy with their new leader. Their leader stalked around the pond making great noises and attracting great attention. Their joy turned to sorrow, however, and ultimately to panic, for, in a very short time, the stork began to eat its subordinates."

The Lord does not want His leaders to be like logs who allow the people totally to run the Church. Neither does the Lord want His leaders to be like storks that eat up the people and only take advantage of them. May the Lord grant His leaders the divine balance that He so greatly desires.

God is restoring a truly biblical emphasis in Church leadership. In the next chapter, The Call of Leadership, we will examine the call in detail. We will see how it fits into God's pattern of organization for the Church. And you will see that whatever your gift and ministry is, God has a call for you as well.

CHAPTER 3
THE CALL OF LEADERSHIP

Most of the divine encounters throughout the Bible have related directly to God's call on the men and women of God. For the Christian leader, the call of God is the point of revelation, the personal foundation for ministry.

The same is true for every Christian, though not every ministry requires as much time or energy as governmental ministry. Our first goal and identity as Christians is to know Christ and to serve the Body of Christ. In this regard, much of your individual, personal identity as a Christian comes from your calling and ministry from God. As you give your life away to Christ and His Church, you will discover it.

This chapter will open the mystery of God's calling. It will explain what God's calling is to a believer, and how God uses the calling as part of His plan to build the Church. If you have not heard God's calling for your life yet, it will help you discover God's calling. If you have received your calling, you'll learn more about how it establishes your place in the Body of Christ.

"For even Christ came not to be ministered unto, but to minister, and to give His life as a ransom for many." With that same spirit, let's begin the process of discovering God's assignment for each of us in the Body of Christ.

The Necessity of the Divine Call

Through the years, numerous theologians have pondered, discussed and taught on the subject of the call of God. Magazines have published countless articles and testimonies on the necessity of God's call. Every Christian must be called to a specific ministry. It is the governmental ministries, however, because of their highly visible, public nature, which are most often coveted and pursued without God's calling.

Unfortunately, many leaders over the years have managed to enter positional ministries without receiving a divine call from God. Through their failures, these people have discovered that victory in the ministry hinges upon this initial call from God. Some entered governmental ministry in presumption. Some entered with innocent and noble motives, others in the same way they would enter any other profession in the world.

Many scriptures in the Old Testament describe the phenomenon of so-called leadership without the call of God. Every passage comes to the same conclusion: going forth on their own initiative, without the Lord sending them, these men failed.

The book of Jeremiah develops the subject of God's call very clearly. His warnings come at a pivotal time in Israel's history, when the remnant of Judah is threatened with captivity in Babylon. Jeremiah speaks out against the false prophets, the spiritual leaders of Israel who are leading the country to believe a lie--that God won't punish His people for disobedience. These prophets grew in favor by telling the people what they wanted to hear, directly contributing to Judah's disaster. Yet they were so popular that even after the captivity, the people continued to listen to them, hoping for an early end to captivity, when Ezekiel was called to respond.

"I sent them not, neither commanded them, therefore they shall not prosper this people at all" (Jeremiah 23:21,32).

" 'I have not sent them,' saith the Lord" (27:15).

"Then said the prophet Jeremiah unto Hananiah the prophet, 'Hear now, the Lord hath not sent thee, but thou makest this people to trust in a lie' " (28:15).

" 'They prophesy falsely, I have not sent them,' saith the Lord" (29:9,31).

" 'They have seen lying and vain divination,' saith the Lord, 'and the Lord hath not sent them, they have made others to hope that they would confirm the word' " (Ezekiel 13:6).

God Rejects False Leadership

Throughout Scripture, we encounter the Lord's judgment, "I have not sent them." Leaders down through the ages have run without a divine call, and God's people have suffered for it. They were not sent by God. Who sent them? Were they sent by the devil, or by the will of man, or did they send themselves?

In the Old Testament, it was a very serious offense to presume upon the office of any ministry without a divine call. If a man was called to be a priest, he dare not presume upon the king's office. If a man was called to be king, the priest's office was off-limits to him. Such presumption always resulted in the judgment of the Lord. No man ever entered the presence of the Lord without a divine commandment. God called Moses to come to see the burning bush. The Lord said, "Take off your shoes, for the place wherein you stand is holy ground" (Exodus 3:5). God ordained the high priest once a year on the Day of Atonement to come into His presence in the holy of holies. For a man to take this upon himself was literally to take his life into his own hands.

In the same manner, it is presumptuous for a person who is not called by God to go out and say that he is the Lord's representative. There must be a divine encounter with the Lord before a person can be sent out by the Lord. God must call the person and equip him before he goes forth. There must be an appointment by God.

There are three ways that a man can be appointed to an office. First, God can appoint him; second, man may appoint him; third, a person may appoint himself. In the world today there are many leaders appointed by themselves and by man, and few appointed by God. Let's look separately at each one of these sources of calling.

Self-appointed Leadership: Korah

A self-appointed leader takes upon himself the authority and responsibility of a spiritual office into which he has not been divinely called. The man Korah is an Old Testament example of self-appointed leadership. Numbers 16 and 17 provides the background and history to this story. Korah rebelled against the divinely-appointed leadership in Moses and tried to advance himself as a leader.

Korah followed a clearly defined process of self-appointment, which anyone will follow in pursuing a position to which God has not called him.

1. He caused others to rise up against existing spiritual leadership (Numbers 16:2).
2. He publicly criticized and questioned the existing leadership: "*Ye take too much upon you seeing the congregation are holy, every one of them, and the Lord is among them, wherefore lift ye up yourselves above the congregation of the Lord?*" (Numbers 16:3).
3. He accused leadership of what he himself was guilty (16:3).
4. He was not satisfied with the position that he had been given. He continually wanted more authority and a higher position (16:10).
5. He continued to murmur against the existing leadership (16:11).

The epistle of Jude, verse 11, refers to three men as examples of false ministries: Cain, Balaam and Korah. Jude states that in these last days, some men will go the way of one or all of these false ministries. The way of Korah is the man who will appoint himself to a divine office without the call of God. He represents self-willed and presumptuous men who want authority that is not given to them. They rise up against God-ordained leadership, as Korah did against Moses.

Man-appointed Leadership: Saul

Man-appointed leaders claim to receive a call from God, but the call is by the authority of human vessels who are not speaking by the unction of the Lord.

Man-appointed leadership is very common in our society today. The strong trend of humanism in the world makes people man-centered rather than God-centered. The humanistic spirit, which exalts the might and wisdom of man, has infiltrated the Church and her leadership. As a man calls himself into a position of authority in the Church, he puts much reliance on his own strength and ability, his academic degrees, training and education. Churches today are coping with this kind of leadership. But education, good as it is, cannot replace the call of God which alone brings anointing and the true authority of God upon an individual's life. The Church today does not need man-made or man-called or man-trained leadership.

Man-appointed leaders look toward the ministry as a professional (e.g. a dentist) looks toward his career. But ministry is more than a good career in a nice institution. Some of our modern theological institutions, which claim to train young men and women for the work of the ministry, have almost lost the concept of a divine encounter with the Lord. Thank God for those colleges and seminaries that make the divine call of utmost importance!

Man is not the one to choose the profession of the ministry. God is the one who exercises the choice, man responds. It is presumptuous to enter the ministry simply because one can speak several languages and pass written examinations on history, world religions and other subjects. Many in this category have run, but God has not sent them. Man can fill the mind and say, "Go forth and speak." But only God can give the anointing and the authority of the Holy Spirit to bring forth fruit and change lives through Jesus Christ.

The first king of Israel is an example of a man-appointed leader. The background to this story is found in I Samuel 8-10. In I Samuel 8:1-4 we find Samuel appointing his own sons as judges over Israel. Samuel's sons, however, had not followed their father in the ways of the Lord. The people, therefore, rejected them as leaders. They asked Samuel to give them a king like all the other nations. Up until that time, Israel had no king but Jehovah. Israel had a theocracy, but now they wanted a man to rule over them. Samuel, very displeased, went to God.

The Lord told Samuel to give the people of Israel what they wanted--a man to rule over them. The Lord said they had not rejected Samuel as their leader, but that they had rejected Him. Samuel returned to the people and gave them their request, a leader appointed only with earthly authority, a ruler who could draw only upon earthly resources. Samuel described the kind of leader they would have. Taken from I Samuel 8:11-17, the description applies to the man-appointed leaders in the Church world today.

"He will take your sons and appoint them for himself" (I Samuel 8:11).

"He will appoint many men to work his ground, to harvest his crops, to make his instruments of war and his chariots" (8:12).

"He will take your daughters to be confectionaries, cooks and bakers" (8:13).

"He will take the best of your fields, vineyards and oliveyards and give them to his servants" (8:14).

"He will take the tenth of your seed and of your vineyards and give it to his officers and servants" (8:15).

"He will put to work your servants, maid-servants, godliest young men, and your asses" (8:16).

"He will take a tenth of your sheep, and you shall be his servant" (8:17).

The key phrase to those portions of Scripture is, "He will take." The man-appointed leader is destined to rob and spoil the people of the Lord. He is out to get what he wants and what he needs, at the expense of the sheep. He is not concerned with the needs of the sheep. This is a picture of the hireling, who is the opposite of the true shepherd. The shepherd will die for the sheep, whereas the hireling lives off the sheep. A man-appointed leader is more interested in his own selfish desires than with the people whom he is supposed to serve.

In I Samuel 10 we have the account of Saul's anointing by the prophet Samuel. Samuel anointed Saul with oil poured out from a vial. All other kings were anointed by the oil poured forth from the horn of an animal--not a vial. The vial was a man-made bowl containing drinking water. The horn was taken from an animal that gave its life to produce it. Saul, a man-made ministry, was anointed with a man-made instrument, the vial. David, on the other hand, being God's choice, was anointed with the divine oil poured forth from the horn of an animal. God's leaders are anointed with a horn and not a vial; by God's Spirit and not by man's.

God-appointed Leadership

After looking at two of the most common errors in appointing leadership, we will now look at the Biblical pattern. The Bible is still the handbook for the believer, setting the guidelines needed for all areas. God appoints leaders to function in a given capacity. They are God's choice, God's appointed and placed ministries. The following words--appoint, separate, call and send--will provide scriptural insight into God Himself calling His leaders.

Appoint. The Hebrew word for "appoint" means to oversee, to care for, to watch over. The following are some examples of those whom God appointed:

Numbers 1:50	*"Thou shalt appoint the Levites."*
Numbers 3:10	*"Thou shalt appoint Aaron to his office."*
II Samuel 6:21	*"God chose and appointed me David ruler over the people."*
I Chronicles 15:16	The Levites were to appoint their brethren.
I Chronicles 15:17-19	*"The singers, Heman, Asaph and Ethan, were appointed to sound with cymbals of brass."*
Numbers 27:16,19,22	Joshua was the set (appointed) man over the people.
Acts 6:3	The apostles appointed deacons over the business of serving the tables.

Separate. The Hebrew word for "separated" means to set off by boundaries, to appoint to set aside. The following are some examples of those whom God separated:

Deuteronomy 10:8	*"The Lord separated the tribe of Levi."*
Deuteronomy 32:8	The Lord *"separated the sons of Adam."*
I Chronicles 23:13	*"Aaron was separated, that he should sanctify the most holy things."*
Romans 1:1	*"Paul . . . called to be an apostle, separated unto the gospel of God."*
Galatians 1:15	Paul had been *"separated from his mother's womb."*
Acts 13:2	*"The Holy Ghost said, 'Separate me Barnabas and Saul'."*

It is the Lord who calls and separates. Many people may help to develop a ministry through the preparation process, but the Lord must initially call people to His work. Through the hand of the Lord, through the dealings of God, a person's life service to God is set aside. All of the priests, kings, prophets and apostles, being chosen vessels of God, experienced a divine separation.

Call. The Hebrew word for "called" means to accost a person, to call out by name. The word "called" is used in the following references:

Exodus 3:4	God called (Moses) from out of the bush.
Exodus 31:2	*"I have called by name Bezaleel."*
I Samuel 3:4,18	*"The Lord called Samuel."*
Romans 1:1	*"Paul . . . called to be an apostle."*
I Corinthians 1:1	*"Paul, called to be an Apostle of Jesus Christ."*
Mark 1:20	*"Jesus straightway called the disciples."*

Send. The Hebrew word for "sent" means in the Hebrew to send away for a specific reason. The following are some references in which the word "sent" is used:

Genesis 45:7	*"God sent me before you to preserve you."*
Exodus 3:12-18	*"The God of Abraham, Isaac and Jacob hath sent you."*
Jeremiah 1:7c	God told Jeremiah that everywhere he would serve Him, he would go.
Zechariah 2:8	*"The Lord hath sent me unto the nations."*
Luke 4:18	*"He hath sent me to heal the broken-hearted."*
John 1:6	*"There was a man sent from God."*
John 4:34	*"My meat is to do the will of him who sent me."*

Each one of these words was chosen to illustrate the divine power of God in choosing and calling His leaders. Moses was set aside to establish the tabernacle for God. No other man at that time was given that responsibility. God gave him a special call with a specific job. David was marked to be the king of Israel. He was not man's choice, but God's. Man would not have chosen a young shepherd to lead the nation as king. But God put his hand upon David and called him to fulfill a divine destiny.

All of the servants of Jehovah received a specific call from the Lord for their work. The Lord has never lowered His standards in calling his servants; He alone must appoint the leaders He chooses. If the Church settles for man's choice of leaders, the will of God will not be accomplished in this generation.

All Believers Called to a Specific Function

The call of God has two sides that make a perfectly balanced whole. The necessity of a divine call cannot be stressed enough, when we have many presuming upon the ofices of the governmental ministries described in Ephesians 4:11. Unfortunately, the Church herself has helped create some of the confusion. She has over-emphasized the five gifted ministries, and has not taught enough about every-member ministry. Some people believed that governmental ministries were the only ones available. They falsely assumed that if they wanted to serve God and His Church, they had to aspire to one of the governmental ministries.

The Bible does not teach that the apostle, prophet, evangelist, pastor and teacher are the only ministries in the Body of Christ. The New Testament lists many more ministries. But sometimes the Church over-reacts to certain doctrines, and goes to an extreme in its practices. The call of God to governmental ministries is balanced by the call of God to congregational ministries.

Right now, the Church is over-reacting to its earlier over-emphasis on governmental ministries. The truth of every member having a ministry in the Body of Christ is being emphasized strongly. The Church today is hearing much about the priesthood of all believers, and the whole Body functioning in some realm of responsibility. But when we say that all members have a ministry and a responsibility, we should make the responsibilities of each ministry very clear. The responsibility to practice oversight of the Body of Christ is given only to the governmental ministries, and not to all members of the Body of Christ.

There is a great difference between the governmental ministries and the congregational ministries. Governmental ministries are given divine authority to rule the Body of Christ through the offices invested in them, the offices of apostle, prophet, evangelist, pastor or teacher. To function in one of these offices, a person must receive a divine call from God, and under His authority, to carry out His purposes. To function in a congregational ministry, a person must understand his position of responsibility and his limitations. Each part of the Body of Christ has received a call from God, but not necessarily to function in a governmental ministry.

Some people in the Church live all their lives waiting for an angelic visitation that will put them in some profound globe-trotting apostolic ministry. They are waiting for that divine call from God to some office they feel they should have. Most of the Body of Christ, however, must understand it has already been called to function as a shower of mercy, or a ministry of helps, or hospitality, or exhortation, or any other congregational ministry. Such a call is no less important. A ministry of helps is just as important as a ministry of an apostle. A ministry of hospitality is just as important as a ministry of a prophet. Though there are different callings in the Body, all of the callings are important and necessary. The difference lies in function, not in importance.

It is of the utmost importance for all Christians to realize that they have an important calling from God. The following scriptures illustrate this fact:

II Timothy 1:9	*"He saved us and called us with a holy calling."*
II Peter 1:10	*"Give diligence to make your calling and election sure."*
I Thessalonians 2:12	*"Who hath called you unto his kingdom and glory."*
Hebrews 3:1	*"Ye are partakers of the heavenly calling."*
Romans 1:6,7	*"Ye are called of Jesus Christ."*
I Corinthians 1:26	*"For ye see your calling, brethren."*
Ephesians 1:18	*"That ye may know what is the hope of his calling."*
Ephesians 4:1	*"Walk worthy of the vocation wherewith ye are called."*
II Thessalonians 2:14	*"He hath called you."*

The wisdom of God in calling different ones to function in different positions is past human understanding and human legislation. It is established in God's Word. The Church does not need to wait for further voices or visions from heaven to know that each member is called by God to some form of service.

Some Christians suffer from an inferiority complex. They cannot believe that God could call them to a place of ministry. In his epistle to the Corinthians, however, Paul states this doctrine of God's calling in a very clear way:

"For ye see your calling, brethren, how that not many wise men after the flesh, not many mighty, not many noble are called. But God hath chosen the foolish things of the world to confound the wise, and God hath chosen the weak things of the world to confound the things that are mighty. And the base things of the world, and the things which are despised, hath God chosen, yea, and the things which are not, to bring to nought things that are. That no flesh should glory in his presence" (I Corinthians 1:26-29).

Every Christian can see himself in that passage. Not many of us are wise after the flesh, not many mighty, not many noble. The world at large describes us as the foolish things, the weak things, the base things. We are the despised things, and the things which are not. Yet God has used us, and will use us, to confound the wise and the mighty, and "to bring to nought things that are."

The Nature of the Call

What is God's call? Does God's call on your life contain certain elements that can be examined and understood? Does God's call on you have some things in common with His call on all other members of the Body of Christ? We can answer these questions with a brief study of several New Testament words that bring us further understanding in the area of God's call to every member of the Body. These words are: ministry, talent, grace, gift and office.

Ministry. The word "ministry" in the New Testament Greek is "diakonia," which means to be a servant and to serve in menial tasks. The following is a list of scriptures in which this word is used:

Colossians 4:17	*"Take heed to the ministry which thou hast received"*
I Corinthians 16:15	*"Addicted to the ministry of the saints"*
II Corinthians 5:18	*"Has given to us the ministry of reconciliation"*
Romans 12:7	*"Let us wait on our ministry"*

All Christians have the ministry of being servants in the house of the Lord. The word ministry has already been discussed in the last chapter. We only reiterate here that the Church must continually root up, pluck out and pull down the false concepts of this word, which lead us to believe that "ministry" is only for a select few.

All Christians receive the command to serve. While public and pulpit ministries don't have room for all Christians, there is always room for dedicated Christian service. Do a quick mental inventory of needs in your church, your neighborhood, your home, your family, your job, your school. You know someone who needs Jesus, who needs your help--and you may be the only person who can provide it.

Talent. The word we translate as "talent" from New Testament Greek means to bear a weight, or refers to that which is weighed. To our English vocabulary, this word has provided the meaning of an abundance of ability.

In Matthew 25, Jesus teaches us several things through the parable of the talents. People receive talents (abilities and opportunities) in different degrees. But each member of the Body of Christ has received at least one talent or ability from the Lord. And every believer has the responsibility to develop the talent he has been given and use it for the kingdom of God.

Grace. The New Testament Greek word for "grace" carries the meaning of divine influence upon the heart, and its reflections in the life of the receiver. It also means the deposit of God within a Christian, an enablement that makes him come forth in some area of service to the Body of Christ. It is this deposit of grace in the life of Paul that caused him to describe himself as "a debtor," with an obligation to go preach the Gospel in Rome (Romans 1:13-16).

The word "grace" is used 150 times in the New Testament. The following is a list of some of the scriptures that use the word grace:

Luke 2:40	*"The grace of God was upon him."*
John 1:14	*"Jesus was full of grace and truth."*
Romans 1:5	*"Paul . . . received grace and apostleship."*
Romans 12:3	*"There is grace given to every man."*
Romans 12:6	*"Gifts differing according to the grace."*
Ephesians 4:4-7	Grace is given to the body of Christ.

The grace of God is freely given to each member of the Body of Christ, that each might minister freely to all of the Body. In this way, the grace of God fosters growth in the Body.

Gift. In Greek, the word "gift" means an endowment and a blessing of God. In this case, however, the recipient is not the focus of the gift. The focus is on all of the other people beyond the recipient, whom God will bless through the recipient's exercise of the gift. The following is a list of some of the verses using this word:

Romans 1:11	*"Impart unto you some spiritual gift"*
Romans 12:6	*"Having then gifts differing"*
I Corinthians 14:1	*"Desire spiritual gifts"*
I Corinthians 14:12	*"Be zealous of spiritual gifts"*
I Timothy 4:14	*"Neglect not the gift that is within you"*
II Timothy 1:6	*"Stir up the gift that is within you"*

The apostle Paul commanded the church at Corinth to be zealous of spiritual gifts, and to covet them. This same exhortation should be applied to the Church of the 20th century. Each member of the Church today needs to ask the Lord for a gift that will bless and build the Body of Christ. Your spiritual gift or gifts from the Lord are not given casually. And they are not to be a tool for attracting attention or admiration, as talents are among the worldly. Instead, they must be sought through intense prayer, and they must be faithfully used to serve those whom the Lord wants to help through you.

Office. The word "office" refers to a deed or official right to do or practice something. It denotes a specific action, function or involvement. The following is a list of some of the verses which use this word:

Exodus 29:1	*"Minister unto me in the priest's office*
I Chronicles 9:22	The porters were ordained by the priest to their set office
I Chronicles 23:28	The office of Levites was to wait upon the sons of Aaron
Nehemiah 13:13	*"Their office was to distribute unto the brethren"*
Romans 11:13	Paul the apostle magnified his office
Romans 12:4	*"All members have not the same office"*
I Timothy 3:1	*"If a man desire the office of a bishop"*
I Timothy 3:10	*"Let them use the office of a deacon"*

"First the natural and then the spiritual" is a principle Scripture uses (I Corinthians 15:45-49) in teaching spiritual truth through physical analogies. The natural picture of the human body at work is a perfect illustration of the office of every member at work in the Body of Christ. All members of the Body do not have the same office or the same function. Furthermore, if all members of the Body are not each doing their part, the whole Body suffers. Each part must know its office to fulfill, and must be faithful to that station.

The Church — the Body of Christ

The New Testament writers many times used the human anatomy to explain the function of the Body of Christ. They knew that it is a very tangible analogy for grasping a great mystery, the complex operation of the spiritual Body of Christ. And human anatomy is itself complex, an analogy worthy of the Body of Christ.

Even with today's advanced medical technology, man is still amazed at the structures and functions of the human body. Aptly, and with divine revelation, did David the prophet say of his own human body, *"I will give thanks to Thee, for I am fearfully and wonderfully made"* (Psalms 139:14a). Similarly, it is beyond our human understanding to grasp totally the greatness of the spiritual Body of Christ, and the various functions of its ministries and gifts.

Scientifically speaking, the study of anatomy concerns the structure and organization of any living thing. In a complementary way, the study of physiology describes the uses or functions of any living organism. Physiology explores each bodily organ and notes how it is integrated in the whole. The natural science of physiology can show the Church the spiritual principle of how each member of the Body is called to function in its particular place. As each member of the Body of Christ functions in its own place, the whole Body becomes healthy and beautiful.

This functioning of the Body of Christ is similar to the operating of the human body, which is composed of trillions of cells, a complex bone structure, musculature, digestive system, gland systems, a nervous system, heart and lungs at the hub of a complex circulatory system, and a magnificent brain--all vital to the life of the whole. All of these parts of the human body are so very different in their function and activity, yet all are so very necessary for the body to operate normally and healthfully.

The following verses present the Church in the imagery of the Body:

Ephesians 1:22-23	*"He gave him to be the Head over all things to the Church which is his body"*

Ephesians 4:12	*"For the edifying of the body of Christ"*
Ephesians 3:6	*"Fellow heirs of the same body"*
Ephesians 4:4	*"There is but one body"*
Ephesians 4:16	*"Whole body fitly framed together"*
Ephesians 5:23-30	*"For we are members of his body"*
I Corinthians 12:12	*"For as the body is one and hath many members"*
Colossians 1:8	*"He is the Head of the body"*
Colossians 2:19-23	*"All the body by joints and bands"*
Colossians 3:15	*"Ye are called into one body"*

The Fullness of the Spirit

Two key words, "fullness" and "measure," reveal a foundational principle that will help us understand the operation of the many parts or ministries in the Body of Christ. "Fullness" has the meaning "to be complete, filled up, to render full, not lacking anything." The Greek word for "measure," by contrast, describes a state of degrees, of incompletion.

Fullness of Christ. In Scripture, the word "fullness" is used to describe the Head of the Body, the Lord Jesus Christ. Only the Lord Jesus Christ has the fullness of divine blessing. As the Head of the Body, Christ received the fullness of the Spirit. He did not receive the Spirit in partial measure, as a believer does when baptized in the Holy Spirit. Christ received the fullness of God's Spirit. The following verses demonstrate the principle that Christ received the fullness of God's Spirit, while the believer receives only a portion of the Spirit:

John 1:16	*"Of his fullness have we all received"* (Amplified Bible)
John 3:34	*"For God giveth not the spirit by measure unto him"*
Ephesians 1:23	*"The fullness of him that filleth all in all"*
Ephesians 3:19	*"That we might be filled with all the fullness of God"*
Ephesians 4:13	*"Unto the measure of the stature of the fullness of Christ"*
Colossians 1:19	*"It pleased the Father that in him should all the fullness of the Godhead dwell"*
Colossians 2:9	*"For in him dwelleth all the fullness of the Godhead bodily"*

John the Baptist testified that Jesus received the Spirit of God without measure (John 3:34). Jesus was unique from any prophet or man of God that had ever come to Israel. Others had been sent with a message of repentance or judgment from God. Jesus in Himself was the message of God, the Word of God in the flesh. The Spirit was not given to Christ to enable Him to work the miracles of God on special occasions. He Himself was the fullness of the Spirit, God in the flesh.

Throughout Israel's history, many had come who were characterized as deliverers, men with a distinct message from God. They had intermittently experienced the power of the Spirit upon their ministries. They were inspired on different occasions to go forth and speak for God. But this man, the Lord Jesus Christ, was God the Son, sent forth from the Father to do the work of eternal redemption and reconciliation. Jesus did not merely receive the Spirit of life or the Spirit of power. He was and is the source of all life and power. No believer in this life or in the life to come will ever have the fullness of the Spirit as does the Head of the Body, the Lord Jesus Christ. Only He is the incarnate and only begotten Son of God with the fullness of the Spirit. Only in Jesus is God's fullness.

Measure in the Church. The word "measure" refers to a part or portion of the whole. The Bible applies it often in describing the Body of Christ. The Christian believer, through faith and obedience to the Word of God, receives a limited measure of the fullness of the Head.

It is one of the great mysteries of the Church that, in spite of this limitation, the world may still see the fullness of the Head. This happens when every member of the Body of Christ is filled with its apportioned measure of the Spirit, and shows forth that measure in harmony with the rest of the Body. It is a miraculous testimony to the world.

Here are some of the scriptures concerning the Body of Christ receiving a measure of the fullness of Christ, the Head of the Body:

John 1:16	*"Of his fullness have we all received."*
Romans 12:3	*"He has dealt to every man a measure of faith."*
Ephesians 4:7	*"Unto every one of us is given grace, according to the measure of the gift of Christ."*
Ephesians 4:13	*"The measure of the stature of the fullness of Christ."*
Ephesians 4:16	*"According to the effectual working in the measure of every part"* (Amplified Bible).
I Corinthians 12:11	*"All these worketh that one and the self-same Spirit, dividing to every man severally as he will."*

It is God's will, in due time, that His Body be filled with all the fullness of God (Ephesians 3:19). He has ordained this to happen when each member of the Body functions in its proper place, with the measure of grace that God has given to it. The following comparison chart will bring into sharp focus this concept of the fullness of the Lord Jesus Christ and the measure in His many-membered Body. Don't be surprised if you find one of your own gifts named there, as a corresponding reflection of the fullness of Christ.

CHRIST, THE HEAD THE FULLNESS

1. Fullness of the Spirit
2. Fullness of grace
3. The Word made flesh
4. Fullness of power
5. Fullness of the fruit of the Spirit
6. Fullness of ministry
   apostle in fullness
   prophet in fullness
   evangelist in fullness
   pastor in fullness
   teacher in fullness
7. Fullness of the gifts of the Spirit
   Spirit of wisdom
   Spirit of knowledge
   Spirit of faith
   Spirit of healing
   Spirit of miracles
   Spirit of prophecy
   Spirit of discernment
   Spirit of tongues
   Spirit of interpretation

THE CHURCH, THE BODY A MEASURE

1. Measure of the Spirit
2. Measure of the Spirit of grace
3. Measure of the Word in a word from God
4. Measure of the Spirit of power
5. Measure of the fruit of the Spirit
6. Measure of ministry to different members
   some apostles
   some prophets
   some evangelists
   some pastors
   some teachers
7. Measure of the gifts of the Spirit
   word of wisdom
   word of knowledge
   word of faith
   gift of healing
   gift of miracles
   gift of prophecy
   gift of discernment
   gift of tongues
   gift of interpretation

8. Fullness of the Spirit of intercession

9. Fullness of the ministry of mercy

10. Fullness of anointed preaching

11. Fullness of the Spirit in binding up the broken-hearted

12. Fullness of the Spirit in proclaiming liberty to the captives

13. Fullness of the Spirit in opening the doors of the prisoner

14. Fullness of the Spirit in proclaiming the acceptable year of the Lord

15. Fullness of the Spirit in comforting those who mourn

16. Fullness of the Spirit in giving beauty for ashes

17. Fullness of the Spirit in giving the oil of joy to those who mourn

18. Fullness of the Spirit in giving the garment of praise for the spirit of heaviness

19. Fullness of the Spirit of counsel, might, power and the fear of the Lord.

8. A measure in different ministries of intercession

9. Measure of mercy in various ministries

10. A measure in various anointed preachers

11. A measure in certain ministries of compassion

12. Measure of deliverance through certain ministries

13. A measure in different spiritual keys to open the doors of the prisoner

14. A measure in proclaiming the last days and the good news of Jesus Christ

15. Measure of comfort through different ministries in the Body

16. Measure of restoration through each ministry in the Body

17. Measure of the oil of joy, manifested through the different gifts and ministries in the Body

18. Measure of praise through the various ministries of song, praise, thanksgiving, music, instruments and worship in the Body

19. Measure of counsel, might, power and the fear of the Lord through various ministries in the Body

Your Call from God

Now that we've explored the gifts and ministry of the Holy Spirit, you may have some urgent questions. What's my gift? To what ministry am I called? What's my place in the Body of Christ? What grace is operating in me right now? Even if you're a mature Christian with a well-defined ministry, you can be more fruitful when you understand your calling. Your gift and ministry make up an important part of your identity as a Christian.

The chart below, "Gifts and Ministries in the New Testament Church," can help you answer questions about your gift and ministry. It may help you see yourself--and others--as you never have before.

Somewhere in the chart, your gift and ministry is described, because it is a complete list of all Church gifts and ministries. Key sections of Scripture listed with your gift will help you see what the Bible says about you and your personality as a believer. The function of your gift is included, letting you know the activities where your gift excels. This may confirm that you are already beginning to function in your ministry, if you are actively involved in serving the Body. The definition of your ministry, also included, will give you an idea of where your gift fits in the Body of Christ. It may also help you identify Christians who share your gift and ministry, people who can help you grow into your area of service to the Body of Christ.

But the process of discovering your gift and ministry also involves a personal encounter with God. Once your faith has been instructed and you see what may be your gift and ministry, you need to hear from God. Only He can call you to your place in the Body of Christ. Only He can establish His choice of gift and ministry for you. You'll discover the biblical pattern of God's call to His servants in Chapter Four, "Man's Response to the Call of God."

GIFTS AND MINISTRIES IN THE NEW TESTAMENT CHURCH

GIFT/MINISTRY	SCRIPTURES	DEFINITION	FUNCTION
Apostle	Ephesians 4:11 I Corinthians 12:28 Acts 2:43	One sent forth with orders A delegate or ambassador Bearer of a commmission	To establish local churches To ordain elders To bring forth revelation of the Word To train and discipline ministries To bring adjustment to counselors To be a spiritual father to others
Prophet	Ephesians 4:11 Ephesians 2:20 Acts 11:27-30 Acts 13:1-4	Foreteller of God's Word and future events Forthteller of God's Word under inspiration of the Spirit Mouthpiece or spokesman for God An interpreter of God's Word	To function in the office of a prophet To pronounce judgment To confirm direction of ministry To travel with apostles in team ministry confirming local churches
Prophetess	Exodus 15:20 Luke 2:36	Female foreteller of God's Word A woman inspired by the Holy Spirit in the Word of God	To prophesy
Evangelist	Ephesians 4:11 Acts 21:8 II Timothy 4:5	Preacher of the Gospel (messenger of good news) Preacher having a harvesting ministry	To train soul-winners To win the lost through preaching and miracles To work with apostolic teams in starting and establishing local churches
Pastor/ Shepherd	Ephesians 4:11 John 10:16 John 21:16 I Peter 5:2,3	Herdsman of God's people An overseer of the Church One who tends, guards, feeds and guides the flock of God	To feed the flock To counsel the flock To lead the flock To identify with the flock To oversee a local flock
Teacher	I Corinthians 12:28 I Timothy 3:2 II Timothy 2:2,24	Instructor in God's Word One who imparts systematic knowledge A teacher of other teachers	To establish truth and doctrine from God's Word To teach others how to teach To correct doctrine To balance the prophet's inspirational ministry
Prophesy	Romans 12:6 I Corinthians 12:10 I Corinthians 13:2 and 14:3	To occasionally foretell future events To speak under the inspiration of God's Spirit A gifted member who inspires, confirms and reinforces revealed truth	To exhort, edify and comfort through inspirational speech To encourage Christians through the anointing of the Spirit

GIFT/MINISTRY	SCRIPTURES	DEFINITION	FUNCTION
Ministry	Acts 6:1 Romans 15:31 II Corinthians 4:1 Romans 12:7	One who attends as a servant A servant to the household of faith One who renders service, aid and relief to others	To serve in any capacity available To show a willing spirit to meet needs at any time To minister to others' needs and desires
Teaching	Romans 12:7 II Timothy 2:2	One who instructs others One who instills doctrine into another	To lay out material for the edification, exhortation and comfort of others To instruct others in a supportive role to a true ministry
Exhortation	Ephesians 4:11 Acts 20:12 I Corinthians 14:3 II Corinthians 1:4,6 Titus 1:9	One who consoles, encourages, strengthens others One who comforts others on a personal level One who encourages the Church with short words of edification	To warm, console or admonish the believers To cheer or comfort the Church in times of stress or need
Giving	Romans 1:11 and 12:8 Ephesians 4:28	One who liberally shares and imparts to others what he has to give One who gives to others out of the abundance that God has given to him	To meet others' needs through giving To believe God for blessings so that others may receive them in turn To give financially and sacrificially to meet the needs of the Church
Ruling	Romans 12:8 I Thessalonians 5:12 I Timothy 3:4,5,12	One who presides over various Church functions One who leads by good example and service One who organizes, facilitates and administrates church activities	To protect or guard the flock with a leader's instinct To be a support ministry to the elders of a local church To organize and carry out activities and programs
Mercy	Romans 12:8 Matthew 5:7 and 6:2-4 James 3:17	One who feels the hurts of others One who is loving and compassionate One who shows sincere, gracious favor to others One who is motivated to encourage and cheer	To minister to the sick, elderly, shut-in and needy To show kindness and gentleness to the hurt To anonymously give to meet needs

GIFT/MINISTRY	SCRIPTURES	DEFINITION	FUNCTION
Word of Wisdom	Matthew 21:25 and 22:21 John 8:7 I Corinthians 12:8	One who receives supernatural revelation and wisdom from God for situations One who is anointed by the Spirit to give specific counsel to others that meets their needs	To perceive and communicate how the ways of God apply to a specific situation To function and speak under a supernatural mantle of wisdom and prudence To receive specific understanding from the Lord about the best way to handle a situation or problem
Word of Knowledge	I Corinthians 12:8 and 5:3-5 Acts 5:3 and 9:10 and 8:23	One who receives from God supernatural facts and information which would be humanly impossible to know	To speak forth by divine revelation the specific facts about a situation To speak to others God's mind toward a specific situation To reveal to individuals or groups their specific needs or provision by divine revelation
Faith	I Corinthians 12:9 Matthew 21:19	One who can believe God for the impossible One who has the special gift of faith for what God has promised to do; an ability to see God's promises come to pass	To speak the word of faith with results To receive from God supernatural power to believe Him for miracles
Healing	I Corinthians 12:9, 28,30 Acts 4:22-30	One who is used by God as the vessel through which He imparts healing to the physical body at times of His choosing	To be the instrument through which God brings a healing or cure To lay one's hands on others and see them restored to health, by the power of the Spirit, on a regular basis To be the instrument through which God's power frequently heals a particular kind of sickness
Miracles	I Corinthians 12:28 and 4:19,20 II Timothy 1:7 Romans 1:16	One who performs what is naturally impossible through the power of God One who has been gifted with a ministry of power and deliverance	To perform the supernatural through the power of God To do something not normally possible, to the glory of God

GIFT/MINISTRY	SCRIPTURES	DEFINITION	FUNCTION
Discernment	I Corinthians 12:10 Acts 16:16-18	One who recognizes what spirit (divine, evil or human) is causing a certain manifestation or activity	To judge accurately what is of the Spirit of God and what is not To have a gifted sensitive spirit that distinguishes between truth and error To know the spiritual source behind something or someone
Tongues	I Corinthians 12:10 and 14:5,6,18, 21-23,27,28,39 Acts 2:4,8-11 and 10:46 and 19:6	One who speaks forth a language he does not understand One who speaks by the Spirit in a language that he has not previously learned	To speak out a supernatural utterance which is interpreted by the same or different person in a public gathering for the edification of the Church To speak forth a language not previously learned by formal education, yet is understandable to its hearers To speak forth a heavenly language as a sign of the reception of the Baptism of the Holy Spirit for one's personal edification is not the same as the gift of tongues
Interpretation of Tongues	I Corinthians 12:30 and 14:6-14,27,28 Acts 10:46	One who is given supernatural understanding to interpret the meaning of a message in tongues to the Church	To interpret the meaning of a message given by the gift of tongues in a congregation
Governments	I Corinthians 12:28 Romans 12:8 I Timothy 5:17	One who steers, directs or pilots an activity in the Church or a local church	To guide some of the affairs of the Church To operate in the gift of administration
Helps	I Corinthians 12:28	One who gives relief and help One who lightens the load of leaders by doing certain practical things for them	To help the local church in practical ways To relieve some of the everyday needs of the people in the Church To relieve those who serve in the Word of some of their routine responsibilities

GIFT/MINISTRY	SCRIPTURES	DEFINITION	FUNCTION
Intercession	Isaiah 59:16 Romans 8:26,27,34 and 11:2 I Timothy 2:1	One who confers with or entreats another person One who goes to meet a person for conversation, consultation or supplication	To pray for others with a supernatural revelation of their needs To bring the needs of the Church before the Lord with a special fervency and frequency To have a deep prayer life and ministry which God uses as a speaking vessel to bring certain needs before Him
Elder	Acts 11:30 and 14:23 I Timothy 4:14 and 5:17-19	One who is older, or a senior One who has advanced and matured in life	To lead and rule the people of God To shepherd the people of God
Bishop/ Overseer	Acts 1:20 Philippians 1:1 I Timothy 3:1-8 Titus 1:7 I Peter 2:25	One who watches over, curates or guards others	To watch over the Church To guard, protect and help the flock
Deacon	Acts 6:1-6 Romans 16:1 I Timothy 3:8,12	One who serves guests food and drink at table	To serve others in practical ways To do menial tasks in the Church To usher, serve communion, or take the offering in a local church service
Singer	I Chronicles 15:16-27 II Chronicles 5:12,13 and 9:11 and 20:21 and 23:13 Ephesians 5:19 Colossians 3:16 Hebrews 2:12	One who supports the priestly function through music One who makes melody to the Lord with his voice	To glorify God in a song To be an active member in the church choir To lead the church's song service To inspire others to sing the Song of the Lord To sing the Song of the Lord with the anointing of the Spirit To edify the Church in song as a soloist
Teacher of Song	I Chronicles 15:22, 27, and 25:6	One who instructs and leads others in the use of their ministry of singing unto the Lord	To teach others to sing the Song of the Lord To instruct the congregation to sing and to play their instruments in harmony unto the Lord To lead a church choir To be an instructor in voice

GIFT/MINISTRY	SCRIPTURES	DEFINITION	FUNCTION
Musician	I Chronicles 15:16 and 16:42 II Chronicles 5:13 and 7:6 and 23:13 and 29:26 and 29:27 and 30:21 and 34:12 Psalm 150	One who glitters from afar (in eminence) One who is a superintendent of the music in the temple services	To play an instrument skillfully unto the Lord Through music, to inspire others to play or sing unto the Lord To edify the people of God through music To be a skillful member of the church orchestra
Doorkeeper	I Chronicles 9:17-26 and 15:18,23,24 and 16:38,42 and 26:1 Psalm 84:10	One who waits at the threshold (the vestible)	To warmly greet visitors arriving at a church To help people find seats in the church as an usher To serve the congregation at church in similar practical ways
Priest	I Peter 2:5,9 Revelation 1:6 and 5:10 and 20:6 Hebrews 13:15,16	A born-again Christian in the Church of Jesus Christ	To offer spiritual sacrifices of praise to God as a Christian To offer sacrifices of money, fellowship and services to God as a Christian

CHAPTER 4
MAN'S RESPONSE TO THE CALL OF GOD

To a young man or woman, receiving God's call is the most exciting event in life. Blessing in ministry confirms the call, and helps establish a leader's confidence in his call. In the face of failure and criticism, every genuine Christian leader is taken back to his call. "Did I hear God correctly? Am I where I should be? What must I do to return to God's original call, to come under His hand of blessing?"

Every believer is called to his or her ministry, whether it be governmental or congregational. And whatever your ministry, you probably will be called to act in a leadership role at some time. It may be in a major work of service, or in a more temporary work. Though perhaps less sweeping and dramatic, your call to serve as a leader will contain some of the elements of the calls we will study next--the call of Moses, Jeremiah and Gideon.

The Call to Governmental Ministry

God has called certain men to govern His Body. In Ephesians 4:11,12 Paul clearly states that only some of the Body of Christ are called to this governmental function. Paul states, "And He (Jesus) gave some as apostles, and some as prophets, and some as evangelists, and some as pastors and teachers . . ." The principle of leadership here is that only some members of the Body are called to governmental ministry. Each member of the Body has a calling, each calling is unique, and each calling is perfectly rewarding and satisfying to the Christian who is living in faith.

Not only does every Christian have a unique calling, but each is called in a unique way. This is especially true of God's leaders. The Bible provides a long list of leaders who were called in a unique fashion. Though some patterns are repeated, each call happens under its own circumstances and follows its own rules. In the following list of men who served in various governmental capacities, notice the great diversity in God's method of calling.

Abraham was called by God (at the age of 70) through the word of the Lord (Genesis 12:1-5).

Aaron was called by God through Moses (Exodus 3:13-17).

Joseph was called by God through the word of the Lord in a dream (Genesis 37:1-10).

Jacob was called by God through the hand of the Lord being upon him from the time of his birth (Genesis 25:22-26).

Moses was called by God through an angel in the burning bush (Exodus 3:1-6).

Joshua was called by God through the words of Moses (Exodus 17:9-11).

Samuel was called by God through God's audible voice (I Samuel 3:1-10).

Saul was called by God through the word of the prophet Samuel (I Samuel 10:1,2).

David was called by God through the word of the prophet Samuel (I Samuel 16:11-14).

Solomon was called by God through his father David and a dream from God (II Chronicles 1:1-12).

Ezekiel was called by God through the word of the Lord (Ezekiel 1:1,3).

Jeremiah was called by God through the word of the Lord (Jeremiah 1:1-10).

The apostles Peter, Andrew, James and John were called by God through the words of the Lord Jesus Christ (Matthew 4:18-22).

Paul was called by God through visitation by the Lord Jesus (Acts 9:1-9).

Timothy was called by God through his family upbringing and the hand of Paul (I Timothy 1:2,18; II Timothy 1:2,5,9 and 2:1).

These fifteen examples show us that God calls His leaders to governmental ministry in different ways. He calls some through a "burning bush" experience. Some will receive a definite spiritual visitation from the Lord. Others will have a dream, vision or prophetic word. Still others will be called by God through deep inner desires which He has planted in their hearts. All of these calls are unique but real to the people who have received them. They are all valid calls of God.

Men and women of God should not judge the means of another's call just because it may be different from their own. Furthermore, people who are called by God should not feel condemned if their calling was not exactly like someone else's. The same is true regarding the calls we will study in this chapter, the call of Moses, Gideon and Jeremiah. They are useful patterns to study the human response to God, not laws for measuring the validity of God's call.

Each Christian has a unique and valid calling from God. It is ironic that some of those who are not truly called by God to a governmental ministry sometimes desire one fanatically. And some of those who are truly called by God sometimes resist it the most. We will now look at this ironic fact of ministry calling, in the lives of three great governmental leaders of God: Moses, Jeremiah and Gideon.

The Call of Moses

Moses is one of the most interesting men of the Old Testament. Dueteronomy 34:10 states, *"And there arose not a prophet since in Israel like unto the man Moses, whom the Lord knew face to face."* Moses was obviously a man with a unique relationship with the Lord.

Hebrews 11:23 states, *"By faith Moses, when he was born, was hid three months by his parents, because they saw he was a proper child, and they were not afraid of the king's commandments."* Moses was born of faith. His parents had a living faith in the God of their fathers. We have the Old Testament account of this in Exodus 2:1-10. The verses immediately following do not tell us what transpired during the early years of the life of Moses. But with the help of Scripture and history, we can begin to understand a portion of what happened.

The Youth of Moses

Moses was adopted and raised in the house of the daughter of Pharaoh, which meant he lived in the royal household. Acts 7:22 states, *"And Moses was learned in all the wisdom of the Egyptians, and was mighty in words and deeds."* From this verse we see that Moses had all the education of the known world available while in the royal house of Pharoah. Any university or tutoring scholar, as it were, would have deemed it a privilege to tutor the son of Pharoah's daughter.

Egypt was, at that time, one of the most productive and progressive countries of the known world, with educational achievements far above any other land. Their economic and social life, too, was highly developed. Even today, Egypt's colossal pyramids, with their mathematical precision, confound the understanding of the most educated builders in the world. This was the environment in which Moses was raised from his youth.

The ancient Jewish historian Josephus gives one account of Moses which provides an insight into his power and ability. Josephus says that Ethiopian armies attacked, and were on the verge of inflicting a terrible defeat on Egypt. Moses, apparently, was appointed to go forth and command the armies of the Egyptians in an attempt to save the country from a disastrous downfall. Moses reportedly lead the armies into battle and brought a great victory. If true, this account gives us a good glimpse of the man that Stephen described as *"the man which was mighty in words and in deeds"* (Acts 7:22).

As we look at the scriptures concerning Moses, it is evident that the Lord must have spoken to him sometime during the early years of his life. Hebrews 11:24-26 states, *"By faith Moses, when he had grown up, refused to be called the son of Pharoah's daughter, choosing rather to suffer affliction with the people of God, than to enjoy the pleasures of sin for a season."*

This reference makes it very clear that Moses faced a very difficult decision in life. He had to choose between royalty and peasantry. Moses had to choose between all of the wealth, power, influence and glory of Egypt and the slavery of his own people Israel. Would he identify with the royalty of Egypt or the bondage of his own people?

Hebrews 11:27 tells us that *"By faith Moses forsook Egypt, not fearing the wrath of the king, for he endured, as seeing Him who is invisible."* Moses was at the age of forty when he made this life-changing decision. Moses' decision challenged and changed his life, to say the least. In saving a Hebrew from a cruel beating, he slew the Egyptian who was beating him. This led Moses directly into a personal forty-year period of wilderness wanderings. Why would God use a wilderness to prepare the leader of His people? God's ways are always different and sometimes opposite to man's ways, especially when it comes to dealing with His servants.

The Stripping Process

A transition from the royal courts of Pharoah to the backside of the desert would have been a drastic change for anyone. But God had a purpose in it for Moses' development; God was going to put Moses through some years of divine stripping. Moses had been a long forty years in the courts of Pharoah learning all of the wisdom, ways, power and tools of men. He had, in a sense, all of the academic degrees that Egypt could offer him. But the Lord God of Israel was not going to use these Egyptian methods to free His people from their bondage. God was going to strip Moses of all his Egyptian wisdom, and begin to mold him for a task that only God's wisdom could accomplish through him.

For forty years, Moses was on the backside of the desert, where he shepherded his father-in-law's sheep. He could not claim to possess so much as his own sheep. He was just a comman herdsman of another man's flock. In addition, Moses' wife was just an ordinary woman of the desert. She was a far contrast from the royal young maidens that he could have married in Egypt. The question naturally arises at this point, "What was God's purpose in all of this?" God was totally stripping the man whom he was going to use greatly.

The effectiveness of all of God's strippings were very evident in the way that we see Moses respond to God's call at a later time. As we shall soon see, Moses was stripped of self-confidence and Egyptian pride. These attitudes would have made it impossible for him to accomplish what God had called him to do. In the great task that Moses was going to face, he would need to know that God, not man, was the source of his strength. As with Moses, God has a desert for all of His servants that He is going to use in a mighty way. The stripping process ia part of the plan of God for all who will respond to the call of the Lord. A leader dare not challenge God's processes of calling and preparation.

The Burning Bush

In Exodus 3:1-11, we read about the call of Moses. When he was called, Moses was on the backside of the desert. Moses was tending sheep in the dry desert, as any other day's work would normally have required him to do. Exodus 3:2 states, *"And the Angel of the Lord appeared unto him in a flame of fire out of the midst of the bush: and behold the bush burned with fire and the bush was not consumed."*

The fact that the bush was not consumed was the fascinating attraction that caused Moses to turn aside to see what this strange thing was. Exodus 3:4 states, *"And when the Lord saw that he turned aside to see, God called unto him out of the midst of the bush and said, 'Moses, Moses.' And Moses said, 'Here am I.'"* When God revealed himself to Moses out of the burning bush, He told Moses to draw near so that He might speak to him.

The Lord told Moses of His plan to deliver the children of Israel out of their Egyptian bondage. God told Moses how the children of Israel were in great distress, affliction and mourning because of their Egyptian taskmasters. Because Moses already understood the sad plight of the children of Israel, he did not hesitate to agree with the Lord that Israel greatly needed help. Moses' agreement with the Lord showed that he had a definite burden for his people.

The Failure of Moses

Moses had already tried once to deliver his people in his own might but had failed (Exodus 2:11-15). Now the Lord was saying to Moses, in essence, *"I am going to deliver the people this time by my own power, and in my own way."* Because God told Moses that He Himself was going to deliver the people, it must have come as a real shock to Moses when he heard God say to him what seemed to be just the opposite: *"Come now therefore, and I will send thee unto Pharoah that thou mayest bring forth my people, the children of Israel, out of bondage"* (Exodus 3:10).

Similarly, all men and women of God experience times when they fail to deliver the Church from her bondage, because they try to do it in their own power and their own way. After breaking them down, God consequently arises to give them the same commission as before. Only the second time, God delivers the Church through His servant by the power of His Spirit. In doing so, God humbles His servant so that He Himself can receive all of the glory from His mighty deliverance of His people.

Moses received a direct call from the God of Abraham, Isaac and Jacob. He did not doubt that his call was from the Most High God, because he heard it with his own ears. But how did Moses respond to this call? In the following section, we will observe the different responses that Moses had to God's call upon his life. Throughout history, men and women of God have responded to the calling of the Lord in these very ways.

The Response of Unworthiness

Moses' first response to God's call was a response of unworthiness. It is found in Exodus 3:11, where the Scripture states, *"And Moses said unto God, 'Who am I, that I should go unto Pharoah, and that I should bring forth the children of Israel out of Egypt?'"* Moses said that he was not worthy of the great task to which God was calling him. Moses' feeling of unworthiness was a feeling of being undeserving, useless, valueless and inadequate.

This sense of inadequacy was probably a real contrast to Moses' personality forty years earlier. At that time, he may have been the commander of the armies of Pharoah. He was the man who was mighty in words and in deeds and had been reared in the royal house. Moses probably never felt unworthy in the royal house. All of Pharoah's servants bowed to him and waited upon him as they did for all of the royal family. But in spite of all this royal heritage, the Lord had so stripped Moses that when he heard God's voice out of the burning bush, he could only exclaim, *"I am not worthy of the work of the Lord."*

In response to Moses' statement of unworthiness, God said, *"Certainly, I Am will be with thee"* (Exodus 3:12). Although many men who are called of God feel unworthy of the calling, God's divine enablement and protection causes them to respond fully to God's call, as Moses eventually did. The "I Am" in Hebrew carries the idea of "I will be all you need when you need it."

The Response of Fear of Rejection

Moses' second response to God's call was a fear of rejection. It is found in Exodus 3:13-16, where the Scripture states, *"And Moses said unto the Lord, Behold, when I come unto the children of Israel, and shall say unto them, 'The God of your Fathers hath sent me unto you'; and they shall say to me, 'What is his name?' What shall I say unto them?"* Moses feared that Israel would reject him if he did not know the specific name of God, who had called him to deliver the nation. Because Israel knew the specific names of the Egyptian gods, Moses wanted to tell the people that the one and true God of Israel had sent him.

Moreover, Moses feared that the people would not respond to the authority in which he was coming to them. He remembered what was said to him the last time he tried to deliver the children of Israel (Exodus 2:12-15). When Moses told an Israelite that he was wrong in fighting a brother Israelite, the man replied, "Who made thee a prince and a judge over us?" The rejection had made a lasting impression. Consequently, Moses asked the Lord to give him something to tell the people when he went to them this time.

The answer that the Lord gave to Moses is in Exodus 3:14. *"And God said unto Moses, 'I AM THAT I AM. Thus shalt thou say unto the children of Israel, I AM hath sent me unto you.'"* God sent Moses forth in the name of the Lord (Yahweh), the great I AM. In giving to Moses His name, God gave Moses the key to overcome his fear of rejection. Moses had not only been rejected by the Egyptians, but he had also been rejected by his own people. Therefore, he needed a strong and encouraging word which would enable him to overcome this feeling of inferiority. In essence, the Lord told Moses was that if the people rejected him, they would be rejecting God Himself. In the confidence of God's name, Moses would take courage and go forth to deliver God's people.

An important theological fact is illustrated through this: God will not let His name be ridiculed. God will uphold His name in whatever ministry He has chosen. Just as Moses did not go forth in his own name or strength, so every man called by God to lead should only go forth with such a divine accompaniment. It is a Bible principle that applies to all who are called to the work of the Lord. All that are called must ask themselves, "Am I going forth in the name of the Lord, or am I going forth in my own name?" The presence of a divine commission makes all the difference in the spiritual productivity of a ministry. Self-sent, self-made or self-empowered ministries, who are not commissioned by the Lord, are sure to fail. The confidence of the call and name of God, however, are keys to helping a leader overcome the fear of rejection.

The Response of Unbelief

Moses' third response to the Lord's call was that of unbelief. Exodus 4:1 states, *"And Moses answered and said, 'Behold they will not believe me, nor hearken unto my voice, for they will say, 'The Lord hath not appeared unto you.'"* We can see again how the previous years of Moses' experience in the land of Egypt had affected him. The people of Israel had not hearkened to him forty years earlier. Why would they hearken to him now? This unbelief was not the familiar voice of the mighty Moses as he had been in the land of Egypt. He had been very mighty and bold in both words and deeds, but now he was afraid that his people would not even listen to him.

In response to this, the Lord gave Moses three signs. The first sign was of the rod turning into a serpent. The second sign was of his hand becoming leprous. The third sign was of the water turning to blood. In each of these signs, a spiritual lesson is learned. These signs illustrated the conversion of the natural into the supernatural, and the normal into the miraculous. By these signs, God demonstrated to Moses the power by which he was to deliver the children of Israel: His Spirit. Zechariah 4:6 clearly states this principle of God's power, *"Not by might, nor by power, but by My Spirit; saith the Lord of Hosts."*

The Lord told Moses to look at what was in his hand. Moses saw that it was his old, familiar rod with which he had daily tended the sheep. The point was that the Lord's provision for Moses was in his hand at the very time that he was questioning the Lord. God told Moses to cast the rod down and to step back. Moses obeyed the Lord, and the rod turned into a serpent. Moses was startled at the sight of the serpent, but the Lord told him to pick it up. Moses knew from his Egyptian background that the only way to pick up a serpent was by the head, so that it could not bite him. However, the Lord told Moses to pick it up by the tail.

In the very act of his picking up the serpent by the tail instead of by the head, Moses was learning obedience to God's commands in contrast to the ways of Egypt. Moses was learning that it was not going to be by Egyptian reasoning or logic that he would deliver Israel, but that if he would deliver the nation at all, it would have to be by God's Word and Spirit. The fear and unbelief that Moses showed was answered by God through his miraculous experience with the rod. The other two signs of leprosy and blood also showed Moses that the most common things in the hands of man become opportunities for the Lord to show forth His power when they are submitted to His command. In a similar way, God must teach every one of His leaders that His Spirit is the key to ministry success.

The Response of a Lack of Eloquence

Moses' fourth response to the call of the Lord was that he was unable to speak. Exodus 4:10 states, *"And Moses said unto the Lord, 'I am not eloquent, neither heretofore, nor since thou hast spoken to thy servant: but I am slow of speech, and of a slow tongue'."* This inability to speak is quite a contrast to the Moses of forty years earlier who was a man "mighty in words." Moses had lost all confidence in himself as a spokesman.

We can logically ask, "Where were Moses' past skills? Did not the Lord choose him because of what he had learned in the land of Egypt? Did not the Lord want to use all of his Egyptian training and degrees?" Apparently not. God wanted a man that would obey His word and depend upon His Spirit. He wanted a vessel through which He should show His Glory--not Moses' glory. God's response to Moses' feeling of non-eloquence was simply, "Who made man's mouth?" In asking this question, the Lord told Moses that He would teach Moses what to say. We can apply this principle to all of God's leaders. The Lord will give all of his leaders the words to speak and the ability to speak them, when they will speak out of their weakness, to His glory.

The Response of Inferiority

Moses' fifth response to the calling of the Lord was an attitude of inferiority. Moses believed that the Lord had made a mistake in His choice. Exodus 4:13 states, *"And he said, 'O Lord send, I pray thee, by the hand of him who thou wilt send.' "* The Amplified Bible translates the verse in this way: *"And he said, 'O Lord, I pray you, send by the hand of some other whom you will send.' "* Moses attitude was one in which he would rather have seen someone else take his place of leadership.

This was a form of inferiority, in which Moses was not acting like the proud prince of the Egyptian kingdom he had once been. He was now acting like a humble shepherd from the backside of the desert who had been stripped of all his pride and self-confidence. In the end, God did give Moses his brother Aaron to be his mouthpiece, not out of His wisdom, but simply to satisfy Moses' endless requests. Moreover, Aaron would always be a reminder to his brother that he must always depend upon God's help and strength in his ministry. Similarly, God reveals to all of His leaders their own inadequacy, that they might depend on Him. God also gives his leaders specific ministry assignments to show them that they cannot be "one-man bands," but must depend on Him and one another for help.

The Response of Unfruitfulness

Moses' last response to God's calling was his accusation against the Lord because of no apparent fruitfulness in what the Lord had told him to do. In Exodus 5:21-22, Moses asked, *"Lord, wherefore hast thou so evil entreated this people? Why is it that thou hast sent me?"* Moses had gone to Egypt as the Lord had commanded him, and had even spoken the words that the Lord had told him to speak. What Moses had expected to happen did not happen, and he was profoundly disappointed.

Indeed, instead of any sign of progress in the situation of the nation of Israel, things became worse. Pharoah did not hearken to the word of the Lord through Moses and Aaron. Pharoah had the taskmasters beat the children of Israel because of what Moses had said. Moses was displeased because of this apparent unfruitfulness in his ministry. But at this point, the Lord was testing Moses to see what kind of reaction he would have. The Lord was in control of the whole situation all the time that it was "getting worse." Moses expected results sooner than the Lord wanted to give them. Moses was learning patience.

All leaders must learn that everything works according to God's plan and God's timing. Leaders may feel impelled to hurry to get everything done, but the Lord demands patience in waiting for things to come to full fruition. All ministers have to learn to restrain anger or impatience with God when the fruit of their ministries is slow in coming, or comes in unexpected ways.

Leaders must remember, above all, to Whom their ministries belong in the first place.

The Call of Jeremiah

Jeremiah is one of the most interesting prophets of the Old Testament. His book gives us more details about a prophet's life, ministry, message, methods and reaction from the people than we have concerning any other prophet.

Jeremiah lived during a time of national apostasy, and a time of great international strife. His prophetic ministry to the nation of Judah continued for approximately forty years before and during the Babylonian captivity. During this time, he saw the reign of the last five kings of Judah, which literally composed the darkest hours in the history of the nation. The history of these last five kings of Judah (Josiah, Jehoahaz, Jehoiakim, Jehoachin and Zedekiah) is found in the Second Book of Kings.

In Jeremiah's time, all things in Judah were rushing to God's final judgment, which would result in their seventy-year captivity in Babylon. With the spirit of the times causing great emotional reactions in Jeremiah, there is no doubt as to why he was called "the weeping prophet." Jeremiah was a man with a burdensome task before him. He had to speak to his own people at a time of national and spiritual catastrophe. Because of the message that Jeremiah had to bring to his people, he underwent many intense persecutions and sufferings.

The Trials of Jeremiah

Looking first at some of Jeremiah's trials and persecutions will explain why he needed such a specific and powerful call from the Lord. Any man of God who was to suffer the things that Jeremiah suffered needed a divine, landmark call. Every leader can gain insight from the following list of some major persecutions in Jeremiah's life.

Not permitted to marry (16:1-2)
Jeremiah lived a life of solitude and loneliness, without the joys of a family or the security of loved ones near him.

Beaten and put into stocks (20:1-3)
This was the nation's response to his message of judgment. Through all of his rejections, however, Jeremiah never chose to relieve his suffering by rejecting the message that God had given to him.

Imprisoned in a dungeon of miry clay (38:1-6)
In this dungeon, a religious leader of God's people was treated worse than murderers and thieves. There is some evidence that this was a nearly-dry well, and that Jeremiah was faced with an agonizing death by slow suffocation.

Called to a ministry of opposition (1:18,19)
Jeremiah was not a popular ministry. People did not flock to hear him say that they were wicked, backslidden and headed for judgment in exile.

Publicly disgraced to depict the judgment of Israel (27:1-3)
God told Jeremiah to put bonds and stocks around his neck. He was to do this publicly to depict the yoke of Babylon that was going to come upon His people for their disobedience.

Preached from the Book of the Covenant (11:1-10 and 12:1-7)
Jeremiah's message for Israel was based on the Book of the Covenant (possibly Deuteronomy).

While revered during the reign of the good king Josiah, this message now aroused tremendous hostility, and even helped cause his own family to conspire to kill Jeremiah.

Rejected by priests and prophets (26:1-24)

Jeremiah's life was preserved only by the Lord Jehovah. He was beaten more than once, and priests and prophets were implacably set on punishing or even executing him.

These are just a few of the trials and persecutions of Jeremiah during the time of his ministry. With this greater understanding of Jeremiah, let us now proceed to the actual reception of his divine call.

The Word of the Lord

The call of Jeremiah appears in Jeremiah 1:4-10. The Lord called Jeremiah by His Spirit before Jeremiah was born, and God confirmed His call upon him by the Word of the Lord coming to him when he was approximately seventeen or eighteen years old (1:4). By contrast, God called Moses through a burning bush and Gideon through an Angel. The differences between Moses', Gideon's and Jeremiah's calls is indicative of the fact that God always has a special and unique way to call each one of his leaders and ministries. Not all of God's leaders can claim to have received their call from a burning bush, an angel, or the Word of the Lord. But the point here is that God chooses the way in which a ministry is called.

It is significant to note that several other biblical leaders also received their call through the Word of the Lord. These were:

Ezekiel (Ezekiel 1:3 and 3:16)
Hosea (Hosea 1:1)
Joel (Joel 1:1)
Jonah (Jonah 1:1 and 3:1)

It may be significant that all five of these men who received their divine call through the Word of the Lord were prophets. These leaders ministered in the same realm as they had received their call. As prophets, they were to minister the Word of the Lord, having received their call through the Word of the Lord. It may be interesting to note how many of the specific ministries of God's leaders directly relate to the way they received their calling from God.

Jeremiah's Ministry Foundations

Jeremiah's appointment by Jehovah as a prophet to the nations (Jeremiah 1:5) is one example of the fact that each of God's leaders has been essentially predestined to fill a particular place in the kingdom of God. This fact of a special and unique plan for each one of God's leaders should dispel all envy of other ministries who differ in their function because of God's divine plan. It should also excite every Christian leader to seek the Lord with all his heart, to have the Lord reveal His special place of service for him.

Jeremiah was sanctified from his mother's womb to be a prophet of God (Jeremiah 1:5). This illustrates an important truth: everything that happens to Church leaders, from the point of birth, is either directly planned by God or will definitely be used by Him to cause His servants to fill a place in His divine will.

Jeremiah was ordained and set apart by God to be a prophet to the nations (Jeremiah 1:5). This should excite every leader to whom God has given a specific and direct call to rejoice in that it was God (and not another human being) who called him into governmental ministry.

The hand of the Lord touched Jeremiah's mouth to give him the particular divine words that he was going to speak (Jeremiah 1:9). This should encourage all Christian leaders to know that they can trust the Lord to open His Word to them and enable them to feed the people of God.

Jeremiah had the words of the Lord to speak to the people (Jeremiah 1:9). This should stand as a warning to all Christian leaders that their ministries must be based on God's word and not man's word. Before they speak to God's people, they should know they have heard God's word, and are speaking nothing else.

The Lord set Jeremiah over nations and kingdoms (Jeremiah 1:10). This should encourage all of God's leaders to remember that their promotion does not come from the East or the West, but it comes from the Lord. After they have humbled themselves before God, He will exalt them in due time.

Jeremiah was called *"to root out, to pull down and to destroy"* (Jeremiah 1:10). This should encourage all of those called by God, that as they preach and teach against sin and unrighteousness, the Lord will enable them to build righteousness and purity in their place.

God warned Jeremiah that Israel would fight against him (1:17-19). This reinforces the words of the Lord Jesus to all of those who are called to be leaders in the Church:

> *"If the world hate you, ye know that it hated me before it hated you.*
> *If ye were of the world, the world would love his own, but because ye are not of the world, but I have chosen you out of the world, therefore the world hateth you.*
> *Remember the word that I have said unto you, 'The servant is not greater than his lord.' If they have persecuted me, they will also persecute you, if they have kept my saying, they will keep yours also. But all these things will they do unto you for my name's sake, because they know not him that sent me."* (John 15:18-21)

Jeremiah had three major excuses when the Lord called him to the office of prophet.

The Excuse of a Lack of Eloquence

Jeremiah's first excuse to God's call echoed an excuse of Moses: *"Lord, I cannot speak"* (Jeremiah 1:6). It is interesting that a prophet like Jeremiah, who would spend most of his ministry speaking forth the word of the Lord, would feel an inferiority in this area of his ability to communicate. In a way, of course, he was right. No amount of oratorical skill can generate the true spiritual impact of the words of God.

But the Lord already had an answer for Jeremiah: *"All that I command you, you shall speak . . . [and] Behold, I have put my words in your mouth"* (1:7b,9b). Jeremiah was not required to use his own oratorical skill to accomplish God's objectives, but simply to speak the words which God would give him. The Lord will always put His words into the mouths of those He is equipping for ministry. It was because the Spirit of the Lord came upon Jeremiah that he fulfilled his divine calling. The same will be true for all of God's spokesmen.

The Excuse of Youth

Jeremiah's second excuse to the call of God was that of youth. Youth was also an excuse of Gideon. Jeremiah explained, *"Alas, Lord God! Behold, I do not know how to speak, because I am a youth"* (1:6). Jeremiah feared the people who had attained more age, experience and education than he had.

To God, however, these were not the most important factors. The most important factor was his willingness to obey the word of the Lord. God abruptly replied to Jeremiah's complaint with these words: *"Do not say; 'I am a youth,' because everywhere I send you, you shall go"* (1:7). In such cases, men and women of God have only to put aside their excuses of age and obey God's word to them.

The Excuse of Timidity and Fear of Rejection

Jeremiah's final excuse to God's calling was that he was too afraid to go because of the rejection that he would sense even by the expression on the people's faces. The Lord knew what was in Jeremiah's heart, and so He commanded him, *"Do not be afraid of their faces, for I am with you to deliver you . . . Behold I have put my words in your mouth"* (1:8,9).

Jeremiah probably knew instinctively that he was going to face some very difficult situations. All of God's leaders, however, can be assured that God probably will not reveal His total plan for a ministry to the person involved all at once. God knows that if he saw some of the things through which he would have to go, he would certainly turn back in trepidation. All of God's leaders can also be assured that God will give abundant grace for them to meet every fearful situation as they call upon Him in prayer. It is the fear of God, and not the fear of men, that should be the primary concern of ministries. As to Jeremiah, so to all of His ministries, God assuredly says, *"Do not be afraid of them, for I am with you . . ."* (Jeremiah 1:8).

The Call of Gideon

Our final example of a governmental leader who responded to the call of God in a unique way is Gideon. Like Moses, Gideon responded to God's call with six excuses.

The background to Gideon's call is found in the Book of Judges. This book covers the backsliding and apostasy of the nation of Israel after they had come into the land of Canaan. The book's setting is after the death of the great leader Joshua. The main theological lesson we can learn from the Book of Judges is that of the possibility of losing one's spiritual inheritance through idolatrous compromise. Judges has aptly been called the book of failure, because it clearly and repeatedly presents Israel's cycle of disobedience to God. At least six times in the book, the Lord had to raise up new men and women called judges or deliverers, to lead the nation out of their constant self-inflicted bondages.

The Angel of the Lord

At the time of Gideon's call from God, the Midianites had oppressed Israel for seven years (Judges 6:1). To escape the terror of the enemy, Israelites had been hiding in mountains, dens, caves and strongholds (Judges 6:2). Because the Israelites had planted their own crops, and their enemies had reaped the harvest (Judges 6:3-5), Israel was greatly impoverished. In this state, the Israelites cried unto the Lord (Judges 6:7), and in response, they heard a prophet of the Lord pinpoint their disobedience to God as the reason for their sad condition (Judges 6:8-10).

Immediately after this, God called Gideon.

> *"And there came an angel of the Lord, and sat under an oak which was in Ophrah that pertained unto Joash the Abiezrite: and his son Gideon threshed wheat there by the wine-press to hide it from the Midianites. And the angel of the Lord appeared unto him and said unto him, 'The Lord is with thee, thou mighty man of valour.' "* (Judges 6:11,12)

Gideon received his call from the Lord through an angel and not a burning bush as Moses did. The principle of leadership here is that even though God uses many different ways to call His leaders, all of them are personally called by Him. Let us now observe Gideon's different responses to God's call through the angel.

The Excuse of Circumstances

Gideon's first excuse came in the form of a question concerning Israel's circumstances. Gideon was not startled at the appearance of the angel, or the angel's declaration. Gideon simply wondered, *"If the Lord be with us, why, then, is all of this befallen us?"* (Judges 6:13).

We can safely assume that because Gideon had probably heard the prophet declare the reason for Israel's oppression was her disobedience to God. He probably knew very well the reason that all of the bad circumstances had befallen Israel. But he was not going to accept the state of their captivity without a promise of total deliverance from the angel, who represented the Lord. Similarly, all of God's leaders must take the attitude, "If the Lord be with us, how can we allow this oppression to continue?"

The Excuse of No Miracles

Gideon's second excuse was the question, *"Where be all the miracles our fathers told us about?"* (Judges 6:13). Gideon was asking about the previous spiritual revivals that the nation had experienced. Where, he wondered, was the famous power of God about which he had heard.

Gideon was not interested only in stories about the past. He wanted the same God who had moved in the past to move in his generation. God knew that Gideon greatly desired to see the same power of God against these Midianites, as was demonstrated by Moses and Joshua in the wilderness journey to Canaan. Therefore, God sent an angel to Gideon to give him the opportunity of seeing the God of the past work in the present. Similarly, God will send visitations of His Spirit upon those who believe that He has moved in past generations, but also desires to move in the present one as well. God is looking for leaders who will rise up in faith and ask, "Where are all of the miracles of which our fathers spoke? We desire them, too."

The Excuse of Unbelief and Frustration

Gideon's third excuse was a statement of honest frustration. Gideon bewailingly stated, *"The Lord has forsaken us and delivered us into the hands of the Midianites"* (Judges 6:13). Gideon was very frustrated about the situation in which Israel found herself. His cry of unbelief was that God had forsaken His people.

It is significant that the Lord did not directly respond to Gideon's cry of frustration. Instead, and because He knew that Gideon had a desire to see Israel set free, the Lord merely said to him, *"Go in this thy might and thou shalt save Israel from the hands of the Midianites. Have not I sent thee?"* (Judges 6:14). Similarly, God challenges all of His leaders to put aside their feelings of unbelief and frustration, and instead to go onward to defeat the enemy, because He Himself has sent them.

In passing, note the phrase the angel spoke, "Go in this thy might." What was Gideon's might? He could not tolerate the oppression of Israel by her enemies. This was evident in his efforts to risk his life to salvage some of the wheat harvest. Already, Gideon's heart was at least partly identified with God's intention to free Israel. Because of that, the call of God came in the form of a release, a warrant to do what Gideon's inner man already desired--"Have not I sent thee?"

Even so, Gideon had his doubts and fears. The angel of the Lord had to provide more answers before Gideon's call was complete.

The Excuse of Inferiority

Gideon's fourth excuse to the call of the Lord was his own sense of inferiority. Gideon lamented, *"O my Lord, wherewith shall I save Israel?"* (Judges 6:15). Gideon was saying, in essence, "Lord, I see the situation, but I am not the one for the job."

This feeling of not being the right one for the job is very common among leaders whom God chooses for governmental ministry. God's leaders may see all of the problems with the Church, and what the enemy is doing to God's harvest of souls. But they still do not always think that the Lord can use them. As with Gideon, many of God's leaders hide their potential. It was precisely because God saw such a spiritual potential in Gideon that the angel addressed him as, "Thou mighty man of valour." All of God's leaders must remember that the Lord always looks at the potential works that he sees in them as they are clothed with His Spirit.

The Excuse of Family Background

Gideon's fifth excuse was a depreciation of his family background. He exclaimed, *"Behold my family is poor in Manasseh"* (Judges 6:15). Here Gideon exposed an underlying attitude that many leaders have when the Lord calls them to a positional ministry. Many ask, "What about my family background? What about the family from which I came?" In essence, Gideon was probably thinking, "Since there have not been any deliverers in my family tree, how can I respond to God's call to deliver His people?"

Gideon was indeed a very average person in Israel. He was not from a rich family that had tremendous political influence. He suffered the same poverty and problems as all of the people around him. The fact is that the Lord does not call men on the basis of their family background, their past, their education, or their wealth. He chooses those He desires to choose for His own good pleasure. In condensed form, I Corinthians 1:23-27 states, *"Not many mighty, not many noble, not many wise after the flesh; but the foolish, the weak, the base, the despised things and the are-nots hath the Lord chosen."*

The Excuse of Youth

Gideon's last excuse to the Lord's call was connected with the excuse of the insignificance of his family background. Gideon continued, *". . . and I am the least (youngest) in my father's house"* (Judges 6:15). Not only was Gideon of low status, he was also the youngest in his family.

But neither his financial status nor his youth stopped the Lord from calling Gideon. God clearly said to Gideon, *"I will be with thee and thou shalt smite the Midianites as one man"* (Judges 6:16). At the right time, *"the Spirit of the Lord came upon Gideon and he blew a trumpet"* for the battle (Judges 6:34). Because it was God who had called Gideon to deliver Israel, God's Spirit came upon Gideon. In spite of all of his excuses, Gideon did that for which the Lord had called him.

Your Call

Be assured that sometime during your life as a Christian, God will call you.

He will call you to your ministry, whether it be governmental or congregational. And He probably will call you to act in a leadership role at some point, whether for a major undertaking, or a short-term project.

How will you respond? Don't be surprised if you're nearly paralyzed by feelings of inadequacy. After all, leadership in the Church is an issue of primary importance. The more you care about the needs of the Church, the more intensely you'll react and respond to the call. If you believe you have been called or are being called to leadership in the Church, work through the "Ministry Calling Evaluation" chart below. It will help you understanding God's calling, and your own response to it.

The ministry that God gives to each believer is one of the many treasures He puts in our lives as Christians. The call to service, and possibly to leadership, will change your life as nothing else will.

Ministry Calling Evaluation

If you believe God has called or is calling you to leadership in the Church (whether temporary or permanent), work through this chart. Include events, dates, precise scriptural references, names of people, and other specific information. You are constructing a brief personal history that can help you understand God's calling on your own life, and your response to it. To receive guidance and confirmation, discuss your personal calling with your pastor.

Type of Ministry (taken from "Gifts and Ministries In The New Testament" at the end of Chapter Three):

_____

Type of Call
- Deep internal desire
- Hand of the Lord--
  blessing on an activity
- Prophecy by another

- Word of the Lord

- Audible voice

- Dream
- Vision

Other (describe):

_____

Circumstances of the Call
Personal state: describe your spiritual, emotional, intellectual, physical, financial circumstances at the time of the Call

_____

_____

Corporate state: describe the state of those whom you are called to serve (spiritual, emotional, intellectual, social, financial, physical)

_____

_____

Your Response to the Call
The desires of your heart: _____

_____

Your existing qualifications: _____

_____

Your fears and perceived inadequacies: _____

God's Dealings in the Call
Personal Scripture promises: _____

_____

Spiritual and/or material provision: _____

_____

Other dealings of the Spirit: _____

_____

The Church's Reaction to the Call
   Confirmation by leadership: _____
_____

   Assignment to ministry responsibilities: _____
_____

   Rejection, nature and reason: _____
_____

Your Current Status in Your Calling
   Receiving it _____
   Receiving confirmation _____
   Preparing to fulfill it _____
   Initiating service _____
   Regularly serving a local Body _____
   Temporary leadership role completed _____
   Indication of changes/new callings _____

CHAPTER 5
THE HEART QUALIFICATIONS OF LEADERSHIP

We have already studied the nature of leadership, and the call to leadership. We have discussed the critical importance of leadership in the Body of Christ. It has become apparent that at some point in your own service to the Church, whatever the nature of your own ministry calling, you will probably be called to act in a leadership role.

Will you qualify? Will you be ready for one of the greatest adventures of a lifetime?

To a large degree, it's up to you. While God is committed to help you grow in faith, your level of cooperation is the releasing factor that leads to a qualified heart. He is looking for people He can trust, people who share His own heart's love and concern for the Church.

This chapter deals with the heart qualifications of leadership that all Christians must have: the heart of a father and the heart of a servant. If you are called to a governmental ministry, they are your prerequisites and the foundation for the performance of your ministry. In a congregational ministry, they are the "modus operandi," the very soul of your service. They are qualities of the heart that we all rely upon to achieve our full stature as Christians.

Definition of the Word "Heart"

What does God mean when He asks His ministers to give Him their hearts? To the Western mind, the word "heart" may generally mean (beyond the vital physical organ) the emotional feelings of a person. For example, when we in the western hemisphere say that a man loves a woman "with all of his heart," we generally mean with intense feelings.

Hebrew Meanings. To the ancient Hebrew mind, however, the meaning of "heart" encompassed not only a person's emotions, but also his spiritual, mental and physical life. The Hebrews viewed man as a total unit, and the word "heart" was understood in that context. The Hebrew word for heart is "labab," which in a general sense means the midst, the innermost, or the hidden parts of anything. The Bible uses such phrases as *"the heart of the sea"* (Exodus 15:8), *"the heart of heaven"* (Deuteronomy 4:11), *"the heart of a tree"* (II Samuel 18:14), and *"the heart of the earth"* (Matthew 12:40).

In the Hebrew, therefore, the word "heart" comes to mean, by extension, the seat of man's collective energies and the focus of his personal life. The heart would be the very throne upon which life itself sits. In relating this to the ministry, when the Lord asks a man for his heart, he wants that person to be involved in the Lord's work from the very core of his being.

Greek Meanings. In the English Bible, one of the most common Greek words that is translated as "heart" is the word "kardia." In general meaning, "kardia" refers to the center and seat of both spiritual and physical life. It carries the connotation of both soul and mind. "Kardia" was often used to refer to the mind as the fountain and seat of human thoughts, passions, desires, appetites, affections, purposes and endeavors. The Greek scholar H.W. Robinson believes that this Greek word (used 250 times in the New Testament) refers to the personality and the inner life and character of an individual.

From these studies, we can reach a general definition of the word "heart" as the core of a person's body, mind, emotions, personality, character and spirit. When the Lord tells His leaders to give Him their hearts, then, He is asking of them their entire lives.

Importance of the Heart

Physically speaking, the heart is the most important bodily organ. Without it, the body's various organs, processes and functions would cease, and life would end. We can draw many parallels between the physical heart and the spiritual heart, showing its utmost importance in the leader's spiritual life and function.

Parallel:

The Physical Heart	The Spiritual Heart
The physical heart is located approximately in the center of a man's breast.	The spiritual heart (or the heart of the Spirit) should be located in the very center of a leader's thoughts, words, actions and ministry, motivating everything in his life.
Every physical heart is approximately the size of its owner's clenched fist.	Every leader's spiritual heart is only really as big as the works of his hands show it to be.
The blood in a physical heart is composed of different nutrients contained in the food consumed by its owner.	The life in a leader's spiritual heart is composed of what he consumes through his mind and experience. The purest life is obtained from "eating" the Word of God.
The pumping system of a physical heart is based on a reception/release method. Blood is received through one part of the heart, and other blood is released through another part of the heart.	The outflowing of spiritual life from a leader is based on his own personal reception of God's love and forgiveness, and then its subsequent release to those around him.
The physical heart pumps blood from one end of the body to the other, if it is functioning properly.	The spiritual heart of a leader circulates the life of the Holy Spirit throughout the Body of Christ, if he is functioning properly.
The physical heart pumps blood throughout the body, cleansing the body from its impurities.	The spiritual heart of a leader knows and preaches the cleansing power of the blood of Jesus Christ, continually purifying the spiritual Body of Christ.

The healthy physical heart beats automatically, without the conscious effort of its owner.

The physical heart is more prone to some forms of heart disease and attack on a high-fat diet, in an overweight body.

The physical heart is more prone to disease and attack in a body that consumes alcoholic beverages.

The physical heart is more prone to disease and attack in a body that gets little exercise.

The physical heart will be more prone to disease and attack the more tension and stress its owner experiences.

The physical heart is more prone to disease and attack the more heart defects its owner inherited from its parents at birth.

The healthy spiritual heart of a leader shows the love, joy and peace of God naturally, spontaneously, and without any conscious effort or insincere "put-on."

The spiritual heart of a leader is more prone to spiritual sickness as the leader takes in rich truths of the Word of God without practicing them and making them an active part of his life and the lives of others.

The spiritual heart of a leader is more prone to spiritual sickness as he dabbles with the wine of the pleasures and cares of this world.

The spiritual heart of a leader is more prone to spiritual sickness the less he actually performs the will of God as expressed in God's Word.

The spiritual heart of a leader is more prone to spiritual sickness as he lives a high-adrenalin, high-stress lifestyle by not entrusting all cares into the Lord's hands.

The spiritual heart of a leader is more prone to spiritual sickness the more spiritual problems he has for which he did not truly repent as the time of spiritual rebirth by the Spirit.

All of these physical parallels clearly demonstrate the importance of the spiritual heart in the life of God's leadership.

Guarding the Heart

Biblically speaking, a leader has at least three reasons to guard his heart. The first reason is that his heart is the very source of all his attitudes and actions. We see this in the following verses:

Proverbs 4:23

"Keep thy heart with all diligence for out of it are the issues of life" (King James Version).

"Keep your heart with all vigilance (and above all that you guard it) *for out of it flow the springs of life"* (Amplified Bible).

"Guard your heart more than any treasure, for it is the source of all life" (New English Bible).

"Above all else, guard your affections for they influence everything else in your life" (Living Bible).

Philippians 4:7

"The peace of God which passeth all understanding shall keep your hearts and minds through Christ Jesus" (King James Version).

"The peace of God which transcends all understanding shall garrison and mount guard over your hearts and minds" (Amplified Bible).

In these passages, the leader is exhorted to guard his heart as a soldier guards the city gate. The leader must watch over his affections, to prevent an invasion of foreign values. He must maintain the alertness and discipline of a sentinel who guards over a camp or castle to protect his king within.

The second reason a leader must guard his heart is because it is the source of all that he ministers or speaks. We see this in Matthew 12:34b,35:

"Out of the abundance of the heart, the mouth speaketh" (King James Version).

"Out of the fullness, the overflow, the superabundance of the heart, the mouth speaketh. The good man from his inner treasure flings forth good things, and the evil man out of his inner evil storehouse flings forth evil things" (Amplified Bible).

Each leader is the guard in charge of the storehouse of his own heart, which is full of either good or bad treasures. It is out of this storehouse that the leader brings forth good or evil to the open treasure boxes of the people of the Lord. The Old Testament provides some beautiful illustrations of this. In the history of Israel, many storehouses full of grain, wine, oil or weapons were designated for the benefit and protection of the people. Both Solomon and Hezekiah were very proud of the wealth in their storehouses (I King 9:19; II Chronicles 32:28).

In the same way, every leader must ask himself if he is proud of the contents of the storehouses of his heart. From them, he must feed and protect the people of the Lord. Solomon stored grain, wine, oil and weapons for the defense of Israel. Today, the spiritual leader must store in his heart the Word of God, the joy of the Lord, the anointing of the Spirit and the full armor of God (Ephesians 6:13-17).

The third reason a leader must guard his heart is to prevent it from causing spiritual defilement to himself or God's people. You can see this in the words of Jesus:

"And when he had called all the people unto him, he said unto them, 'Hearken unto me every one of you, and understand: there is nothing from without a man, that entering into him can defile him: but the things which come out of him, those are they that defile the man. If any have ears to hear, let him hear.' And when he was entered into the house from the people, his disciples asked him concerning the parable. And he said unto them, 'Are ye so without understanding also? Do ye not perceive, that whatsoever thing from without entereth into the man it cannot defile him: because it entereth not into his heart, but into his belly and goeth out into the draught, purging all meats?' And he said, 'That which cometh out of a man, that defileth the man. For from within, out of the heart of men, proceed evil thoughts, adulteries, fornications, murders, thefts, covetousness, wickedness, deceit, lasciviousness, an evil eye, blasphemy, pride, foolishness: all these evil things come from within, and defile the man.' " (Mark 7:14-23, King James Version)

The Lord Jesus Christ said that the unguarded heart of a leader can become the source for a long list of terrible things: base and wicked thoughts, sexual immorality, murders, stealing, covetous desires, dangerous and destructive wickedness, unrestrained and indecent conduct, an eye that looks for evil, an abusive mouth that slanders and makes malicious misrepresentations, a heart that is uplifted in pride against God and man, and a reckless love of folly.

It is the tragedy of the Church that at some periods in its history, this list of shame has become the agenda for some of its most influential leaders. What went wrong? Both the leaders and those who followed them left their hearts unguarded. Instead of shepherding God's flock, these leaders were foremost among those who "like sheep have wandered away." Grazing from one pleasure to another, they have lost all track of God's will for the Church.

Qualities of the Heart

Thus we see that the qualities of a leader's heart are very important to God. God is continually trying (Deuteronomy 8:2), searching (Jeremiah 17:10) and pondering (Proverbs 21:2) the hearts of His leaders. It is a leader's responsibility to maintain a pure heart before the Lord (James 4:8).

What's the condition of your heart? In large part, that will be determined by your reaction to the Lord, to people and events around you. When you see a big need in someone's life, do you have a willing heart to help? Or do you have a hardened heart that says, "This just can't be fixed"? When the Lord confronts you with your own sin, do you have a tender heart? Or do you have a hypocritical heart that says, "Please, Lord, not now. I'm in the middle of something important now. Could we just straighten it out later"? When you hear an inspiring scriptural truth in a good sermon, do you have a retaining heart that makes plans to implement the truth later in the week? Or do you have a double heart, that enjoys the thrill of discovering a new idea, but fails to follow through with action?

This chart of "Spiritual Heart Qualities" contains a list of heart qualities, with Bible verses describing both the positive and negative sides to each quality. This is an excellent tool for evaluating the condition of your own heart. Through the Spirit and the Word, God can use it to help you pinpoint and adjust any unhealthy conditions in your spirit. If you are or desire to be a Church leader, it should be part of your "spiritual curriculum." Moreover, anyone will profit by reading and praying through the list. The list of positive qualities is a distilled inspirational message from God's Word.

Spiritual Heart Qualities

Positive

Grieved Heart . . . . Genesis 6:6
Willing Heart . . . . Exodus 25:2
Stirred Heart . . . . Exodus 35:21
Wise Heart . . . . Exodus 35:35
Another Heart . . . . I Samuel 10:9
Perfect Heart . . . . I Chronicles 12:38
Tender Heart . . . . II Chronicles 34:27
Sorrowful Heart . . . . Nehemiah 2:2-12
Faithful Heart . . . . Nehemiah 9:8
Soft Heart . . . . Job 23:16
Upright Heart . . . . Job 33:3
Communing Heart . . . . Psalm 4:4
Heart of Wax . . . . Psalm 22:14
Pure Heart . . . . Psalm 24:4
Broken Heart . . . . Psalm 34:18
Panting Heart . . . . Psalm 38:10
Failing Heart . . . . Psalm 40:12
Proclaiming Heart . . . . Psalm 45:1
Fixed Heart . . . . Psalm 57:7
Living Heart . . . . Psalm 69:32
Established Heart . . . . Psalm 112:8
Understanding Heart . . . . Proverbs 2:2
Retaining Heart . . . . Proverbs 4:4,21
Sound Heart . . . . Proverbs 14:30
Merry Heart . . . . Proverbs 17:22
New Heart . . . . Ezekiel 18:31/36:26

Negative

Evil Heart . . . . Genesis 6:5
Hardened Heart . . . . Exodus 4:21
Deceived Heart . . . . Deuteronomy 11:16
Non-Perceiving Heart . . . . . Deuteronomy 29:4
Proud Heart . . . . Chronicles 32:35
Presumptuous Heart . . . . Esther 7:5
Hypocritical Heart . . . . Job 36:13
Lifted-up Heart . . . . Deuteronomy 8:14
Firm, Hard Heart . . . . Job 41:24
Iniquitous Heart . . . . Psalm 41:6
Wicked Heart . . . . Psalm 58:2
Erring Heart . . . . Psalm 95:10
Proud Heart . . . . Psalm 101:5
Fat and Greasy Heart . . . . Psalm 119:70
Desolate Heart . . . . Psalm 143:4
Despising Heart . . . . Proverbs 5:12
Deceitful Heart . . . . Proverbs 12:20
Bitter Heart . . . . Proverbs 14:10
Backslidden Heart . . . . Proverbs 14:14
Foolish Heart . . . . Proverbs 15:7
Human Heart . . . . Proverbs 15:11
Abominable Heart . . . . Proverbs 26:25
Double Heart . . . . James 1:8
Wounded Heart . . . . Psalm 109:22
Evil Heart . . . . Matthew 15:19
Rebellious Heart . . . . Jeremiah 5:23

Fleshly Heart .... Ezekiel 11:19	Arrogant Heart .... Isaiah 9:9
Purposeful Heart .... Daniel 1:8	Deceitful Heart .... Jeremiah 17:9
Pondering Heart .... Luke 2:19	Whorish Heart .... Ezekiel 6:9
Forgiving Heart .... Matthew 18:35	Stony Heart .... Ezekiel 11:19
Unblameable Heart ..... I Thessalonians 3:13	Weak Heart .... Ezekiel 16:30
Blood-sprinkled Heart .... Hebrews 10:22	Despiteful Heart .... Ezekiel 25:15
Nourished Heart .... James 5:5	Bitter Heart .... Ezekiel 27:31
Sanctified Heart .... I Peter 1:22	Beastly Heart .... Daniel 4:16
Assured Heart .... I John 3:19	Divided Heart .... Hosea 10:2
Honest, Good Heart .... Luke 8:15	Gross Heart .... Matthew 13:15
Burning Heart .... Luke 24:25-32	Heavy Heart .... Proverbs 31:6
Single Heart .... Acts 2:46	Reasoning Heart .... Mark 2:6-8
One Heart .... Acts 4:32	Envious, Striving Heart .... James 3:14
Opened Heart .... Acts 16:14	Lustful Heart .... Psalm 81:12
Obedient Heart .... Romans 6:17	Troubled Heart .... John 14:1
Circumcised Heart .... Romans 2:29	Uncircumcised Heart .... Acts 7:51
Believing Heart .... Romans 10:9,10	Darkened Heart .... Romans 1:21
Steadfast Heart .... I Corinthians 7:37	Hard, Impenitent Heart .... Romans 2:5
Enlarged Heart .... I Corinthians 6:11	Anguished Heart .... I Corinthians 2:4
Caring Heart .... I Corinthians 8:16	Blind Heart .... Ephesians 4:18
Singing Heart .... Ephesians 5:19	Unknowing Heart .... Hebrews 3:10
Established Heart .... Hebrews 13:9	Evil Heart .... Hebrews 3:12
	Condemning Heart .... I John 3:20
	Overwhelmed Heart .... Psalm 61:2
	Evilly-exercised Heart .... II Peter 2:14

The Leader and the Heart of a Father

Greek Meanings. *"For though ye have ten thousand instructors in Christ, yet have ye not many fathers"* (I Corinthians 4:15).

In the original Greek language, the word for instructor meant "A boy leader, tutor, guide, guardian or servant whose office it was to take the children to school." Among the Greeks and the Romans, an instructor could also be a trustworthy servant or steward who was charged with supervising the lives and morals of boys in the higher classes of society. The boys were not allowed to step out of the house without their instructor until they reached the age of manhood. The word carried with it the idea of severity; an instructor was a stern censor and enforcer of proper morals for the young men.

This Pauline verse uses the word "instructor" to present a strong contrast. Paul wrote to the Corinthian Christians that they had many tutors or instructors (those who freely offered them strict teaching and rigid rules) but not many fathers. The word instructor denotes a student-teacher relationship of instruction, whereas the word father denotes a father-son relationship of love. The Book of Proverbs was built on this concept of the father-son relationship. The father's wisdom, knowledge and understanding of life is transmitted to the son in a loving father-son relationship.

Hebrew Meanings. The voice in much of Proverbs is that of the father speaking to his son. It illustrates the attitude of a father's heart:

"My son, hear the instruction of thy father" (1:8).
"My son, if sinners entice thee, consent not" (1:10).

"My son, walk not thou in the way with them" (1:15).
"My son, if thou wilt receive my words" (2:1).
"My son, forget not my law" (3:1).
"My son, despise not the chastening of the Lord" (3:11).
"My son, let them not depart from thy eyes, keep sound wisdom" (3:21).
"My son, attend to my words, incline thy ears to my sayings" (4:20).
"My son, keep thy father's commandment" (6:20).

The Church Today

As in Paul's day, so it is true in our day, that the Church has ten thousand instructors, but not nearly as many fathers. The Church has many scholars and professional ministers, but not nearly as many spiritual fathers. Many scholars and professional ministers in the Church today can deliver eloquent, impressive sermons that touch our minds and thoughts. But where are the fathers? Some religious colleges and seminaries today seem bent on mass-producing teachers. But who is attempting to produce spiritual fathers?

Will the Church allow a leadership of orators, educators and instructors to forever rob her of the spiritual blessings which only spiritual fathers can bring her? The world has the service of thousands of erudite scholars, but the Church is still crying out for the ministry of true spiritual fathers. The Church does not need any more computer-like men with memory banks full of dry biblical information to instruct the unlearned in the ways of the Lord. She needs true spiritual fathers who can lead her in the ways of the Lord. The Church needs men who have a heart for the people of the Lord and a compassion for the needy.

A computer presents information without love, mercy or understanding. A leader will show as much love, mercy or understanding as a computer shows, if he does not have the heart of a father. The Church needs more than just biblical knowledge or instruction. She needs the very heart and life of her spiritual fathers to be imparted to her. The impartation of spiritual life, however, can't be taught from a college textbook in a college classroom. Spiritual life can only be learned in a close relationship with God, God's people, and the spiritual example of true fathers in the faith.

The Father's Heart of Jesus

Let's first look at the characteristics of a father's heart in the life of the ultimate example to all leaders, the Lord Jesus Christ. Jesus was the full expression of the heart of the heavenly Father on earth. His words, His ways, and His actions all manifested the heart of the Father. Accordingly, Jesus said, *"I and the Father are one"* (John 10:30) and *"He who has seen me has seen the Father, how do you say 'Show us the father?' . . . The Father abiding in me does his works"* (John 14:9c,10c). The list below shows some of the father's-heart attitudes of the Lord Jesus Christ, who is the example to all of God's leaders.

Compassion.	*"When he saw the multitude, he was moved with compassion"* (Matthew 9:35,36).
Concern.	A Pharisee asked one of Christ's disciples, *"Why eatest your master with publicans and with sinners"* and Jesus replied, *"They that be whole need not a physician, but they that are sick"* (Matthew 9:11-13).
Willingness.	*"There came a leper and worshipped him, saying, 'Lord, if thou wilt, thou canst make me clean.' And Jesus put forth his hand and touched him, saying, 'I will; be thou clean.' "* (Matthew 8:1-3).
Humility.	Jesus gave us a new definition of humility: *"Except ye be converted as a little child, ye shall not enter the kingdom of heaven"* (Matthew 18:3; also see Philippians 2:5-10).
Warmth.	*"Mary has chosen the better part,"* Jesus said to Martha, in explaining

	why Mary shouldn't have to leave her listeners' place at the feet of Jesus to busy herself with service. (Luke 10:38-42; also see John 12:1-8).
Forgiveness.	Jesus also gave us a new definition of forgiveness. On the cross: *"Father, forgive them for they know not what they do"* (Luke 23:34). In the tale of the prodigal son: *"When the son was a great way off, his father saw him and had great compassion on him and ran and embraced him, and kissed him"* (Luke 15:32). To a prostitute taken in sin: *"Neither do I condemn you, go and sin no more"* (John 8:11).
Brokenness.	Jesus laid down all His heavenly authority in coming to earth, and was the model of brokenness for all leaders. *"He groaned in his spirit and was troubled . . . and Jesus wept"* (John 11:33-36). *"O Jerusalem, Jerusalem,"* He lamented, *". . . how often would I have gathered thy children together, even as a hen gathereth her chickens under her wings, and ye would not!"* Matthew 23:37).
Self-Sacrifice.	Jesus showed us how to pay the ultimate price. *"I lay down my life for the sheep"* (John 10:15).
Service.	Jesus also showed us that no service was unimportant or without dignity. *"If I then, your Lord and Master, have washed your feet, ye also ought to wash one another's feet"* (John 13:14).

Fatherly Gentleness

In I Thessalonians 2:7 Paul states, *"But we were gentle among you."* In the Amplified Bible, this verse reads, *"But we behaved gently when we were among you, like a devoted mother nursing and cherishing her own children."*

The word "gentle" in the original Greek means to be affable, mild or kind. Greek writers freqently used this word to characterize a nurse with crying children, or a teacher with difficult pupils. This word describes a nursing mother.

Gentleness is another attitude to be found in the heart of a father. Gentleness describes the loving, fatherly touch that all children must have during their development. Without this gentleness, children will be imbalanced. The Bible requires gentleness of all those who are going to take responsibility in the house of the Lord. Without gentleness, a strong leader will injure the people of God.

This list of scripture references on gentleness will exhort every leader to allow the Lord to develop this quality in his life.

II Timothy 2:24	*"The servant of the Lord must not strive but be gentle,"* Paul told his disciple Timothy.
Titus 3:2	*"They are not to be brawlers, but to be gentle."*
James 3:17	*"But the wisdom from above is first pure, peaceable, gentle."*
II Corinthians 10:1	*"I, Paul beseech you by the meekness and gentleness of Christ."*
Galatians 5:22	*"The fruit of the Spirit is . . . longsuffering, gentleness, goodness and faith."*

A spiritual father in the house of the Lord must develop gentleness. This heart attitude will allow the leader to teach sensitive and difficult subjects in the Church without spiritually hurting or permanently offending the people of God. Gentleness will cause the people to listen and to respond to the more serious admonitions that a leader feels he must give.

Fatherly Nursing

I Thessalonians 2:7 states, *"but we were gentle among you, even as a nurse cherisheth her children."* In the New Testament Greek, a "nurse" nourishes children, to the point of fattening them, cherishing them with choice foods. This word denotes a mother who nurses her children before they are weaned. It describes the mother would would take the most anxious and tender care of her little ones.

In the context of this scripture, we have the apostle Paul speaking to a church he had begotten in the gospel. In the next verse (I Thessalonians 2:8), Paul described the outworking of a father's heart. He said, *"So being affectionately desirous of you, we were willing to have imparted unto you, not the gospel of God only, but also our own souls, because ye were dear unto us."*

The apostle Paul imparted to the Thessalonians not only the gospel, but his own life and energy as well. What Paul gave to these Christians can be seen in the feelings expressed by a mother who nurses her own child. This is the true picture of a "nursing father," in the masculine sense, as it relates not only to the apostle Paul, but also to every leader.

Acts 13:18 gives us an account of how the Lord nursed His people Israel in Old Testament times. This verse states, *"God suffered their manners in the wilderness."* The Septuagint translation puts it this way: *"God bare, as a nursing Father, the people of Israel."* Similarly, Deuteronomy 1:31 states, *"In the wilderness where thou hast seen that the Lord my God bare thee as a man doth bare his son."*

The Hebrew word for "bare" means to build up, support, foster (as a parent), to nurse or render firm or faithful in all dealings. Numbers 11:12 speaks of Moses in this sense of the word. Moses was a nursing father to the Israelites (cf. Isaiah 40:11 and 49:23).

For all that the nation of Israel did to offend the Lord, He was still patient with them and cared for them. He was a nursing father unto the people. Moses was a nursing father to Israel, also. This attribute of being like a nurse was worked into the life of Moses through all of the experiences of the people of Israel. Moses never wanted to trade Israel for a better nation, though the Lord proposed it. Moses never asked the Lord to judge them too harshly. He was a true father-nurse. May it be the same with every leader.

Fatherly Cherishing

Paul stated that he treated the Thessalonian Christians "as a nurse cherisheth her children." The Greek word for cherish means to warm, to brood over and foster, to cherish with tender love, care for with tender love, and to show compassion. The Septuagint uses this word to describe a bird caring for its young by spreading its feathers over them in the nest (see Deuteronomy 22:6 and Matthew 23:37).

A spiritual father in the family of God will spread his protective and loving wings over the small or weak of the flock while they are still in the nest, to protect them from the attacks of vultures. This is another expression of the father's heart in the work of leading. (For examples, see I Thessalonians 2:8,11; Philippians 2:22; I Timothy 3:1; Ephesians 5:29.) We think of leading as handling adults adroitly and running a "tight ship." But God thinks of leading as nursing, caring, being gentle, serving, teaching and loving children.

The Example of Husbandry

The tender care and feeding of a young plant so that it grows properly to a healthy maturity is another beautiful illustration of the words gentleness, nursing and cherishing.

Plants may suffer from many different maladies during their lives. They may suffer from vegetation diseases, insect damage, environmental changes, or damage from sheer neglect. Some plants are more tender than others. Some will suffer severely by neglect, where others will appear to thrive on it. But even an old sturdy standby plant can be affected drastically by neglect or environmental change.

A plant's appearance and growth indicate the state of its health. Early stages of ailment and ill health are usually very subtle. Unless the gardener knows the plant through close relationship, he will not discern the problem until devastating symptoms occur. Stages of severe defoliation and withering are not the time for the gardener suddenly to examine the plant for causes of ill health. Unfortunately, this kind of emergency help is found too often in the vineyard of God's people!

To prevent his plants from reaching a state of emergency, the gardener must discern the need of the plant in its early stages. In doing so, the gardener will save his plant from death--and perhaps others around it. The husbandman must use preventative measures to ensure the health of his vineyard.

Applying the wrong therapy to any plant problem is very wasteful. And if the supposed remedy is too strong, the plant might not survive it. As a discerning father, the husbandman must be alert to meet the various needs of his plants. Some plants will need to be re-potted. For others, re-potting could be a sure end. Some plants need more room for their roots to reach maturity. Others need their roots trimmed and even to be put into a smaller pot. Needs vary, and rule-of-thumb gardening simply doesn't work.

Some plants may appear very beautiful on the surface, but beneath the soil have rotten and dead roots. Surprisingly enough, over-watering can cause this. A husbandman may also kill his plants by too much exposure to sunlight. Every plant needs water and sunlight in different amounts. To meet every plant's needs according to its nature and level of maturity requires a wise and experienced husbandman.

All that can be said of the natural elements of plant husbandry can also be said of leading the children of the Lord. A father-hearted Christian leader will discern and minister to the different needs and maturity levels of the people of God. This ability is the fruit of a father's gentle, cherishing and nursing heart of love. The following chart on "Spiritual Husbandry" illustrates the parallels between husbandry and spiritual leadership.

Spiritual Husbandry Principles

The Wise and Experienced Husbandman Gives to the Plants	The Father-Hearted Leader Gives to the People of God
Sunlight	Light of God's Word
Water	Water of God's Spirit
Cultivation	Training for ministry
Pruning	Fatherly discipline
Proper environment	Proper church atmosphere of God's presence
New pot and soil	New lifestyle in Christ
Treatment for ailments	Help and counsel for problems
Early detection of disease	Observation of any problems in their early stages
Room for growth	Room to grow and exercise ministry

Spiritual Husbandry Application

A spiritual husbandman, who has a father's heart, will therefore pursue the following practices in caring for God's people:

Provide the spiritual nourishment for balanced Christian growth

Deal tenderly with the people of the Lord

Discern the needs of the children of God at any stage of their development

Be gentle and loving in relationships with the people of the Lord

Consistently attend to the spiritual, emotional, physical or mental needs of the children of God

Fatherly Nurture and Admonition

Ephesians 6:4 effectively expresses the fatherly attitudes of nurture and admonition:

"Ye fathers, provoke not your children to wrath, but bring them up in the nurture and admonition of the Lord" (King James Version).

The Amplified Bible translates this verse:

"Fathers, do not irritate and provoke your children to anger--do not exasperate them to resentment--but rear them (tenderly) *in the training and discipline and counsel and admonition of the Lord."*

In this chapter, the apostle Paul was teaching about raising a family. He was giving principles a father must follow in bringing up his children. The attitudes and principles a natural father needs to raise his natural children are those a spiritual father needs in raising his spiritual children. The house of the Lord needs these guidelines to rear its children in a balanced way. Paul used two words, "nurture" and "admonition," to illustrate this balance.

A study of the Greek word for "nurture" brings out an entirely different meaning than we find in today's English. In the New Testament Greek, the word "nurture" meant to promote the development of a child by teaching, supporting and encouraging him during the different stages of his growth. It meant to tutor or educate a child by training, discipline or correction. To nurture was to chastise with the intent of molding character into the child. The word included the idea of training and educating children, of cultivating their minds and/or morals by correcting and reproving them with words and actions.

Nurture. The word "nurture" is translated several different ways in the King James Version, with three primary forms being instruction, learning and chastening. (See II Timothy 3:16; I Timothy 1:20; II Timothy 2:25; Hebrews 12:5; Acts 7:22 and Revelation 3:19.)

Jesus illustrates the heart attitude of nurturing in His teaching. The Lord Jesus was a man of true love and compassion for all people. This did not stop Him from speaking the truth in a way that sometimes offended many people. He offended not only the hypocritical religious leaders of Israel, but also His own disciples. (See Matthew 15:12, Mark 14:27 and John 6:60-62 for examples.) In the New Testament, nurture does not mean gently nursing to maturity, but the strong teaching a child needs to mature in the Lord.

In Ephesians 6:4, Paul was not focusing on a father's love for his children, though that was not absent from the verse. Paul was focusing on the responsibility of a father to teach his children. Paul was giving an important charge to fathers: if they desire to raise their children correctly, they must have the "heart and the hand" to teach them in a very firm manner.

The ministry of a spiritual father includes strong teaching. A true spiritual father must be prepared to strongly correct his spiritual children. He must mold the charater of the child through teaching that is hard and grievous for the child at times, but that is still necessary. The word "nurture" that Paul used in Ephesians 6:4 was not the tender word that many people think it was. Today, the Church desperately needs spiritual fathers who have the courage to nurture her to full maturity by discipline, correction and chastening.

Admonition. The word translated "admonition" in Ephesians 6:4 meant calling attention to something by mild rebuke, warning and exhortation (as from the Lord). Literally, it meant putting into the mind. The word involved training by verbal encouragement, or, if necessary, verbal reproof and remonstrance. The Greek word translated as admonition or warning is "noutheto." The following list of scriptures shows the different ways in which the New Testament translates this word:

Acts 20:31 — *"ceased not to warn every man night and day"*
Romans 15:4 — *"able to admonish one another"*
I Corinthians 4:14 — *"but as my beloved sons, I warn you"*
Colossians 3:16 — *"admonishing one another in psalms and hymns"*
I Thessalonians 5:12 — *"those that admonish you"*

"Admonition" is a strong disciplinary word describing a very important attitude of a spiritual father. A spiritual father must put into the mind of the child the teachings that he alone knows the child needs for spiritual development and a healthy future. It takes constant exhortation and strong encouragement in righteousness to reach this goal.

All spiritual fathers in the Lord must decide to admonish. God's children need strong rebuke at times to reach maturity. Many teachers today would prefer to teach only what is pleasing, and will keep people coming back. That is not always what people need. A spiritual father must discern the precise needs of God's people. Through strong exhortation and teaching, he must impart it to them.

A Balanced Father's Heart

Every leader must balance the heart attitudes of a spiritual father that have been presented in this chapter. Nurture and admonition must stay in balance with gentleness, nursing and cherishing. Nurture and admonition are strong words which describe a leader's ministry of correction and discipline to God's people. These are needed, but are incomplete by themselves. The people of the Lord will not respond to the leader who speaks only rebuke and warning, who has hardened his heart in a one-sided pursuit of discipline. God's leaders must weep with the people. They must feel their burdens and heavy hearts in order to minister effectively. Gentleness, love, mercy and warmth must go with discipline.

The life of the apostle Paul demonstrates all of these attitudes. His ministry, a powerful one, was not composed exclusively of rebuke, chastisement and discipline. He also had a heart of gentleness, love, mercy and compassion. The parallel columns, below, show this balance by contrasting fatherly attitudes at work in his ministry. Like two sides of the same coin, each of the balanced attitude areas in this list must go together to make a complete whole.

Fatherly Heart Attitudes of the Apostle Paul

To Nurture and Admonish	To Love and Cherish
Discipline	Responsibility
"I have decided to deliver such a one to Satan" (I Corinthians 5:1-8)	*"In Christ Jesus I became your father through the gospel"* (I Corinthians 4:15)
Rebuke	Love

"I praise you not" (I Corinthians 11:17)

Chastisement
"I made you sorry with a letter" (II Corinthians 7:8)
Correction
"If I come again I will spare not" (II Corinthians 13:1,2)
Forthrightness
"O foolish Galatians, who hath bewitched you?" (Galatians 3:1-3)
Responsibility
"Yet to remain on in the flesh is more necessary for your sakes" (Philippians 1:24)

"That you might know the love that I have especially for you" (II Corinthians 2:4)
Relationship
"I speak unto you, my children" (II Corinthians 6:11-13)
Gentleness
"I, Paul, beseech you by the meekness and gentleness of Christ" (II Corinthians 10:1)
Reconciliation
"Restore such a one in a spiritual gentleness . . . bear ye one another's burdens" (Galatians 6:1,2)
Compassion
"Now I tell you even weeping" (Philippians 3:18)

The illustration of a balance shown below depicts the balance of discipline and love each leader must maintain in his ministry. If developed, both of these important sides of a leader's life will together maintain balanced growth for the Church.

A Balanced Father's Heart

1. Nurture
2. Admonition
3. Instruction
4. Correction
5. Chastisement
6. Authority
7. Rebuke
8. Warning
9. Truth
10. Judgment

1. Love
2. Gentleness
3. Nourishment
4. Forgiveness
5. Patience
6. Nursing
7. Kindness
8. Praise
9. Mercy
10. Justice

The heart of a spiritual father normally appears only in older people. Both years and experience are required to develop its characteristics. A younger person gains a father's heart only through early cultivation of certain attitudes and principles in his life.

In our day, many groups emphasise the academic and social preparation of a leader. The Bible, however, puts a far greater emphasis on the character and attitudinal preparation of a leader. It is possible to prepare a person's intellect for the ministry without preparing a person's heart. To successfully lead in a governmental ministry, a leader must have a prepared heart. The person who desires to help the people of God mature spiritually will seek God's help in developing the heart attitudes of a spiritual father.

The Leader and the Heart of a Servant

A leader, most people would say, is a person who directs, administrates, organizes, makes decisions, delegates responsibilities, and plans for the future. This definition lacks a very essential part of true leadership: a leader is one who serves. A leader of God's people must have the inner attitudes and motivations, and the outer service, of a servant.

Hebrew Meanings

The Old Testament translates several Hebrew words as "servant." Each presents a certain portion of truth concerning the heart of a servant.

"Ebed." Our first Hebrew word for servant, "ebed," generally means a slave or a servant. It is used in several applications, all of which apply quite well to a definition of a ministry of leadership.

"Ebed" applies to a person who is at the complete disposal of another person (Genesis 24:1-67). A leader of God's people must be at the complete disposal of the Lord Jesus Christ, and of those whom he is called to serve.

A person who works for a master is also described as "ebed" (Deuteronomy 15:12-18). In the same way, a leader must work for his master the Lord Jesus Christ. All his work is offered as a labor to Christ, and also to those whom he is called to serve.

This word also applies to a slave who has given up all of his personal rights to serve his master (Deuteronomy 15:12-18). A Church leader must give over all his personal rights to the Lord Jesus Christ, and to those whom he is called to served.

An "ebed" is also a slave in the service of a king (I Kings 1:9,47). A Christian leader must be a love-slave of the Lord Jesus Christ, who is the king above all earthly kings.

Finally, this word also applies to a person who serves in attendance to the temple sanctuary (I Samuel 3:9). A Christian leader must tend the true temple of God, the Church, with his worship toward God and his service to God's people. (For further studies on "ebed," also see Genesis 26:15,24 and 32:4,5; Numbers 12:7; Deuteronomy 7:8; Joshua 1:1,2,13,15 and 24:29; I Samuel 3:9,10 and 29:3; Isaiah 20:3 and 49:3; Jeremiah 33:22; Joel 2:29; Zechariah 1:6 and 3:8.)

"Abad." Another Hebrew word for servant, "abad," generally means to work and (in any sense) to serve. This word also has a variety of applications which help define Church leadership.

A person who tills the ground is an "abad" (Genesis 2:5; 3:23). A leader of God's people must work at breaking up the fallow ground of their hearts so that they can receive the seed of the Word of God.

This word also applies to a person who dresses or keeps a garden (Genesis 2:15). A leader of the Church must dress and keep God's vineyard, the Church of Jesus Christ.

The name of "abad" also applies to a priest who serves the people (Numbers 18:7,23). A Christian leader must lay down his life in sacrificial service to those whom God has called him to serve.

(For further studies on "abad," see Exodus 23:25; Deuteronomy 4:19, 28; Joshua 22:5,27; I Samuel 12:14,20; Psalm 22:30 and 72:11; Joel 2:22,23; Jeremiah 34:14; Ezekiel 29:20 and 36:9; Malachi 3:18.)

"Sakiyr." A third Hebrew word for servant, "sakiyr," generally means a person who works for wages by day or by year. This word has a variety of useful applications in defining conditions of Church leadership.

The "sakiyr," as a hired servant, could not eat the Passover of his master's family (Exodus 12:3-45). A leader of the Church must forsake the attitude of "paid professionalism." To eat of the true Passover lamb, Jesus Christ, he must by faith enter into the relationship of love-slave to the Lord, rather than paid servant.

The hired servant was not a love-slave (Leviticus 25:39-42). A Christian leader must come to a point in his life where he forsakes a religion of legalism that protects his rights. He must move into a personal relationship with God through faith in Jesus Christ, where his total self is given in exchange for Christ.

A "sakiyr" was not worth half of the amount that a love slave was worth (Deuteronomy 15:18). A leader must realize that ministry and activities not motivated by the love of God are not worth half as much as those motivated out of a love relationship.

A "sakiyr" may also be a sojourner who is taken into a house as a slave (Leviticus 25:6). A leader of the Church must recognize that he was once only a wandering stranger before Jesus Christ bought him with His own blood and established him in the house of God. (Other scriptures which use the word "sakiyr" are Exodus 22:14,15; Leviticus 19:13 and 22:10 and 25:40,50,53.)

"Sharath." A fourth Hebrew word for servant, "sharath," usually means a person who is a doer of menial and insignificant tasks.

A priest who ministers or serves in his priestly office is called a "sharath" (Exodus 28:35-43). A leader of the Church must perform seemingly insignificant tasks to fulfill his role as a servant-priest.

This word also applies to a priest who ministers continually before the ark of the covenant (I Chronicles 16:37). A leader is held responsible to continually receive power for service by entering into the presence of the Lord with praise and worship.

Joshua was a "sharath" to Moses (Exodus 24:13; Numbers 11:28). A leader of God's people has authority only as he is under proper authority, serving those over him with a servant's heart.

Greek Meanings

The New Testament uses a Greek word for servant, "doulos," which gives us a very good word picture of a servant's heart. Generally, "doulos" signifies bondage, but most commonly applies to a servant who has willingly bonded himself to a master, by some legal obligation. Paul the apostle uses this word to describe himself in several of his epistles:

Romans 1:1	*"Paul a servant* (doulos) *of Jesus Christ."*
Philippians 1:1	*"Paul a servant* (doulos) *of Jesus Christ."*
Titus 1:1	*"Paul a servant* (doulos) *of God."*

The Love-slave

The Old Testament provides the Hebrew background for this concept in Deuteronomy 15:1-23. When it came time for a master to release a slave after six years of service, according to the Mosaic Covenant, the slave had two options. The slave could accept his total freedom with no legal obligations to his master. Or he could stay in his master's house as a love-slave. If he chose to stay in his master's house as a love-slave, he was far more valuable to his master than the slaves who worked only to fulfill a debt or some other legal obligation. The servant who became a love-slave said to his master, in essence, "Because it is well with me as your slave, and because I love you and your household, I will serve you forever on the basis of my deep love for you."

Paul was this kind of a servant of the Lord Jesus Christ. He, like any other leader of the Church, was bought with the price of the blood of Jesus Christ. He realized he could never pay back this debt by working with a "for-hire" mentality. He desired nothing less than a relationship where his work and service was motivated purely from willingness and love.

The most effective leaders in the kingdom of God are those who serve the Lord only out of a desire to love Him. Such leaders do not serve for money, reputation, position, power or selfish advantage, even though their service means long hours of pressure and sacrifice. The leader with a servant's heart, who is secure in his personal relationship with the Lord and does not have to prove himself, is able to serve sincerely with no desire for personal profit or fame.

The New Testament Concept of Serving

Several Greek words in the New Testament present the concept of serving. From these several Greek words, the English word most commonly used is the word "deacon." Today, a large portion of the Church world does not properly understand the New Testament concept of deaconship or servanthood.

Some people erroneously think deaconship is limited to a small group of worthies in the local church who take the offering or serve communion. They believe it is the mere conferral of a title for the performance of some symbolic religious functions. But the true meaning of deaconship goes far deeper. The early Church appointed men as deacons only after they already manifested the qualities of a deacon: a good reputation, being full of the Spirit, and being full of wisdom (Acts 6:3). Before recognition as deacons, they had to be functioning in the requirements of the office already.

First, a Servant. Any leader, moreover, must first be a deacon (servant) in the true sense of the word. On the basis of servanthood, he is able to lead. The ministries of Jesus and His apostles were all founded on a servant's "people-conscious" heart. Jesus said that He came to serve, not to be served (Mark 10:45; Luke 22:27). He told his ambitious, position-seeking apostles that *"He that would be greatest among you, let him be your servant"* (Matthew 23:11). To every leader, Jesus is the supreme example of servanthood.

Today, however, some leaders would still repeat the selfish words of some of Jesus' disciples, who said, *"Master, do what we desire"* and *"Grant that we may sit on your right and left hand in your kingdom"* (Matthew 20:20-28). The selfish disciples desired a position for themselves, but there is no room for such an attitude in any of Christ's leaders.

Christ's leaders must desire to serve, not to be served, to give, and not to take. They must find true happiness in pleasing God and the Church. To put one's own happiness first would violate the heart of a servant. Selfishness is contrary to the law of the love-slave (Romans 1:1; Deuteronomy 15:1-23). It is contrary to the laws of promotion in God's kingdom (Matthew 23:12), love (I Corinthians 12:4-6), eternal life (Luke 10:25-27), wisdom (Proverbs 22:9), the Gospel (Luke 9:24-26) and humility (Philippians 2:3-5; I Corinthians 10:24,33).

The Deaconship. Let's take a closer look at the word "deacon" (servant) in the New Testament.

The word deacon can be applied in two ways. First, it can be applied to all Christians who are called to serve Jesus Christ and His people. This is seen in the broadbased ministry of household servants. Second, it can be applied to the official appointment of certain deacons as representatives of the local church, and as set into that office by the local leadership (Acts 6:1-4). Stephen and Philip were two appointed deacons (Acts 6:5-8:40). Both had powerful ministries, which should forever stamp into our minds that the office of deacon was never intended by God to be a despised or weak office in the New Testament Church.

If you are a Christian, whether or not you have been appointed as a deacon, your ministry will profit from studying the principles of deaconship. The qualifications for deaconship are a part of the qualifications for all Christian leaders. And the ministry of deaconship is the foundation of all congregational ministries.

The early Church believed that an official capacity of serving the people of God was very important. The Church outlined certain qualifications for deacons and their wives (I Timothy 3:8-14), and appointed people to the office (Philippians 1:1). Paul exhorted the deacons to use their office in the right way, implying that their office was invested with enough authority to create the possibility of improper use (I Timothy 3:10,13). Paul admonished the deacons to live up to the title of their office, that of "servant to God's people."

Three key words in New Testament Greek develop the idea of being a minister to God's people.

The word "diakoneo" (I Timothy 3:10,13) is a verb which means to be an attendant, to wait upon. It is usually used in a domestic setting, as the work of a household servant.

The word "diakonia" is a noun, which refers to the aid or service that a servant or official renders to someone else.

The word "diakonos" (Philippians 1:1; I Timothy 3:8,12) means to run errands, to attend on someone, or to do any menial task.

These three words describe all the primary elements of the deaconship: the act of service, the service itself, and the one who serves.

The New Testament writers borrowed the Greek word "deacon" and developed it as a part of their vocabulary. Originally, the word referred to waiting on tables (as the deacons did in Acts 6:1-4). Later, it broadened to include the idea of providing or caring for any need of another person. Even later, the word was used to refer to the service or act of showing love to another person in a personal way, as from one friend to another. All of these meanings applied to every Christian in the house of God.

To the Jews, however, the idea of menial service was abhorrent. May the Lord deliver us from such attitudes and give us true servants' hearts.

The following material on deaconship is in general outline form, to help the reader study this subject in greater detail.

"Diakoneo." The following scriptures use the word "diakoneo," and show different examples of the "act of serving" in the early Church. Each of these scriptures can be applied in principle to the duties of service required of every Christian in the Body of Christ.

Matthew 4:11	*"angels came and ministered* (diakones) *unto Him"*
8:15	*"she arose and ministered"*
20:28	Jesus *"came not to be ministered unto, but to minister"*
25:44	*"in prison and did not minister"*
27:55	*"many women . . . ministering unto him"*
Luke 10:40	*"my sister hath left me to serve alone"*
12:37	*"servants . . . will come forth and serve them"*
22:26	*"he that is chief, as he that doth serve"*
22:27	*"he that sitteth at meat or he that serveth"*
22:27	*"I am among you as he that serveth"*
John 12:26	*"any man serve me let him follow me"*
Acts 6:2	*"leave the word of God and serve tables"*
Romans 15:25	*"to minister unto the saints"*
I Timothy 3:10	*"let them use the office of a deacon"*
3:13	*"for they that have used the office of a deacon"*
II Timothy 1:18	*"how many things he ministered unto"*
Philemon :13	*"he might have ministered unto me"*
Hebrews 6:10	*"in that ye have ministered to the saints and do minister"*
I Peter 1:12	*"unto us they did minister the things"*
4:10	*"even so minister the same one to another"*
4:11	*"if any man minister, (let him do it)"*

Let us look further at some verses in that list. After being healed of sickness, Peter's mother-in-law "arose and ministered unto" Jesus and the disciples (Matthew 8:15). On the day of judgment, said Jesus, service to the needy would be likened to service to Christ Himself. " *'Lord, when saw we thee an hungered, or athirst, or a stranger, or naked, or sick, or in prison, and did not minister unto thee?'* . . . *'Inasmuch as ye did it not to one of the least of these, ye did it not to me' "* (Matthew 25:44,45).

"*But now I go unto Jerusalem to minister unto the saints,*" said the apostle Paul (Romans 15:25). He knew it might well lead to his death. "*As every man hath received the gift, even so minister the same one to another, as good stewards of the manifold grace of God . . . if any man minister, let him do it as of the ability which God giveth,*" said the apostle Peter (I Peter 4:10,11b). This last verse from the apostle Peter clearly establishes that all Christians are called and empowered to serve (minister).

"***Diakonia.***" The following scriptures use the word "diakonia" (which along with "diakoneo" occurs 70 times in the New Testament), showing us "the service of ministry."

Acts 1:17	"*had obtained part of this ministry*"
1:25	"*he may take part of this ministry*"
6:1	"*neglected in daily ministrations*"
6:4	"*apostles not to wait tables but to pray and minister the word*"
11:29	"*determined to send relief unto the brethren*"
Romans 12:7	"*ministry* (let us wait) *on* (our) *ministering*"
15:31	"*that my service which (I have)*"
I Corinthians 12:5	"*are differences of administrations*"
Ephesians 4:12	"*for the work of the ministry*"
Colossians 4:17	"*take heed to the ministry*"
I Timothy 1:12	"*putting me into the ministry*"
II Timothy 4:5,11	"*Make full proof of your ministry; for he is valuable to me for the ministry*"
Hebrews 1:14	"*spirits sent forth to minister for them*"
Revelation 2:19	"*I know your works, and charity and service*"

The above verses, using the noun form for "service" or "ministry" establish the office of the deacon. In Acts 1:24,25, the apostles asked God to *show whether of these two* (Joseph or Matthias) *thou hast chosen, that he may take part of this ministry and apostleship, from which Judas by transgression fell.* The apostle Paul admonishes Archippus to *take heed to the ministry which thou hast received in the Lord* (Colossians 4:17). From prison, Paul asks his disciple Timothy to bring Mark to him on Timothy's next visit, *For he is profitable to me for the ministry* (II Timothy 4:11). In Revelation, the message to the church in Thyatira was, *". . . I know thy works, and charity, and service, and faith"* (2:19).

"***Diakonos.***" As a description of one who serves, the Greek word "diakonos" appears 30 times in the New Testament. It comes from the word "diako," to run errands. It is translated with three English words: minister, servant and deacon. From its use, it is apparent that not only those who are officially designated as "deacons" are to serve others, but that all Christians are to serve. For further study, the list of verses where "diakonos" appears is:

MINISTER	SERVANTS
Matthew 20:26	Matthew 23:11
Mark 10:43	Matthew 22:13

Romans 13:4
Romans 15:8
I Corinthians 3:5
Ephesians 3:7
Colossians 1:25
I Thessalonians 3:2
II Corinthians 3:6
II Corinthians 6:4
II Corinthians 11:15
II Corinthians 11:23
Galatians 2:17
Colossians 1:7
Colossians 1:23
Colossians 4:7
I Timothy 4:6

Mark 9:35
John 2:5
John 2:9
John 12:26
Romans 16:1

DEACONS
Philippians 1:1
I Timothy 3:8
I Timothy 3:12

Particular Forms of Ministry. Service is coupled with other words to describe a particular form of ministry.

The *"ministry of the word"* (II Timothy 4:5) reminds us that a preacher is one who serves up the bread of life (Acts 6:4).

We hear of *"the ministry of reconciliation"* in II Corinthians 5:18.

Self-effort to keep all the requirements of the law is called *"the ministry of death and condemnation,"* but the life of faith is a *"ministry of the spirit and a ministry of righteousness"* (II Corinthians 3:7-9).

Several verses use "diakonos" to show that people can be servants of many things. It is possible to be a servant of Satan (II Corinthians 11:14-15). God wants us to be, instead, servants of God (II Corinthians 6:3), of Christ (I Timothy 4:6), of the Gospel (II Corinthians 11:23), of the new Covenant (II Corinthians 3:6), of the Church (Colossians 1:25). God desires us, as servants, to perform any task that the Spirit tells us to do, whether it appears menial or important.

Example Servants

Leaders can sometimes become isolated. They may think they are the only ones trying to fulfill the ministry of service to God, Christ, the Gospel, the New Covenant and the Church. Fortunately, this is wrong. The New Testament presents an inspiring list of individuals and groups who were and are called to serve God and the Church in their own particular ways.

1. Timothy and Erastus (Acts 19:22; diakonos I Timothy 3:2 and 4:6)
2. Onisiphorus' service to Paul at Ephesus (II Timothy 1:16-18)
3. Apostles' service to the Church (II Corinthians 3:3)
4. Old Testament prophets to the Church (I Peter 1:10-12)
5. Paul ministering to needs of the saints at Jerusalem (II Corinthians 8:19; Romans 15:31)
6. Ministry of saints in general (Ephesians 4:11; Hebrews 6:10)
7. Household of Stephen devoting themselves to the service of the saints (I Corinthians 16:15)
8. Ministry of angels (Hebrews 1:14; Mark 1:13)
9. Archippus (Colossians 4:17)
10. Tychicus (Ephesians 6:21; Colossians 4:7, diakonos)
11. Epaphras (Colossians 1:7, diakonos)

The Lord Jesus Christ provides us the best example of servanthood. In His earthly ministry among the Jews, He totally overturned their negative attitudes toward servanthood by becoming a servant in every way. He served from His birth to His death. The Church must make sure that she does not stumble over the requirement to serve, but instead she must follow the example of her Master Servant, Jesus Christ. Let's explore the teaching and life example of Christ the servant in the following verses:

Luke 12:37	*The Lord will reward men and women who keep a constant watch for opportunities to serve Him, by serving them Himself: "He shall gird himself, and make them to sit down to meat, and will come forth and serve them."*
Luke 22:27	*"Which is greater, one who sits at the table or one who serves? I am among you as one who serves."*
John 13	*In this chapter, Jesus takes the place of a slave, and washes the disciples feet.*
Mark 10:43	*"Not lording it over them . . . whosoever will be great let him be your servant. The first must be a slave."*
John 12:24-26	*"If anyone serves me, he must follow me, and where I am, there shall be my servant. Also . . . if anyone serves me, the Father will honor him."*
Philippians 2:8	*"Jesus took the form of a servant and humbled Himself unto the death on the cross." Jesus had bound Himself to be God's servant, and accepted the full measure of labor and suffering required to complete His service.*

In all of these verses (with the exception of John 13, where the example of Jesus says all), some form of the word "diakonos" is employed for "servant." May every leader develop a servant's heart like Christ's.

Conclusion

If you earnestly desire to know your spiritual calling, pursue the qualifications that make you the candidate to receive one. Develop the heart of a father, and the heart of a servant. You will discover your calling in the Church as you serve with a healthy attitude.

If you have received your calling, continue to cultivate these qualities of the heart. They will directly influence your ability to grow in your calling and serve the Body of Christ. If you want to see your ministry established to the glory of God and the edification of the Church, continue to cultivate these qualities of the heart. Your service depends on them.

If you are a leader with an established governmental ministry, tenaciously cling to the father's heart and the servant's heart. Satan wants to separate you from them, that he might tear down your life's work and once again capture the people you have helped liberate from his domain.

The next chapter, "The Leader and the Heart of the Shepherd," will complete our study of the heart qualifications for leadership. It is important for you to understand this fundamental quality of a governmental leader's heart. As a governmental ministry, it is the point that distinguishes your function from all others in the Body of Christ. As a congregational ministry, your understanding of the heart of the shepherd will equip you to pray for and support your pastor and other leaders.

CHAPTER 6
THE LEADER AND THE HEART
OF A SHEPHERD

As we study the shepherd's heart in this chapter, you may see Jehovah and the Lord Jesus Christ in new ways. That's because the heart of a shepherd is the heart of the Lord for His Church.

A shepherd's heart is a required attitude in all leadership ministries, and especially in governmental ministries. This does not make it either less desirable or less valuable in a congregational ministry. What better way to be a Christian, a "Christ-like one," than to love the Church as Christ loves her? If you want to understand Christian leadership, if you want to know Christ, you'll want to study what the Bible has to say about the heart of a shepherd.

"Shepherd" as a Leadership Title

God's leaders are given many titles in both the Old Testament and the New Testament. Some of these titles are bishop, presbyter, priest, preacher, minister and shepherd. Each word has a history and significance of its own. But the term "shepherd" has a particular importance to God.

Interestingly, the word "shepherd" has probably seen the least use of all these titles throughout Church history. Such infrequent use of the word shows that many of the leaders of the Church have not fully experienced or practiced true shepherding. Let's survey each of the titles above, and see how they all fall short of truly representing God's idea of the shepherd-servant.

"Bishop." The word "bishop" came into the Church from the Gentile world. It is used to designate a leader who oversees or superintends the flock of God. In the Apostolic era, all local churches had bishops. Since the word directly calls up images of authority and administration, however, many Church leaders have abused this title for dictatorial ends. Even in its original form, "bishop" does not completely describe the meaning that God invested in the word "shepherd."

"Presbyter." The word "presbyter" came into the Church from Judaism. As far back as the time of Moses, Jews had this kind of leader. The New Testament uses "bishop" and "presbyter"

interchangeably, even as the early Church combined the Gentile and the Jewish worlds. In the early Church, presbyters (elders) were primarily men of some years. The word "presbyter" is based on age and experience, which does not take in the full scope of the meaning in "shepherd."

"Priest." The word "priest" has a long history in both Judaism and paganism. In Judaism, the priest represented the people to their God, and God to His people. Jesus and His disciples used this word very little in the New Testament. The ultimate New Testament meaning of "priest," as it applies to individual Christians, was given to Peter. Peter called the Church *"a royal priesthood"* (I Peter 2:5,9). But since the office of priesthood involves the work of representing and mediating, it misses the important element of guidance that "shepherd" contains. The term "priest" has been one of the most abused terms when applied to Christian leadership, producing spiritual bondage for many people--a far cry from the intent of the shepherd.

"Preacher." The word "preacher" has a great tradition in the Church of describing the public speaking aspect of the shepherd (pastor). The meaning and high value placed on this title has led, unfortunately, to the false belief that success as an orater equates with success in shepherding the flock. But since the concept of "preaching" depends heavily on a pulpit/pew kind of relationship, it is very far from the process of shepherding.

"Minister." The word "minister" has been applied to Church leaders (particularly pastors), whether the leaders are professionally ordained by man or spiritually ordained by God. Our applications of the word sometimes give no distinction between a true servant of God and a man who falsely dons the same title. Even if a man is not divinely called, even if he is neither willing nor able to serve God's people, he can be ordained and called a "minister" by the state government.

An unfortunate attitude rising from the Church's misuse of the term "minister" is that only the one man called "minister" is the servant of God. Instead, God calls each Christian to a particular ministry function. This confusion over the definition of "minister" has led to the idea that only an ordained minister is competent to do the spiritual work of the Church. Thus the word "minister" has been given an idea of professionalism which clashes with the true meaning of "shepherd."

"Shepherd." Finally, we have the beautifully descriptive title of "shepherd." Throughout her history, the Church has probably used this title of ministry least, because it represents the ministerial function most lacking in the Church. At times, the Church has obviously lacked the true ministerial function of the "shepherd": tender, sincere, intimate, loving, spiritual care of a shepherd for his flock. Fortunately, God is again greatly emphasizing this most significant title of ministry.

Everyone who wants to fulfull his or her area or responsibility in the kingdom of God must have the heart qualifications of a leader. He needs the heart of the father, to nurture the people of the Lord to maturity. She needs the heart of the servant, to sacrifice time and life to minister to every need of God's people. Now we come to the heart attitude of the Shepherd. Everyone involved in the work of the Lord must have a shepherd's heart--it's not just for the "full-time" minister.

Periodically, the Church passes through seasons of great need for true shepherds. When Church leadership is immature or failing, the sheep are scattered, wounded and bruised just as were the Children of God in different times during Israel's history.

Numbers 27:15-17   When Moses' leadership of Israel was ending, he asked the Lord to *"set a*

	man over the congregation . . . that the congregation of the Lord be not as sheep which have no shepherd."
I Kings 22:17	When the prophet Micaiah prophesied a military defeat at the hands of Syria: *"I saw all Israel scattered upon the hills, as sheep that have not a shepherd."*
Ezekiel 34:4-6	*"My flock became meat to every beast of the field, because there was no* (true) *shepherd . . . I will deliver my flock from their mouth* (of false shepherds), *that they may not be meat for them."*
Zechariah 10:2	*"They were troubled because there was no shepherd."*
Zechariah 13:7	*"Smite the shepherd and the sheep will be scattered,"* a prophecy of Christ's death.

Jehovah as the Great Shepherd

A shepherd is "a man who takes care of the sheep, a person who cares for and protects the sheep; a spiritual guide, friend or companion." This describes a natural shepherd's work of protecting, guiding, and feeding the flock. A spiritual shepherd does the same spiritual work of protecting, guiding and feeding God's people. The Lord is called a shepherd of His people many times throughout Scripture. He is our example, the source of the true definition of what He wants us to be and do as shepherds. He is the Great Shepherd of our souls:

Psalm 23:1	*"The Lord is my shepherd."*
Psalm 80:1	*"Give ear, O shepherd of Israel."*
Ezekiel 34:12	*"I will search for my sheep as a shepherd does a flock."*
Isaiah 40:11	*"He shall feed his flock like a shepherd."*
Psalm 77:20	*"Thou leadest thy people like a flock."*

Actions of the Great Shepherd

The Lord of the Old Testament is the Great Shepherd to His flock Israel, and more. He also illustrates, to all spiritual shepherds throughout all ages, the proper attitudes and actions of a shepherd of God's people. The list below names some of the actions that arose from the shepherd's heart of the Lord in the Old Testament.

Searched out the lost sheep	Ezekiel 34:11-16
Delivered the captive sheep	Ezekiel 34:12
Gathered the dispersed sheep	Ezekiel 34:13
Fed the hungry sheep	Isaiah 40:11, Ezekiel 34:13
Rested the weary sheep	Psalm 23:1-3, Ezekiel 34:15
Bound up the hurt sheep	Ezekiel 34:16
Strengthened the weak sheep	Ezekiel 34:16
Guided the directionless sheep	Psalm 23:3
Carried the broken sheep	Isaiah 40:11
Restored the soul of the tired sheep	Psalm 23:3
Comforted the agitated sheep	Psalm 23:4
Prepared a table for the frightened sheep	Psalm 23:5
Anointed the needy sheep	Psalm 23:5

Jesus as the Good Shepherd

In the New Testament, we find the revelation of God in the flesh, the Lord Jesus Christ, as the Good Shepherd of the sheep. Jesus displays all of the attributes of God's shepherding heart. As we see His life unfold in the New Testament gospels, we see the heart of Jehovah made manifest. Jesus Christ was the good shepherd of His sheep in the gospels as Jehovah was the Great Shepherd of Israel in the Old Testament. The following scriptures show Jesus as the Good Shepherd of the New Testament:

John 10:11,14	*"I am the good shepherd"*
Hebrews 13:20	*"Jesus, the great shepherd of the sheep"*
I Peter 2:25	*"Return unto the shepherd and bishop of your souls*
I Peter 5:4	*"When the chief shepherd shall appear"*

As we listed the heart attitudes of the Lord in the Old Testament, so we list the heart attitudes and actions of Jesus Christ, the pattern Shepherd in the New Testament. Most of these insights are derived from John 10. Jesus:

Matthew 9:35,36; John 10:15b	Cares for the sheep.
John 10:3	Relates to the sheep.
John 10:1	Condemns all who reject the Door of the sheepfold, and enter some other way, as thieves and robbers.
John 10:8	Condemns all who came before Him as thieves and robbers.
John 10:1	Provides a sheepfold for the sheep.
John 10:3,4	Leads the sheep.
John 10:2	Enters by the Door Himself.
John 10:3a	Has the doorkeeper open to Him.
John 10:6	Provides spiritual insight for the sheep.
John 10:3b,27a	Makes His voice plain to His sheep.
John 10:3c	Calls His own sheep by name.
John 10:3d	Leads His own sheep out into pasture.
John 10:4a,b	Goes before His own sheep as He leads them out.
John 10:4c,27c	Has the sheep follow Him.
John 10:4d	Has the sheep recognize His voice.
John 10:7,9a	Is the Door of the sheep.
John 10:9	Feeds the sheep.
John 10:10b	Gives life to the sheep by protecting them.
John 10:10b,11b,15c,17	Gives His life for the sheep.
John 10:11a,14a	Is the Good Shepherd of the sheep.
John 10:12a,13a	Is a true shepherd of His sheep and the opposite of a hireling.
John 10:12c	Is the owner of the sheep and not a hireling.
John 10:12d	Sees when the wolf comes to destroy the flock.
John 10:12e,f	Stays near the sheep when the wolf comes in contrast to the cowardly hireling.
John 10:14b,27b	Knows His own sheep.
John 10:14c	Is known by His own sheep.
John 10:15b	Knows the Father.

John 10:15a	Is known by the Father.
John 10:16a	Has other sheep in other folds.
John 10:16c	Brings in the other sheep also.
John 10:16d	Is heard by the other sheep as well.
John 10:16e	Is the One Shepherd and owner of all folds.
John 10:17c	Takes up His life again because He laid it down.
John 10:18abc	Lays His life down freely and of His own initiative.
John 10:18d	Has the authority to lay down His life because God Himself has commissioned Him to do so.

The Lord Jesus showed us the attitude and actions of a true shepherd throughout His entire ministry. He set forth an example for all the shepherds of God's flock. Jesus was a man of compassion and love. He did not rely on crowds and multitudes of followers to measure his success in shepherding. On the contrary, He looked for the the sheep with needs, and He identified those needs. Then, He was not satisfied until He met the individual needs of each sheep.

Today, how do the shepherds of the Church see the people of the Lord? Do our shepherds see the people of God as a crowd of sheep, hungry for rich food and entertainment? Or do they see them as broken people in great need of love and compassion? Today, unfortunately, the majority of Church leaders are not doing the work of a true shepherd. The Church desperately needs true shepherds, who will lay down their lives for the sheep, as Jesus did. The Church needs spiritual shepherds to heal the broken-hearted and bind up the wounds of the hurt. The contemporary Church has enough theologians who love to write or verbalize the knowledge of God. She needs shepherds who have true spiritual ministries to God's people.

Relational Pictures of a Leader

In short, the Church needs leaders who themselves have an intimate relationship with God, and who can bring others into the same communion with God. The Bible uses many different pictures (described below) to demonstrate this need for relationship, pictures that can guide spiritual shepherds in relationships with their sheep.

Father and Child Relationship. This is a picture of the warm, loving relationship between a father and his children. In this relationship the children love and respect the father, and respond to his corrective hand. Here we see the shepherd, like the father, whose primary purpose is to cause his children sincerely and without fear to love him, their mother, their brothers and sisters, and those outside of the family. Fathers also seek to mature their children in all of their relationships in life.

Husband and Wife Relationship. This is a picture of the love relationship of Christ with His Church, the bond of marriage with all its sacred meaning. The husband provides the home and supports his wife in love. The wife receives and responds to his love. Here we see how the shepherd must be the initiator in giving his love to his sheep, and how he must provide them with a good spiritual home.

Head and Body Relationship. This is a picture of a relationship of governing and protecting. Just as Christ governs and protects His Church, which is His Body, so the shepherd must take his rod and staff in hand and govern and protect his local church body. In both of these pictures, the head is the covering for the body. The body is many-membered, but the head is singular. As a body has only one head, the shepherd must remember that Christ continues as the only Head of the Body. The under-shepherd takes up his leadership responsibility in service and support of the Head, Christ.

Vine and Branches Relationship. The Lord Jesus presents this picture of a relationship between Himself and the Church in John 15. In these verses, He is the vine and His people are the branches. All of the life, source and power for the branches must come from the vine. There is such a close relationship between the vine and the branches that one cannot always discern where the vine ends and the branches begin. Jesus said the branches must bear fruit, or they will be purged by the husbandman. If need be, the husbandman will take his sharp knife and cut away the worthless parts of a branch. So it is with the shepherd, who should develop such a close relationship with his sheep that they will allow him to sheer away some of the unprofitable areas of their lives.

Husbandman and Vineyard Relationship. This is the picture of a vineyard meticulously cared for by a husbandman or farmer. At times, the vineyard is overgrown, and so the husbandman must come and clean out all the debris. At ties he must skillfully use his tools to harvest the vineyard's fruit. Similarly, God's shepherds must be sensitive enough to his sheep that he can discern the spiritual times and seasons in their lives.

Potter and Clay Relationship. This is a picture of the hand of God which forms His vessel, the Church. The potter's hand is in complete control of the clay. The clay cannot ask the potter what he is doing. This is the way the Lord deals with His people. Similarly, the shepherd should be able to so relate to his sheep that he can help form Christ's character in their lives.

Captain and Army Relationship. The picture here is one of discipline and authority. The army of the Lord is a place of correction and training. The army must experience many drills in order to be useful to its captain in warfare. At this time, the Church is under the hand of the mighty Son of David, the Captain of her salvation, Jesus Christ. Similarly, the shepherd must train and discipline his sheep to fit them for their tasks.

Creator and Creature Relationship. God is the all-powerful Creator at Whose words the worlds were brought into being and framed. At His word, all that is in the heavens and earth were formed. This is a picture of the mighty God reproducing His own image and likeness in His creation. The relationship here is not a very personal one, because man alienated himself from God through disobedience. Through obedience, however, man can enter again into a relationship with his Creator. Similarly, the shepherd should be the instrument through which God can create new life in His people.

Shepherd and Sheep Relationship. This last picture of the shepherd and the sheep is a picture of warmth and beauty. Love, compassion and tenderness are exchanged. This is demonstrated in the shepherd carrying his small, hurt lamb upon his shoulders to safety. Since this illustration is also shown in one of the titles of God (the Great Shepherd), it holds a tender picture of true ministry.

The Shepherd-Watchman

The requirements for a natural shepherd apply directly to the spiritual shepherds of God's people. Natural shepherds, as watchmen over their flock, build observation towers to scan the countryside for advance warning of dangers to the flock. Flash floods can sweep through the hills and destroy everything in their path. Predators may raid the flock; lions, bears, jackals or wolves could sneak in and claim a straying lamb or wounded sheep. These predators, in fact, are a threat to the shepherd himself. Vultures or eagles might swoop down to wound the young of the flock, and return later for the kill. The shepherd must be a far-seeing watchman, constantly alert to potential dangers around him and the flock. He dare not be a lazy or unseeing watchman.

Paul exhorted the Ephesian elders, in his farewell address, to watch over the flock in just this way (Acts 20:28-31). Paul's letter to the Corinthians exhorts them to watch and stand fast (I Corinthians 16:13). Other examples of the call to shepherdly watchfulness:

"Watch ye and stand fast" (I Corinthians 16:13)
"Continue in prayer and watch" (Colossians 4:2)
"Let us not sleep, but let us watch" (I Thessalonians 5:6)
"But watch thou in all things" (II Timothy 4:5)
"Obey them who have rule over you . . . for they watch for your souls" (Hebrews 13:17).

A leader over the flock must be a most diligent watchman. The Church has many enemies that would attack the house of the Lord in these last days. Lazy shepherds leave the Church open to attack. And false shepherds have inflicted some of the Church's worst wounds. Not only do they steal from God's people, but they often bring forth a response of misguided over-regulation from government. True and watchful shepherds of spiritual Israel are the Church's hope of protection from spiritual destruction in these perilous times.

The Shepherd-Protector

Closely related to the role of watchman is the shepherd's role as guard, protector and defender of the flock. Sheep are among the most defenseless of animals. They have no natural weapons for attack. Their docile disposition leaves them very unlikely to bite, kick or scratch. They are one of the only animals that depend almost completely on a human protector. The shepherd is the flock's main (if not the only) guard and protector against hazards and enemies. At times, the shepherd must risk his own life for the life of the sheep.

Sheep are also very ignorant about personal survival in the wilderness. The shepherd must exercise constant watch over the sheep in the wilderness, where they invariably wander into trouble. In the wilderness, shepherds used to build a sheepfold with walls that could repel the strongest predators. Shepherds slept by the door to provide complete security for the flock. If an enemy came first, he would have to step over the shepherd to get to the sheep. In meeting the sheeps' enemies first, the shepherd was willing to lay down his life for the sheep.

The Lord, the Great Shepherd of the sheep, gives us His standard and His example of how to defend the flock. In Psalms 121:3, we are assured that *"He that keepeth thee will not slumber."* Other verses that give us the Lord's standard and example for His under-shepherds in being a true defender of the flock:

Psalm 7:10	*"My defense is of God."*
Psalm 59:16	*"Thou hast been my defense and my refuge."*
Psalm 62:6	*"He is my defense I shall not be moved."*
Zechariah 9:15	*"The Lord of Hosts shall defend them."*
Psalm 121:3	*"He that keepeth thee shall not slumber."*
Psalm 12:7	*"Thou shall keep them, O Lord."*
Psalm 31:20	*"The Lord shall keep them safely in his pavilion."*

Psalm 127:1   *"Except the Lord keep the city."*
John 17:11   *"Holy Father, keep them through thy own word."*

The Lord Jesus is the Great Shepherd who shall keep His people from all trouble. In the same way, each of His shepherd-leaders must do all he can to protect the sheep from their enemies.

The Shepherd-Guide

A shepherd must perform another important role for the sheep, that of guide. To say the least, sheep are not independent travelers. They have no sense of direction. Astray from the flock, they wander in circles until taken by predators. When grazing, they keep their noses to the ground as long as there is grass, but never look up to see where their grazing takes them.

Conditions in the wilderness are not kind to sheep. Good pasture is often in spots and small strips, and is hard to find. Streams may be few in number and hidden in some areas, making the land parched and unyielding. Without a shepherd, sheep would wander aimlessly until they died of starvation or thirst. The shepherd must wisely select grazing range for the sheep, out of personal, first-hand knowledge. The lives of the sheep depend on his guidance.

Sheep are sensitive animals that cannot endure hard driving. They are meant to be led gently, and the wise shepherd does so. Some weak, sickly or injured sheep would die if the shepherd drove them too far or too fast. The wisdom of the shepherd can save the lives of many sheep. The patriarch Jacob illustrates this truth. In Genesis 33:9-15, we have the acount of Jacob guiding his flock as he went back to his home country. He demonstrated many important attitudes as a shepherd over his flock.

TENDERNESS
Genesis 33:13   *"The children are tender."*

SENSITIVITY
Genesis 33:13   *"The flocks and the herds have young with them."*

GENTLENESS
Genesis 33:13   *"The flock will die if men overdrive them in one day."*

OBSERVATION
Genesis 33:14   *"The flock must be led softly."*

PATIENCE
Genesis 33:14   *"The flock must only be lead as much as the youngest can endure."*

These verses in Genesis 33 clearly show the heart of a true shepherd. Jacob was willing to go slowly in order to save the young and the tender of the flock. He did not drive the flock, though he had the power to do so and it would have had its benefits. Similarly, the Church of the Lord Jesus has many young and tender sheep. These cannot be driven hard by forceful men. They must be gently guided by true shepherds.

God has promised to help His shepherds guide the flock effectively. He will be their Great Shepherd, the One whose example and guidance the under-shepherd can follow.

Promises for the shepherd:

Psalm 23:2   *"He leadeth me beside the still waters."*
Psalm 77:20   *"Thou leadest thy people like a flock."*
Psalm 78:52-54   *"He led forth his own sheep and guided them in the wilderness like a flock."*

The Shepherd-Physician

The shepherd must also be a physician to his sheep. The English word "physician" means a person that heals, relieves or comforts. In the Hebrew language, the concept of physician is one who mends by stitching, cures, causes healing, repairs and makes whole. In the Greek language, the concept means to make whole, and to set free by curing.

These various definitions capture the shepherd's ministry. The spiritual shepherd is to heal the broken-hearted and mend the torn. This is the true work of those who have a shepherd's heart. Like people, sheep may suffer from a variety of maladies and diseases. Consequently, they need shepherds who are competent as physicians. The spiritual shepherd must have spiritual discernment regarding the problems that can overtake his flock. He must correctly diagnose and treat these sicknesses, or they may prove fatal to the sheep.

Jesus showed His concern for the hurting sheep of Israel when He visited the "publicans and sinners." To the Pharisees who objected to this, He replied, *"They that be whole need not a physician, but they who are sick"* (Matthew 9:12).

Many sick people in the Church today need a shepherd-physician. They suffer in any number of ways--emotionally, spiritually, mentally, physically. It takes a true spiritual physician to heal God's flock, not an over-intellectual academic. The ability to cooperate with the Holy Spirit in the healing of souls requires experience in the school of the Spirit, and a knowledge of the Word of God's practical application to everyday life.

Job rejected would-be physicians who attempted to meet his needs through inadequate human understanding and knowledge. *"Ye are all physicians of no value,"* he said (Job 13:4). We must ask ourselves, "How many shepherds are in this same category?" Unfortunately, too many "ministers" are of little value to the flock of God, because they cannot discern the spiritual needs of the sheep.

What practical value does a shepherd have, without the ability to meet the practical needs of hurting sheep? Preaching well does not negate the need for shepherd-physicians. Without an understanding of the main purpose of a shepherd's work, understanding all of the brilliant professors of the past and the knowledge of many languages have no value. The sheep need shepherds who can stitch up the wounded and bind up the brokenhearted. The need today is for God-anointed shepherds with skill and wisdom as spiritual physicians, who can diagnose and treat the sheep of God.

Like other creatures, sheep have unforeseen accidents and misfortunes. They may break their legs, get cut, fall into pits, or bruise themselves. At different seasons, they are prone to different diseases or conditions. Different environments and different food effect sheep in different ways. Sickness can overtake a sheep even if it does nothing wrong. The shepherd must not always blame the sheep for their suffering; he must guard his attitude toward the sheep, and not become hardened to their cries.

A sensitivity to the sheep is a must for the shepherd's work of ministry. A shepherd must not beat a sheep for falling into a hole, or punish a sheep for getting bruised in a thicket. Our Chief Shepherd, the Lord Jesus, never showed a hastiness to condemn the sheep. A true shepherd feels the hurt of the sheep, suffers a sheep's bruises as if they were his own. A shepherd accepts the problems of the sheep. They will fall into pits and holes. They will catch colds and need special attention. It is the responsibility and the very life of the shepherd to meet such needs. If all the sheep were well, there would be less need for the shepherd's ministry. The sheep that are sick need a physician, not the ones that are whole.

Some shepherds want a flock that is healthy and without needs. This is virtually impossible. The true shepherd, on the other hand, is always looking for sheep with needs. He looks for a broken leg, a bruised heel, a cut foot, a bad eating habit. The true shepherd finds his very fulfillment in tending the needs of the sheep! The spiritual shepherd should always remember that a needy sheep, that limps from a foot wound or does not feed due to an infirmity, should receive more abundant care and attention. God's Church is not a business, with a "spiritual sales quota" on every "employee." The Body of Christ is the flock of the Great Shepherd. The shepherd is called by God to heal the brokenhearted, not to condemn those who need his help.

Sheep Diseases

The shepherd must watch over his flock, alert for signs of common sheep diseases and maladies. The following list of sheep diseases can also serve as a warning list to God's spiritual shepherds. It will explore how each of these diseases is analogous to a spiritual disease or problem that can occur in the Church.

THE NATURAL DISEASE	THE SPIRITUAL APPLICATION
Overeating Disease (may come from) A sudden change of food	Spiritual Truth A sudden change of teaching, or spiritual food of any kind can be fatal to many people; change must come slowly and progressively.
An excess of high energy food	To give the people a rich, potent teaching diet continually is to spiritually overfeed them. A variety of teaching and preaching is needed.
Irregular feeding times	To upset regular feeding times does harm to the people. They need a definite feeding time to be consistently satisfied.
Increasing amount of food too rapidly	To increase the amount of ministry, teaching or preaching too quickly will harm the people. The spiritual shepherd must discern the people's growth level and meet them where they are.
Feeding lambs of varying sizes together	All people do not have the same spiritual need. The flock has different levels of growth and maturity. Each different level of the people requires a specialized ministry.
White Muscle Disease (may come from) Vitamin deficiency	Spiritual Truth The people must be kept on a straight, nutritional diet of the Word of God exclusively.
Imbalanced diet	The people must have a balanced diet of practical, devotional, spiritual, inspirational and instructional food for proper growth.
Death of offspring (result)	Spiritual reproduction of the people will be stifled if their diet is imbalanced.
Twin Lamb Disease (may come from) Low blood pressure due to stress	Spiritual Truth Undue pressure upon the sheep may cause ill spiritual births.
The ewes with a tendency toward this disease	The most productive members of the flock need

can be discovered when the shepherd even gently drives the sheep, and they show no energy to be driven.

Grass Tetany Disease (may come from)
Low magnesium in the blood, due to lush grass

Not enough variety in the food

Pneumonia (may come from)
Excessive stress on the sheep

Foot Rot Disease (may come from)
Too much time in wet pasture

Threatens the mobility of the sheep

Bloat Disease (may come from)
Feeding on lush legumes and pastures, which disturbs the sheeps' digestion

Parasitic Disease
Parasites may attach either to external or internal parts of a sheep's body

The result is an unhealthiness in the walk of the sheep.

Poisonous Plants Diseases
Poisonous plants are usually hidden among nutritional plants

Sheep generally do not know the difference between poisonous and nutritional plants

close attention, including a double portion of food and energy.

Spiritual Truth
A mixture of lush spiritual food with dry food is needed when the sheep are fed with the Word. Too much of the same kind of teaching or preaching will cause illness in the people.

Spiritual Truth
The shepherd must not be guilty of oppressing the flock. The shepherd must not overdrive those under his authority.

Spiritual Truth
Dry spiritual periods are needed, as well as wet periods, as the people are washed in the water of the Word and follow the Spirit on a daily basis.

Excessive watering with the Word, without balance, cripples the walk of the people.

Spiritual Truth
Too much rich teaching that cannot be put into action causes problems in the life of the people, and will result in immediate spiritual death.

Spiritual Truth
The shepherd must at times inspect the people for hidden areas that will bring spiritual death. He must also be aware of the outward involvements that may be sapping all of the strength out of the people's relationships with God.

If this problem goes unchecked, it will weaken the lives of the people and their dedication to the Lord and His work.

Spiritual Truth
The shepherd must carefully examine all the sources from which his people receive their teaching and preaching.

The people must learn to recognize the difference between good and bad teaching through the teaching of their shepherd.

Types of Sheep

The shepherd-physician should be aware of the different kinds of sheep in his flock. Different sheep are prone to different problems. We will look at three different sheep "personalities" that have applications in spiritual truth for the spiritual shepherd.

Solitary sheep. This sheep constantly strays from the flock, and it does not eat with the flock. He is the loner of the flock. The shepherd may not notice his straying unless he identifies the sheep each time it strays. In spiritual analogy, this sheep has some real inward problems. He may have suffered deep emotional wounds, causing a lack of trust in the other sheep or in the shepherd. The solitary sheep might feel the other sheep are too mature or immature for his fellowship. All three of these attitudes are unhealthy and need the shepherd's help and correction.

Fear of exposure is common among solitary sheep. The exposure of past sins, habits or hurts keeps this sheep from healthy fellowship. Some solitary sheep, on the other hand, are merely looking for attention. They will do anything, even separate themselves, to be noticed and attended by the shepherd or other sheep. Such an attention-seeker needs immdiate help, because avoiding fellowship can cause many serious problems.

Hermit sheep. Though similar to the solitary sheep in some ways, the hermit sheep avoids the flock for different reasons. The hermit sheep stays away from the flock to avoid being sheared or clipped by the shepherd. It has an uncanny way of knowing when shearing time is approaching. It will do anything to avoid the clipping process.

The shepherd must continuously watch for the hermit sheep so it cannot hide. The uncut wool of the hermit sheep will eventually grow long enough to cover his eyes and blind him. In this condition, he will surely run into serious problems. Predators, thickets and pits are just a few of the dangers he can no longer avoid. His unclipped wool becomes heavy enough to slow him down, making him fall behind the flock and become an easy target for predators. When the flock is moved to better pasture, the hermit sheep is left behind so that he does not influence the other sheep.

God intends for all of His people to bear fruit. In the analogy of the hermit sheep, we see a Christian who wants to keep all the blessings and fruit in his life for his own enjoyment. Money is one example. But time, talents, relationship, and service to the Church are all areas where a spiritual hermit sheep needs to give. God's economy is not like the world's economy, where scarcity rules and storing up blessings is the natural response. In God's economy, His people must be givers, and more will be given to them. Though we give with the intention to bless God and bless others, it is also true that we receive more when we are giving more.

Wandering sheep. He is among the most dangerous of all. To the wandering sheep, the grass is always greener somewhere else, so he's always looking for a way out of the sheepfold or pasture. He spends all of his time looking for escape, and he usually finds an opening in the fence, a hole in the ground, or a gate left open.

The wandering sheep never settles down to enjoy the present pasture, and he breeds discontent among the other sheep as well. Because his bad influence especially affects the young of the flock, he is removed from the flock. In the Church, that wandering spirit must be broken and harnessed to a healthy purpose. The shepherd must accomplish this before the wandering sheep destroys himself, and many others.

These three types of sheep are only examples of the many problem personalities that the spiritual shepherd should know. He must discern the needs and problems in his sheep, and learn how to minister to them effectively.

Hireling vs. Shepherd

The opposite of a true shepherd is a hireling. Inherent in the word "hire-ling" is the essence of its meaning: "One that is hired for wages by day or by year." Technically, most people fit in that category today. Most people are paid to work for a set time period. To express the difference in today's terms, the difference between a hireling and a shepherd is like the difference between someone who has only a job (no matter how important the position) and someone who has a healthy career.

The person who has only a job assigns a dollar value to the mere passing of time. He may even cheat his employer in any number of ways to increase his "earnings." The person with a healthy career values all of his work relationships, and tries to increase his productivity, in order to build a better future.

Even that comparison, however, fails to capture the great contrast the Old Testament makes between the concepts of hireling and shepherd. The concept of a hireling is applied in the Old Testament to the following areas:

Ordinary laborers (I Samuel 2:5; II Chronicles 24:12)
Mercenary soldiers (II Samuel 10:6; II Kings 7:6; I Chronicles 19:6)
Goldsmiths (Isaiah 46:6)
Bands of loose fellows (Judges 9:4)
False priests (Judges 18:4)
Balaam (Deuteronomy 23:4; Nehemiah 13:2)
Hostile counselors (Ezra 4:5)
False prophets (Nehemiah 6:12)

In contrasting the general concept of a hireling with that of a shepherd, we could say that a hireling, as a leader, receives payment for his job but has no heart for it. A hireling is ambitious for position, power and financial support, but he does not have a real love for God's people. A hireling certainly does not have a call of God or a shepherd's heart--the very existence of this attitude in his life is proof of that.

The following is a list of some of the obvious scriptural contrasts between a hireling and a shepherd.

Hireling vs. Shepherd

Labors only for money (Matthew 20:7)	Labors out of love
Has no heart for the people	Has a heart for the people
Leaves when trouble comes (Jeremiah 46:21)	Gives his life for the sheep (John 10:11)
Is unfaithful to his master	Faithfully serves his master
Feeds himself, and not the sheep (Ezekiel 34:3)	Feeds the sheep
Neglects the sheep	Tenderly cares for the sheep
Lacks mercy (Ezekiel 34:4)	Is full of mercy
Is harsh, cruel and forceful	Is gentle, kind and loving
Drives the people too hard	Leads the people wisely
Scatters the sheep	Unites the sheep
Is not willing to make personal sacrifices (Ezekiel 34:2)	Is always willing to make personal sacrifices
Is ambitious for position, but avoids responsibility	Is not oriented to position, but has a servant's heart
Does not take the time to bind up the sheeps' wounds	Binds the brokenhearted and heals the bruised
Domineers the sheep	Leads the sheep lovingly

Does not care about the sheeps' needs	Discerns needs of the sheep
Produces unfruitfulness in the sheep	Causes the sheep to be fruitful
Is anxious at the close of day	Is peaceful and watchful (especially at night)
Has no part in the master's inheritance	Receives the flock of God as his inheritance
Makes no personal investment in the sheep	Invests his life in the sheep, at the highest price he can pay
Has no balance in discipline: too harsh, or not at all	Disciplines with the rod and the staff of God in love
Limits his work to a given time period (Isaiah 16:14; 21:16	Gives himself to his work full-time, because it is his calling and his lifestyle
Forgets the lost or those driven away	Seeks out the lost and those driven away
Is a work of men's hands (see Psalm 135:15-18; 115:4-8)	Is a work of God's hands
Has a mouth that speaks not	Has a mouth that speaks spiritual things
Has eyes that see not	Has eyes to discern spiritual things
Has ears that hear not	Has ears to hear spiritual things
Has a nose that senses not	Has a nose to sense spiritual things
Has hands that do not touch or feel	Has hands that touch spiritual things
Produces his same unfeeling, undiscerning and carnal nature in the people	Produces his same feeling, discerning and spiritual nature in the people

May every spiritual shepherd forsake the way of the hireling and truly shepherd the flock of God.

Guard Your Heart

The heart of the shepherd is the closest thing to the heart of God for His Church. The Christian leader must do more than understand it--he or she must live it. People in congregational ministries sometimes operate with this attitude. It is undeniably required of all governmental ministries.

To its great loss, the leadership of the Church tends to follow leadership trends in society at large. During a time of economic expansion, the shepherds of God's sheep may adopt an "easy money, quick fix" attitude. They fail to build true spiritual strength in their churches, opting for a show of growth in new buildings, membership drives and other outward displays of blessing.

Unfortunately, the heart condition of such leaders may erode a great deal further. During prosperous years, the drive to build and expand personal kingdoms in the Church goes on with a vengeance. In the middle of it all, some of the most successful Church leaders became some of the most carnal. They fail to guard their hearts. Their carnal sins may even grow more disgusting than anything committed by their "peers" in society at large.

When such a broad and far-reaching epidemic of sin begins in the Church, it does not quickly run its course. Other Christian leaders who also fail to guard their hearts live a similar lifestyle, and adopt the ways of the world around them. It is not the purpose of The Making of a Leader to condemn these people. It is the purpose of this book to give the Church the biblical resource it needs to rebuild a sound leadership that restores the Church to health.

But it would be a great failing if this book neglected to hold up their example as frightening proof that our leaders must guard their hearts. Christian leaders are on the front line of the war with Satan. They must never forget that they can pass from the status of victor to the ranks of vanquished in a matter of moments. And when that happens, many in the Church will pass with them.

You may be one of the leaders who is raised up to help rebuild the Church for the 20th century and beyond. Even as a congregational ministry, you can exert a tremendous influence for good over the leaders of the Church. Your prayers are the daily defense that saves Christian leaders. It's quite likely that a lack of supporting prayer has been a major factor in the dissolution of some major governmental ministries.

Have you ever watched the demise of a Christian leader, and said to yourself, "Now I realize that I saw it coming. There were signs of spiritual illness all along." Don't put your leaders on a pedestal and leave them there to die alone. Love them, pray for them, and correct them privately--before major problems develop--in a way that shows how much you support their ministries.

Let us all guard our hearts, and ask the Lord to develop in us His own heart, the heart of the shepherd.

CHAPTER 7
CHARACTER QUALIFICATIONS OF LEADERSHIP

"If you create an act, you create a habit. If you create a habit, you create a character. If you create a character, you create a destiny." Andre Maurois

"If I take care of my character, my reputation will take care of itself." D.L. Moody

What begins in the heart must be carefully cultivated to come to full fruit in action. The heart qualities we have studied in the last three chapters must be diligently pursued to pave the way for character development.

This chapter will define the character qualifications of leadership. It will explain the ways that God deals with His leaders, to develop their character so they may be vessels of honor for His use, and effective in their ministries. While the gifts of the Spirit are given freely, character development comes only with time, at great personal effort. Each Christian is a responsible partner with God in this life-long process.

This chapter will help you begin the process of growing character with eternal value.

God's Purpose for Man
Many times throughout the Word of God, the Lord states His purpose for man. The following scriptures describe God's high purposes for man:

Genesis 1:26-28   *"Let us make man in our image and after our likeness and let them have dominion."*

Matthew 5:48   *"Be ye therefore perfect, even as your father in heaven is perfect."*

II Corinthians 13:9   *"This also we wish, even your perfection."*

Galatians 4:9   *"I travail in birth until Christ be formed in you."*

Ephesians 4:13   *"Until we all come . . . unto a perfect man."*

II Timothy 3:17   *"That the man of God be perfect."*
II Peter 1:3   *"Hath called us unto glory and virtue."*

God purposes to make man into the image of His Son, the Lord Jesus Christ, the God-Man, the Word made flesh. This purpose has never changed. In the beginning, God created man in His image, and that is still His desire. The fall of man did not change this plan and purpose of God

Since the first man, Adam, failed to maintain God's image, God sent His Last Adam, the Lord Jesus Christ, who would not fail. The Lord Jesus did not fail in God's plan because He was God's perfect Son, the express image of God Himself. The Lord Jesus was the eternally existent Son of many sons yet to be created. These sons and daughters of God will develop to be like the Pattern Son. Hebrews 2:10 says, *"For it was fitting for him, for whom are all things, and through whom are all things, in bringing many sons to glory, to perfect the author of their salvation through suffering."*

"Character is perfectly educated will." Novalis

God's Purpose for the Church

God's purpose for the Church is to bring many sons to glory. For the Church to reach this goal, her leaders must lead the way. The leaders of the Church must be the first partakers of the glorious plan of God in maturing His sons. Generally, He must develop the character and personality of the Lord Jesus in the Church leaders before He can form it in His people at large.

Many churches have emphasized the gift and power of a leader, far above his character development. This imbalance has caused many problems in the Church, including the backsliding of many leaders. Today, however, God is bringing us back to a balance between gift and character. The Lord is not concerned with a leader's gift and anointing only. He also cares deeply about a leader's lifestyle and character. He desires a balance between gift and character in every one of His true leaders. The following diagram illustrates the truth found in this balance.

GIFT	CHARACTER
DEPOSITED	DEVELOPED

▲

"A false balance is an abomination to the Lord, but a just weight is his delight" (Proverbs 11:1).

The Definition of Character

If there must be a balance between gift and character, what is character? The following descriptions display the different aspects of a definition of the word "character":

Character is the seat of one's moral being.

Character is the inner life of man. It will reflect either the traits of the sinful nature (being influenced by the world) or the traits of the divine nature (being influenced by the Word of God).

Character is the combination of qualities distinguishing any person or class of persons.

Character is displayed in the action of an individual under pressure.

Finally, character is the sum total of all the negative and positive qualities in a person's life, exemplified by one's thoughts, values, motivations, attitudes, feelings and actions.

"Talents are best nurtured in solitude. Character is best formed in the stormy billows of the world." Johann von Goethe.

"Character is that which can do without success." Ralph Waldo Emerson.

Greek Meanings. The Greek word for character offers much insight. In the King James Version, this Greek word, "charakter" is translated as "image." "Charakter," a noun, is derived from the word "charasso," which means a notch, indentation, a sharpening, scratching or writing on stone, wood or metal. This word came to mean an embosser and a stamp for making coins. From this, it came to mean the embossed stamp made on the coin, or a character styled in writing. This Greek word appears in the New Testament only in Hebrews 1:3. Here, the writer states that Christ is the very character of God, the very stamp of God's nature, and the one in whom God stamped or imprinted His being. Consequently, we derive the meaning of our English word "character" as a distinctive mark impressed, or otherwise formed, by an outside (or internal) force upon an individual.

What Character Is Not

To help define what character is, we should also see what it is not.

1. Character is not just what a person will ideally be in the future. Character is what a person is at this present time. When pressure comes to a person's life, the real person surfaces. A person may act and think one way under the blessings of the Lord, but quite another way when the trials and heat of life are his portion.

2. Character is not only how a person acts. Character also includes a person's inner thoughts, motives and attitudes. Thoughts, though hidden, indicate the real character of a person. Motives, too, are true expressions of the inner man. To change the character of a person, one must go deeper than action.

3. Character does not appear without pressure. The pressures of life test what the Lord has really accomplished in a person's character. When the heat is upon a person's character, his true character surfaces. The common irritations of everyday living expose the weaknesses in every person's life. How do you respond to the disappointments and pressures of everyday life? Character is formed under such pressures and circumstances. The qualities that are truly part of a person's character are consistent, whether the heat is on or off his life.

4. Character is not only that which other people see on the external. Character is what other people do not see. People may see only the side of a person that a person wants to display, but God sees the real person. An individual cannot hide his weaknesses from the Lord. Man may look at the external, but the Lord looks at the heart. The Lord commands good works from each one of us, but these must proceed out of a godly character. A person can do many outward religious works, and still be ungodly. Works are not always a sign of good character.

5. Character is not limited to having wisdom to comment on the behavior of others. Intellectually knowing how to act, think and feel consistently with Bible principles may be a far cry from actually living in harmony with those principles. A person with true character doesn't just verbally tell other people what to do, but lives as an example worthy of following.

6. Character is not limited to relationships between Christians. To believe that it does not matter how a Christian acts toward non-Christians is a deception. Character shows forth godly principles in every situation and toward all people. For example, a Christian worker must give the same respect to an employer whether he is Christian or not.

7. Character is not limited to a person's relationship with his spiritual family. It also shows in how he treats his natural family. A Christian must demonstrate his faith and love in the way he treats his immediate family. A person's character can be discerned by the way he respects and honors his mother and father. A Christian with an unbelieving natural family can win his family to Christ by having a mature, loving character toward them.

Character is like a tree, and reputation like its shadow. The shadow is what we think of it, but only the tree itself has the substance of reality.

The Need for Character

The Bible warns of an onslaught of wickedness and perversity in the last days of the world. This great onslaught only increases our need for godly character. The standards of the world are obviously becoming more and more corrupt. In the midst of these evil days, however, the Bible also says the Lord will raise up a people with the righteousness of the Lord Jesus Christ. Their lives will testify to the power of the Holy Spirit.

Even as the character of the world becomes more corrupt, the Lord is causing the character of the Church to be matured. More than ever, the Christian needs to develop his character to resist being conformed into the different molds of this world. If the Church is to achieve and retain the image of the Lord Jesus, her leaders must lead the way. We need strong, godly character to stand against the attacks of the enemy.

Many scriptures identify the time period in which we now live as "the last days." According to the apostles and the prophets, this last-day time period extends from the ascension of the Lord Jesus to His second coming. The following diagram illustrates this.

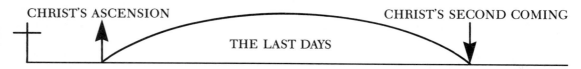

CHRIST'S ASCENSION   CHRIST'S SECOND COMING

THE LAST DAYS

In the last days, wicked men will grow more and more perverse. The occult will continue to grow, and the morals of many are already being shaken. The world system is challenging, shaking and changing the spiritual values of many young people. Today's Church leadership must give a clear word to the Church. They must see the need to develop godly character, for themselves as well as the House of the Lord.

The following list of negative character traits, now on the increase in these last days, was taken from Isaiah 2:1-4, Joel 2:28-30, Acts 2:19-23, II Timothy 3:1-4, I Timothy 3:1-12 and 4:1-7. It provides a description of the spirit of our times, and how that is expressed in our own behavior, thinking and lifestyles.

Negative Character Traits and Their Expression

1. Perilous times (difficult, hard to bear and troublesome days): the Church should have a healthy fear of the perverse days in which she is living.

2. Men shall be lovers of their own selves: self-centered and in willful pursuit of sin.

3. Covetous (fond of money, in love with money): to have a wrong value system, wanting something that belongs to someone else.

4. Boasters (braggarts, empty pretenders): to boast about ungodly or false things in an ungodly pride of self.

5. Proud (haughty, appearing above others): to have the wrong evaluation of oneself and others; to be blinded to the truth of one's lowliness.

6. Blasphemous (disrespectful against God or man): To have no respect of the value of anything, to slander the things of God, the Church, and all positive values ordained by God.

7. Disobedient to parents: to become a part of the spirit of the day, which is rebellion and lawlessness.

8. Unthankful (lack of gratitude): to ungratefully, unthankfully take advantage of others.

9. Unholy (profane, immoral): to live only for the satisfaction of one's sensual desires.

10. Without natural affection (sexual perversion, abortion, child beating, unfeeling): to pervert what is good and natural in order to assert one's self; homosexuality, sodomy, lesbianism, incest.

11. Truce-breakers (cannot keep promises): to be untrue to one's promises, to cause a distrust in one's word.

12. False accusers (liars, bribers): to oppress others with unverified, undocumented criticism.

13. Incontinent (without self-control or moral restraint): to be so far lost in love of sin that one impulsively sins, and has no control over one's moral behavior.

14. Fierce (untame, savage): to behave as a passionate, unthinking beast toward others.

15. Despisers of those who are good: to belittle or to treat shamefully the righteous actions of others.

16. Traitors (betrayers): to lack a sense of loyalty to the true laws of friendship.

17. Heady (rash, reckless, headstrong): to be ruled only by one's will, to be a reckless thinker, to have a darkened mind.

18. High-minded (conceited, proud): to be blinded by the pride of the intellect; to have pride in one's knowledge.

19. Lovers of pleasure more than of God (fulfilling one's own sinful desires): to have a wrong perspective on life, a value system overcome by temporal influences.

20. Having a form of godliness (external religiosity without a changed life): a hypocritical lifestyle.

21. Scoffers (mockers, ridiculers): to consistently mock and ridicule the righteous and holy.

22. Some shall depart from the faith: to backslide and reject God's plan for one's life and basic Bible teaching.

23. Giving heed to seducing spirits (to cause to wander, to lead astray): to allow oneself to be deceived, to invite the devil to lead one astray from the truth.

24. Doctrines of devils (teachings from the pit of hell): to require abstinence from meats or lifetime celibacy, to add unbiblical rules to the Church.

25. Speaking lies in hypocrisy: to teach false doctrines and not be a genuine believer.

26. Having a seared conscience (no inner sense of right and wrong): to lose one's sensitivity to the inner promptings of the Holy Spirit through continued sin.

This list of negative character traits supplies the leader with a mirror for judging his own and others' character. Sincere reflection on the list can be discouraging; you must remember that character is cultivated after a person comes to Jesus, and that character is not a freely given gift of the Spirit. There are no shortcuts--character development comes only from discipline of the flesh. It takes time and dedication. When you can see your own need of character development, you have reached the beginning of that development. A leader must open every area of his life to change from the Lord, so that he will be more able to minister change to others.

"To enjoy the things we ought, and to hate the things we ought, has the greatest bearing on excellence of character." Aristotle

God's Dealings in Character Development

A reading of II Peter 1:1-11 in the Amplified Bible will help the reader understand God's process of developing character in a Christian's life. The following diagram gives a general outline of these verses:

PROVISION OF DIVINE NATURE THROUGH CHRIST	PROCESS OF ADDING THROUGH OBEDIENCE	PURPOSE OF PERFECT CHARACTER THROUGH DILIGENCE

                                                                    Love
                                                        Brotherly Kindness
                                              Godliness
                                  Patience
                        Temperance
            Knowledge
      Virtue
Faith
Diligence

DIVINE NATURE RECEIVED (II Peter 1:4,9)	DIVINE PROMISES GIVEN (II Peter 1:4) DIVINE POWER GRANTED (II Peter 1:3)	DIVINE NATURE MATURED (II Peter 1:3)

II Peter 1:8   *"If ye do these things ye shall not be barren or unfruitful"*
II Peter 1:9   *"He that lacketh is blind and cannot see afar off"*
II Peter 1:10   *"If ye do these things ye shall not fall"*

The Believer's Responsibility

Repentance from sin and faith in Jesus Christ is the responsibility of every believer. The provision of the divine nature through the power of the Holy Spirit belongs to the divine sovereignty of the Lord. Every believer is responsible to apply this provision, and to pursue fulfillment of the goal of God's provision. God has positionally given believers all things pertaining to life and godliness. Believers have all that it takes to develop a mature Christian character as they follow the Lord. But if Christians do not do the things necessary for these promises to be fulfilled, the Scripture speaks of them losing what could have been their own.

Such disobedience or misunderstanding has made many Christians and ministries barren and unfruitful in the Body of Christ today. Many leaders are blind and have no vision from the Lord because they have not obeyed the Word of God. Leadership, as well as the Body of Christ at large, must develop character through the inner disciplines of the Holy Spirit.

The "adding" of a series of disciplines referred to by Peter describes the Christian's walk and growth in Christ. The power to accomplish these disciplines is provided through Jesus Christ. But the process of actually accomplishing them is determined by each Christian's attitude of response to the dealings of God in his or her life. God wants to develop character. When a believer lacks the discipline to develop his character, the Lord Himself will provide learning experiences and circumstances to help him. This learning process is commonly called "the dealings of God."

In II Timothy 2:6, Paul exhorted Timothy to be the first partaker of the fruit, since he was the husbandman of it. This is a natural illustration, borrowed from the farmer being the first to taste his crops. It has a spiritual application in the work of the Lord. If the Body of Christ is going to be developed in character through the dealings of God, the leader must be the "first partaker." That is, he must be the first to allow God to change his character.

Faithfulness of God's Dealings

The following scriptures shed light upon the development of character through the dealings of God:

Philippians 1:6
"I am convinced and sure of this very thing, that He which began a good work in you will continue until the day of Jesus Christ our Lord (right up to the time of His return) *developing that good work in you and perfecting you, and bringing you to full completion."* (Amplified Bible)

Psalm 32:4-5
"For day and night thy hand was heavy upon me."

Hebrews 10:32
"But call to remembrance the former days, in which, after ye were illuminated, ye endured a great fight of affliction."

Psalm 18:30
"As for God, his way is perfect, the word of the Lord is tried."

Psalm 12:6
"The words of the Lord are pure words, as silver is tried in the furnace of the earth, purified seven times."

Psalm 119:67
"Before I was afflicted I went astray, but now I have kept thy word."

Hebrews 12:7
"If ye endure chastening, God dealeth with you as with sons."

Most if not all of God's leaders experienced the real development of character through the dealings of God. Abraham, Moses, Elijah and even the Lord Jesus Christ all experienced the deep dealings of the Lord.

Now, let's look at four different aspects of the dealings of God. First, we will look at the need for the dealings of God. Second, we will define words describing the process. Third, we will discover the purpose of these dealings. Finally, we will see what attitude responses one should maintain to guard and foster God's dealings in the formation of character.

The Need for God's Dealings

Fallen Nature. All of us are born in iniquity and shaped in sin. We all have a fallen nature with which we must cope throughout our lives. The fallen nature of man is not in harmony with any of the things of the Lord. Scripture frequently refers to man's fallen nature as "the old man," the "carnal self" and "sinful nature," or "the flesh." At times, this degenerate nature of man will cause us to grow cold concerning the things of God. At times the Christian goes through complacency and indifference, even though the Lord has set before us the glorious goal of perfection.

Spiritual maturity is the biblical goal for all of us who are in Christ Jesus. But during times of discouragement, man's lower nature urges us away from this goal. At times, man's carnality does not want him to develop his character as the Scripture commands. This unspiritual laziness in man's nature is the first reason why we need the dealings of the Lord. Every Christian needs the dealings of God to motivate him on to spiritual perfection (Hebrews 6:1-3).

Secret Sins. The second reason why every Christian needs the dealings of God is a need for the revealing of hidden areas of sin in his or her life. God reveals these concealed areas of sin to help us grow. The Scripture tells us that God is the revealer of such secrets. Examples of this:

Deuteronomy 29:29	*"The secret things belong unto the Lord"*
Daniel 2:22,28	*"God is the revealer of secrets"*
I Corinthians 3:13	*"All things will be revealed by fire"*
Matthew 10:26-27	*"Fear them not therefore: for there is nothing covered that shall not be revealed; and hid that shall not be known. What I tell you in darkness, that speak ye in light: and what ye hear in the ear, that preach ye upon the housetops."*

God must reveal our secret sins to prevent them from destroying us and our ministries. It is not enough that He Himself knows these areas; He reveals them to us because it is our responsibility to forsake them. To do this, however, the Christian greatly needs the grace of God, because human nature only seeks to cover up its weaknesses and faults.

Man's desire to hide his sins continually sets him in conflict with the nature of God. Our situation is still the same as Adam and Eve, who hid themselves from God as soon as they realized they had sinned against Him (Genesis 3:8). God has given Christians the Holy Spirit to reveal their areas of spiritual need.

The Holy Spirit searches every Christian's heart to reveal sins that must be abandoned. The word "reveal" means to take off the cover. The word "conceal" means to hide by covering, to veil from sight, or to cover over a matter. God is trying to take the cover off man's sin, while man tries to hold onto that cover. The Bible not only declares God as the revealer of secrets, but also describes man as the concealer of secret faults:

Psalm 19:12	*"Cleanse thou me from secret faults"*
Psalm 90:8	*"Our secret sins are revealed in thy presence"*
Psalm 51:6	*"Thou desirest truth in the inward parts, in the hidden parts thou wilt make me to know wisdom"*
Psalm 32:3,5	*"When I kept silence about my sin, my body wasted away, but I acknowledged my sin to thee, and my iniquity I did not hide"*

Several men in Scripture illustrate the fact of secret sin. The beginning of their lives, unfortunately, were in great contrast to their ends. They started well, but ended tragically. Man bears the image of God; men can begin well. But if men hide secret sins in unrepentance, they end by destroying their lives or ministries. Leaders, especially, should take note of this truth.

Secret sins have caused the fall of many of the Lord's leaders, at the end of their ministries, or even in the very height of their service. The scriptural observation, *"How are the mighty fallen!"* is an ever-present cry of the Spirit of God. In the account of David's mourning for Jonathan and Saul (II Samuel 1:17-27), three times David cries out, *"How are the mighty fallen!"* In this lamentation, David describes "the mighty" in the beginning of their lives and ministries as:

Beautiful	(v. 19)
Mighty	(v. 19)
Lovely and pleasant	(v. 23)
Swifter than eagles	(v. 23)
Stronger than lions	(v. 23)
Able to clothe others in scarlet	(v. 24)
Able to put ornaments of God on others	(v. 24)

How many men of God have started out this way! Many ministers of the Lord have been beautiful in the sight of the Lord and the Lord's people at the beginning of their ministries. Many were mighty and strong in the Lord. Unfortunately, however, many of their mighty exploits have only ended in ruin and shame. Why? One of the main reasons why is because they did not forsake their secret sins when the Lord revealed them to their hearts. If every leader would only remember that the purpose of the dealings of God–to prevent a fall by rooting out secret sins–every leader would seriously and immediately respond to the inner convictions of the Holy Spirit.

We will now study some Bible characters that began well but ended in tragedy. This list will show their good beginnings, their names, their secret sins, and their tragic endings.

THE TRAGEDY OF SECRET SIN

GOOD BEGINNING	SECRET SIN	TRAGIC ENDING
I Samuel 10	**SAUL**	**I Samuel 31**
1. Anointed king	(independent	1. Stripped of kingdom
2. Strong, mighty man	spirit)	2. Tried to murder David
3. Great warrior		3. Sought after withcraft
4. Excellent leader		4. Disloyal to his own son
5. Humble in heart		5. Committed suicide
I Samuel 17	**DAVID**	**II Samuel 11; Psalms 32 & 51**
1. Anointed king	(lust)	1. Disloyal to his men
2. Mighty warrior		2. Committed adultery
3. Musician of the Lord		3. Committed murder
4. Faithful, loyal man		4. Tried to cover great sins
5. Great leader		5. Brought judgment on his
6. Built tabernacle of David		whole family
II Chronicles 1:7-12	**SOLOMON I**	**Kings 11; Ecclesiastes 1**
1. Anointed king	(pride; greed;	1. Turned his heart from God
2. Humble person of prayer	wrong values;	2. Became an idol worshipper
3. Temple builder	self-	3. Vexed by vain philosophy
4. The greatest kingdom	confidence)	4. Sinned in sight of the Lord
5. The greatest throne		5. His kingdom taken away
6. The greatest wisdom		6. Sought to kill Jeroboam
7. The greatest wealth		7. Wrote "Ecclesiastes," book
8. Author of 3,000 proverbs		about the vanity of life
9. Author of 10,005 songs (including Song of Solomon)		

Judges 14-16

1. Dedicated to God
2. Great warrior
3. Exceedingly strong
4. Man of faith
5. Killed a lion
6. Killed 30 Philistines
7. Killed 10,000 soldiers
8. Broke strong bands
9. Carried off gates of Gaza

SAMSON

(lust; gullibility to a woman)

Judges 16:20-27

1. Deceived by a woman
2. Hair shaved; lost his dedication to God
3. Had eyes burned out
4. Imprisoned
5. Left by the Lord
6. Mocked and ridiculed
7. Loved a strange woman
8. Never fulfilled potential
9. Lost his anointing

Judges 6-8

1. Chosen by God
2. Had angelic visitation
3. Hated idols
4. Destroyed idols
5. Great deliverer
6. Great man of faith

GIDEON

(power and greed)

Judges 8

1. Rejected by God
2. Made an idol
3. Caused Israel to sin
4. Became a stumbling stone
5. His good ruined by his evil

Ezekiel 28; Isaiah 14:12-20

1. Full of beauty
2. Perfect
3. The anointed cherub
4. One who covered the Throne
5. Song leader and musician of heaven

LUCIFER

(lust for pride and power)

Revelation 12:9 & 20:2,3,10

1. The serpent
2. The source of all sin
3. The devil, and the spirit of deception
4. Cast down to the pit
5. Destroyer of the Church

All of these mighty leaders of God began with the splendor of success, but ended with the tragedy of defeat. It is important to note that they all began with many good qualities in their lives and their ministries: humility, wisdom, faith, knowledge, anointing and a heart after the Lord. This fact makes for an even stronger warning for today's Church leaders. Beginning with strong qualities only requires one to grow even more sensitive and obedient to the Lord.

In I Corinthians 9:23-27, Paul spoke of the man who runs the race for the prize. In these verses, Paul said that he did not want to be like the man who, after having preached to others, would become a castaway, rejected and of no value. All leaders must maintain a continual alert against the secret sins that can so easily destroy their lives and ministries.

God's Dealings Defined Scripturally

The Bible uses many words to describe God's dealings in a person's life. Here we will list five of the more commonly used words, their definitions, and scriptures in which they are used.

1. Distress (to assault, trouble, hem in; Psalms 4:1,2 and 18:6; Isaiah 25:4; I Corinthians 7:26)

2. Affliction (to bruise, to be heavy, to press heavily; to melt)
    a. Affliction of souls (Leviticus 16:29-31 and 23:27)
    b. Land of affliction (Genesis 41:52)
    c. Bread of affliction (Deuteronomy 16:3; I Kings 22:27)
    d. Cords of affliction (Job 5:6 and 36:8)

      e. Furnace of affliction (Isaiah 48:10)
      f. Day of affliction (Jeremiah 16:19)
3. Purge (to refine, purify, clarify by heat; Isaiah 1:25; Psalm 51:7; Malachi 3:8)
4. Pressing (to squeeze, push on, come down upon, crush; Psalm 38:2; II Corinthians 1:8)
5. Fire (intense heat)
      a. Brings out the sweet smell (Leviticus 1:7-17)
      b. Fire is in Zion (Isaiah 31:9)
      c. For the believer to walk through (Isaiah 43:2)
      d. To burn up the chaff (Matthew 3:11-12)
      e. Likened to the Word of God (Jeremiah 23:29)
      f. Burns off bondages (Daniel 3:22-27)
      g. Part of the believer's baptism (Matthew 3:11-12)
      h. Reveals a man's works (I Corinthians 3:13)
      i. Tries our faith (I Peter 1:7; Revelation 3:18)
      j. God is a consuming fire (Hebrews 12:29)

The spiritual application of the principles embodied in these words can be seen in Israel, the Church in the wilderness. They can also be applied to the Christian life. Israel's tabernacle furniture, tabernacle proper, and its sacrifices all demonstrate these truths.

The incense used for the altar of incense had to be crushed before it could be used as an offering to the Lord. Similarly, every Christian (and especially Church leaders) must first experience God's crushing dealings before their lives can bring forth a sweet fragrance unto the Lord.

The golden candlestick also illustrates the necessity of the dealings of God. The candlestick was made of one single beaten piece of work. The candlestick was a single beaten piece of gold that was taken through the fires of purification before it could be used as a vessel of light in the tabernacle. Likewise, God has a furnace for each Christian.

All of the boards in the sanctuary had to undergo a stripping process before their use in the tabernacle. They were ground and carved until they came to the shape desired for them as part of the House of the Lord. All Christians, and particularly Christian leaders, are in the formative stages. We can be confident that the Lord will bring forth a beautiful work in due season, if we faint not.

The Purpose of God's Dealings

The Image of Christ. God's first purpose in His dealings is to change us into the image of the Lord Jesus Christ. This process is described in II Corinthians 3:18, *"But we all with open face behold as in a glass* (mirror) *the glory of the Lord, are changed into the same image from glory to glory, even by the Spirit."*

The word "changed" here in the Greek language is "metamorpho," which means a complete change from one form to another. This Greek word is the root of our English word "metamorphosis," which scientists use to describe the caterpillar's process of changing into a butterfly. The process takes much time and energy. The caterpillar changes from one form into a completely different form. Christians also are going through a metamorphosis. Christians are people with a sinful lower nature. But each day, the Christian who follows the Lord is more and more transformed into the image of Jesus Christ, Who is perfect in body, soul and spirit.

"Character building begins in our infancy, and continues until death." Eleanor Roosevelt

To Purify. Second, God's purpose in His dealings is to purge away all dross from our lives. The word "purge" means to refine, to make pure, to change by heat. The Lord constantly puts heat on His people today, through His dealings. All over the world, there is much pressure and heat upon God's people. God has ordained this heat to purge His people, as the preparation of precious metals. All of the filth and foreign matter is brought to the surface for disposal.

The word "dross" means the scum, that which is thrown off, waste matter, the useless part. God is removing all waste matter and scum from His people, and particularly from His leaders. He wants to develop character in all His leaders. (For examples of this, see Proverbs 25:4; Isaiah 1:22,25; Ezekiel 22:18-19; Psalm 51:7; Daniel 11:35; Matthew 3:12; II Timothy 2:21; John 15:2.)

To Cleanse Our Spiritual Garments. Third, the purpose of God's dealings is to cleanse and wash our spiritual garments. The background for this purpose is contained in some important prophecies about Christ. Malachi 3:1-3 speaks of two messengers. The first is John the Baptist: *"Behold I will send my messenger, and he shall prepare the way before me."* (Matthew 3:3 correspondingly states, *"The voice of one crying in the wilderness, 'Prepare ye the way of the Lord, make straight his paths.'"* See also John 1:19-28.)

The second messenger is the Lord Jesus Christ. Malachi 3:1,2 prophetically states, *"And the Lord whom ye seek, shall suddenly come to his temple, even the messenger of the covenant, whom ye delight in, behold he shall come, saith the Lord of Hosts . . . For he is like a refiner's fire and like fuller's soap."* The Lord Jesus Christ, the messenger of the New Covenant, came suddenly to the Jewish temple. Ever since, He has been like a refiner's fire and like a fuller's soap to His people.

Some cultural background is necessary to interpret this verse. The fuller was a tradesman who cleansed all the fibers of a piece of material so that it could be made into a beautiful garment. The fuller would take the material down to the nearby water brook and lay it upon flat stones. He would then begin to beat the raw material with a fuller's club. This club was huge and had iron teeth in it to beat the filth out of the material. As he would beat the raw material, all of the debris and dirt would rise to the surface, and the water would wash it away. This process cleansed the material, which would then be ready for the craftsman to make into a beautiful garment.

Frequently, this saying has come from Christian pulpits: "God is not some big monster sitting upon His throne with a club, waiting for His people to make a mistake so that He can clobber them." This is generally correct, because such a brutal attitude would be inconsistent with God's nature. However, God does have a club that He uses to bring all the filth out of Christians' lives! The good thing about this is that He knows how to "beat" us without hurting the incorruptible good seed of His Word within us. God does not use His club merely to flaunt His power, but to cleanse the spiritual garments and lives of His children.

To Bring Forth Fruit. Fourthly, the purpose of God's dealings is to cause His peoples' lives to bear fruit. In John 15, we have an allegory given by the Lord Jesus Christ, the master teacher. In this allegory of the vine and the branches, the husbandman who dresses the vine must at times use his pruning shears. He removes dead, fruitless branches so that they do not draw away any of the necessary sap needed by the living branches. Fruitless branches are removed, while fruitful branches are pruned to bear more fruit. God will prune, purge, refine and cut the fruit-bearing branches to increase their fruitfulness. God's purpose is always positive and redemptive. Those leaders through which God desires to produce the most fruit will have to be pruned the most.

To Prepare Vessels for Service. Fifth, the purpose of God's dealings is to prepare vessels for service. In II Timothy 2:19-20, Paul states that a large house has many vessels. Some vessels are made of gold or precious metals, while others are made of clay. Some vessels are reserved for the more honorable tasks, but all vessels have a use.

Making a vessel involves much work in every step of the formative process, from the shaping of the clay until it is pulled out of the oven. At times, the potter's hands upon the vessel are rough and firm. But the potter's wheel and the furnace, as well as the potter's hands, are all vital parts of the vessel's preparation. This is true of God's spiritual shaping in our lives, as well. The purpose of all this work is to mold a vessel of honor, fit for its intended use by the Lord (Jeremiah 17:1-10).

Vessels that were not properly prepared, but contained a flaw, were thrown out into the potter's field. In the potter's field, you could find many "would-be" vessels of great use. Their problem was that they had not formed properly on the wheel, or they had not responded well to firing. An irreversible flaw formed in them.

Scripture seems to indicate that Judas, the fallen apostle and betrayer of Christ, hung himself in the potter's field (see Matthew 27:1-10). In this field, a rejected, maimed and corrupted human vessel of dishonor was found along with many marred vessels of clay. Something was missing in Judas's preparation as a leader. The purpose of God's dealings with Judas, as well as with every potential leader, is to expose the flaws in the vessel soon enough so that they can be reformed and used for a specific purpose. It is a measure of God's great wisdom that He found a valuable purpose even for Judas, that vessel of dishonor, though his end was destruction.

To Enlarge Our Lives. Sixth, God's purpose in His dealings is to bring enlargement to our lives. Isaiah 54:2 and Genesis 9:27 describe God's desires for His people to be enlarged. Isaiah proclaims, *"enlarge the place of thy tent,"* which figuratively means that God wants His preparing leadership to enlarge their capacity to receive more from the Lord. II Samuel 22:37 states that the Lord can enlarge the steps (i.e., the walk) of His leaders. Isaiah 60:5 says that a person's heart can be enlarged (see also Psalm 119:32; II Corinthians 6:11,13 and 10:15). In His dealings, God purposes to enlarge us in many ways. God desires to enlarge our ministries and our functions in the House of the Lord, as well as our character. To summarize all these areas, we could say that God is enlarging:

Our habitation (capacity) for God	(Isaiah 54:2)
Our vision	(I Chronicles 4:10; Proverbs 29:18)
Our steps	(I Samuel 22:37)
Our hearts	(Isaiah 60:5)
Our borders	(Exodus 34:24)
Our confession	(I Samuel 2:1)
Our chambers	(Ezekiel 41:7; Proverbs 24:3,4)
Our ministries	(II Corinthians 6:11,13 and 10:15,16)

To Provoke Us to Seek Him. Seventh, the purpose of God's dealings is to provoke us to seek God in prayer and the Word. The Lord will bring pressures and heat upon His leaders at specific times to cause them to seek Him. His pressures do not turn them away or against God, but toward Him. Many times, the leader in preparation misinterprets hard circumstances and trials. When God deals with them this way, it is to cause them to turn to God as their only stronghold. A leader must learn how to find God in troublesome times, so that he may help others do the same. Every leader must know by experience how to respond to the person who comes and asks,

"Lead me to the rock that is higher than I."

The prophet Hosea reminds us of this truth in Hosea 5:15, where he writes, *"In their affliction they will seek me early."* This is a truth that natural Israel illustrates to us many times. For example, when God put the pressure on Israel through Assyria or Babylon, Israel was quick to turn to the Lord. Jonah also is an example of turning to the Lord in time of trouble (Jonah 1:17 and 2:1ff). In any affliction, pressure or heat, a leader must learn where to turn.

"Character is long-standing habit." Plutarch

To Produce Spiritual Wine. The eighth purpose of God's dealings is to produce more spiritual wine in us. Scripture depicts wine as a type of the Spirit of rejoicing, and the Holy Spirit (Matthew 9:17; Acts 2:13-16; Ephesians 5:18). A study of the Hebrew method of wine making yields many rich truths concerning God's dealings. Harvest was a joyful time for all the people. After long labor and waiting for harvest, the whole family would reap the harvest.

Women and children would bear the vintage upon their heads in baskets. They would bring the grapes to the large stone wine vat where the treaders of grapes waited barefooted. The reapers would come and dump their full baskets of grapes into the vats and the treaders would walk upon the ripe grapes, squashing the juice out of them. As the treader worked, he held onto a beam of wood that was attached to the center pole in the middle of the vat. This rested most of his weight on the beam, so that he did not tread too heavily upon the grapes. If he treaded too heavily on the grapes, he could crush the seed along with the grape, making the wine bitter and fit only for the animals.

We can derive a beautiful spiritual truth from this custom. God is the treader of grapes, and we are the grapes. Since He wants the new wine of His Spirit to flow from our lives and our ministries, He crushes us. This is a hard, painful process, but God will never crush our spirits (i.e., the seed of the grape) to make us bitter. A bitter life (as with bitter wine) is good for no one, and no one will seek after it. God does not want bitter leaders. He wants the fresh and new wine of the Spirit to flow through their lives. The leader should welcome the crushing process, for it yields much fruit (in this context, see the different ways that God deals with His people in Isaiah 28:23-29).

Provide New Focus and Perspective. Ninth and finally, the purpose of God's dealings is to give us a new focus and perspective. Paul states this truth in II Corinthians 4:16-18: *"For this light affliction which is but for a moment works for us a far more eternal weight of glory."* All of our afflictions, pressures and trials now create something in us that is far more eternal. We should not focus on the present dilemma, but on the eternal fruit that it will produce in us and in others. Gifts are freely given by God, but character is developed over time. Character is of eternal value, for it goes with us into eternity (I Corinthians 13:8-13). What we develop in our character now is far more important than the afflictions of this life that we must endure to produce it.

Attitudes That Embrace the Dealings of God

Our attitudes are the root causes for us either embracing or rejecting the dealings of God. The following list of attitudes will give a leader another mirror for reflection. A leader must maintain these attitudes when he undergoes a trial or affliction:

Prayerful attitude	(James 5:13)
Contrite attitude	(I Peter 4:19)
Reflective attitude	(Hebrews 12:3)

Praising attitude	(Psalm 74:21)
Enduring attitude	(Matthew 10:22; I Corinthians 10:13; I Thessalonians 1:4,5; Hebrews 12:5-7; I Peter 2:19)
Joyful attitude	(Matthew 5:12; Romans 5:3; II Corinthians 7:4 and 12:10; Hebrews 12:2; James 1:2; I Peter 4:13)

Endurance. Let us look more closely at the attitude of endurance. Endurance generally means to hold or be stable under adversity. The following three Greek words are translated as "endurance":

Avekomai — to hold oneself up against, to endure the act of holding up or sustaining (I Thessalonians 1:1-5)

Hupomeno — to stay under, remain, undergo; the act of continuing to dwell in a location (Hebrews 12:5-7)

Hupophero — to bear from underneath, carry away, bear with the shoulders (I Corinthians 10:13)

Jacob illustrates a proper attitude in response to the dealings of God. Throughout Scripture, God identified Himself with three particular men: *"I am the God of Abraham, Isaac and Jacob,"* He has said at many times. As the *"God of Abraham,"* He is the keeper of His covenants. As the *"God of Isaac,"* He is the God of miracles. But when Scripture proclaims that He is also the *"God of Jacob,"* the meaning is less clear. Nevertheless, as the *"God of Jacob,"* He could be spoken of as the God of change, for God changed Jacob's name and nature from Jacob ("deceiver") to Israel ("prime"). This title speaks of God as the God who can take a person with major character flaws and change him into a godly person. Jacob gives hope to us all.

The good attitude that God developed in Jacob is best explained in Isaiah 41:14-16 where God says, *"thou worm Jacob."* Why does God call Jacob a worm? This would effectively describe Jacob's response to the crushing hand of God upon him at Peniel (Genesis 32). Along the same lines, the Psalmist prophetically calls the Messiah a worm in Psalm 22:6 (see also Job 17:14 and 24:20 and 25:6).

In response to the heavy hand of God upon Him, Jesus had the same attitude as Jacob. Both men yielded and submitted to God's dealings. What we might call a "worm attitude" directly opposes the "serpent attitude" that we find in Satan himself. Some leaders respond to God as a worm, while others respond to His pressures as the serpent. The following chart contrasts the two attitudes:

A Worm:	**A Serpent:**
1. Crushes underfoot	1. Strikes when treaded upon
2. Has no defense	2. Defends with venom
3. Squirms, but gives up its life	3. Fights to the death

Let us carefully examine our own attitude responses to the dealings of God in our lives. Do we react to God like a worm or a serpent? God has to wait many times for us before He can develop character in our lives, when we react to His dealings as a serpent. The struggle for character development is surely great. But the consequences are even greater, if God's goal for us is not reached due to the hardness of our own hearts.

Major Character Areas

The Christian leader today must develop his character in these eight major areas of life in order to achieve God's goals for him:

1. Spiritual life — A leader's relationship with the Lord is built upon a godly character as well as a depth in God's Word and prayer.

2. Personal life — The habits, lifestyle and patterns which a leader develops will have a great influence upon the ministry he or she has received from the Lord.

3. Home life — A leader's personal family life will form the basis for his ministry to the family of God. A leader must first have his own home in order. This is based upon his character, for without character he will have no successful family life.

4. Social life — A leader's friendships reflect his character. A leader must develop character to have successful social relationships. Loyalty and acceptance are two great factors required in friendships. If a man has character, he will have the needed elements for a normal and good social life.

5. Educational life — Education by itself is not enough to build good character. But if character is developed through the disciplines of life, education can be a powerful force in the life of a leader. A good character enables a leader to receive a good education in and out of the classroom.

6. Ministerial life — Character is the very root of all that a governmental ministry does. Ministry function is, in itself, a manifestation of a leader's character. What he is will come out in what he does in his ministry. I Timothy 3 and Titus 1 list character qualifications as the basis for a leader's ministerial life.

7. Marital life — A leader's marital life will succeed only as he has a mature and developed character. A man without a developed character brings his deficiencies into the home with him. A leader's married life will blossom only if his character is cultivated; otherwise, he will never be able to meet the needs of his wife.

8. Financial life — Jesus Christ Himself said that if a man did not know how to take care of money, that God would not commit to him the true spiritual riches of the kingdom. A leader's frugality, wisdom, true desires, values, self-esteem, and ability to give are all demonstrated by how he uses the money that he has (though not necessarily by how much money he earns).

"Character, in great and little things, means carrying through what you feel able to do." Johann von Goethe

Recognition of Character

What is a man of God? How do we recognize a spiritually mature person? When Timothy stayed in Ephesus to support the apostle Paul and help the church mature, he often worked with men who wanted to be teachers and spiritual leaders in the church. In I Timothy 3:1, Paul commended those who wanted to lead, *"It is a fine work he desires."*

Immediately after that, however, Paul gives a long list of qualifications. Obviously, he wanted Timothy to select a certain kind of man to be a church leader. Paul's teaching to Timothy and Titus forms a powerful profile for testing a Christian's maturity level.

A man of God does not "suddenly appear." He is cultivated by the Holy Spirit in a slow process. Timothy in Ephesus and Titus on the island of Crete had to test many who aspired to leadership. Paul's letters to them provided the character tests for leadership, which are a yardstick for measuring Christian character development in general.

In I Timothy 3:1-13 and Titus 1:5-9, the standards of character maturity are many.

Above Reproach (I Tim. 3:2, Titus 1:7). Blameless, having unquestionable integrity, irreproach-able — "not to be taken hold of," having such character that no one can rightfully take hold of the person with a charge of unfitness. The conduct of an elder must be an example to the flock of God, and free from the taint of scandal and accusation. Therefore, an elder must conduct himself so well that any accusation is rendered absurd and unfounded from the outset.

A person above reproach is:

"One that cannot be called to account, unreprovable or unaccused," (I Tim. 3:2, Thayer)

"One that gives no ground for accusation" (3:2, Amplified Bible)

"Of blameles reputation" (Titus 1:7, Phillips)

"Of unquestionable integrity and irreproachable" (1:7, Amplified Bible)

Husband of One Wife (I Tim. 3:2; Titus 1:6). This does not mean that an elder must be married (Paul was not), but that he be married to one wife. A husband of one wife is:

Not a bigamist
"One wife's husband" (Lenski)

As "one wife's husband," a man has nothing to do with any other woman. He must be a man who cannot be accused on the score of sexual promiscuity or laxity. At different times and in different churches, "one husband's wife" has had spiritual meanings as well.

To the Roman Catholic Church, the bishop's one wife is the Church, to whom he must remain faithful. Some European churches prohibit widowers who have remarried from serving as bishops. Early Church fathers allowed a man already married to be ordained, but if he was single when ordained, he must remain so all his life. Some Church leaders maintain that any record of divorce, even if before conversion, would disqualify a man from taking office.

The morals and social environment of Paul's day certainly made this character standard an important one. Pagan temple prostitutes were used regularly by many, without social stigma. "Companion" girls were often used by both married and unmarried men. Many men openly kept mistresses.

But in requiring bishops to be "the husband of one wife," Paul required them to be intimately related to only one woman. And Jesus Himself had earlier set an even higher standard: he who "looks on a woman to lust" (greatly desires for a sexual, physical relationship) is guilty of sin. Note, however, that this standard differentiates temptation, with much less personal involvement, from the sin of lust.

In the environment of Paul's day, a happily married man handled the many available sexual temptations better than the man with a bad marriage. Paul is thus saying that a leader must have a strong marriage, with a healthy sex life, and must not deliberately expose himself to sexual temptations (such as today's pornographic magazines). A man and woman must work hard to cultivate a tremendous unity and love in their marriage. A man should never share his private struggles with another woman, only with his wife or mature men of God. Single men should never share their struggles with other single women, and sometimes not with some single men, either.

Temperate (I Tim. 3:2; Titus 1:8). This character quality denotes keeping oneself in hand, self-controlled and disciplined. An elder must be able to control (rule) himself in all respects:

"Self-controlled over appetite and affection" (Concordant Literal)

"A man who is discreet" (Titus 1:8, Phillips)

Free from extremes

Having power over or control of a thing (Robertson)

Some related meanings are worth developing. The exhortation to be sober (I Thessalonians 5:6,8) is a call to temperance. In II Tim. 4:5, Paul exhorts Timothy to *"endure . . . do the work . . . make full proof."* A temperate man has a clean perspective on life, and a correct and fruitful spiritual orientation. A temperate man does not lose his physical, psychological, spiritual balance. He is stable, steadfast, always thinking clearly, and doesn't lose his perspective under pressure. He does not get caught up in false security of the day; he has a proper perspective.

Prudent (I Tim. 3:2). This is to be sober minded, prudent, sensible; not given to fanciful thinking or emotional irrationality; using sound judgment. A prudent person is:

Safe in mind and judgment

"Fair-minded" (I Tim. 3:2, Phillips)

"Disciplined" (Titus 1:8, NIV)

So many religious fads, fancies and unstable ways are offered to leaders today. Leaders with a safe, sane steady mind in all matters of life will not easily shake from God's path.

Dictionary definitions of "prudent" commonly include these elements: caution, practical wisdom, carefulness over the consequences of actions, to wisely forsee the future through understanding the present.

In Proverbs, a prudent man "covereth shame" and "looketh well to his ways" and "responds to correction" and is "hungry for training." See Proverbs 12:16,23 and 13:16 and 14:8,15,18 and 15:5 and 16:21 and 18:15 and 19:14 and 22:3 and 27:12.

Respectable (I Tim. 3:2). Of good behavior, having a modest, orderly, disciplined, respectable lifestyle. A respectable person is:

Orderly or moderate

Not light or vain

Has a composure that brings no reproach upon the ministry or the Lord

The Greek word for "respectable" should be understood in its broadest sense as denoting a character quality, and goes well beyond a refined, courteous, polite person. A respectable man lives a well-ordered life. The verb form of "respectable" in Greek is "kosmeo." It is used to describe a well-ordered house (Matthew 12:44), a decorated tombstone (Matthew 23:29) and well-trimmed lamps (Matthew 25:7).

Paul is saying here that a man who is respectable has a lifestyle that adorns the teachings of the Bible in his speech, his dress, his appearance at home, his office, or the way he does business. God is a God of order. A man of God, too, should be orderly and proper.

(Other scriptures: I Thessalonians 4:10-12; Colossians 3:23,24; I Tim. 6:2; Colossians 4:5,6; I Peter 2:12; Philippians 1:27).

Hospitable (I Tim. 3:2; Titus 1:6). Quite simply, this means "fond of guests" (strangers). It means more than simply taking people into your home. It means being fond of and kind to them while they are there. An elder must enjoy having guests into his home and being a help to strangers.

Fond of guests; enjoys the company of others, especially believers (I Tim. 3:2).

Loving and a friend to believers, strangers and foreigners (Titus 1:6 Amplified Bible).

"(If the) stranger resides in your home, do him no wrong . . . (he) shall be as your native

among you, love him as yourself" (Leviticus 19:33,34).

"Let love be without hypocrisy . . . be devoted to one another in brotherly love" (Romans 12:9,10).

"Let love of brethren continue . . . do not neglect to show hospitality" (Hebrews 13:1,2).

"Be hospitable to one another without complaining" (I Peter 4:9).

Apt to Teach (I Tim. 3:2). That is, a skilled teacher. The Greek word does not mean simply to teach, it means to teach in a skillful manner.

"Instructive or able to communicate" (I Tim. 3:2).

Able to teach, resulting from having been taught.

Implied as having the ability to aprove the critic and unbeliever wrong, with the result being a proper communication of the truth of God's Word (Titus 1:9).

The Greek word used here "didakitkos" means able to impart truth. It could also be translated as "teachable." It refers to a quality of life: humble, sensitive, desirous to know the will of God.

The "didakitkos" does not look for arguments or stir them up. He is sensitive to people, even those who are confused, obstinate and bitter. When verbally or even physically attacked, he does not reciprocate with cutting words and putdowns. This is a self-controlled lifestyle.

Those who are apt to teach are also apt to learn. They learn more of the Word (II Tim. 2:2). They progressively believe more of the Word (Titus 1:9). And they progressively live more of the Word (II Tim. 2:24,25).

Not Given to Wine (I Tim. 3:3; Titus 1:7; Proverbs 20:1). Literally, not tarrying at wine or staying near wine.

"One who sits long at his wine" (Robertson)

One who drinks alcoholic beverages often and in large amounts

Would Paul condone drinking at all? In this passage, he is not speaking of total abstinence. He uses a word, "paoinos" that definitely refers to excess, meaning that he is talking about the kind of drinking that causes one to lose control of his senses and be brought into bondage. Paul here is talking about overdrinking. And the consequences of this are indeed terrible (Proverbs 23:29-34). A higher law rules us in this matter: we should not do "anything by which your brother stumbles" (Romans 14:21).

Not Self-Willed (Titus 1:7). An elder must not be dominated by self-interest, self-pleasing, stubbornness or arrogance. He must submit to proper authority, seek to please God and others, and not become "set" in his ways.

Not insubordinate

"Self-pleasing and arrogant" (Thayer)

"Not stubborn" (Williams)

"Arrogant or presumptuous" (Amplified Bible)

"Not given to self-gratification" (Concordant Literal)

"Self-centered and wants to do as he pleases" (Beck)

A self-willed person is set on having his own way, never seems to lay down his desires in order to serve another, and when he finally does, he does it grudgingly. The self-willed man builds the world around himself. The self-willed man is his own authority (II Peter 2:2,3,10,14,18)!

That probably couldn't describe any of us reading this book. But just to be sure, ask yourself these questions.

Do you usually or always get your way?

Do you have difficulty admitting your mistakes?

Do you rule your own home with authoritarian leadership--"Do it because I told you to do it"?

As a child, were you overindulged, and did you have problems with being conceited or spoiled?

Self-will and strong willed are two different things. The spiritually mature person will not dominate others, even if he does have a strong will.

Not Quick-Tempered (Titus 1:7). Not soon angry, not prone to anger or quick-tempered. An elder must not be irascible, cranky or irritable.

Not easily provoked or inflamed
"Not quick-tempered" (Titus 1:7 Amplified Bible)
Capable of governing your own spirit (Kevin J. Conner)

The person who is not soon angry doesn't have a "short fuse," doesn't "fly off the handle." Our guide in dealing with anger is Ephesians 4:26, *"Be angry, and sin not."* Some feelings of anger are inevitable in this fallen world. But if we quickly release and forsake them, they will not harm us. Brooding anger hurts the spirit; smoldering, revenge-seeking anger causes a man to lose perspective. Those who are "slow to anger" (James 1:19,20) will find it much easier to cooperate with the moving of the Holy Spirit.

Not Pugnacious (I Tim. 3:3; Titus 1:7). No striker, not violent, combative or pugnacious. A pugnacious man carries a chip on his shoulder and is always ready for a good argument--perhaps even just a good theological tussle!

Not quarrelsome

Not disposed to arguments or fighting

A pugnacious person loses control of his senses and is controlled by anger. He is always ready to fight, with a combative, belligerent nature. He cannot always avoid engaging in physical violence.

Be comforted in this fact: God has helped and used some people who had a problem with anger. Moses had a history of anger. He killed an Egyptian (Acts 7:20-29); he threw down and broke the Tablets of the Law which God gave him; he angrily smote God's rock of provision in the wilderness, contrary to God's command (Numbers 20:1-13). In spite of all this, the Lord used Moses in a mighty way. Peter also was rash in word and deed; he cut off the ear of the high priest's servant on the night of Christ's arrest (John 18:1-27).

Uncontentious (I Tim. 3:3). Not contentious, not a brawler. This signifies someone who is not quarrelsome and contentious, but is peaceable. An elder must be a man of peace.

"Not to be withstood; invincible" (Thayer)
Peaceable (I Tim. 3:3)
Easily corrected

The contentious person domineers others, but in reality is insecure and defensive. He struggles against others, has to compete and debate others. He is not happy unless he is in charge, and not willing to serve or come under anyone else. He is not willing to bend, not flexible: "It's my way or no way!" Such people, usually jealous and selfish, are motivated by pride. He is apt to contend and argue, and loves controversy, strife, conflict, struggle and discord.

By contrast, the peaceable character quality that makes a person a good bishop seeks peace. "With all that lies within you...live at peace with one another" is his motto (Romans 12:16,18). This person is easily corrected.

Gentle (I Tim. 3:2). Patient, that is, gentle, kind, considerate, and forbearing. A gentle person:

Has a mild disposition.
Is gentle or considerate (Robertson).

In Philippians 4:5, this same word is translated in various versions as "moderation" and "forbearance" and "sweet reasonableness." This Greek word, "epiekes" means "trench," and, by extension, "yielding." It is used in the context of not insisting on one's legal rights; legal rights can become moral wrongs when a person takes advantage or has the upper hand on somene else too often.

In a noble and generous spirit, a superior person will even yield to the lesser. Galatians 6:1 tells us to restore people "in a spirit of gentleness."

Free From Love of Money (I Tim. 3:3). This person is not greedy of money. Basically one word in the Greek, it means not acquiring money by dishonest means or acquiring dishonest money by any means. This person is:

Not fond of money (Concordant Literal)

Not pursuing dishonest gain (I Tim. 3:3, NIV)

Free from the love of money (Titus 1:7)

Also, this person is not covetous of other possessions as well. He is not a lover of (fond of) money, not avaricious, or simply "not greedy." An elder must be free from the love of money and the things it can obtain. Being insatiable for wealth and ready to obtain it (Tim. 3:3 Amplified Bible) by questionable means obviously disqualifies someone from the office of bishop. It renders spiritual growth impossible.

Rules His Own House Well (I Tim. 3:4; Titus 1:6). An elder must preside over and manage his own household (family members, finances, possessions, etc.) in an excellent manner. The ruling aspect includes the concept of concerned (caring) management. This requires more than just watching the overall direction, but also requires helping to conduct the affairs of the family. The word "well" in the Greek is a strong term, meaning beautiful or excellent, as opposed to just pretty or fair.

"Children in subjection with all gravity" is holding or keeping children under control (in obedience, submission). The term "all gravity" could apply to the elder or to his children or both. "All gravity" means true dignity, respect, reverence, venerableness.

"Faithful children" refers to "believing children," or children who believe in Jesus Christ as their savior (that is, they are Christians). Elders' children are to be Christians.

Children in subjection (I Tim. 3:4)

Controlling his own household (Concordant Literal)

Whose children are well-trained and are believers, not open to accusation of being loose in morals and conduct or unruly and disorderly (Titus 1:6 Amplified Bible).

This passage does not speak of very small children. These little ones will go through phases of difficulty, but if there is not willful, loose living, time will tell if the parents trained well. "Dissipated rebellion" could only speak of older children who have reached the age of accountability. Riotous and improper living is characteristic of the common rebellion among older teenagers and young adults. In I Samuel 2:12, the two sons of Eli are disqualified from the priesthood because their riotous living made them *"sons of Belial"* (2:17). To truly love our wives and children, we must discipline them in love (Ephesians 5:25; I Peter 3:7).

A Good Reputation With Those Outside the Church (I Tim. 3:7). This is the result of living an excellent testimony for those outside of the church (the non-Christian community). A reputation may exist in areas of business, community relations and civil law. An elder must be a respected person "on the job" as well as in the church.

An example of Christian virtue in the community in regard to integrity, honesty and purity

"Behave properly toward outsiders" (I Thessalonians 4:11,12)

"Conduct yourself with wisdom toward the outsiders" (Colossians 4:3,6)

"Give none offense, neither to the Jews, nor to the Gentiles" (I Corinthians 10:31-33)

"Having your conversation honest among the Gentiles" (I Peter 2:12)

Lover of Good (Titus 1:8). Although the King James Version has "lover of good men," the Greek word here is much broader than that. It means being fond of good--good men, good activities, things, thoughts, etc. An elder's desires should be toward the good things of God, and not set on evil, questionable or less important things.

"One who loves good things and good people" (Titus 1:8 Amplified Bible)

"One who loves what is good" (Titus 1:8 New International Version).

A promoter of virtue.

This mindset is described in detail in Philippians 4:8, which lists many good things for the believer to dwell on: *"whatsoever things are true . . . honest . . . just . . . pure . . . lovely . . . of good report . . . any virtue . . . any praise."*

Just (Titus 1:8). That is, righteous, equitable and upright. This entails not only right standing before God, but also doing what is right and just in one's dealings with other people. It is conduct that meets the approval of the divine Judge. The just man is:

Equitable in character

Fair in decisions (Titus 1:8)

Right in judgment

Upright and fair-minded

The just man can make mature decisions and proper judgments. God blessed Solomon exceedingly because rather than asking for wealth, he prayed this prayer: "Lord, give me an understanding heart." Other examples of just men: Joseph (Matthew 1:19); Cornelius (Acts 10:22); John the Baptist (Mark 6:20).

Devout (Titus 1:8). A devout man pursues holiness, and pleases God and is set apart for His service. The opposite of this character quality is worldliness and carnality.

Essential nature and character in relationship to God (Kevin J. Conner)

Benign (Concordant Literal)

A devout man and religiously right (Titus 1:8 Amplified Bible)

A devout man actively and consistently practices righteousness. He maintains his moral and religious obligations.

Not a Novice (I Tim. 3:6). That is, not a newly-converted Christian.

Not a new convert (I Tim. 3:6 Amplified Bible)

One who is newly planted (Robertson)

Hopeful beginners who have ministry qualifications still lack the maturity in the faith that is needed. This refers not to a young man's age, but to his spiritual maturity.

Such a leader can easily become "conceited," which in the Greek means to wrap in smoke, or "besmoked" pride that covers him like a smoky fog. In this fogged position, the devil can easily make him stumble.

In America, the Church quickly elevates to spiritual leadership newly-saved television and cinema stars, and "chief sinners," almost immediately after their conversion. This violates the Bible command in I Tim. 3:6. Some of these "hothouse growth" leaders survive this mistake, some are ruined for life, and others never seem to find a balanced role in ministry.

Holds Fast the Faithful Word (Titus 1:9). An elder must have a firm grip and a strong hold on the Word of God as it was taught to him. He must know the scriptures and the proper teaching (sound doctrine) he received. See also II Tim. 2:2. Holding fast the faithful Word involves:

Never being willing to compromise truth (Kevin J. Conner)

A deep conviction of the infalibility and authority of Scripture

Not Double-Tongued (I Tim. 3:8). This involves:

Not being shifty or a double-talker, but being sincere in what you say (I Timothy 3:8)

Not standing between two persons, saying something to one person, and then saying the complete opposite to the other.

For Self-Evaluation

The following list of questions will provide the shepherd or potential leader with a means of evaluating his own character development. What is God looking for in my leadership today? What specific qualities must I have to be a balanced leader? Am I a spiritual man? As you honestly reflect through the following questions to your own character, you will be able to assess your own development of leadership character.

Do I stay in close communion with the Holy Spirit?

Do I accept the Bible as the Word of God?

Do I love God's people?

Do I identify with God's people in a specific local church?

Do I willingly submit to authority?

Do I love the sinner and the backslider?

Do I truly worship God with all of my heart?

Do I have a strong prayer life?

Do I have a mature attitude in pressure situations?

Do I let another person finish a job that I began without feeling any bitterness toward that person?

Do I listen to and receive criticism?

Do I accept it when someone else is assigned a job for which I am better qualified?

Do I gloat self-righteously when someone else makes a mistake?

Do I allow other people's opinions, or do I always have to argue for my point of view?

Do I have inner peace during times of turmoil?

Do I forgive someone who deliberately ignores me?

Do I control my anger?

Do I pass up certain present pleasures to achieve long term goals?

Do I finish the projects that I begin?

Do I put others before myself?

Do I face unpleasant disappointments without any bitterness?

Do I freely admit when I am wrong?

Do I keep my promises and complete my commitments?

Can I hold my tongue when it is best to do so?

Do I accept and live in peace with the things I cannot change?

To Evaluate Co-laborers

The following list identifies some of the most important character qualities that a shepherd should look for when he chooses co-laborers:

Integrity	Guards a secret
Sharing the same spirit and burden	A spirit of sacrifice
Faithfulness	Does not require a salary of the Church
Commitment to the Church	Successful in a secular job
Right attitudes	Lives consistently with Bible principles
A shepherd's heart	Not addicted to the gods of this world
Stability	Good habits
An ability to get along with people	Doer of the Word
Deliberation in making decisions	Teachable spirit
A lover and enjoyer of other people	Love for God's House
Not domineering	Receives correction and changes
Gracious	Supportive, not competitive, toward others
Not a respecter of people	Submissive spirit
A servant's heart	Humble heart
Not a busybody	Transparent, open and honest nature

May every leader strive to develop these attitudes and qualities in his or her own life. May every leader allow the Lord to mold him into the image of His dear son, Jesus Christ.

If that is your personal prayer, you are ready to move into the next stage in our leadership study: Chapter Eight, "A Leader's Preparation." Christian character development has its most demanding expression in the preparation of God's leaders.

CHAPTER 8
A LEADER'S PREPARATION

Every leader whom God uses in any capacity must first be prepared to function in that capacity. Proper preparation is the only assurance of a leader functioning effectively for God. Many leaders greatly desire to function effectively, but far fewer are willing to pay the price of being made ready for the task. God prepared nearly every leader in the Bible before he began to do his full work for the Lord. Some were in preparation longer than others. Each was trained differently. God Himself has a tailor-made education for each one of His leaders, depending upon the work to which He has called him or her.

The act of preparation is to make ready for a special purpose, to make suitable, to fit, to adapt, to train, to equip or to furnish. The Greek idea of preparation emphasized the act of making something ready to function properly. The following extended synonyms help us appreciate the full meaning of the verb "to prepare":

to provide properly for
to foresee problems
to predispose a certain reaction
to rehearse ahead of time
to train for a specific task
to educate with special knowledge
to set the groundwork and foundation of
to cultivate for fruitful reproduction
to mellow and mature the character of
to arm or fit out with the necessary weapons of warfare

The great importance of preparation is stamped indelibly in the very fiber of three areas: nature, craftsmanship and Scripture.

The Law of Preparation in Nature

Preparation is stamped upon the world of nature in many different ways. First, by instinct, the animals themselves prepare their food for winter by their discipline of gathering food during the harvest seasons. If God has given the animals an instinct for preparation, how much more should man feel the same for the ministry of the Spirit.

Second, the ground is prepared by nature and the farmer to bring forth fruit. The rains, the snow and the sun all help to prepare the ground for spring. Nature is continually preparing itself for its next cycle of life and reproduction.

Third, stones are prepared by nature in rivers. Stones are continually tossed and turned in the river until they are very smooth. Nature has a beautiful way of developing her stones for human use. In I Samuel 17:35-50, the shepherd boy David was faced with the humanly impossible task of slaying the giant, Goliath. As David approached Goliath, he stopped by a stream and carefully chose out five smooth stones, one of which would find its place in the forehead of the giant. David merely used a smooth stone which nature herself had prepared.

The Law of Preparation in Craftsmanship

Skilled craftsmanship and professions provide an excellent example of the need for preparation. All technical occupations in society require a certain level of technical training. A mechanic be trained to quickly grasp the relationships in a complicated diagram. He must understand how chemical, mechanical, electrical and electronic component systems work together. Most professions require years of education and training, and constant updates.

Medical general practitioners must have at least eight years of university training. Who would visit a medical doctor who had no medical education?

Great skill in a craft, trade or profession demands years of apprenticeship, practice, on-the-job training and consultation. How much more do we need seasons and years of preparation for spiritual ministry unto the Lord, in the school of the Holy Spirit and the Word of God.

The principle of preparation in craftsmanship also has a biblical illustration. Throughout Scripture, the analogy of the potter and the clay is used (Romans 9:20,21; Isaiah 45:9 and 64:8; Ephesians 2:10 and Jeremiah 18:1-4; II Timothy 2:2-,21). Both clay and potter must receive much preparation before the potter can produce beautiful works of pottery. The following is a partial list of preparation for potter's clay. Clay must be:

1. dug from the ground, blasted out and separated
2. washed and soaked in water
3. smitten and thoroughly worked by the potter's hands
4. investigated for air bubbles by a thin wire
5. perfectly centered on the wheel for shaping
6. stretched and pulled up and down to be molded seamlessly
7. set aside on the shelf to dry and harden
8. undergo firing in the kiln to develop ceramic qualities

Just as a craftsman follows all of these steps to prepare clay for a beautiful vessel, so God follows comparable steps in preparing each one of His ministers.

The Law of Preparation in Scripture

God has also demonstrated the principle of preparation in His Word. Scripture describes many things that must be prepared to fulfill their specific purpose. The following list--each a study in itself--contains many of the principles God follows in readying His leaders for effective service.

Preparation of a habitation for the Lord (Exodus 15:2; Psalm 107:36).

Preparation of offerings for the tabernacle of Moses (Numbers 15:3-12 and 23:1,2).

Preparation of the people to pass over the Jordan (Joshua 1:11).

Preparation of a man's heart to seek God (I Samuel 7:3; Psalm 10:17).

Preparation of the materials for Solomon's Temple (II Chronicles 2:9; I Chronicles 22:3-14).

Preparation of the ant for winter (Proverbs 30:25).

Preparation of the way for the Messiah (Isaiah 40:3; 62:10; Matthew 3:1-3 and 11:10).

Preparation of the Levites (II Chronicles 35:10-20).

Preparation of the horse for battle (Proverbs 21:31).

Preparation of an honorable vessel (II Timothy 2:20-21).

Preparation of the Messiah's natural body (Hebrews 10:5).

Preparation of the Bride of Christ (Revelation 19:7 and 21:2).

In all of these Scripture examples, we can see the importance of the law of preparation. It is obvious that God is a God of preparation. All whom God will use must go through God's process of preparation.

The Church greatly needs prepared and trained spiritual leaders. The Church does not need mainly "degreed" people, however; she needs those who have been trained and prepared by the Lord. The Church needs those who have been shaped and fired to be formed into godly leaders.

The Season of Preparation

The following diagram illustrates a leader's life-span, and shows where his or her preparation fits into the process. Paul wrote in I Timothy 3:10, *"And let them* (future leaders) *first be tried* (investigated, proven)."

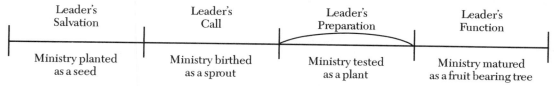

Leader's Salvation	Leader's Call	Leader's Preparation	Leader's Function
Ministry planted as a seed	Ministry birthed as a sprout	Ministry tested as a plant	Ministry matured as a fruit bearing tree

Every leader can find himself at some point on this diagram. From spiritual rebirth to natural death, he is maturing in the Lord. It should be clearly noted that this diagram must begin with salvation; no one can hope to be a spiritual leader in the Church without it. Without being saved, a person has no spiritual capability of leading God's people. Taking their salvation experience for granted, some leaders would have to admit that, unfortunately, they have never matured past that point to identify or fulfill their specific calling in the Lord. Some identify their call, but fail to prepare for their ministries. Still others receive their call and proceed into the preparation period, but fail in the process. Unfortunately, some leaders die in the wilderness at some point along the way in their development.

Isaiah 49:1-3.

The prophet Isaiah gives a beautiful picture of preparation in Isaiah 49:1-3. The prophet gives a word that applies to himself, to the Messiah, and to all of the Lord's servants. In this particular prophecy, Isaiah speaks about an arrow hitting the mark. There are five important points about preparation in these verses.

1. "The Lord called me from the womb."

A sense of destiny was on Isaiah, since God's calling was evident from his mother's womb. Before birth, the purpose for this child had been determined. This kind of calling was fulfilled in Isaiah and the Lord Jesus Christ. It is fulfilled in all of God's servants. All of God's leaders have been called from the womb to fulfill a purpose in the Lord. All of God's leaders have a divine destiny.

The Lord Jesus Christ was called from the womb with a specific purpose for His life (Isaiah 7:14 and 9:16 and 11:1-3). The believer also has been called forth from the womb and destined for a particular task in life (Ephesians 1:4-5 and 5:25-27; Romans 8:28-29; Ephesians 3:1-10). Every servant of the Lord must determine with confidence that he has indeed heard the true call of the Lord that has been from eternity.

2. "He makes my mouth like a sharp sword."

This particular point speaks of the Word ministry of a servant of the Lord. The Word of God is spoken of as a sword in the Epistle to the Ephesians 6:17). The Word is a sword that cuts under the flesh and the soul, down to the very intentions of the heart (Hebrews 4:12). A leader, however, must not use this sword to injure the people of God. The Lord must make a leader's mouth like a sharp sword, but one that does not bring death to the Church as the leader speaks.

The apostle John on the isle of Patmos saw the Lord Jesus in a vision (Revelation 1:10-18). In this vision, John saw the Lord Jesus with a two-edged sword coming forth from His mouth. Even though the Word of God that proceeded from the lips of the Lord Jesus was a sharp sword, the Lord Jesus never used this Word in His earthly ministry to destroy people or to condemn them beyond redemption. As did the Lord Jesus, every leader should learn to use God's Word for edification and not destruction (Ephesians 6:17; Proverbs 6:2 and 18:21; Matthew 10:34; Revelation 2:12 and 19:13-15; Isaiah 51:16 and Romans 3:10-14).

3. "In the shadow of his hand hath he hid me."

This speaks of the veiling of the servant of the Lord during his time of preparation. During this time of training, the servant of the Lord is hidden from the eyes of the world, and sometimes even from the eyes of the Church. Many of the leaders in the Bible experienced a hidden period. Moses, the great deliverer, was hidden forty years on the backside of the desert before he lead his nation forth from Egypt. During this time, the Lord prepared a shepherd's heart in Moses to lead the nation of Israel.

Psalm 91 speaks about hiding under the shadow of the wings of the Almighty. All the leaders of the Lord must learn to abide under the shadow of the Almighty, in that secret place of preparation, without a spirit of impatience or distrust. Jesus, the Pattern Son, was under the shadow of the Almighty for thirty years until His unveiling at the river Jordan. He was not released into His mighty ministry, to the nation and ultimately to the world, until after His thirty "hidden" years. Moses, David, Elisha, Jesus, Paul and many more leaders experienced this period of overshadowing.

This principle still applies to the preparation of a leader today. Many leaders are going through this overshadowing right now. Some are chaffing under it, others are taking advantage of it. What the Lord works into a leader during this period, He will reveal at the time of the leader's release.

Every servant of God should learn well during this time. It is an important period of preparation for his future.

"In the shadow of his hand" can also speak of the five-fold ministry referred to in Ephesians 4:11,12 under which leaders are developed. All leaders must come under the hand of the Lord through these governmental ministries in order to be trained properly. These ministries are given to the Body of Christ to help prepare her potential leaders. They provide covering, protection and preparation. No leader should chaff when he finds himself being hidden by God, for a season, under His dealings through His anointed ministries.

4. *"He also made me a polished shaft."*

Here the prophet brings forth a word picture of an arrow. He states that the shaft of the arrow must be polished before its use. The shaft is one of an arrow's most important components. If the shaft of the arrow is warped or misaligned in any way, the arrow will not hit its mark. A crooked shaft renders an arrow useless. The arrow's sharp head would be of little value if a malformed shaft made it miss the mark.

On the other hand, an arrow would have little value if it reached its mark but a dull head rendered it unable to stick. Arrow shaft and arrow head are of equal importance. The shaft of the arrow can speak of the character of a servant of the Lord, while the head speaks of his ministry. Both the character and the ministry of a servant of God must be properly prepared.

The word "polish" means to clarify, to examine, to purge so as to brighten. Isaiah wrote that God had made him a polished shaft. The shaft must undergo the purging, sanding and polishing process to play its role in producing an arrow that will hit the mark.

During Isaiah's time, preparing an arrow was a detailed process. Acacia wood, a strong but very rough, crooked and knotted wood, had to be carefully straightened and sanded. First, all of the leaves were plucked from the chosen piece of wood. Next, the naked piece of wood was left in a frame using tightly-placed pegs that would slowly straighten it. The shaft was then anointed with oil to soften the wood before the final sanding. After sanding, the shaft was then ready to receive its tip.

All of these steps in the preparation of a natural arrow speak of many spiritual truths in the process of preparing a leader. In a similar way, the Lord will take every leader through a stripping process before He uses him to hit the mark for which he was prepared. Every leader will experience character preparation (the straightening of the shaft) and ministerial preparation (sharpening of the head). This is a very painful and long process at times. But every leader can encourage himself in the knowledge that the more God plans to use an arrow, the more demanding will be its preparation.

5. *"In his quiver hath he hid me."*

The quiver comes to rest and enjoys a long wait until the chosen time that it goes forth. The "quiver experience" is very hard for most leaders, because they feel they have already totally experienced the progressive steps of preparation to be sent forth. This is especially hard for those who have endured bitter experiences successfully. They have responded correctly to their calling, their word, their preparation, their hiding under God's hand, and their polishing. But now they ask, why the waiting period?

This is a time when the leader learns patience. Because of this important lesson, the quiver is no less a place of preparation than the sanding block. The main importance in the quiver experience, now, is not the external but the internal. This is always the hardest test for any leader of the Lord. Each must realize that God has a perfect time when, as an arrow, he is shot forth to hit the mark God ordained for him.

Paul stated in the epistle to the Galatians that the Lord Jesus was shot forth "in the fullness of time" (4:4). Jesus came to earth in the perfect moment of history. This arrow had been waiting for at least four thousand years to be sent forth. But Jesus, who was the Lamb slain before the foundation of the world, waited patiently for the moment at which He would be revealed in human space and time.

Moses was destined to be the great leader of Israel, but there was a perfect time for the release of that arrow that only God knew. When Moses killed the Egyptian, it was not the perfect time for him to be revealed as Israel's great spiritual leader. Moses had to be in the quiver for another forty years.

David was destined to be a king of Israel. He was anointed when he was about seventeen years of age, but did not receive the throne until he was thirty. David had to wait in the quiver for thirteen years. Several times David could have killed Saul to gain the throne by natural means, but the Lord gave him the grace to know that He would open the throne to David in His own way. David chose to wait for God's timing and not man's.

For every one of His leaders, God has a special season of hiding in the quiver, and of revealing only at His appointed time. Temptations and pressures will come to every leader, from without and from within, urging him to go ahead of God's timing. The potential leader must take great care to avoid tampering with the perfect timing of the Lord. There is no set age for the release of a leader. There is no detailed, set pattern for every leader to follow in his release into ministry. The time and the manner of the release is different for every leader. This is why no leader should compare himself to another, but each should wait patiently for the timing of the Lord, for He is the only perfect marksman.

CONCLUSION

In the next chapter, we'll take an in-depth look at the preparation of two great leaders of Israel, Joshua and Samuel. Both led during times of major transition in Israel, Joshua during the period of entry into the promised land, Samuel during Israel's transition from a federation of tribes into a kingdom. Both will illustrate that preparation is a life-long process, though some periods of life are more intensive than others. They are both an encouragement and a challenge to the potential leader.

If you think you may never meet the requirements to fulfill your ministry, be encouraged, because your fears are well-founded! Even for both of these great men, preparation never ended. You can then be relieved to know that you don't have to reach complete maturity in a moment, or in a short time.

If you think you're nearly prepared to be a leader already, or that you are, in fact, fully prepared, you need to be challenged by the lives of Joshua and Samuel. They were never fully complete, but always growing into their ministries. So it will be for every one of God's leaders. How else could it be, for the most demanding, important work in the universe?

CHAPTER 9
THE LIFETIME PREPARATION OF JOSHUA AND SAMUEL

The Bible gives us a wealth of information about how Joshua and Samuel were prepared to fulfill their important ministries in Israel. In both cases, preparation was not limited to the early adult years that the diagram in the last chapter referred to as "A Leader's Preparation." In fact, preparation is not limited to one period in a leader's life, though it is often most intense during one period. Preparation is a lifetime process, with most leaders going through several major cycles, and numerous minor cycles. These cycles follow important events in the fulfillment of the leader's overall commission.

The Preparation of Joshua

Whether you are a potential leader in preparation, or an established leader, you'll find Joshua's life a useful and inspiring study in God's preparation. As we follow his life through the books of Exodus, Numbers, Deuteronomy and Joshua, we will see that God prepared Joshua to be:

A WARRIOR (Exodus 17:9-11)

Joshua was probably born during the Egyptian captivity. He was never trained in the military arts of warfare. When we first see Joshua as a leader, however, he is a warrior against the Amalakites. Joshua, as a man of great courage, was chosen to lead the armies of Israel into battle. Thus, he begins as a leader of warriors and progresses to become the leader of all Israel. Joshua already must have manifested the qualities of a good leader to become a general.

All potential leaders must begin as good spiritual warriors. Each must have a cause and a vision in the heart to defeat the enemy and bring victory for the Lord (John 18:36; I Corinthians 9:25-26; I Timothy 6:12; II Timothy 4:7). A leader can progress in ministry only from a warrior's beginning.

A WORD-BEARER (Exodus 17:14; Acts 9:10-22)

Joshua received a prophetic word from the Lord immediately after the battle, concerning his lifetime ministry to Israel. Moses was to "rehearse" this word in the ears of Joshua. What was he to rehearse? He was to rehearse the victory of the battle, the way God answered prayer, and the way He fought for Israel. Joshua was destined to be the military leader of Israel, for he had received a word from the Lord.

All leaders in the making must receive a definite personal word from the Lord. Each needs assurance of who God is, what He can do, and that He has indeed called them into the ministry. A leader must bear this personal word of the Lord in his heart.

A SERVANT (Exodus 24:13 and 33:11)

Joshua was known in Israel as "the servant of Moses," his official title. He was not called "the servant of Jehovah" until the book of Joshua, after Israel had entered Canaan. The words "to minister," used throughout the Old Testament concerning Joshua, meant to attend as a menial worshipper, to contribute, to serve another, to wait upon others. The word for servant in Exodus 24:13, *"Moses and his servant Joshua,"* would be equivalent to the New Testament Greek word "diakonea," or deacon. Joshua was willing to serve Moses and be known as Moses' deacon. The leadership principle found here in the life of Joshua is for a leader to be faithful to others as servant. Afterward, this ministry will realize its full potential in direct service to God.

In Joshua 5:14, Joshua replies to the Angel who appears to him, *"What saith my Lord unto his servant?"* The word "servant" here is a completely different Hebrew word from the one previously mentioned. It means "a love-slave, or a bond servant." This shows us that Joshua had become Jehovah's love slave only after he had been Moses' servant.

Joshua is a tremendous example to all leaders in the area of preparation. All leaders need to learn how to serve others first, and must be known as ministers (servants) in their local church.

A FAITHFUL CO-WORKER (Exodus 32:17)

When God called Moses to the meeting on mount Sinai, Moses took Joshua. Joshua, however, was stationed at the half-way point as Moses went on to the top. Moses went to the summit, to be encompassed round about with the presence and glory of God. For forty days, he received revelation of the laws and commandments of the Lord, in face-to-face communication with Father God.

But Joshua was half-way down the mountain, with no cloud, no voice, no presence of God and no Moses. His mountain experience was not as glorious as Moses's. Joshua might have seen the cloud or heard something, but he did not experience it himself. The people became weary of waiting for Moses and made themselves a golden calf. Aaron, Moses' brother, should have stopped them, knowing that God forbade idol worship. Instead, Aaron was the master overseeing those who made the calf. Though not with the people, Joshua could probably hear them. He could have joined the people in their sin. No doubt, he grew bored in his mountain experience, and his attention wandered. But Joshua was faithful to Moses and to God. He remained forty days, waiting faithfully while the people were unfaithful--the mark of a truly good leader (see also Genesis 16:1,15,16 and I Samuel 8:5-7).

A LOVER OF GOD'S HOUSE AND GOD'S PRESENCE (Exodus 33:11)

Moses met with God many times in the door of the tabernacle. There God would speak to him and guide him with His presence. Joshua would go with Moses to the tent. During this period, he would not want to leave the tent when Moses had finished, and he would stay on. He loved the presence of the Lord, he loved the house of the Lord.

This characteristic of Joshua as a young leader is of the utmost importace. It is possible for a leader to fall in love with his gift or ministry and never fall in love with the presence of the Lord! Moses must have deeply impressed Joshua when he said to God, *"Except thy presence go with me, I will not go"* (Exodus 33:15). Joshua learned from Moses the importance of the presence of the Lord.

The following scriptures on the presence of the Lord will amplify the importance of this to every leader:

Genesis 4:16	*"Cain went out from the presence of the Lord."*
Exodus 33:13,14	*"My presence shall go with thee."*
Psalm 16:11	*"In thy presence is fullness of joy."*
Psalm 31:20	*"Thou shalt hide them in the secret of thy presence."*
Psalm 51:11	*"Cast me not away from thy presence."*
I Corinthians 1:29	*"That no flesh should glory in his presence."*
II Corinthians 3:17,18	*"Where the Spirit of the Lord is, there is liberty."*

Leaders need to fall in love with the presence of the Lord, as Joshua did. They are not to be like Cain, who went out from the presence of the Lord. How many leaders today do not love His presence? May every leader say with the Psalmist, *"Cast me not away from thy presence!"*

A MAN OF ZEAL

The presence of the Lord had come down upon the camp of Israel here in a marvelous way. God's presence was so strong that two young men ran down into the camp and began to prophesy. Joshua became so concerned that he ran to Moses and forbade the two young men. The zeal of Joshua at this point, however, surpassed his knowledge of God. For Moses answered, "I would that all of God's people were prophets."

The zeal of young ministries (remember our use of this word to refer to people who minister) must be balanced with a mature knowledge of God and His moving. In John 18:10, we see the zeal of Peter in cutting off the soldier's ear. Yet Jesus humbly put the ear back on, and told Peter to put his sword away. Peter had zeal but not knowledge.

In Luke 9:51-56, James and John desired to call fire down from heaven and destroy the city that rejected Jesus. But Jesus' humble reply was, *"You know not what manner of spirit you are of."* They did not understand that Jesus came to save men, not to make burnt offerings of them! Zeal without knowledge is dangerous.

In Mark 10:35-45 James and John desired the right and left hand of the Lord's throne. Jesus could not give them what they desired, but He could give them the ministries that they were destined to become: the ministries of suffering servants. Their desire for position was zeal without a true knowledge of the source or meaning of that position.

In Acts 19:13-16 we have the sons of Sceva, probably a Jewish high priest or a man using such a title to propogate his own magical arts. They found a man with demons, and in their zeal wanted to cast them out. Instead, the demons whipped them soundly and cast out the sons of Sceva. Why? Because they had zeal without a knowledge of Jesus Christ as their Lord.

Young leaders usually have a good dose of zeal, but lack wisdom and knowledge. This is not, however, a totally negative characteristic. God does want zeal in His leaders, but zeal must be balanced with the knowledge and wisdom of older and more mature ministry.

A MAN OF CHANGED CHARACTER (Numbers 13:16)

Scripture makes a close tie between a name change and a character change in a person. Note this in the following characters.

Abram's name ("father") was changed to Abraham ("father of a multitude"). God changed Abram's name after confirming with him His covenant that his seed would be as the sand and stars, without number.

Sarai ("heady and domineering person") was changed to Sarah ("princess and noble one"), as she trusted God to work His perfect will through her husband Abraham. In this, she became an example of faith to all women.

Jacob ("supplanter") became Israel ("prince having power with God"). This name change took place at the same time that Jacob's character was changed.

Joshua's original name, Oshea ("deliverer, helper") became Joshua ("God helps, Jehovah saves"). God changed his name to teach Joshua that he would be a victorious general only by God's strength and help.

REJECTED BY HIS BRETHREN (Numbers 14:6-12)

In any contest, three against three milion is not desirable odds. Here, in Numbers 14, Joshua, Caleb and Moses stood against all of the rest of Israel. Israel wanted to stone Joshua and Caleb to reject their good vision and report about Canaan. Here, the same people that Joshua had led into battle against the enemy now wanted his death. His own people rejected his leadership and his abilities. This rejection was not from Amalek or some other uncircumcised heathen, it was from Joshua's own brethren. All of Israel opposed him.

Many of God's leaders in the Bible experienced rejection by the brethren. The following chart will show their names, their periods of wilderness rejection, and their destinies. Every leader of God's people can take courage that, even though rejection will come, God will use it in His plan.

THEIR MINISTRY REJECTED	THEIR MINISTRY FULFILLED
REJECTIONS, WILDERNESS EXPERIENCES, PRISONS	
Paul . . . . . . 14 years of obscurity	Apostle
Joseph . . . . . . 13 years of prison	Throne
Moses . . . . . . 40 years of wilderness	Deliverer
Joshua . . . . . . 40 years of wilderness	Captain
Jesus . . . . . . 3.5 years of rejection	King

SUBMISSIVE TO THE LAYING ON OF HANDS (Deuteronomy 34:9; Numbers 27:18; I Timothy 4:14)

God told Moses to lay his hands on Joshua because Moses had the Spirit of God in him. In doing this, Moses identified Joshua as a leader in Israel, and also imparted to him his own spirit of wisdom.

Similarly, the leaders of the Church today should submit themselves to God and to the presbytery for the laying on of hands. This act both identifies a person's ministry and imparts spiritual gifts, which must be continuously stirred up and used for the Lord. If a leader truly has a ministry, he need not fear to receive the laying on of hands by the presbytery, because God always confirms His true ministries. The laying on of hands helps better prepare a leader for spiritual battle because it gives him sure words of prophecy upon which he can stand and believe God.

SET BEFORE THE PRIESTHOOD (Numbers 27:19a)

After receiving the laying on of hands by Moses, Joshua was set before Eleazar the priest. This speaks to today's leader of the necessity for other ministries to recognize his position. When Moses commissioned Joshua, it was in front of Eleazar. Joshua took his charge from Moses in a fully responsible way, as being under a higher authority and ministry. He also valued (on a horizontal plane) recognition of his ministry by his peers in ministries of similar importance.

Likewise, all Church leaders should be secure enough in their own ministries to submit to other leaders in the Church. If a leader cannot submit to other leaders, he will not be prepared properly to submit to God in the future.

SET BEFORE THE CONGREGATION (Numbers 27:19b)

Joshua was given his commission by a higher ministry, recognized by equal ministry, before the entire congregation of Israel. This process cultivated in Joshua the ability to relate to others in a horizontal type of relationship, as well as the vertical.

As with Joshua, all of God's leaders will undergo a "fishbowl" experience, in which all of their lives are open and exposed before the people of their church. Such a type of commissioning process makes the taking of authority upon a leader a very serious business. It also calls for a holy, exemplary and transparent life on the part of the leader. This is a vital part of a leader's training, because every leader must realize that it is to such a congregation that he will minister.

RECEIVING A COMMISSION (NUMBERS 27:19)

Joshua did not have a proud or independent spirit about his ministry. He waited until he received a formal commission from the hand of Moses and before the priesthood and the people.

This is not to say that a leader cannot preach the gospel without ordination papers. It simply means that all of God's leaders must recognize that they will receive specific responsibilities by those over them in the Lord. The word commission here means a charge, responsibility or constitution. Paul used similar language when he addressed his faithful servant Timothy (I Timothy 1:18 and 5:21 and 6:13,17). All leaders must be willing to receive a special charge, given to them from the Lord through those over them in spiritual authority.

SHOULDERING RESPONSIBILITY GRADUALLY (Numbers 27:20)

God told Moses to place some of his authority upon Joshua, so that the congregation would obey him. God did not tell Moses to put all of his authority upon Joshua in an instant. Joshua had to take his authority and responsibility gradually, as it was given to him.

Too many leaders want full authority immediately, but this is very unwise. The reception of authority comes from a proper recognition and obedience of authority. The verb "to obey" literally means "to hear under." God was the authority over Moses, and Moses had to obey what God spoke to him. Similarly, Joshua was under the authority of Moses.

Likewise, today's leaders must learn to take their responsibility gradually, as those over them in the Lord give it to them. They must learn not to demand too much too soon, which may well lead to their own pride and destruction.

OBTAINING GUIDANCE THROUGH THE WORD OF THE LORD (Numbers 27:21)

Receiving authority by Moses before the congregation did not relieve Joshua from the need of seeking the Lord's guidance. Moses told this young leader that He must go to Eleazar the priest to receive guidance from the Lord through the urim and the thummim, even as any other member of the congregation.

This process of receiving guidance from Eleazar was a foreshadowing of today's direct guidance by the Godhead. Urim ("lights") is comparable to the Father, thummim ("perfections") is comparable to the Holy Spirit, and the guidance of Eleazar is comparable to the working of Jesus Christ. The New Testament tells us that the Father is *"the father of lights"* (James 1:17), that the Holy Spirit brings the Church to perfections of truth (John 14-16), and finally, that Jesus Christ is the final high priest over the household of God (Hebrews 1:5). Thus, every leader must continually realize that no matter how much authority or responsibility he has, he still must seek the Lord for guidance and direction, just like all of the rest of the congregation.

THE FIRST TO OBEY THE COMMAND OF GOD (Numbers 27:15-23; II Timothy 2:6)

Moses declared that both Eleazar and the congregation would go in and out at the word of Joshua, as he received guidance from the Lord. Joshua was not suddenly commanding the people arbitrarily to go out and come in. Joshua, as a shepherd husbandman (or farmer) had already put into practice what he was now commissioning the people to do (Numbers 27:17).

Just as Joshua himself had already actively served in the congregation, every leader must make sure that he first does what he asks his people to do.

AN EXAMPLE TO THE CONGREGATION (Numbers 32:12; I Timothy 4:12)

God told Israel that none who were over twenty years of age would go in to see the promised land except Caleb and Joshua. Why? Except for these two young leaders, all Israel refused to have faith about entering into the land. God declared that Caleb and Joshua "followed the Lord fully." In this, and in encouraging Israel to possess the land of Abraham, they were excellent examples of true believers.

Joshua stood as a man of faith and confidence in God's promise for the nation to inherit the promised land. So every one of God's leaders should ask himself, "Am I an example of faith and confidence in God that others can follow?"

CONSULTING WITH THE ELDERS (Numbers 32:28)

Joshua was among the assembly of elders when Moses spoke with the tribes of Reuben, Gad and the half-tribe of Manasseh about possessing Canaan. Moses gave command concerning these tribes to Eleazar the priest, to the heads of the fathers households, and also to Joshua.

Similarly, the more a leader follows the Lord, the more he will find himself invited and commissioned to consult with the elders. In addition, spending time among the elders will greatly benefit the Christian leader. The Bible says, *"He that walks with wise men will be wise, but a companion of fools will suffer harm"* (Proverbs 13:20). Even older leaders need each others' counsel.

CAUSING OTHERS TO POSSESS THEIR INHERITANCE (Deuteronomy 1:38; Joshua 21:43-46 and 11:23 and 18:10; Ephesians 1)

Moses told Israel that the Lord had told him that Joshua would enter into the promised land and cause Israel to inherit it. In fulfillment of this, the Bible states, *"So Joshua took the whole land, according to all that the Lord had spoken to Moses, and Joshua gave it for an inheritance to Israel according to their divisions by their tribes. Thus the land had rest from war"* (Joshua 11:23).

Similarly, every leader must cause Christians to possess their spiritual inheritance in Jesus Christ. A leader must be as concerned about helping others obtain their promised spiritual land as he is about inheriting his own.

RECEIVING ENCOURAGEMENT FROM OTHERS (Deuteronomy 3:21-28)

Joshua received spiritual encouragement from Moses, who promised him that God would give him victory in claiming the promised land. Many leaders, however, are too proud or too full of self-pity to openly receive encouragement and comfort from others. Every good leaders realizes that because he is human, he needs times of spiritual uplift and edification.

The verb "to encourage" means to fasten upon, to seize, to be strong, to repair and to fortify. Similarly, "to strengthen" is to be alert both physically and mentally, and to be steadfastly minded. Every leader needs these influences in his own spiritual life now and again. As with Joshua, so every leader needs to admit that he frequently needs to welcome the words of Moses, *"Do not fear them, for the Lord your God is the one fighting for you"* (3:22).

RECEIVING PROGRESSIVE REVELATION ON HIS MINISTRY (Exodus 17:14; Numbers 27:17; Deuteronomy 31:7 and 34:8,9; Joshua 1:1-9)

God did not reveal to Joshua the full extent of his ministry at one time. He revealed it to him gradually. We first saw Joshua as a warrior, then as a leader, then as a man who caused Israel to possess her inheritance, and now finally as the chief shepherd over the entire nation. God did not reveal the full extent of Joshua's ministry, because he might have destroyed both his life and his ministry by trying to help God fulfill it.

Similarly, every leader should accept the progressive revelation of his ministry.

FILLED WITH THE SPIRIT OF WISDOM (Deuteronomy 34:9; Ephesians 1)

A spirit of wisdom was upon Joshua, because Moses had laid his hands upon him to impart it, but also because he had observed Moses very carefully, and had thus learned much wisdom from him. All leaders must learn that every day (not just time in the class) is a rich opportunity for them to gain wisdom through observing people, life and leaders. The nation obeyed the commands of Joshua because it saw the imparted and learned wisdom in him. The Bible says, *"Wisdom is justified by her children"* (Matthew 11:19).

Similarly, every leader will have willing followers if he seeks the Lord for true wisdom, and observes the events and people around him to gain wisdom.

IN COVENANT RELATIONSHIP WITH GOD (Joshua 1:1-9)

When God told Joshua to rise and cross the Jordan River, He referred to His covenant name. He said, *"to the land which I AM giving to them"* (Joshua 1:2). Joshua could not succeed in the land without his own covenant relationship and promises from the Lord. God promised him, *"Every place on which the sole of your foot treads, I have given it to you"* (1:3). God also confirmed His covenant relationship with Joshua with the words, *"Just as I have been with Moses, I will be with you; I will not fail you nor forsake you"* (1:5). The God of Abraham, the God of Isaac, the God of Jacob, and the God of Moses was now becoming the God of Joshua.

Similarly, every leader should have a close covenant relationship with God through Jesus Christ and the New Covenant. Through this, the leader will receive special promises and revelations of the will of God. But it all starts with the leader being a man of covenant, the New Covenant in His blood.

LEARNING FROM BAD EXPERIENCES (Joshua 2)

In Numbers 13-14, Moses sent twelve spies to spy out the land of Canaan. When they returned, only Caleb and Joshua gave a good report of the land. Remembering what happened to Moses, Joshua this time sent forth only two spies, rather than twelve. Joshua did not want to repeat

Moses' bad experience of having the majority of a group of spies come back with an evil report of the land. From the bad experience of Moses, he learned to send forth only two men.

Similarly, all of God's leaders should learn from the mistakes of his own life as well as of others, and especially of those over them in the Lord. Why should a young leader have to repeat a misfortune of an older leader? This little epigram sums it up well: "Experience is expensive; wisdom is far, far cheaper."

FUNCTIONING WITH ORGANIZATION AND PRINCIPLES (Joshua 3)

When the children of Israel were ready to cross over the Jordan River into the promised land, Joshua used both organization and principle. His organizational ability is evident in the physical arrangements to cross the river. First, he told the priests to pass over the river before the people, with the ark of the covenant upon their shoulders (v. 6). Then he had the people follow after the ark when they saw it go before them (vs. 2,3), and put a space of two thousand cubits between the ark and the people so the entire nation would know which way they were to go (v. 4).

Joshua followed principles when he obeyed the voice of the Lord, which told him to command the priests to stand still in the river when they came to the brink of it (vs. 7,8,13). Thus Joshua showed himself as a leader who knew how to obey the Word of God and His principles.

Similarly, every leader must combine both organizational and spiritual principles in his life. Some leaders can organize and administrate, but do not know how to hear and obey God's voice. Others know how to hear and obey God's voice, but are failures at administration. God desires a balance of both in the lives of His leaders.

RECEIVING PROMOTION (Joshua 3:7; I Timothy 3:6)

God told Joshua, just before the nation was to cross the Jordan, *"This day will I begin to magnify thee in the sight of all Israel, that they may know that, as I was with Moses, so I will be with thee"* (3:7). Here God was beginning to exalt Joshua above the nation of Israel as its chief ruler. Many times when God begins to do this with men, they will grow proud and fall. But Joshua had allowed God to so humble him that he did not get haughty. At times, God will not promote people in the ministry because He knows they have too high of a pride level. Every leader should learn from this that one must keep his heart humble before the Lord.

A PREACHER OF VICTORY (Joshua 3:9-11)

Joshua told the children of Israel, "Hereby ye shall know that the living God is among you, and that he will without fail drive out from before you the Canaanites, and the Hittites, and the Hivites, and the Perizzites, and the Girgashites, and the Amorites, and the Jebusites. Behold the ark of the covenant of the Lord of all the earth passeth over before you into Jordan." Here Joshua listed the seven nations that God was going to help them defeat in the land of Canaan. Notice how he preached victory for the people of God in a very positive way. He declared that the Lord was a living God to Israel. He asserted his confidence in the Lord as the one who would bring these victories, stating that His presence in the ark would ensure it.

Every successful leader needs to have a fresh and living vision of the Church of Jesus Christ as a victorious army--not as a defeated one. To follow in the steps of Joshua, every leader must imprint a positive message of faith in God, trust in His Word, and identification with His Church upon God's people.

HANDLING GOD'S TEST OF BLESSING (Joshua 5:10-12)

Until Israel first celebrated the feast of Passover in Canaan, she had lived on manna and quail.

To Israel, manna was a "proving bread," a means by which God kept the nation dependent and obedient to His word. But now in Gilgal, two days after they had celebrated the Passover, the "proving bread" stopped, and they began to eat directly of the fruit of the land (v. 12). This was the test of blessing from the Lord, for the land itself would now supply their needs, instead of the Lord's "morning dew." Would Israel be able to love the Lord, even though He was now blessing them with the fruit of Canaan itself?

Every leader should be aware when trials of the Spirit seem to be ending, and blessings start flowing in. Times of blessing are great times of temptation for leaving the Lord, because it does not appear that one needs the Lord anymore. Just the opposite is true. As a leader, Joshua was able to handle blessings. But there is no telling exactly how much Joshua's next experience with the Lord helped him to continue trusting His God.

RECEIVING VISITATION FROM THE LORD (Joshua 5:13-15)

Near Jericho, Joshua received a visitation from the Lord of hosts. This was, in reality, a theophany appearance of the Lord Jesus Christ, the Captain of the Lord's hosts. Moses' visitation from the Lord in the burning bush preceded his delivering of Israel from Egyptian bondage. Joshua's visitation preceded his possessing all of the promised land. When Joshua realized that this visitation was from the Lord, he confessed Him as his personal Lord, fell down, worshipped, and loosed his shoes from off of his feet because of the revelation of the holiness of God.

Similarly, every leader should be prepared for a visitation by the Lord Jesus through His Spirit. This requires an attitude of readiness to make Jesus the full Lord of his life, to humble himself before Christ, worship Him, and allow an understanding of the Lord's holiness to shake every impure fetter from his life. Such visitations have the purpose of purifying a leader to be a vessel of honor for the Lord's work.

OBEYING INSTRUCTIONS BEYOND NATURAL UNDERSTANDING (Joshua 6:1-20)

Joshua had a humble trust for the Lord. When God told him to ensure Jericho's defeat by compassing the city seven times, with seven priests blowing seven rams' horns before the ark of the covenant, he believed. This certainly must have seemed a strange way of taking Jericho and its king! Nonetheless, Joshua did not rely upon his own understanding of how to make war (which was considerable, by now). He obeyed God, Who brought the walls of Jericho crashing to the ground.

Every leader must learn how to obey the voice of God in his heart even when, at times, it will run counter to his own understandings. The Lord is committed to keeping His servants dependent upon Him and His resources. If a leader can remember this and live by it, he will save himself much wasted time, and destroy many enemy strongholds for the Lord.

COMFORTED AND STRENGTHENED TO DEAL WITH SIN (Joshua 6:17-27; 7:1-26)

During the victory over Jericho, an Israelite named Achan disobeyed the Lord's command, by taking of "the accursed thing," religious items marked for destruction. The anger of the Lord was kindled against the entire nation. Israel experienced a very sad defeat in their next campaign, with Ai. At the defeat of his nation, Joshua tore his clothes, and in discouragement fell to the earth before the ark of the covenant. In response, the Lord simply asked Joshua why he was lying face down, instead of getting up and finding out who in the camp had sinned against the Lord's commandment.

Similarly, a leader should never forget that many times there is a simple answer to a Church problem of destructive sin. God simply will not bless sin. When a leader finds that his people cannot win any spiritual victories in their lives, he must turn to the Word of God and ask the Holy Spirit to reveal which of God's principles have been violated.

USED IN HIS AREA OF EXPERTISE (Joshua 8:18)

God made a similar request both to Moses and Joshua: to stretch forth before Him what they had in their hands. Moses had a shepherd's staff, Joshua had a spear. The stretching forth of his spear was Joshua's signal to the other part of his army to ambush. Beyond this, God was asking Joshua to use his training in warfare in His service. God was asking him to use his background, knowledge, skill and what was presently at his disposal for His kingdom and purposes.

Similarly, God asks every one of His leaders to make available for His use all of his past knowledge, training, skill and experience. Sometimes leaders become discouraged by thinking that they have nothing to offer to the Lord for His service. But God takes what a leader does have, no matter how small it is, and uses it. As Jesus did with the five loaves and two fishes, God will bless it, break it, and multiply it to feed others. God multiplies whatever is sincerely offered to Him.

REMEMBERING THE LORD DURING BLESSING (Joshua 8:26-35)

Joshua did not forget the Lord during times of blessing. After Israel had just experienced a wonderful victory over Ai, Joshua remembered to build an altar to the Lord, to give Him all the glory for the victory. He built an altar on Mount Ebal ("cursing") because he had just cursed the enemy. He built the altar acording to the Law through Moses, *"an altar of whole stones, over which no man hath lifted up any iron"* (v. 31; Deuteronomy 27:5).

Joshua also set some of the tribes of Israel before Mount Ebal (cursing) and Mount Gerizim (blessing) according to the command of Moses (Deuteronomy 27:11-13; 11:29). In representing peace offerings unto the Lord, the following tribes were on the mount of blessing:

Simeon (a people who has heard)
Levi (joined)
Judah (praise)
Issachar (reward)
Joseph: Ephraim (doubly faithful) and Manasseh (forgetting)
Benjamin (son of the right hand)

To represent Israel's burnt offerings unto the Lord, the following tribes were stationed on the mount of cursing:

Reuben (behold a son)
Gad (one of a troop)
Asher (joy)
Zebulun (dwelling)
Dan (judge)
Naphtali (wrestling)

This reminds the leader in God's house to remember the Lord during times of blessing, and to recite to his people both the curses and blessings of God's covenant promises. Since human nature is tempted to become self-confident and loose-living when we are blessed, times of blessing especially require a remembering of God's Word. (The leader would do well by taking the background, history and meaning of each tribe's name and seeing why it is found either on the mount of blessing or on the mount of cursing.)

FALLING TO THE SIN OF SELF-CONFIDENCE (Joshua 9:1-27 and 14 and 15)
After Joshua's great victories over Jericho and Ai, he received a visit from the men of Gibeon. They came disguised as strangers from a far country (they were actually natives of the land), seeking to avoid destruction by Israel. When approached by this ruse, Joshua did not "ask counsel of the Lord," but made a league with them. It is very likely that, in the glow of his victories, Joshua felt confident that he could discern the truth of this situation without inquiring of the Lord for insight.

Self-confidence is a temptation for every leader who has experienced any successful ministry in the Lord. Two keys in resisting self-confidence: to dismiss the importance of past achievements, and to give all of the glory for victory to God.

EXERCISING FAITH WITH AUTHORITY (Joshua 10:1-14)
Adonizedek, the king of Jerusalem, planned an attack against the Gibeonites after he learned of their league with the destroyer of Jericho and Ai. Joshua, however, helped the Gibeontes win the war, because the Lord fought with them. As the enemy fled, Joshua commanded the sun and moon to stand still until Israel had full revenge on her enemies, and this happened. Joshua had faith and authority to command miracles, even though he had recently disobeyed the Lord (9:15).

Every leader should so build the Word of God into his life that he can speak with faith and authority, without becoming overly discouraged by mistakes. If a leader obeys God, he can believe the Lord to do mighty miracles through him to set captive people free from the enemies of sin and unbelief.

GATHERING ISRAEL UNTO A PLACE OF VISITATION (Joshua 10:1-14; Genesis 12:6-8 and 18-20)
Now old in years, Joshua gathered all of the tribes of Israel to Shechem, along with all of their leaders, judges and officers. There he rehearsed what the Lord had done for Israel and made a covenant with the people that they would serve the Lord. Joshua probably chose to meet with Israel in Shechem because it was a place of past spiritual visitations for Abraham and Jacob.

It is important for all leaders to remember that they must never forsake the Biblical truths of the past. Yet they must also remember that they need a fresh, personal encounter with God, even if this occurs on the much-visited ground of the past. Every generation must have its own Shechem experience.

USING HISTORY AND PROPHECY TO ADMONISH ISRAEL (Joshua 24:1-28)
In Shechem, Joshua spoke to the people of what the Lord had done to Israel, and exhorted them to serve the Lord only. He used his prophetic gift: *"And Joshua said unto all the people, 'Thus saith the Lord God of Israel' "* (v. 2). And he also used his knowledge of salvation history. He referred to the book of Exodus (vs. 5-7), to the book of Numbers (vs. 8-10), and to his own history with Israel. In this way he edified and exhorted the people to follow the Lord in the present, with all of their hearts.

Similarly, every leader must combine of knowledge of Bible history with his gift of teaching, preaching or prophesy to help the Church today put away her idols and follow on to know the Lord. A leader should use the Old and New Testaments to edify God's people (I Corinthians 10:11).

LOOKING BACK OVER A LIFE OF SUCCESSFUL MINISTRY (Joshua 24:29-31)
Joshua died and went on to be with his fathers at one hundred and ten years of age. The Bible

records a remarkable testimony concerning his life and ministry: *"And Israel served the Lord all the days of Joshua, and all the days of the elders that outlived Joshua"* (v. 31).

Every leader in God's kingdom should deeply desire such a testimony when he is taken on to be with the Lord. To have the people's obedience to the Lord under one's leadership, and the continued obedience to the end of one's own generation, is a marvelous witness to a leader's ministry. May it be that of every leader.

The Preparation of Samuel

Samuel led Israel through a transition that was second in importance only to her entry into the promised land. Samuel was Israel's spiritual father and shepherd during her transition from a federation of tribes into a united kingdom. He was both a judge and a prophet. He suffered with Israel through times of sin and defeat, and he never lived to see the full flowering of Israel as a kingdom under David. Samuel was faithful in all of his dealings with Israel, and so he was a vessel of honor that God could use to accomplish a great work with His people. His lifetime of preparation illustrates that the more important God's ministry is for you, the more demanding your preparation will be.

THE MIRACULOUS BIRTH OF SAMUEL

Before we look at the lifetime preparation of Samuel, we need to look at Samuel's mother, Hannah. I Samuel 1:1-2:10 gives us the main section in which Hannah appears as a woman who has had no children. The following list shows us the depth of sorrow that Hannah experienced before she gave birth to her first-born son, Samuel. Hannah:

Had no children because God had closed her womb (I Samuel 2:4,5).
Had an adversary who provoked her (v. 6).
Fretted (v. 6).
Wept (v. 7).
Did not eat (v. 7).
Grieved in her heart (v. 8).
Was bitter in her soul (v. 10).
Experienced affliction (v. 11).
Had a sorrowful spirit (v. 15).
Was complaining and grieving (v. 16).

For a Hebrew woman to be childless was one of the worst things possible. She would have felt that the judgment and curse of God had come upon her. In Hannah's case, the Lord had closed her womb (v. 5), not to judge her, but to manifest His miraculous power in the birth of Samuel.

Samuel was born out of all of this sorrow and affliction in his mother's life. He was born out of hardship, prayer and grief of soul. Yet after he was born, Hannah faithfully declared, *"I will give him unto the Lord all the days of his life"* (v. 11). Since Samuel was born of God, Hannah gave him back to God.

Hannah, taken in one way, can represent the condition of a leader before his ministry is brought forth by God. Samuel is the ministry that is finally brought forth. Just as Samuel, Hannah's ministry or gift to God was born out of much spiritual affliction. So are the ministries of many leaders. To release God's power to work in a leader's life, and for God to be greatly glorified, many times ministries must come forth in human weakness, prayer and sorrow. This prevents a leader from glorying in himself when his ministry succeeds, and helps him give all the glory to the Lord. Hannah's prayer illustrates her glorying in God and not herself. Note how many times she gives all the glory about Samuel's birth to God and not to herself:

"My heart exalts in the Lord;
My horn is exalted in the Lord . . .
Because I rejoice in thy salvation,
There is no one holy like the Lord,
Indeed, there is no one besides thee
Nor is there any rock like our God . . .
The Lord makes poor and rich:
He brings low, he also exalts,
He raises the poor from the dust
He lifts the needy from the ash heap . . ."

(I Samuel 2:1-10, selected)

In causing ministries to be born out of adversity, God receives all the glory to Himself. He also causes every leader whose ministry is birthed in this way to continually depend on Him for its continuation. May every leader allow God to bring forth a Samuel out of his or her own suffering and pain (Proverbs 24:10; Isaiah 30:20).

Samuel played a special role in the history of Israel. He was the last of Israel's judges and the first of her prophets. To indicate that Samuel was a special child, God caused his mother Hannah to bear Samuel in a miraculous birth (I Samuel 1:20). After this special birth, Samuel was consecrated to God by becoming a holy Nazarite (1:1). The young man was thus separated unto God's service. Even so, he found himself functioning under corrupt religious leadership (chapters 1-2), and was surrounded by the corrupt influence of the fornications of Hophni and Philehas (2:14-17). In spite of all of this, Samuel was a righteous priest even as a youth (2:11,18). Because he was a righteous man, Samuel had a balanced growth in his ministry, as he related well both to God and to man (2:26).

God caused Samuel's ministry to be right on time for the present situation (3:3). Samuel did not lose his servant's heart (3:21), even though his ministry was one of receiving the word of the Lord (3:21) and revelation from God (3:3,4). This ministry was obviously confirmed by God (3:19-21). Thus, we have before us a man of God who was not only a priest (7:3-12), a judge (7:15-17) and an intercessor (12:6-25), but also the chosen prophet of God who anointed both Saul and David as king.

Samuel's birth can be compared to a Church leader's miraculous spiritual birth into the kingdom of God by faith in Christ. Indeed, each aspect of this previous character sketch on Samuel can be applied in varying degrees to every leader. The characteristics from Samuel's lifetime of preparation we will now apply to today's Church leader. In the following sections, we will see the spiritual application from Samuel's preparation:

AS A NAZARITE (I Samuel 1:11)

Hannah, in her prayer to the Lord, told Him that if God would give her a son, she would totally dedicate him to God's service. She said, "I will give him to the Lord all the days of his life, and a razor shall never come upon his head." In this statement, she was declaring that her son would be under the vow of a Nazarite (Numbers 6). As a Nazarite, Samuel would be separated unto the Lord, and separated from sin.

As a Nazarite, Samuel was under a vow of abstinence from intoxicating liquor. Samuel was to stay away from that which would dull his senses and cause him to be unaware of things and events around him (Proverbs 20:1 and 23:20,29-31 and 31:4). Similarly, every leader of God should abstain from all of the intoxicating things of this world, from "the lust of the flesh, the lust of the eyes and the pride of life." In this way, the leader will keep his spiritual senses exercised and alert, and thus be able "to discern (perceive) both good and evil" Hebrews 5:14.

As a Nazarite, Samuel was also to exercise self-denial. He was to maintain self-control over his spirit, mind and body. The Church leader desires this today, since self-control is a fruit of the Holy Spirit (Galatians 4:22,23). Every leader should remember what the Lord Jesus said about self-denial: "If any man come after me, and hate not his father, mother, wife, children, sisters and brother, yea, even his own life, he cannot be my disciple" (Luke 14:25-27). To follow Jesus, a leader must deny himself.

The apostle Paul spoke to this point also in the words, *"love seeks not her own way and is not selfish"* (I Corinthians 13:5). Concerning his disciple, Timothy, Paul stated *"I have no man like-minded, who will naturally care for you, for all seek their own things, and not the things that be of the Lord"* (Philippians 2:20-22; see also chapters 2 and 4; Colossians 3:1). Each leader must deny his own personal desires in order to serve the Lord and His people.

As a Nazarite, Samuel never allowed a razor to come to his head. He had long hair, an indication of the total dedication of his mind and life to God (Numbers 6:5). The Nazarites wanted to completely submit to God's control, so they did not cut the hair on their heads, since the head represents the authority of God over them. Similarly, every leader should totally submit his mind to God, knowing that the mind submitted to God (Romans 12:1) is a necessity in bringing the body under God's dominion as well.

In relation to the Church, every leader must be submitted to the Head of the Body, Jesus Christ. Jesus is the head of the Body (Colossians 1:18; Ephesians 1:22,23 and 4:15; I Corinthians 11:3). All plans, decisions, ministries, activities and thoughts of a leader must be directed by the Lord.

Samuel was also to avoid all contact with dead bodies, signifying an absolutely pure life unto the Lord. Similarly, every Church leader today must avoid contact with everything in the world-system that is tainted with death. This requires that a leader must be a man of character and value, as well as a man of ability. These scriptures exort all Christians, and the leader especially, to lead holy lives:

Matthew 5:48, *"Be ye perfect, even as your father in heaven is perfect."*
Ephesians 1:4, *"We should be holy and without blame before him in love."*
I Timothy 2:8, *"Lifting up holy hands unto the Lord."*
(See also Psalms 18:26 and 22:3 and 24:4; Luke 23:4; Hebrews 7:26; I Peter 1:16; Titus 1:15 and Revelation 3:15)

A leader can spiritually fulfill Samuel's Nazarite vow only by the working of the Lord Jesus through His Holy Spirit. Before the Lord Jesus established the kingdom of heaven on earth, the Spirit enabled two other men to fulfill this vow. They were Samson (Judges 13:5) and John the Baptist (1:15). Both of these Nazarites pointed to the Lord Jesus Christ.

Jesus came "from Nazareth" (Matthew 2:23), and therefore was called "a Nazarene." He spiritually fulfilled the holy requirement of a Nazarite (Hebrews 7:26). In this sense, Jesus Christ is the spiritual fulfillment of the vows of the Nazarite. In being from Nazareth ("a branch, stem or germ," see also Isaiah 11:1), Jesus becomes the insignificant stem from which would grow the worldwide tree of faith. In being called a Nazarene ("a despised one" see Isaiah 11:1 and 53:1-3; Matthew 2:23; Acts 22:8), Jesus becomes the despised one who was hated and crucified for the sins of the world. In being the personal fulfillment of the holy requirements of the Nazarite vow (separated, consecrated, devoted, coming from the root meaning of "crowned"), Jesus was able to fulfill all of the vow in a spiritual way through the cross.

The Nazarite believed that his hair was the crown of God upon him; Jesus was "crowned with glory and virtue" through His inward life of righteousness. The Nazarite could not touch dead bodies lest he become unclean. Jesus could touch and heal the sick and dead (Mark 5:41; Luke 7:14; John 11:14), because He was the total fulfillment of the reason for this prohibition, the call to holiness. Only Jesus could touch a dead body and remain undefiled. The Nazarite could not drink wine. Jesus was accused of being a winebibber, a glutton and a friend of sinners (Luke 7:34) because He fulfilled the spiritual purpose in this law of the Nazarite. Through the person and work of Jesus Christ, every leader can fulfill the true spiritual purpose of the Nazarite law.

AS LIVING UP TO THE MEANING OF HIS NAME

Samuel's name means "heard of God," in contrast to Eli's name, which means "lofty" or "to ascend." Samuel's name also means, by extension, to hear intelligently and to hear with attentiveness and obedience. The root of his name is in the Hebrew word for strength and might. The meaning of Samuel's name was fulfilled in God hearing Hannah's prayer for a son. It was also fulfilled in that Samuel heard God's voice, and God heard Samuel's voice. Every leader needs to hear God's voice in his inner man, and to obey the meaning of his own spiritual name, which God has given him as a challenge to his own character development.

AS HAVING A MIRACLE BIRTH (I Samuel 1:19)

Samuel's birth was miraculous, because the Lord had for several years closed the womb of his mother, Hannah. Samuel was the miraculous answer to Hannah's deep prayers. In addition to Samuel, Samson, John the Baptist and Jesus all had miracle births. In the same way, every Church leader must have a miraculous new-birth experience by faith in Jesus Christ before he can do anything to build the kingdom of God.

AS TURNING TO GOD IN HIS YOUTH (I Samuel 2:22)

Samuel ministered before the Lord as a growing boy and showed respect and submission to Eli, the leader over him, even though Eli was corrupt. In the same way, God desires every leader to turn to Him at an early age in life, and to respect the position of their leaders, even if they are not wholly following the Lord.

AS UNHINDERED BY SIN AROUND HIM (I Samuel 2:12-17)

In addition to the corrupt leadership of Eli, Samuel was also surrounded by the sins of Eli's sons, Hophni and Phinehas. They were described as "sons of Belial" (the devil, v. 12). Samuel remained in submission to Eli, though he was a poor father, with a corrupt home, who did not correctly discipline his sons (2:22-25). Faithfulness and stability were already in evidence in the life of Samuel (2:18).

Every leader will have sin in his environment, which he must resist, to grow up righteously before the Lord. The leader must reject behaviorism and every other fatalistic world view that says he needs only a change in environment to change his thoughts and behavior. Every leader must squarely address his own responsibility for his own life.

Though Adam and Eve were located in the ultimate, beautiful garden environment, they sinned against God (Genesis 3). Though David slept in lovely palace surroundings and had every possible need satisfied, he still descended to the bed of adultery. No leader can blame a bad environment, poor leadership or surrounding sin for stunting his spiritual growth. Growth before God is a matter of our own personal choice and responsibility. Moreover, evil influences, when resisted, can even become a dynamic catalyst for seeking the Lord and developing godly character.

AS A PRIEST (I Samuel 2:18)

Though Samuel was not a priest by family descent, he ministered to the Lord as a Levite, in the priestly office and girded with the priestly garment of the linen ephod. As he continued to minister to the Lord, he continued to grow. His ministry to God, in fact, was his means of growth in God.

Every leader must accept his first responsibility as a New Testament priest (I Peter 2:5,9), to offer up spiritual sacrifices of thanksgiving and praise to God (Hebrews 13:15). Out of this spiritual relationship with God, every leader grows into his or her ministry.

AS GROWING IN BALANCE

Samuel's growth into leadership was balanced. He grew in his relationship with God, and also with people. In this way, Samuel's spirit grew. Luke 2:40,52 describes this balanced growth process in Christ Himself: *"and the child grew, waxed strong in spirit, was filled with wisdom, and the grace of God was upon him...Jesus increased in wisdom and stature, and in favor with God and man."*

Similarly, every leader needs to develop relationship with God and with man. He cannot afford to go to either extreme. He must remember that after Jesus came down from hours of prayer with God on a mountain, He always came down into a valley to meet people's needs. In growing both with God and man, the leader will grow strong in spiritual wisdom and practical ministry.

AS A RIGHT-ON-TIME MINISTRY (I Samuel 3:1,3)

Before the full manifestation of Samuel's ministry, Israel was spiritually desperate. Her leadership was spiritually dead and blind, and the lack of spiritual vision in those days is represented in the words, *"and the lamp of God was nearly out in the temple."* Just before the lamp had extinguished in the temple, God called Samuel to his ministry. His ministry was right on time to help a desperate Israel. It is important to note that God called Samuel while he was asleep. Samuel was at complete rest and without striving when God called him to His work.

Every leader must realize that God knows exactly where he is, just as he knew Samuel. God will not fail to call a leader at the right time to lead His people. Samuel responded to God with an open and willing spirit, saying, *"Here I am, Lord."* Though he did not totally recognize the voice of God (3:7), God kept calling him. In fact, God had to call him four times before Samuel understood it was not Eli's voice calling to him!

Similarly, all leaders must learn to wait upon God for release of their ministry at the proper time. They will gradually learn to know the voice of the Spirit when He calls.

AS CONTINUING LOCAL MINISTRY ROUTINE EVEN AFTER A POWERFUL PROPHETIC WORD (I Samuel 3:11-15)

After Samuel understood God was calling him, the Lord gave him a tremendous prophetic word about the destruction of Eli's house. Even so, Samuel simply laid back down to sleep and rose in the morning to open the doors of the house of the Lord. He continued his everyday responsibilities, though God had just put a great call on his life. Samuel did not run presumptuously with his word from God. He waited patiently for God to bring it to pass. Samuel, God's anointed, had to wait for Eli to die just as David, Israel's next king, had to wait for king Saul to die. Neither

Samuel nor David was the cause of his leader's death. Each waited for God's right timing.

Similarly, each leader must wait for God to open the door for his ministry, though God may have given him a strong promise or a prophetic word. Even if called by God to replace a corrupt leader who is presently over him, God's leaders must wait for God's proper timing. Without waiting for God's right season, a leader will abort God's original and ultimate intentions. May every leader remember that in God's timing, "a man's gift makes room for him, and sets him before great men" (Proverbs 18:16).

AS A MINISTRY CONFIRMED BY GOD (I Samuel 3:19-21)

Samuel had a successful ministry because the Lord was with him to confirm it. God confirmed Samuel's prophetic ministry by not letting any of his quickened words fail (literally, "fall to the ground"). This demonstrated to all of Israel that Samuel was a true prophet of the Lord. The law of Moses had declared that a man was a true prophet only when his prophesies concerning the Lord came to pass. The Lord also confirmed Samuel by appearing in Shilo again, with a word for Samuel. Because God had His hand upon this young prophet, a place of former sin and fornication again received a visitation from the Lord.

Every leader must realize that if he has a true ministry from God, it will be confirmed by God and recognized by the people. Too many self-made leaders today are running with no divine or human confirmation of their ministries. For their own sake, for the Church's sake, and for God's sake, these unanointed and fruitless efforts should be stopped.

AS HAVING A WORD MINISTRY (I Samuel 3:21)

Through the word of the Lord coming to him, Samuel received a revelation, an unveiling, uncovering and appearing of God. The Hebrew word for "word" here is "dabar," which means a matter which is spoken of. This Hebrew word is comparable to the Greek word "rhema" which also denotes that which is spoken. "Rhema" can be contrasted with the Greek word "logos," because the latter means the expression of a reasoned thought embodying a concept or an idea. "Logos" refers more to the written Word of God in general. "Rhema" refers more to a specific portion of the Word given for the immediate, unique and personal use of the reader or hearer. The following list provides references in which the Greek word "rhema" is translated as "word":

John 3:34	*"For he whom God has sent speaks the words of God."*
Ephesians 6:17	*"The sword of the spirit which is the word of God."*
Acts 2:14	*"Peter said . . .'hearken to my words.'"*
Romans 10:8	*"The word is nigh thee . . . that is, the word of faith."*
Romans 10:17	*"So then, faith cometh by hearing, and hearing by the word of God."*
Jude 17	*"Remember the words which were spoken by the apostles"*

The point here is that Samuel had a word ministry--he received spoken, living, quickened and spiritual words and thoughts from God. In other words, he heard the voice of God speaking directly to him in his inner man.

In a second sense, Samuel had a word ministry because he declared the written law of the Lord, in authority over man's imaginations. Samuel was a man of God who believed, preached and practiced the law or word of God. (See also Deuteronomy 8:3; Psalm 33:4,6 and 56:4,10 and 138:2; John 1:1; Hebrews 4:12; I Peter 1:25; I John 5:7; Revelation 19:13).

Similarly, every leader should develop a word ministry. He should be able to receive a specific, quickened word from the Lord. He should base all of his teaching and preaching on the Bible.

In this way, God will bless his ministry and make it fruitful to His people.

AS MAKING PRIESTLY INTERCESSIONS FOR ISRAEL (I Samuel 7:1-14)

The presence of the Lord in the ark of the covenant had left Israel, and been captured by the Philistines, because of Israel's idolatry. Samuel recognized this. He therefore exhorted Israel that if she would forsake her idols and return wholeheartedly to the Lord, the Lord would defeat the Philistines for her. With Israel initially responding positively to this request, Samuel interceded for Israel and sacrificed a burnt offering for their sins. God heard Samuel's prayer, and sent a thunder storm to confuse the Philistine troops and lead to their defeat. Through Samuel's intercessory prayer, victorious Israel raised a new border-stone between Mizpeh ("watchtower") and Shen, and named the stone Ebenezer ("the stone of help").

Similarly, each of God's leaders must so feel the burden of the Church's sins in this day that he goes to his knees in intercessory prayer seeking God's hand of mercy. Every leader must be convinced of the efficacy of true, Spirit-led intercessory prayer for the Church's victories over her enemies.

AS JUDGING ISRAEL AND RAISING UP SACRIFICE (I Samuel 7:15-17)

Samuel was consistent and faithful in his walk with God and his ministry as a prophet and judge. He *"judged Israel all the days of his life"* (v. 15). After Samuel would complete his circuit as a judge in Bethel, Gilgal and Mizpeh, he would return to his hometown, Ramah. When he reached Ramah, he would build an altar to the Lord, thus maintaining his relationship with God.

Similarly, every leader of God should be forever faithful to the calling that he has received from the Lord. Moreover, he should continue to feed all of the people that the Lord has put in his charge, whether in his hometown or elsewhere. Along with meeting the people's needs, he must maintain a close relationship with his God.

AS PATIENTLY ENDURING ISRAEL'S REBELLION (I Samuel 8:6-11)

Because Samuel's own sinful sons could not succeed him as leaders over the nation, the elders of Israel asked Samuel to appoint a king over them. The Lord told Samuel to do as the elders had requested, even though their request directly rejected God as their king. Consequently, Samuel appointed Saul as Israel's first king, but anointed him with a vial, a man-made instrument, instead of a ram's horn. In this, Samuel showed that the source of Saul's appointment as king was human and not divine. Through this entire period, Samuel showed tremendous patience toward his people Israel.

Similarly, every leader in the Church should have patience and gentleness to his people, even though they may stray from the perfect will of God. A leader must realize that he also has strayed at times from the will of God. He must have compassion on his people when they do the same. This is not to condone anyone's sinful behavior, but simply to help the leader know what attitude to take when his people sin against the Lord. The Church is people, and people are going to make mistakes. With a patient yet firm attitude, a leader can restore his people back to God, and can even prevent them from falling again.

AS MAINTAINING A GOOD REPUTATION THROUGHOUT HIS MINISTRY (I Samuel 12:1-5)

In this chapter, Samuel summarized the course of his years of ministry to Israel. It was obvious to all that he was a man of blameless character. No man could say that Samuel had stolen another man's ox or ass, defrauded anyone, oppressed a man, or taken any bribes to blind his spiritual vision. His character was above reproach.

Every leader should be a man of good reputation, both to those in the Church and to those on the outside (see also I Timothy 3:1-7; Titus 1:6-9). Every leader should also be concerned that he is free of guilt from thievery, defrauding, oppression and bribery--all sins which go beyond financial to spiritual values as well. When a leader reaches the end of his ministry, may he be able to look back and say with Samuel, *"I have walked before you from my youth even to this day"* (v. 2).

AS TRULY ADMONISHING THE PEOPLE (I Samuel 12:6-25)

Samuel truly admonished the people by recalling the ways in which they had brought the judgment of God upon themselves. He did this, however, in a merciful way. When the people asked Samuel to pray for them, he mercifully replied, *"Do not fear . . . for the Lord will not abandon his people on account of his great name, because the Lord has been pleased to make you a people for himself"* (vs. 20,22). Samuel was not only full of understanding and mercy, he was also a leader who prayed for and taught his people (v. 23).

Similarly, every leader must have a merciful heart toward his people. He must not escape from the reality of facing his people with their problems by saying, "I am just going to pray about it." Neither must he think that his ministry of preaching and teaching will meet all of his people's needs, that his prayers are not necessary. A good leader will both teach and pray for his people. He realizes that they need instruction from the Word of God, and also need God's grace to do what they hear.

AS BOLDLY SPEAKING THE TRUTH IN LOVE (I Samuel 13-15)

Samuel was a man of truth and the Word of God. When people disobeyed God's law, he became righteously indignant. In these chapters, Samuel had the forthrightness to prophesy king Saul's destruction. He also openly rebuked the king for usurping the office of a priest by refusing to wait for Samuel, and presumptuously offering a sacrifice to God himself. But even though Samuel saw God's judgment upon Saul, he recognized that God's word must still be obeyed. Thus, on another occasion, he finished the job that Saul should have done, and himself killed the captured Amalekite king Agag (15:32,33).

Similarly, every leader must have a Holy Ghost boldness to speak forth the high standard of the Word of the Lord, no matter who opposes him. Too, the leader must realize that God's work is more important than the workman He uses to accomplish it. Therefore, every leader assuredly should perform what must be done, even if others leave it undone. All of God's enemies must be destroyed.

AS LEARNING GOD'S MASTERY OF EVENTS (I Samuel 16:1)

The Lord had to rebuke Samuel for mourning too deeply and too long over Saul's death. Samuel had to learn how to accept God's decisions and judgments realistically. He also had to learn that God had plenty of anointing oil for the leaders that He desired to equip and use. God still was going to anoint and use David as Israel's king.

Similarly, every leader must learn to accept God's final judgments as righteous and good, without letting his own personal emotions control him. Many leaders need to learn that God's purposes are never ultimately thwarted by the death of any one of His leaders. God always has more men that He can prepare, and more oil with which to anoint them.

AS LEARNING TRUE SPIRITUAL DISCERNMENT (I Samuel 16:7-13)

By this time, Samuel was indeed advanced in years. As he looked at Jesse's sons, he thought that Eliab, the first-born, was surely God's next anointed king for Israel. But Samuel was wrong. God had to tell Samuel not to judge by the outward appearance of physical stature, but to judge by the heart. Samuel had to learn how to judge spiritually and not carnally. When he looked upon the heart and heard the voice of God confirm David as His choice, the prophet anointed this youngest of Jesse's sons as the next king of Israel.

Similarly, no matter how many years a leader walks with God, he still must learn spiritual discernment in all of his decisions. A leader depends upon God's revelation and anointing all of his life. A leader will be surrounded by people who base their judgments on the external. The leader must learn how to judge by the internal, and by the Holy Spirit. The greater a leader's depth in the Word of God and prayer, the greater will be his ability to judge righteously.

God's Preparation in Your Own Life

If God has called you to a ministry, He has already begun to prepare you. It does not matter if He calls you to a governmental ministry, or a congregational ministry, He has already begun to prepare you for your work. Sometimes it can be very hard to see that, however.

Do you have a strong desire to help the Body of Christ experience victory in an area of weakness or defeat? That may be evidence of God's calling and preparation, so pray about it.

Have you already tried to serve the Body of Christ, but had an apparent failure? Only God can determine what is a "failure," and even if you have truly failed, it does not mean that you are disqualified from the call of God. God's preparation is a lifetime process, and He may place you in a leadership role no matter what your age.

Are you called to be a leader? That question must be answered before you try to determine your level of preparation. The principles in this chapter and the next can help you look over your own life, take inventory of God's preparation, and look forward to more refinements as you become one of God's leaders.

CHAPTER 10
PREPARATION PRINCIPLES: ELISHA, DAVID, TIMOTHY

In the last chapter, we took a look at the entire lifetime of leadership preparation that Joshua and Samuel underwent. In this chapter, we will focus on selected principles of leadership preparation at work in the lives of Elisha, David and Timothy.

These men are excellent examples of leadership preparation to us today. We can admire them, and take encouragement in God's work in their lives. The same God who worked mightily through them is alive and ready to do similar works in our own lives. And just as with our example leaders, we also must come under the preparing hand of God, and submit to Him and His principles of preparation.

The Preparation of Elisha

Elisha, a ninth century B.C. prophet of the northern kingdom of Israel, was the disciple and successor of the prophet Elijah. Let us look at the principles of leadership preparation for Elisha, whose ministry included many remarkable miracles that displayed both the power and mercy of God.

God took Elisha through the developmental training and tests that He uses for many of His servants. Elisha underwent the working of several spiritual principles of leadership preparation. This happened between the time when he first touched Elijah's prophetic mantle (I Kings 19:19,20), and the time that he actually received the mantle and a double portion of Elijah's spirit (II Kings 2:13). As with other biblical men of God, Elisha had to experience a time of delay which demanded much perseverance. This period of patience can be diagrammed as follows:

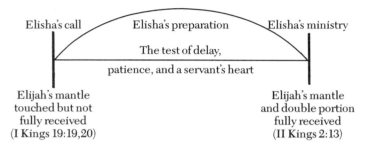

Elisha's call   Elisha's preparation   Elisha's ministry

The test of delay,

patience, and a servant's heart

Elijah's mantle   Elijah's mantle
touched but not   and double portion
fully received   fully received
(I Kings 19:19,20)   (II Kings 2:13)

Between the time of Elisha's call and the time of his ministry, we can see many principles of leadership development. We will follow the events in Elisha's life, and the spiritual principles involved, in two parallel columns.

ELISHA'S CALL

1. Elisha's name means "God is salvation" (I Kings 19:16).

2. Elisha was the son of Shaphat ("a judge") of Abel-meholah ("dancing meadow") (I Kings 19:16).

3. Elisha was anointed by God to be the prophet in Elijah's place (I Kings 19:16).

4. Elisha was used to slay with the sword all that would escape from Jehu's sword (I Kings 19:17).

5. Elijah found Elisha plowing in the field behind twelve other workmen, each with a yoke of oxen, showing that he probably came from a wealthy family (I Kings 19:19).

6. Elisha touched Elijah's mantle before he entered into the full spiritual ministry and function which it symbolized (I Kings 19:19).

ELISHA'S PREPARATION

7. Elijah cast his mantle (a robe used for an upper or outer garment) upon Elisha, symbolizing that he would now receive the personality and rights of a prophet (the hair-shirt mantle was an official part of a prophet's garments; see Ruth 3:9 and II Kings 1:8 and Zechariah 13:4).

8. Called by Elijah, Elisha made a normal request, "Let me first kiss my father and mother" (I Kings 19:20).

LEADERSHIP PRINCIPLE

1. A leader's ministry must be founded upon a spiritual salvation experience with Jesus wherein he can sincerely declare, "Jesus Christ is my salvation!"

2. A leader's ministry must be characterized by a balance of proper judgment and joy.

3. A leader must know the specific ministry and place God is calling him toward, before he can be prepared for that ministry.

4. A leader's ministry must be able to slay his spiritual enemies through the sword of God's Word, even before he enter's formal, positional ministry.

5. A leader must have a servant's heart and not mind doing menial tasks, following the leadership of others and sacrificing his wealth to answer the call to ministry.

6. A leader must patiently wait for God's perfect timing for the full release of his ministry, even if he has already experienced some of what God will do through him in the future.

LEADERSHIP PRINCIPLE

7. A leader must take upon himself the mantle or yoke of Jesus, which means that he will be confirmed into His personality and thus be able to function with some of his divine rights.

8. Though called to minister, a leader must still keep a special respect for the parents which God has given to him. Many times, the way a young

9. Elijah's response to Elisha's request seems to have the meaning, "Go ahead. Have I done anything to stop you?" (I Kings 19:20).

10. Elisha returned, slew some oxen, burned them with his farming equipment as fuel, and had a sacrificial feast with them, all to demonstrate to his family and friends his renunciation of his former life style for his new calling with Elijah (I Kings 19:21; see also I Samuel 6:15; II Samuel 24:22,23).

11. After his sacrificial meal, Elisha arose and became just another one of Elijah's servants (I Kings 18:43,44). Later, Elisha had a servant of his own (II Kings 2:1).

12. As a good student, Elisha went with his teacher Elijah to Gilgal, when it was time for Elijah to be taken away (II Kings 2:1).

13. Elisha persistently followed his master Elijah from place to place, until he saw Elijah taken away from him--even though Elijah kept encouraging him to stay behind. Note the key phrase here that characterized Elisha's identification with Elijah: "So the two of them" (II Kings 2:6,7,8,11). An interesting study of the place names where these interactions happened: Gilgal means "rolling," Bethel is "house of God," Jericho is "place of fragrance," and the Jordan means "to go low."

14. Elijah asked Elisha to ask of him whatever he wanted before he was taken up (II Kings 2:9).

15. Elisha asked Elijah for a double portion of his spirit (II Kings 2:9); similar to the eldest son in an Israelite family receiving a double share of his father's inheritance.

16. Elijah told Elisha that giving him a double portion of his spirit was a very difficult thing, but that if he saw him when he was taken up, then it would be his (II King 2:10).

17. When Elijah was taken up, Elisha tore his clothes in two and cried, "My father, my father, the chariot of Israel and its horsemen" (II Kings 2:12). In this, Elisha was saying that the presence

leader treats his parents represents the way he will treat the people. Yet over and above all, a leader must follow God's call.

9. Although the Holy Spirit will eventually bring men to a leader for training, the leader must never hinder those called to the ministry from fulfilling God's commandment, "Thou shalt honor thy father and thy mother."

10. A leader must make known to his family and friends, in very practical and obvious ways, that he is sacrificing his old life-style to be a slave of Jesus Christ. If a man is afraid to openly witness for the Lord before he is formally "employed" by the Church, he will not be much of a soul-winner afterwards.

11. A leader must never be too proud to be just one of the many common helpers in the local church. If he can humbly fulfill this role, he may eventually receive the same help from others in his own ministry.

12. A leader must be a good student of different teachers in the ministry. A leader must have a teachable spirit and be committed to those who are over him.

13. A leader must show his teachers that he is persistent to learn more of God and His Word, and that he is willing to take up his mantle of leadership from the Lord.

14. A leader must realize that as he is humble and obedient to God, the Lord will purify his heart so that he can make a trustworthy response to the question, "What would you like from me now?"

15. A leader must realize that if he asks humbly, he can ask great things of God for his ministry and for his generation.

16. A leader must realize that in asking things of the Lord, the Lord will sometimes first require spiritual conditions of obedience, relevation or spiritual insight.

of Elijah's spiritual strength was of more value to
Israel's defense than all of her chariots. Later, this
same expression would be used of Elisha by the
king of Israel (II Kings 13:14). (Note that in
referring to Elijah as his father, Elisha was
following the father-son/teacher-student tradition
in the book of Proverbs.)

All of these experiences helped to prepare Elisha for his double portion ministry, which will
be studied in chapter 17, under "The Function of Ministry in Elisha the Prophet."

May every leader trust God to use every experience through which he is now going to prepare
him for his future work.

The Preparation of David

David, the youngest son of Jesse of the tribe of Judah, was the second king of Israel and one
of the most important Old Testament characters. The Bible refers to David more than 1,200 times,
and many times the Lord Jesus Christ was called "the Son of David." David stands as one of the
greatest kings that ever reigned over Israel, the meaning of his name signifying his intimate
relationship with the Lord: "beloved."

David's life can be divided into three main periods: David as shepherd, David as fugitive,
David as king. In the early years of David's life, when he tended his father's sheep as a shepherd,
he was under a time of preparation. In the following thirteen to fourteen years, David was rejected,
and was a fugitive from the hand of king Saul. In his latter years, David was in his time of
exaltation, reigning as king over Israel during some of her most glorious years.

These three periods of time in David's life make a very significant study for every leader. Many
if not most of God's leaders experience similar periods in their lives and ministries. Each one
of these periods in David's life offers the leader many valuable spiritual principles from which
he can learn many things about the dealings of God in his life. David's experiences are prophetic
and typical of the different encounters that all of God's leaders may come to know. All leaders
should diligently apply the principles of this section to their own lives. Nothing is more defiling
to God's kingdom than the deep bitterness in the heart of a leader who believes that God has
misused him or abused him, because he misunderstood God's dealings through a time of rejection.

We can scripturally diagram David's life as follows:

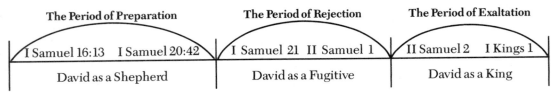

The Period of Preparation	The Period of Rejection	The Period of Exaltation
I Samuel 16:13 I Samuel 20:42	I Samuel 21 II Samuel 1	II Samuel 2 I Kings 1
David as a Shepherd	David as a Fugitive	David as a King

Spiritual Principles of Leadership

We will outline the main points from each of these sections of David's life and then draw some
spiritual principles from them. The astute reader will notice that each one of the following points
from the life of David applies in some way to the life of every leader.

THE STAGES OF DAVID'S LIFE

Preparation

As a shepherd, David's first anointing in the midst of his brethren (I Samuel 16:13).

A skillful harp player (v. 18).

A mighty and valiant man (v. 18).

Considered by others to be a man of war (v. 18).

Shows the character qualities of wisdom and prudence (v. 18).

A comely young man with handsome appearance (v. 18).

Has the favor of the Lord in all of his doings, because David loves Him with all of his heart (v. 18).

Becomes the servant (or armor-bearer) of king Saul (vs. 21,22).

Finds favor in the eyes of Saul (vs. 21,22).

Becomes Saul's court musician (v. 23).

Functions as a shepherd boy at the same time (17:20).

Proves himself to be responsible, brave and testifying by killing both a bear and a lion (vs. 34,35).

Shows the character quality of humility in recognizing his own personal limitations (vs. 38,39).

Demonstrates that he has learned from his past experiences, for he used what he had already learned to do (v. 40).

Manifests his respect for God and His people, and his trust in the name of the Lord, by killing Goliath (vs. 45-51).

Evidences that he can develop intimate spiritual relationships with people (with Jonathan 18:1-3,19,20).

Exhibits an ability to enter into a committed, covenant relationship with others, in his covenant with Jonathan (vs. 1-3,19,20).

Behaves himself so wisely that he is put in command over all of the men of war (v. 5).

Gains a reputation among the people for his mighty exploits, even above the exploits of the one whom he serves (vs. 6-9).

Survives the fierce anger of the one over him in authority, Saul, even to the point of dodging javelins (vs. 6-9,11).

David flees for his life since king Saul continues to threaten his life (19:1,2).

David flees from Saul to the anointed prophet Samuel, who had previously anointed David with oil out of Samuel's horn (v. 18).

Is forced to leave Jonathan and begin his life as a fugitive (20:41-42).

Rejection

Goes to Nod ("wandering"), eats the showbread, and takes Goliath's sword (I Samuel 21), the trophy of former victories.

Travels to Gath ("wine-press") where he must feign insanity to escape (v. 13).

Arrives at the cave Adullum ("a testimony to them") where all of those who are discontented, distressed or in debt come to him (22:1-4).

Goes to Moab ("from father: what father?") from which a prophet tells him to leave (v. 5).

Journeys into the wilderness of Judah ("praise" or "he shall be praised") where he writes Psalm 63 (v. 5).

Goes to Keilah ("let the faint be alienated") where he smites a Philistine ("wallowing") and inquires of the Lord at the ephod through Abiathar ("father of abundance" or "father of a remnant"), the priest (23:1-4).

Travels to the wilderness of Ziph ("melting") where Jonathan ("Jehovah is giver") comes to strengthen him, and they both renew their covenant together (v. 16).

Arrives at the wilderness of Maon ("habitation") where Saul almost kills him (vs. 24-26).

Comes to the wilderness of Engedi ("fountain of the kid") where David cuts off a piece of Saul's garment, and Saul ("requested") repents and goes home (24:1).

Journeys to the wilderness of Paran ("their beautifying"), Samuel ("his name is of God") dies, and David takes wives: Abigail ("mother of joy") and Ahinoam ("sister of pleasantness") (25:1).

David again goes to the wilderness of Ziph ("melting") where Abishai ("father of gift") desires to kill Saul but, instead, David takes the king's spear and cruse. Saul repents and again returns home (26:1ff).

Returns to Gath ("a wine press") and is very discouraged, though Saul seeks him no more (27:1-7).

Receives the city of Ziklag ("enveloped in grief") as a possession from the Philistines ("wallowing") with whom he stays for sixteen months, during which he raids the Geshurites ("proud beholders"), Gezrites ("the cutters off"), and the Amalekites ("the people of lapping or licking up") (vs. 3-12).

Saul goes to the witch at Endor ("fountain of the dwelling") and conjures up Samuel's ("his name is of God") spirit from the dead (28:8ff).

Denied permission to go to war with the Philistines ("wallowing") and therefore returns to Ziklag ("enveloped in grief") (29:1-11).

Pursues the Amalekites ("the people of lapping or licking up") who spoiled Ziklag ("enveloped in grief"); distressed because the people desire to stone him, but encouraged in the Lord and inquires at the ephod through the priest Abiathar ("father of abundance" or "father of a remnant") (30:1ff).

Saul and his sons are killed (31:6).

Orders execution of the Amalekite ("the people licking up") who apparently gave Saul his final death blow, then mourns Saul's death with a song of lamentation (II Samuel 1:1-12).

Exaltation

Anointed for the second time as king over Judah (II Samuel 2:1-4).

David's house grows stronger, and Saul's house weakens (3:1ff; I Chronicles 3:1-3).

Has six sons in Hebron ("communion"): Amnon ("faithful"), Chileab ("sustained of father"), Absalom ("father"), Adonijah ("Lord worshipper"), Shephatiah ("judge of Jehovah"), and Ithream ("excellence of people") (3:2-5).

At 30 years of age, anointed for the third time as king over all of Israel after 7.5 years (5:1ff) and reigns for 33 years.

Takes Zion as his own city (5:7).

Brings back the ark to Zion and sets up the tabernacle of David (6:2).

Receives the Davidic covenant from God (7:1ff).

Commits adultery with Bathsheba, has her husband Uriah killed, receives God's rebuke through Nathan the prophet (11:2-12:14) and writes Psalms 51 and 52.

Flees from Jerusalem at the rebellion of his son, Absalom (15:14).

David dies and his son, Solomon, rules (I Kings 2:12).

SPIRITUAL PRINCIPLES IN DAVID'S LIFE

Many spiritual principles and character qualities for Christian leaders become apparent through the basic facts of David's preparation, rejection and exaltation. Some of the most significant of these principles are the following:

David applied his past experience of killing the lion and the bear to his present problem of Goliath (I Samuel 17:34-36). Every leader must also learn to apply what he has learned from his own experiences to his present challenges and dilemmas.

David did not trust in Saul's armor to bring him the victory over Goliath (vs. 38,39). Every leader must not trust in the ability of the flesh or a religious system, but in the power of the Holy Spirit, to bring victories in his life.

David used a defense he had used effectively in the past to kill Goliath (a sling with five smooth stones, v. 40). So must every leader trust God to use the training he already has in his ministry. In doing so, however, a leader must also recognize the limitations of his ministry and gift.

David came to Goliath in the name of the Lord (v. 45). So must every leader use the name of the Lord Jesus Christ against the power of the devil.

David confessed confidence that he would defeat Goliath (v. 46). So must every leader make the positive confession that he will win total spiritual victory, through the finished work of Jesus Christ.

David doubled the required dowry of 100 Philistine foreskins to marry the princess Michal (he brought in 200, 18:25-27). So must every leader strive to do more than the Lord requires of him.

David remained faithful to his charge of commanding Saul's army, even in the midst of Saul seeking to kill him (19:1,2,8-10). So should every leader remain faithful to the call and ministry which God has given him, even in the face of trials and tribulations.

David kept company with godly people like Samuel (v. 18). Even so should every leader fellowship often with godly Christians and good spriitual leaders in the Body of Christ.

David kept the Lord his God in the midst of his relationships (e.g., with Jonathan, 20:42). So must every leader keep Jesus Christ in the center of all his friendships and associations, recognizing that the devil desires to cause mixture and compromise in his life by keeping him in the company of fools.

David did not show respect of persons in whom he allowed to become a part of his army in the cave of Adullam (22:2). Even so must every leader treat all people equally in the sight of God, and not favor the rich or educated over the poor or uneducated.

David honored his parents by asking the king of Moab to house them comfortably in his palace while David sought the Lord in the cave at Adullam (v. 3). So must every leader honor and think of the needs of his parents, no matter his age or other responsibilities.

David took courage in the Lord when his followers wanted to kill him (30:6). So every leader must gain his strength and joy directly from the Lord at all times. Otherwise he will become discouraged when a different source of strength and joy is taken away from him. (This applies even when a leader's ministry and function is temporarily removed from him. From where does a leader obtain his strength and joy--from Jesus, or from his ministry?)

GODLY QUALITIES IN DAVID'S LIFE

These godly character qualities in David's life made it possible for him to endure preparation, survive rejection, and flourish during exaltation. They will do the same for today's Christian leaders. They are:

Purity (I Samuel 16:7)
Faithfulness (v. 16:11 and 17:26 and 30:11-25)
Responsibility (17:20)
Humility (16:11d and 17:38-39)
Serving (16:11d)
Prudence (16:18e)
Skillfulness (16:18)
Discipline (16:18d,e)
Strength (16:18c)
Boldness (17:32)
Love (18:1)
Commitment (18:2,3)
Graciousness (18:3,4)
Wisdom (18:5,14,15,30)
Respect (18:11 and 22:3,4 and 24:1-6)
Diligence (18:25-27)
Compassion (22:1,2)
Honesty (30:23,24)

David was a godly man of passion who fiercely loved the Lord, and sought Him with intensity. Some of the events and the sins in his life hardly deserve praise. Yet the Bible puts David forth as one of the ultimate examples to all believers, calling him "a man after God's heart." May every leader follow his example. May every leader become an example to the people of God in seeking the Lord with intensity.

The Preparation of Timothy

Timothy takes on special significance because he functioned in team ministry and in a special personal relationship with the apostle Paul.

Timothy had a godly heritage. His mother was a Jewish Christian, his father an unbelieving Greek (Acts 16:1). Along with his Christian mother Eunice, his grandmother Lois (II Timothy 1:5) added to his spiritual background and his knowledge of Scripture from the time of his youth (3:15)

It is not surprising that a believing mother would give her son a name with two positive meanings. First, in relationship to God, Timothy means "one who honors and worships God." Second in God's relationship to him, Timothy means "honored and valued of God." Timothy, moreover, was a man who lived up to the meaning of his name; he both loved God, and was loved by Him. Similarly, every leader should know the cultural and spiritual meaning of his own name, and see how it applies to what God wants to do in and through him and his ministry.

Though Timothy's father was an unbelieving Greek, Timothy still grew up to believe in the Lord Jesus. The many spiritual maladies his father may potentially have had (idol worship, intellectualism, immorality) did little to detract from Timothy's growth in the fear of the Lord which his mother taught him. It is possible that Timothy's Greek father had some significant role in preventing Timothy's circumcision as an infant. And Timothy was raised in the typically heathenistic city of Lystra (Acts 16:1). None of these things stopped him from being called and used of God. Every leader must resist family background or any other environmental factor that would hinder his service to the Lord, as did both Timothy and Samuel.

Timothy's Relationship with the Apostle Paul

Timothy's special and close relationship with Paul are described in some detail in two New Testament letters. Timothy had a good reputation even as a child, and was well-versed in Scripture (II Timothy 3:15). As an older man, he enjoyed "a good report" among the brethren (Acts 16:2).

A Godly Reputation

To Paul, a godly reputation was an important character quality in Timothy. Paul may have specifically desired a man of good repute among Christians and Christian leaders to accompany him on apostolic journeys (Acts 16:3-5 and 18:5 and 19:22 and 20:4). This principle also applied to every Christian leader today. Every man of God should have confidence in his good reputation among Christians and Christian leaders.

Like Father and Son

Paul considered Timothy to be his own dear son in the faith. For this reason, these two men shared a deep relationship and commitment to the Lord, to one another, and to their ministries. Scripture gives several references concerning Paul's choice of Timothy for the ministry of the gospel (Acts 16:3 and 17:14,15 and 18:5 and 20:4; I Corinthians 4:17; I Timothy 1:2; II Timothy 1:2).

One of the richest experiences in life and ministry is a shared spiritual relationship with the brethren. Times of sharing wisdom, prayer, insights and experiences greatly enrich a leader's life in the ministry. Such friendships should be greatly prized by every Christian leader. Neither should a Christian leader become so busy that he forsakes all of his close friends.

Timothy's Ordination by Paul

Paul ordained Timothy into the ministry not for the sake of his deep spiritual unity with Timothy but because of God's calling on Timothy (I Timothy 4:14; II Timothy 1:6,7). How this ordination took place, we do not know. We only know that Paul laid his hands on Timothy and imparted to him some of his own spiritual gift (I Timothy 4:14).

Needless to say, Timothy's ministry and anointing did not come exclusively from the hands of the apostle Paul, but from God. Neither did his rite of ordination give him all of his spiritual ministry. Anointing and ability first came from God--and Paul only confirmed it. This pattern should happen for every man or woman called by God and ordained to His service.

Shared Sufferings of Timothy and Paul

Along with great apostolic confirmation and blessing, however, Timothy also received apostolic rejection and persecution. Paul recognized that Timothy had intimately shared in the persecutions that his father in the faith had received. Thus he gave him appropriate recognition along with exhortations:

"But thou hast fully known my doctrine, manner of life, purpose, faith, longsuffering, charity, patience, persecutions, afflictions, which came unto me at Antioch, at Iconium, at Lystra; what persecutions I endured. Yea, and all that will live godly in Christ Jesus shall suffer persecution. But evil men and seducers shall wax worse and worse, deceiving and being deceived. But continue thou in the things which thou hast learned and hast been assured of, knowing of whom thou hast learned them" (II Timothy 3:10-14).

The following account of a persecution of Paul and Silas, and their rescue by divine visitation, may represent the kind of persecution which Timothy also suffered with Paul:

> *"Now when they had gone throughout Phrygia and the region of Galatia, and were forbidden of the Holy Ghost to preach the word in Asia, after they wre come to Mysia, they assayed to go into Bithynia: but the Spirit suffered them not. And they, passing by Mysia, came down to Troas, and a vision appeared to Paul in the night. There stood a man of Macedonia, and prayed him, saying, 'Come over into Macedonia, and help us.' And after he had seen the vision, immediately we endeavoured to go into Macedonia, assuredly gathering that the Lord had called us for to preach the gospel unto them . . . . And it came to pass, as we went to prayer, a certain damsel possessed with a spirit of divination met us, and cried, saying, 'These men are the servants of the most high God, which show unto us the way of salvation.' And this did she many days. But Paul, being grieved, turned and said to the spirit, 'I command thee in the name of Jesus Christ to come out of her.' And he came out the same hour. And when her masters saw that the hope of their gains was gone, they caught Paul and Silas, and threw them into the market place unto the rulers, and brought them to the magistrates, saying, 'These men, being Jews, do exceedingly trouble our city, and teach customs which are not lawful for us to receive, neither to observe, being Romans.' And the multitude rose up together against them: and the magistrates rent off their clothes, and commanded to beat them. And when they had laid many stripes upon them, they cast them into prison, charging the jailor to keep them safely . . ."* (Acts 16:6-10,23; see also I Corinthians 16:10; II Corinthians 1:1,19).

With Timothy probably experiencing similar situations, we can understand why Paul would tell him, *"Therefore do not be ashamed of the testimony of our Lord, or of me his prisoner; but join with me in suffering for the gospel"* (II Timothy 1:8).

Timothy's Ministry Responsibilities

We can also understand why Paul had to give him a direct command from the Lord regarding his specific calling in God (I Timothy 1:3,18 and 5:7,16,17 and 6:13,17). Paul gave this somewhat timid man (II Timothy 1:7) a general exhortation of duty to Jesus Christ. Paul also laid out very explicit teaching on certain areas: sound doctrine (I Timothy 1), public worship (chapter 2), church offices (chapter 3), false teachers (chapter 4), the church congregation (chapter 5) and the minister himself (chapter 6). Each of these sections contains valuable material for the minister of the gospel to study in fulfilling his work.

Timothy's Character

Paul also chose Timothy because of his godly character. Paul realized that strong character would be required to withstand the onslaught of many trials, persecutions and temptations that come against apostolic team ministry. The apostle knew that gifts and abilities alone could not ensure lasting success in ministry.

Timothy demonstrated many character qualities which every leader should also attempt to develop. Some of these characteristics of the heart are:

A Teachable Spirit

Paul told Timothy to *"continue in the things which you have learned"* (II Timothy 3:14). Timothy had a teachable heart that made him open for truth and instruction.

A Kindred Spirit

Paul told the Philippian Christians about Timothy, *"I have no one else of kindred spirit"* (Philippians 2:20a). Timothy had one spirit and purpose with Paul. Because of this unity of heart and intention in the gospel, Paul had confidence in sending Timothy to help these Christians.

A Sincere Spirit
Paul also told the Philippians that Timothy would be genuinely concerned for their welfare (Philippians 2:20b). There was no sham or put-on to Timothy's life. He cared sincerely and truthfully for the people of God. He was not out to take advantage of them.

A Caring Spirit
Paul told the church at Philippi that Timothy would be concerned for their welfare (Philippians 2:20b). Timothy really cared for God's people. He had a real compassion and understanding of their needs.

A Servant Spirit
Paul was confident in sending this young man to the Philipian Church because he did not selfishly seek his own interests, but rather the interests of Jesus Christ (Philippians 2:21,22). He knew God's values and priorities in life, and he wanted to impart them to God's people.

A Faithful Spirit
Timothy faithfully served wtih Paul in the furtherance of the gospel (Philippians 2:22). Timothy was faithful and loyal to the gospel as well as to Paul. It was because of this faithfulness that Paul knew that he could depend upon him.

A Proven Spirit
Timothy did not have it easy in the ministry. He had endured tests, trials, temptations and persecutions. Thus Paul could say, *"But you know of his proven worth . . . in the gospel"* (Philippians 2:22). God tested and tried Timothy's heart and spirit so that he could be a man in whom Paul could trust (see also I Corinthians 4:17; I Thessalonians 3:2).

A Submissive Spirit
Timothy had a submissive and obedient attitude toward the Lord and toward Paul. Paul could say that he was *"like a child serving his father"* (Philippians 2:22c). Such a father-son relationship speaks not only of a teacher-student relationship, it also speaks of a willingness, loyalty, humility, and submissiveness to serve and obey an older ministry (see also Acts 16:1-3).

Paul could trust Timothy in the ministry, because he had seen these qualities in Timothy's life. Similarly, every leader should allow the Lord to so change his heart and spirit that he, too, would exemplify the same qualities. The leader is encouraged to develop even more of Timothy's character qualities from II Timothy 2, in which Timothy is figuratively described in the following terms: son, teacher, soldier, athlete, farmer, workman, vessel, man, seeker and servant.

Timothy's Ministry
Timothy did not only portray godly character qualities. He was also actively involved in the work and service of the Lord. God developed his character before he was actively serving, but also while Timothy was constructively engaged in labor for Christ and the Church. In what kind of labor, however, was Timothy involved? Timothy was working for the Lord in the following areas:

Establishing churches (I Thessalonians 3:2)
Comforting churches (I Thessalonians 3:2)
Teaching doctrine (ITimothy 1:3)
Exhorting Christians (I Timothy 4:13)

Notice that Timothy was very involved with ministering to local churches. He realized that as he helped to build up Christ's Church, she would go out into the world and win souls for God's kingdom. This is not to say, however, that this young apostle was not also involved in ministering the gospel to lost souls, but it is to say that he spent much of his time ministering directly to God's epeople. Timothy's exhortations most probably centered around the Christine doctrines that Paul so faithfully admonished him to keep and to teach.

To apply this to today, every leader must ask himself how well he is establishing the people of God in the sound Christian doctrines of the Word of God. Establishing the people in the Word of God through sound Bible teaching by Christian leaders is what the Church must have if she is to go out from local churches to reach their world for Jesus Christ.

Paul's Good Example to Timothy

Paul set a good example of Christian ministry for Timothy. This illustrates to all elder ministries their responsibility to set an exemplary life-style for younger men of God. Paul told Timothy about his illustrative life in the following words of II Timothy 3:10,11a,

> *"But you, my son, have followed step by step my teaching and my manner of life, my resolution, my faith, patience and spirit of love, and my fortitude under persecutions and sufferings"* (The New English Bible)

> *"But you have been a faithful follower of mine in every respect: in doctrine, in your whole life and endeavor, in faith, and patience, in love, and constancy, in persecutions and sufferings"* (Greber translation)

Paul did not command Timothy to walk a path that he himself had not walked.

Let us look a little more closely at some of the key words in the previously quoted verses. When Paul told Timothy that he had "known" of the apostles' ways, he meant two things. He meant that Timothy had been able to approve of them through observation, and that Timothy had taken a delight in them through experiencing them himself. In the same way, elder ministries should have such a patterned life that younger ministries may view them transparently, and desire to live the same way themselves.

This desire of young ministries to follow older ministries applies to the kind of Christian instruction or information which they teach. It affects their manner of conduct, how patiently and cheerfully they endure the pressures of rejection and contradiction. It also applies to three other main areas of their lives: purpose, faith and love.

Paul declared that Timothy had observed and experienced his "purpose." He meant that Timothy had seen his obvious and definite proposal and intention in in his service to the gospel of Christ. Paul's purpose in his ministry held nothing secret, confusing or insincere. He knew who he was and where he was going. He did not hesitate to share these intentions with Timothy.

Paul also declared that Timothy had observed and experienced his "faith." He was referring to his firm persuasion and continued conviction in Jesus Christ as Savior and Lord, as seen through his life and actions. Paul's persuasion concerning Jesus did not wane as the years went on. His conviction grew stronger as his life proceeded. Because Timothy and others could see such a faith in Paul's words and actions, Paul could ask them to follow him as he followed Christ.

Finally, Paul expressed to Timothy that the young man of God had observed his "love." He was referring to his deep affection and benevolence for Christ and the Church. The word for love here is "agape," which is the kind of divine, self-sacrificing love that Jesus Himself demonstrated on the cross for the Church.

By imitating Paul's life of obvious intention, firm conviction and sacrificial love, every leader should prosper in his spiritual work for the Lord.

Paul's Exhortations to Timothy

Paul exhorted Timothy on the firm basis of his own Christian behavior, attitudes and works. Conversely, if these qualities had not been in Paul's own life, he could have given Timothy little encouragement about gaining them. A man of God has influence in the kingdom only as far as his life reflects his teachings.

Paul exhorted Timothy in nine main areas: spiritual warfare, conscience, behavior, godliness, age, example, gifts, discipline and faithfulness. Let us look at these admonitions more closely.

Spiritual Warfare. Paul told Timothy, *"War a good warfare according to the prophecies that went over you"* (I Timothy 1:18), and *"Fight the good fight of faith"* (6:12). Every leader must realize that his or her ministry involves military service, expedition, campaign, and duty for the Lord Jesus Christ. Jesus is the commanding officer and all Christians are His soldiers. The weapons of this warfare, however, are not carnal but spiritual (II Corinthians 10:4).

Every leader must be prepared for the testing that will follow a word from God, whether it comes through the laying on of hands or prophecy or any other form of transmission. God may allow many tests to occur between one's reception of a word and its fulfillment. In these tests, one can either progress by faith and perseverance, or digress by unbelief and despair. Paul wanted Timothy to fight this battle of faith so that he might win every battle and move onward in Christ.

Conscience. Paul exhorted Timothy to hold faith and a good conscience (I Timothy 1:19). It is not enough to have faith or firm conviction about God's promises. A leader must also have a clear conscience toward God and man. A leader must live a life of repentance from all sins to keep a clear conscience toward God. A leader must also clear his conscience of all hatred, anger, jealosy, bitterness and unforgiveness toward men, by admitting his wrong attitudes and asking their forgiveness.

Your conscience is like an inner judge who applies the laws of God to every situation in life. Paul told Timothy to hold an immovably tight grip upon a clear conscience. He warned him of others who had let the "conscience-rudder" of their lives swing with the wind. These people had subsequently experienced spiritual shipwreck (I Timothy 6:21; II Timothy 2:18 and 3:8).

Behavior. Paul exhorted Timothy, as well as other Christians, to learn from him how to conduct themselves in the house of God (I Timothy 3:15). Some people do not believe they should maintain a certain kind of orderly behavior in the local church. They feel that anyone should be able to do anything that he feels like doing in a church service, "as he is led by the Spirit." Certain behavior that is claimed to be "led by the Holy Spirit," however, is not in reality led by God at all. While many local churches need a much greater release of the Spirit in their services, everything should be done "decently and in order" (I Corinthians 14:40). Your behavior in and around the church building greatly affects your influence upon the world for Christ. Every leader should conduct himself wisely in the house of the Lord.

Godliness. Paul exhorted Timothy, "But have nothing to do with worldly fables fit only for old women. On the other hand, discipline yourself for the purpose of godliness; for bodily discipline is only of little profit, but godliness is profitable for all things, since it holds promise for the present life and also for the life to come" (I Timothy 4:7,8). Paul's use of the word "discipline" has the thought of practicing vigorously and nakedly for the Olympic games. The idea is to put out of one's life all that would hinder one from reaching his full spiritual potential in God.

Similarly, every leader must remove from his life all things that hinder his growth in godliness and holiness. In doing so, a leader can expect God to bless him not only in the life to come, but in this life as well.

Age. Paul told the young man Timothy, *"Let no one look down on your youthfulness (age)"* (I Timothy 4:12). Paul knew that some people would think against, disesteem and think nothing of Timothy's life and ministry in the Lord, because he was a fairly young man.

Every young man faces the problem of rejection due to his youthfulness. Instead of growing bitter or angry over this, however, a man of God should give even more of his attention to developing character qualities in his life. This will make all of his words and actions above reproach. That is why Paul ends this verse, "but rather in speech, conduct, love, faith and purity, show yourself an example to those who believe."

Example. Paul gave Timothy an alternative to becoming angry and resentful over his lack of acceptance due to his young age. Paul told Timothy to be an example--a stamp, shape, statue, style, model, image and pattern--of and to the Christian believer, in every aspect of his life. Jesus Christ Himself was said to be the example of every believer (I Peter 2:21). In following Christ, every leader's life should conform more fully to the Master's. As it does, the people of God can follow the good example of Jesus through the leader's life.

The Greek picture of being "an example" for something else is illustrated in these ways:

As one's finger makes an impression in the soft wax of a shallow box

As a stylus (a pointed writing object) makes certain marks on parchment

As a pupil traces the written lines of his teacher in wax or parchment

As a hind's rear hooves land in the same previous position as its front hooves when it runs

A leader should be able to say concerning every aspect of his life, "Follow me as I follow Christ." May our words, attitudes, actions and motives preach a living sermon!

Gifts. As Paul usually did for Timothy, he balanced out a teaching about character with a teaching on gifts. He said, *"Do not neglect the spiritual gift within you, which was bestowed upon you through prophetic utterance with the laying on of hands of the presbytery"* (I Timothy 4:14). Paul did not want Timothy to be careless of his spiritual gifts, or to make light of them.

Paul also exhorted Timothy, "And for this reason I remind you to kindle afresh the gift of God which is in you through the laying on of my hands (II Timothy 1:6). Paul desired Timothy not only to be a man of good character, but a man who would freely function in his spiritual gifts as well. Whatever that gift or gifts might have been in Timothy's life, Paul wanted him to keep rekindling them, to let them burn more and more brightly.

Similarly, every leader in God's kingdom should find out what spiritual gifts God has given to him or her. He should learn how to keep them continually functioning through prayer, the Word, worship, witnessing, fasting, and other Christian life principles. The Church needs godly character, but she also needs her gifts to increase and and function continually.

Discipline. Paul exhorted Timothy, *"But flee these things (e.g., the love of money) you man of God, and pursue righteousness, godliness, faith, love, perseverance, and gentleness"* (I Timothy 6:11). Paul told Timothy to flee certain things, and to pursue others.

This process of "fleeing and following" is the Christian process of discipline. Every leader must realize that his entire life and ministry will be a matter of fleeing unrighteousness and following rightousness. Every leader must lead a disciplined life. He must make the most of his time, money and energy to extend the kingdom. He must avoid and run away from the things that would hinder his spiritual life and ministry, and continually follow after Jesus with obedience and perseverance. A man of God will do exploits for the spiritual kingdom of God only through a disciplined life or prayer, the Word, and obedience to God's Word.

Faithfulness. Finally, Paul exhorted Timothy about being faithful. He said, *"O Timothy, guard what has been entrusted to you, avoiding worldly and empty chatter and the opposing arguments of what is falsely called 'knowledge'"* (I Timothy 6:20). Paul wanted Timothy to guard those truths and principles that had literally been "put into his hands" (as into a safe deposit box).

Every leader should guard the spiritual truths that God has committed to him and to his congregation. A leader must protect these spiritual values with his time and care, that they not be lost. The devil comes to "steal, kill and destroy" the truths in the lives of the people of God. But a watchful shepherd-leader sees the wolf coming and prevents theft or destruction. As a leader, you must develop a heart of stewardship and faithfulness to Jesus Christ and the Church to "guard what has been entrusted to you."

Your Preparation as a Leader

Take a moment now to evaluate your own preparation as a leader. Remember, again, that you need not be called to a positional, governmental ministry to be one of God's leaders. You also may lead in a congregational ministry in a major, temporary, or more limited capacity. In fact, it may be easier to evaluate your preparation for such a focused ministry.

Work through this series of questions, which may also stimulate other questions and issues for your own development.

CALLING

It is worthwhile to review the "Ministry Calling Evaluation" at the end of Chapter Four. Focus on the area of confirmation to your calling. Has your calling been confirmed by leaders and the Church at large? These people have watched you grow into your calling, and they can confirm the outward evidence of your calling.

STUDIES

Most leaders who are truly called can't wait for classes to begin; they study on their own. What have you done to study God's Word in preparation for leadership? Under whose authority and guidance are you studying?

RELATIONSHIPS

Most leaders are launched into their ministries through significant relationships with other leaders. Do you have a teacher, a leader, an example to follow? How faithful are you as a disciple? Have you begun to develop solid relationships with younger Christians, so that you can help them grow?

PRACTICAL LEARNING

What have you learned today? Do you see daily progress toward functioning in your ministry-- even if it happens in the school of hard knocks? What are you doing to build on your successes, and to avoid repeating your mistakes? What can you learn in that regard by watching other people?

SERVICE

Have you already begun to function in your unique calling? Ordination or the assignment of responsibility only confirms that you are already functioning in your ministry. What are you doing to minister to the needs of the Church, with or without receiving a formal ministry title?

PROMOTION

Has recognition of your calling and preparation reached the point of your promotion in the

Church? At any point, have you made yourself less available for promotion through pride, or any other damaging attitude or sin? How have you responded to promotion--have you kept the Lord and your ministry in focus throughout this process?

CHAPTER 11
THE TESTS OF MINISTRY PREPARATION

If you truly desire to serve the Lord, in whatever capacity He assigns you, this chapter will be a great comfort. It will be reassuring to understand some of the tests of God that lie before you. It will be encouraging to know that He uses these tests to build and grow you, not to tear you down. You can take great comfort, also, in the spiritual fellowship of the many great servants of God you will read about here. For you as a Christian, they are older brothers, leaders by example, and the truest "mentors" that you could ever hope to find.

From earlier chapters, you know that God has a very special and unique preparation for each one of His leaders. Testing of that preparation is the final step, and it often comes in the middle of the most active ministry. Why do you have to be tested? Doesn't God know if you're ready to minister? Of course He does. But you need to know it, too. The very act of testing is itself the final preparation, and can drive you into a deeper relationship with God as nothing else can.

Though God tests His governmental ministries most rigorously, He uses the tests in this chapter for all of His people. Anyone who desires to serve God will grow through these tests. *"Let them first be proven (tried, investigated)"*

I Timothy 3:10, Amplified Bible

The Bible clearly teaches that God tests and tries every ministry which He uses in His kingdom. When we say that God tests a ministry, we mean that God:

Uses any means which He Himself knows will determine the presence, quality, or genuineness of His call on someone's life.

Assesses and examines the true inner attitudes and motives of those whom He calls, to show whether they are pure or not.

Puts those He calls into difficult situations which will refine them spiritually (like the Latin word for test, "testu," which means to be put inside of an earthen pot with a lid on top).

Biblical Examples of Specific Tests

The Bible is full of examples of God testing His leaders. From the frequency of such instances, God appears to be a God of testing. Hebrews 12:29 states, *"For our God is a consuming fire."* As a consuming and testing fire, God tries the attitudes and motives of each of the people that He uses. This is not simply to expose weaknesses, but to cause them to turn to the Lord for help. God proves His vessels of leadership, already knowing their inner weaknesses, that these might be healed.

God will also test and try a leader to purify him. God will use only pure leaders, whose only motive for ministry is the glory of God and the salvation of souls. Through trials and tough circumstances, God removes impure attitudes of bitterness, selfishness and covetousness from a leader's heart, and replaces them with motives of love.

Producing faithful men and women of God is a primary purpose of God's testing. Men and women who can keep believing and trusting in the living God during problems and difficulties will develop true faithfulness to God and His Word.

Another purpose in God's testing of His leaders is to sort out those who are not truly called by Him. Only those anointed and called of God can sustain the pressures of filling a governmental ministry. God puts His leaders in desperate situations. Those who do not feel a true call of the Spirit upon their lives drop out of the preparation process. This is sometimes the best thing for them and for the Church. God's people can follow only those shepherds who have been divinely appointed to their task.

God also tests His leaders to equip them with the spiritual understanding they need to help His people. All Christians experience a variety of tests and trials. Only the leader who has successfully overcome them himself can help the people.

The different tests of God can and do occur throughout a leader's life. To emphasize their role in preparation, we will study the different tests of ministry in a special preparation period:

THE SALVATION	THE CALL	THE PREPARATION	THE MATURITY
THE SEED OF A MINISTRY	BIRTH OF A MINISTRY	TESTS OF A MINISTRY	FULFILLMENT OF A MINISTRY

The preparation time is the time of God's ordained tests of ministry. To uniquely prepare God's leaders for their various ministries, God puts them through many different tests. This chapter will focus on fourteen of them:

1. Time Test
2. Word Test
3. Character Test
4. Motivation Test
5. Servant Test
6. Wilderness Test
7. Misunderstanding Test
8. Patience Test
9. Frustration Test
10. Discouragement Test
11. Warfare Test
12. Self-will Test
13. Vision Test
14. Usage Test
15. Promotion Test (Chapter 12)

These scriptural tests of God's leaders have some overlap and similarities. We have established fifteen to clarify the many deep valley experiences that every leader in the kingdom must face. Let us now look at each test, with a general definition, purpose and Biblical illustration.

TIME TEST

Definition. In the Time Test, by all outward appearances, God does not seem to be fulfilling the word He gave a leader in the past. The Time Test tries a leader's patience, forcing him to trust God to fulfill his call and ministry in His own time and way.

Purpose. This test gives the leader an opportunity to grow in faith. Every leader has a measure of trust and confidence in God. Because each must lead people to believe in God for every detail of life, however, a leader must be given more faith with which to strengthen his own people.

The Time Test also purifies a leader's motives and attitudes. During times of delay, a leader can see how his own impure, selfish or proud motives and attitudes can cloud his desires before the Lord. God desires transparent motives and attitudes in each of His leaders.

In the Time Test, God proves Himself to be a miracle-working, faithful God to everyone He has called to the service of His kingdom. Many times a leader believes that his own activity and striving can fulfill God's vision for His Church. Though God's leaders must cooperate with God's plan, God always delights in using the weaknesses of men to give Him all of the glory (I Corinthians 1:26-31). During the Time Test, when men's plans can only fail, God arranges a miracle to bring all of the glory to Himself. As He does the miracle, He demonstrates His faithfulness to His leaders.

Biblical Illustration: Abraham (Genesis 12-18). The story of the patriarch Abraham shows the Time Test at work. Abraham was 75 years old when God called him out of Haran to travel to Canaan (Genesis 12:1-9). God promised Abraham to possess all of Canaan from the Euphrates south. Being childless, the patriarch had made his home-born slave, Eleazar, to be his heir. But God promised Abraham that he would have a child of his own as heir (15:4). Abraham did not wait through God's Time Test. At the age of 86, he had a son, Ishmael, through his concubine Hagar (16:1-4). Not until Abraham was 100 did God bring His promise to pass in Abraham's son Isaac (17:1 and 18:10). Abraham had to wait 25 years before he received God's promise of a natural son for his heir.

Many leaders today complain if they must wait five or seven years before seeing God's will fulfilled. With Abraham, they say, *"Oh, that Ishmael might live before Thee!"* (Genesis 17:18). Instead, they must submit to God's Time Test and with patient endurance allow it to work faith and purity into their lives.

WORD TEST

Definition. In the Word Test, the leader experiences circumstances that seem to nullify the written or living Word of God. "How can the known will of God possibly come to pass in my life?" is the leader's cry during this time. Many feel that because they have been filled and called by God's Spirit, they should never experience darkness or confusion as long as they do not fall into sin.

But the Word Test is no accident. In fact, God purposely allows contrary situations in a leader's life and ministry. No leader is exempt from these times of trial and misunderstanding. During the Word Test, God has not forgotten or contradicted His promise. But He desires to accomplish certain purposes that are as yet totally unknown to the leader. If the leader endures with patience, trust and obedience, he will eventually find himself rejoicing in the Lord's wisdom and skill in the planning and use of these seemingly antagonistic experiences.

Purpose. God uses the Word Test to cause a leader to reject his own resources and depend soly on God's strength to bring God's Word to pass. This is a difficult task for a leader, especially for a man of many strengths and abilities. A talented leader can easily trust more in himself than in God.

The Word Test also extends the reach of the kingdom of heaven. A leader may plan to reach a certain number of people with the gospel. But through the Word Test, encouragingly, he will discover that God reached more people after His Word became more than just an untested promise. The trial of God's Word gives a leader further testimony of God's power and faithfulness, to share with more people.

Biblical Illustration: Joseph (Genesis 37-45). Joseph was the eleventh son of Jacob, the first by his wife Rachel (Genesis 30:24), and Jacob's favorite son (37:3). At the age of 17, Joseph received a word from the Lord in the form of two dreams. In one, his family's sheaves bowed down to his sheave in the field. In the other, the sun, moon and eleven stars bowed down to him (37:5-11). Since the two dreams represented his eventual reign over his parents and his brothers, he became an object of jealousy. Joseph's brothers sold him to an Ishmaelite caravan from Gilead, that was traveling down into Egypt (37:25-28). There he was sold to Potiphar, Pharaoh's officer (37:29-36).

Jacob was falsely accused of trying to seduce Potiphar's wife, and was banished to prison (39:7-23). There, one of his last hopes of ever getting a word of reminder to the king about his imprisonment was dashed, when the king's chief cupbearer did not remember to tell the king about Joseph after he himself was released from prison (40:23).

Through all of these contradictory circumstances, God's Word to Joseph was tested. How could he rule over his brethren as an Egyptian slave? How could Joseph rule from a prison cell?

The Psalmist very accurately describes what happened to Joseph and his promise from God. "(God) *sent a man before them, Joseph, who was sold as a slave. They afflicted his feet with fetters, he himself was laid in irons. Until the time that his word came to pass, the word of the Lord tested* (refined) *him"* Psalm 105:17-19.

Joseph waited approximately fourteen years to see the fulfillment of God's word to him. With great patience, Joseph waited in prison until God brought him out through a command of the king (Psalm 105:20,21). During Joseph's experience of the Word Test, God developed character, wisdom and humility in his life.

All leaders must likewise see the instructions of the hand of the Lord during God's Word Test in their lives and ministries.

CHARACTER TEST

Definition. In the Character Test, the leader is surrounded by ungodliness that attempts to pull him in its direction. The leader may be tempted to sin in the lust of the flesh, the lust of the eyes or the pride of life. In order to develop leaders with strong, godly character qualities--love, joy, peace, patience, self-control, faithfulness--God puts His leaders in fiery places so they may learn to stand strong in Him.

Purpose. The Character Test shows to the leader the areas of weakness in his own personality. When God brings a situation into a leader's life which requires much patience, he realizes he must call on more of God's grace. An area of need usually surfaces, where he must allow God to work. Every leader has hidden character deficiencies of which he is totally unaware, until confronted with a specific situation that demands a godly response. To expose his own true inward self to every leader, God uses the Character Test.

The Character Test also motivates a leader to stand up boldly against the powers of darkness around him. Too many leaders are shy about proclaiming the truth. Too many wait until they are attacked from outside before they take the initiative of preaching the gospel. Many need to be confronted with evil so they will stand up boldly for the name of the Lord and His righteousness.

Biblical Illustration: Samuel (I Samuel 2-3). Samuel was the son of a religious Ephraimite, Elkanah, and his wife Hannah. Samuel is regarded as the last and greatest of the judges and the first of the prophets (Acts 13:20 and 3:24). Samuel, however, was born into a corrupt situation.

Eli, the high priest at this time, had grown physically and spiritually dull, and the light in the tabernacle had almost extinguished (I Samuel 2:27-36 and 3:1-3). Eli was a corrupt high priest who did not discipline his sons, Hophni and Phinehas, who committed fornication with women at the very door of the tabernacle of the congregation. Because of this morally corrupt situation, God overthrew Eli's succession and introduced Samuel as the leader of Israel's spiritual and secular affairs.

Though a very young boy in the midst of a corrupt priesthood, Samuel worshipped God and kept himself from sin. The young prophet could have fallen into sin like Eli's sons, but he chose not to. Samuel's story demonstrates that leaders do not have to be corrupted by their environments. Samuel kept himself pure in the midst of sin and immorality. He underwent God's Character Test and remained righteous.

MOTIVATION TEST

Definition. This is a heavenly "examination" in which God exposes to the leader what inner and outer forces influence his decision-making processes. God will arrange situations to reveal a leader's true inner intentions, thoughts, values and priorities that cause him to make choices or act in a certain way.

A leader may not always know why he does something. What appears to motivate him, from an outer inspection, may be a far cry from his true internal motives.

Purpose. God uses the Motivation Test to disclose those inner drives and to purify them into desires for the glory of God, the salvation of souls, and the edification of the Church. A leader may serve God for what he can get out of God, rather than what he can give to Him or His people. A person may use his gifts to glorify himself, rather than God. God puts His leaders through Motivation Tests to expose unrighteous drives, and then to replace them with motives of His Spirit, and true love out of a pure heart.

Biblical Illustration: Balaam (Numbers 22-24). The story of Balaam the prophet shows the Motivation Test at work. Balak, the son of Zippor and the king of Moab, had seen how Israel had defeated all of her enemies in the land. He feared they would destroy his nation as well. Consequently, he offered to pay the prophet Balaam to curse the Israelites to put an end to their victories (22:7). Balaam responded to Balak that the Lord had told him not to go with the elders of Moab to curse the people of Israel.

Balak tried again, sending more numerous and distinguished ambassadors to persuade Balaam otherwise (22:15). This time, the Lord told Balaam to go with the elders of Moab and Midian, but to speak only the word the Lord gave him to speak (22:20). Balaam did go to Balak, but each time he inquired of the Lord, the Lord told him to bless Israel.

Needless to say, this greatly upset the Moabites and Midianites! Through it all, God was testing Balaam's motivation. Would he sell out, or would he be faithful to God's word? God allowed Balak to tempt the prophet's motivation continually, and every time, the size of the bribe grew (22:7,15,17). Unfortunately, it appears that Balaam's motivation did not stay pure, though he initially tried to remain faithful to speaking only the word of the Lord (23:12,26). Balaam failed this Motivation Test from the Lord (II Peter 2:15; Jude 11; Revelation 2:14), who allowed him to be tempted with much money if he would only disobey God and curse God's people.

THE SERVANT TEST

Definition. In the Servant Test, a man is asked to do menial tasks that seem below his high calling in God. No menial task is below any true servant of God. But especially before (or even during) his time of fully giving himself to prayer and the Word instead of "waiting on tables" (see Acts 6:106), God tests a leader to see if he is willing to do menial service.

Purpose. The Servant Test reveals whether a ministry's motivation is simply to be in the public eye and receive service, or if he truly desires to help and serve. Those in authority over that ministry (remember that we use the word "ministry" to refer to a person who ministers) will see how well he passes the test. God may instruct authorities over a ministry to use this test to discern the person's commitment to service. Does a young man think it below his ministry to sweep the church floor? Does a young woman believe it is beneath her calling to sing in a large choir and not to solo? These are revealing questions.

This test also reveals to God's called governmental ministries what it feels like to do different jobs in the local church. How many pastors today cannot appreciate the effort and time a church janitor puts in, unless they experience some of it themselves? How can a man expect to communicate to an adult-level class unless he also relates to college-level groups? Every leader needs personal experience in different jobs in the Church, so he can better understand and communicate with people in those positions when he acts as, for example, a church pastor.

Biblical Illustration: Elisha (I Kings 19). Elisha is a pointed example of the Servant Test. When Elijah found Elisha, who was to become his prophetical heir, Elisha was plowing in the field with twelve yoke of oxen before him. This probably means that Elisha was plowing at the end of eleven other men, each driving a plow and pair of oxen. This was probably a humbling position--following eleven other pairs of oxen would certainly not lend itself to a sweet fragrance, cleanliness or fresh air. The dust of the field was doubtless thick in the air. Was this the proper place for a future prophet of Israel, who was going to do more miracles than his predecessor?

I Kings 19:21 states that after Elisha burned his farming equipment, *"he arose and followed Elijah and ministered to him."* Elisha became the servant of Elijah, though he would succeed him. II Kings 3:11d states, *"Elisha, the son of Shaphat, is here, who used to pour water on the hands of Elijah,"* confirming that his larger ministry began with "menial" service. Ministry does not end servanthood, either. It only means that a leader now must serve even more people in an even greater capacity.

WILDERNESS TEST

Definition. In the Wilderness Test, God directly or indirectly guides a leader (or future leader) into a materially and/or spiritually dry and desolate place. When no fruit comes from his life or ministry, a leader feels he is in this test. In such times, a leader wonders whether he really received a call of God upon his life, because he appears to have no direct involvement in the true, living work of the kingdom of God. Sometimes, a leader is left with no one else to talk to but God Himself.

Purposes. The Wilderness Test increases a leader's appreciation for the good things that God has already put in his life.

This test also teaches the leader how to discern whether the Lord alone sustains his spiritual life, or he draws from his ministry activity to sustain his relationship with God. Does a leader's prayer, word and evangelism activities drop off just because he is not in "full-time" Christian work and supported by a local church? If so, his activities may be sustaining his walk with God, rather than his own personal relationship doing this.

God also uses the Wilderness Test to strip the leader of all the wisdom and ways of the world, and to teach him the ways of His Spirit. Every leader must learn that God's ways are different from his own. Sometimes, the best way to learn this is through dry and lonely desert experiences.

A wasteland experience also drives a leader to cultivate his life in prayer and the Word. Many leaders need dry places to exhaust the reservoir of sheer nervous energy that they draw from to serve the Lord. God desires His leaders not to strive for Him in fearful, nervous energy, but to walk with Him in restful spiritual peace. The Wilderness Test motivates a leader to seek the Lord in a consistent life of prayer and the Word, to find the genuine and must fruitful source of strength: God Himself.

Biblical Illustration: Moses (Exodus 2,3). Moses stands out as an appropriate example of the Wilderness Test. Moses learned that his killing of an Egyptian (who was beating an Israelite, Exodus 2:11) was known to Pharaoh and the palace. He fled across the border to Midian for safety (2:15). There he married Zipporah, daughter of the Midianite shepherd-priest Jethro, and she bore him two sons.

Acts 7:29,30 states that forty years passed before an angel of the Lord called Moses to deliver God's people Israel from Egyptian slavery (Exodus 3:1f). Why was this great men of God kept in the wilderness forty years, shepherding sheep, before God called him to his great ministry as Israel's deliverer and lawgiver? One belief: God took forty years to strip Moses of all his Egyptian learning and prepare him for his work (Acts 7:22). Only then could Moses truly learn God's ways, the only means by which God could lead His chosen people out of the land of bondage.

It is highly unlikely that Moses learned how to hear the voice of God, or to use the rod of God to do miracles, while he was in Egypt. In Egypt he had most probably learned hieroglyphic and hieratic scripts, the reproduction of texts, letter-writing, archery and other "civilized" arts. But he probably did not learn much about the ways of God's Spirit. In forty years in the desert, Moses learned what he needed to know to lead God's people out of Egypt.

Today, some leaders complain much about the far fewer years that God uses a seeming wasteland to teach them valuable spiritual truths. May every leader consider every wilderness test a special class in the school of God's Spirit, from which he can derive much spiritual benefit.

MISUNDERSTANDING TEST

Definition. The Test of Misunderstanding occurs when those hearing a leader do not receive (or reject) the correct meaning he is trying to communicate. People may misinterpret or mistake the true significance of his actions, words, attitudes or motives.

Purpose. The Test of Misunderstanding causes a leader to look for new or better ways of bringing across his feelings. It also causes him to examine his basic attitudes and motivations in communication. Many times people will misunderstand what a person is trying to say just because the communicator has an attitude that is too hard, harsh or angry when he tries to say it.

When a leader discovers major misunderstandings, he is motivated to trust totally in God, and not in his own skills as a communicator. In the New Testament, God was the one who opened the hearts of different people to believe the gospel message. A leader must trust the ministry of the Holy Spirit to quicken the truth of what he is communicating. God desires every leader to trust that His Word, through the Holy Spirit, will accomplish the task of building His kingdom.

The Test of Misunderstanding is especially humbling to leaders because it involves those who are very dear and close to the leader.

To be free mentally, emotionally and spiritually, a leader must make room in his heart for some misunderstanding. Anyone who preaches the Word of God will be misinterpreted at one time or another. The key for every leader in this is to keep his heart free from anger and resentment, and to allow the Lord Jesus to turn the situation into good. Through prayer and trust in God, every leader will learn many lessons of wisdom from times of misunderstanding.

Biblical Illustration: the Lord Jesus Christ. A biblical term for misunderstanding is the word "contradiction." Hebrews 12:3 states this about Jesus: *"For consider him who has endured such hostility* (KJV "contradiction") *by sinners against himself, so that you may not grow weary and lose heart."* Jesus is the prime example of the test of intentional and unintentional misunderstanding. He suffered this not only from the Jewish people in general, but especially by the Jewish religious rulers, and even by His close followers.

When Jesus said, *"Eat my flesh and drink my blood"* (John 6:60), some of His close disciples misunderstood and left Him. Being forsaken by outsiders is one thing, but rejection by one's own disciples over a misunderstanding is another thing. And most of Jesus' own people, the Jews, rejected Him because they did not correctly understand how He fulfilled Bible prophecy.

PATIENCE TEST

Definition. The Patience Test happens when a leader's expectations in God are not fulfilled "on schedule." Patience is one of the fruits of the Holy Spirit (Galatians 5:22). This word comes from a latin word which means "to suffer." In the Patience Test, God challenges a leader to wait patiently, or to endure some tribulation, without complaint. To grow in patience, a leader must bear pain or trouble without losing self-control or becoming a disturbance to others. In portraying this quality, a leader calmly tolerates delay while refusing to be provoked by it.

Purpose. To pass the Patience Test, a leader must have yielded his rights to Jesus Christ already, so that he is able to wait for Him to return his expectations to him in His own timing, and as undeserved blessings. Every leader has certain expectations, not only in his own life and ministry, but also of others. In not attempting to "play God" in his own life or the lives of others, a humble leader will yield to the Lord even some very good and appropriate goals. The leader knows that God will use a delay of fulfillment to accomplish what He desires. A leader must yield rights to the Lord constantly. The Lord will motivate him to do this by using the demands of other people, in the Patience Test.

Biblical Illustration: Noah (Genesis 5-7). Like the other early patriarchs, Noah was given a great many years to live. He was 500 years old when his wife bore their first son (Genesis 5:32), and 600 years old at the time of the Flood (7:11). Noah was probably 480 years old when God informed him of His plan to destroy the earth with water (6:3; I Peter 3:20). It was for some 120 years, then, that he preached repentance to his generation, but to no avail. God allowed a period of 120 years of grace in which Noah was to build an ark for his family and the animals (6:13-22), and preach to his generation about God's coming judgment.

During the entire 120 years of his preaching, Noah saw no one repent of his sins and turn to God for mercy. One hundred twenty years is a long time for any preacher to continue to preach without results. This long endurance required much patience from Noah. He kept preaching and preaching, but without conversions. It was only because God gave divine grace and patience to Noah that he could endure this test so well. At the end of his patience test, only he and his family found themselves safely in the ark which they had built. The scoffers perished in the flood waters outside. Noah's patience paid off for him and his family in the end. Patience will pay for every leader who patiently leaves the results and details of his ministry in the capable hands of the Lord.

THE FRUSTRATION TEST

Definition. A leader undergoes the Frustration Test when he feels that his life or ministry goals cannot be achieved. People or circumstances may prevent him from gratifying his conscious or unconscious desires and goals. A ministry expecially experiences this feeling when he finds no logical or rational reason why his efforts are being baffled, foiled or confused.

Purpose. The Frustration Test causes a leader to re-examine his spiritual priorities. Is he giving enough time to prayer and the Word? Is he giving enough attention to his wife and family? God will many times bring frustration to a leader's life and ministry when his priorities need re-adjustment.

Frustration also causes the leader to put more fervor into his primary spiritual battle against opposition to the simple gospel of Jesus Christ. With his other goals and activities temporarily out of gear, a leader may realize that he has neglected the simple preaching of the Good News to the lost. With that spiritual priority adjust, God will release him from the test of frustration.

Biblical Illustration: Paul (II Corinthians 11). A definite sense of frustration comes through these words from the apostle Paul:

"That which I speak, I speak it not after the Lord, but as it were foolishly, in this confidence of boasting. Seeing that many glory after the flesh, I will glory also. For ye suffer fools gladly, seeing ye yourselves are wise. For ye suffer, if a man brings you into bondage, if a man devour you, if a man take of you, if a man exalt himself, if a man smite you on the face. I speak as concerning reproach, as though we had been weak. Howbeit wherinsoever any is bold, (I speak foolishly,) I am bold also. Are they Hebrews? So am I. Are they Israelites? So am I. Are they seed of Abraham? So am I. Are they ministers of Christ? (I speak as a fool) I am more; in labours more abundant, in stripes above measure, in prisons more frequent, in deaths oft. Of the Jews five times received I (the) forty stripes save one. Thrice was I stoned, thrice I suffered shipwreck, a night and a day I have been in the deep; In journeyings often, in perils of waters, in perils of robbers, in perils by mine own countrymen, in perils by the heathen, in perils in the city, in perils in the wilderness, in perils in the sea, in perils among false brethren; In weariness and painfulness, in watchings often, in hunger and thirst, in fastings often, in cold and nakedness. Beside those things that are without, that which cometh upon me daily, the care of all the churches. Who is weak, and I am not weak? Who is offended, and I burn not? If I must needs glory, I will glory of the things which concern mine infirmities. The God and Father of our Lord Jesus Christ, which is blessed for evermore, knoweth that I lie not. In Damascus the governor under Aretas the king kept the city of the Damascenes with a garrison, desirous to apprehend me: And through a window in a basket was I let down by the wall, and escaped his hands. It is not expedient for me doubtless to glory. I will come to visions and revelations of the Lord." (II Corinthians 11:17-12:1)

We can sense Paul's frustration, especially in verse 28 and 29, where he says, "Beside those things that are without, that which cometh upon me daily, the care of all of the churches. Who is weak and I am not weak? Who is offended, and I burn not?" Paul was a human being like every leader, and he had his time of bafflement and frustration, too. His answer to frustration, however, was a simple trust in the power of the Spirit over the natural. He declared by faith in the midst of frustration:

"We are troubled on every side, yet not distressed; we are perplexed, but not in despair; persecuted, but not forsaken; cast down, but not destroyed; always bearing about in the body the dying of the Lord Jesus, that the life also of Jesus might made manifest in our

body. For we which live are always delivered unto death for Jesus' sake, that the life also of Jesus might be made manifest in our mortal flesh. So then death worketh in us, but life in you. We having the same spirit of faith, according as it is written, I believed, and therefore have I spoken; we also believe, and therefore speak; knowing that he which raised up the Lord Jesus shall raise up us also by Jesus, and shall present us with you. For all things are for your sakes, that the abundant grace might through the thanksgiving of many redound to the glory of God. For which cause we faint not; but though our outward man perish, yet the inward man is renewed day by day. For our light affliction, which is but for a moment, worketh for us a far more exceeding and eternal weight of glory; while we look not at the things which are seen, but at the things which are not seen: for the things which are seen are temporal; but the things which are not seen are eternal." (II Corinthians 4:8-17)

DISCOURAGEMENT TEST

Definition. A leader is going through the Discouragement Test when he allows circumstances or people to dishearten him and deprive him of courage in the Lord. A discouraged leader is deterred from an undertaking which he believed was God's will. During such times, a ministry may lose his confidence or hope in God, His provision, His promises, or His calling.

Purpose. Discouragement causes the leader to go to God in prayer, especially through the Psalms. The Psalms express most of the different conditions of heart that people face during their lifetime. The moods of the Psalms vary from joy over the defeat of one's enemies to the sorrow and depths of despair and discouragement. During the Discouragement Test, a leader should try to find the Psalm(s) that best express the mood of his soul, and then pray through it to God sincerely.

Discouraging times of stress and trial are not wrong. But the attitude one takes toward such circumstances can be, if one persists in self-pity or feelings of discouragement. A leader must learn through these times that his joy comes from delighting himself in the Lord, not delighting only in happy circumstances or positive responses from people. No leader will sustain his ministry without learning how to derive total joy and peace directly from God Himself.

The Discouragement Test also reveals the hidden, bad attitudes in a leader. Many leaders can rejoice in the Lord when everything is going the way they think things should. But how many allow themselves to complain and murmur when things go unexpectedly the other way? During discouragement, the Lord allows the leader to uncover poor attitudes in himself, for which he must ask God's forgiveness. A leader would be far better if God had never revealed these bad attitudes, than if he came to know them but still failed to repent of them. The spiritual principle here: we become responsible to do what God has showed us to do, and failure to obey judges and condemns us.

Biblical Illustration: Elijah (I Kings 19). Elijah became very discouraged when he learned that Israel had forsaken the Lord, and that queen Jezebel planned to kill him (19:2,3). In discouragement, Elijah fled from Jezebel. He left his servant in Beersheba, went a day's journey into the wilderness, sat under a juniper tree, and asked God to take his life (v. 4).

God's response included this statement: *"I have kept for myself seven thousand men who have not bowed the knee to Baal"* (see also Romans 11:4). And God also asked Elijah, *"What are you doing here?"* (vs. 9,13) when the prophet complained that he was the only one who had zeal for the Lord of hosts (vs. 10,14). Many times discouragement comes to a leader when he feels that he is the only one who is totally working for God. This can be alleviated, however, by developing a church along the patterns of God's New Testament gifts and ministries. The congregation can have plurality of eldership, and members of the congregation can be taught how to find and function in their God-assigned spiritual gifts and ministries.

It is valuable to note what God spoke to Elijah during his time of discouragement, and to apply it to the leader today. (Study all of I Kings 19 to understand the context for the following comments.)

In response to Elijah's discouragement, the Lord told the prophet:

TO ELIJAH
"Arise, eat and drink" (vs.5,6).

To apply this spiritual principle to Church leaders today:

TO THE LEADER
In discouragement, a leader's emotional energy is decreased. He may feel like lying down and sleeping just as Elijah did. The leader gains new strength as he arises and eats of the scroll of the Word of the Lord, and thereby also drinks of the Spirit of God. Standing and confessing the Word of God enables a leader to overcome discouragement.

"Arise, eat and drink because the journey to Mount Horeb is too great for you" (vs.7,8).

During discouragement, God desires His leaders to get away and seek His face in prayer. A leader is motivated to pray when he sees that, in himself, he has no strength to do God's will, but that in the Lord he does (as he eats the Word and drinks of the Spirit).

"What are you doing here at a cave on Mount Horeb, Elijah?" (v.9)

During discouragement, a leader is inclined to stop and lodge at a "mountaintop" place where he can hear the still, small voice of God. Every leader must learn how to press into the Lord during such times, until he receives a clear word from the Lord.

"Go forth and stand on the mountain before the Lord. And behold the Lord was passing by!" (v.11)

During this test, the Lord challenges His leaders to stand face-to-face with Him in their distress. A leader should not try to hide his discouragement from God, for He already knows of it.

"What are you doing here (at the entrance of the cave), *Elijah?"* (v.13)

During distress, even after knowing the Lord will speak to him in a still, small voice, the leader is still tempted to run and hide from God. But the leader must not do so when he is discouraged. On the contrary, he must seek the Lord for a word concerning the next action that he should take, and then go do it.

"Go, return on your way to the wilderness of Damascus, and when you have arrived, you shall anoint Hazael king over Syria, and Jehu . . . you shall anoint king over Israel, and Elisha . . . you shall anoint as prophet in your place" (vs.15,16)

When God speaks to the sincere and open leader who is discouraged, He will give him specific assignments. These activities help get a leader's mind off his own problems, and back onto doing the will of the Lord, and obeying His Word in everyday life.

WARFARE TEST

Definition. The Warfare Test happens when a leader encounters violent spiritual opposition to his progress in the Spirit, or in his extending of God's kingdom. Though it happens in the realm of the spirit, it can find natural expressions in conflicts with people, lack of response to one's ministry, or struggles of various sorts (including the feeling of unbearable temptation to sin).

Some people think anointed leaders cannot be tempted like other people can. Recent leadership failures have proved that untrue! And the Bible says that even Jesus "was in all points tempted like as we are, yet without sin" (Hebrews 4:15). The calling of God does not remove human susceptibility to temptation. Leaders must make a conscious effort to *"walk in the Spirit and ye shall not fulfill the lusts of the flesh"* (Galatians 5:16).

Purposes. Spiritual warfare forces the leader to grow stronger in the Spirit. In this, the spiritual realm is like the natural realm, where a muscle becomes stronger only through exercise and resistance. Hebrews 5:14 uses the word "exercise" when it states that solid spiritual food is for the mature, *"who by reason of use have their senses exercised to discern both good and evil."*

Some leaders are not mature because they do not train or exercise their spiritual senses enough. Through spiritual warfare, a leader learns how to use effectively his spiritual weapons of the Word, prayer, praise, and the name of the Lord Jesus Christ.

Biblical Illustration: Timothy (I and II Timothy). Timothy was exhorted by the apostle Paul to give everything he could to succeeding in the tests of spiritual warfare. Due to his youth, the Greek nationality of his father and the heresies of his day, Timothy was a natural target for spiritual attack. The following Scripture references indicate this spiritual fight:

"This command I entrust to you, Timothy, my son, in accordance with the prophecies previously made concerning you, that by them you might fight the good fight" (I Timothy 1:18).

"I have fought the good fight" (4:7).

"Fight the good fight of faith; take hold of the eternal life to which you were called" (6:12).

"Suffer hardship with me, as a good soldier of Christ Jesus. No soldier in active service entangles himself in the affairs of everyday life, so he may please the one who enlisted him as a soldier" (Ii Timothy 2:3,4)

Like Timothy, every leader must fight the good fight of faith. Just like the Christian life, the ministry is a battle to the last breath. Jesus Christ has won the battle for His people through His death and resurrection, but His victory must still be outworked into the full experience of the Church and the world.

The spiritual warfare of a pastor or teacher is to preach the Word of God so powerfully that God's spiritual enemies in darkness will be defeated, and people converted to Jesus Christ. The battle consists also of the leader strongly holding on to his faith in Jesus Christ until the end. Satan tries every means of defeating the proclamation of the gospel and the growth of the Church. But try as he may, the spiritual victory belongs to every Christian leader as he uses the spiritual weapons that God has given him to win the battle.

Please remember that our spiritual warfare cannot be won with natural, carnal, worldly, human or non-spiritual weapons. Throughout history, when the Church has trusted in human violence or unscriptural means of extending the kingdom, the primary goals of saving souls and strengthening the Church have always been lost. Only as today's Church leaders effectively use their spiritual weapons can they win in the tests of spiritual warfare.

SELF-WILL TEST

Definition. When a leader realizes God is asking him to do something that counters his own plans or desires, the Self-will Test has begun. God has to break the self-will and personal ambition of every person He uses, so that He can trust him or her to do whatever He requires in His kingdom.

Even good and appropriate things He asks us to sacrifice at times. God will sometimes even request a man to do something for Him, and give no logical reason for it. In not always explaining His requests to leaders, God is developing a child-like faith and obedience in their hearts. This kind of simple faith is always very pleasing to the Lord. God will even ask His leaders to sacrifice to Him what they know to be God's will. In the case of Abraham, God asked him to sacrifice his son Isaac, God's promised seed (Genesis 22:1ff).

In all of this, a man's desires, thoughts, feelings and plans are put into subjection to God's will. This constant submission to the Lord's will is what true Christianity is all about. God does not necessarily prefer painful sacrifices from His leaders. But when he speaks something contrary to a man's desire, that man must quickly respond to the word.

Purpose. The Self-will Test subjects man's will to God's Word (both the written and the quickened). In doing this, God helps us fulfill the scriptural admonition, *"Let him who boasts, boast in the Lord (and not in man)"* (I Corinthians 1:31). This is why God uses the foolish, despised, unexpected and hateful things of this world for His kingdom, that He might receive all of the glory and credit for what is done (I Corinthians 1:26-31). Man's sinful nature pits his natural will against the spiritual will of God. God must therefore crucify a leader's desires, on occasion, so that He can accomplish His desire in His own way. Isaiah prophesied so appropriately:

"Seek ye the Lord while he may be found, call ye upon him while he is near: Let the wicked forsake his way, and the unrighteous man his thoughts: and let him return unto the Lord, and he will have mercy upon him; and to our God, for he will abundantly pardon. 'For my thoughts are not your thoughts, neither are your ways my ways,' saith the Lord. 'For as the heavens are higher than the earth, so are my ways higher than your ways, and my thoughts than your thoughts!' " (Isaiah 55:6-9)

Biblical Illustration: the Lord Jesus Christ (Matthew 26). The very famous passage of Jesus' final submission to the heavenly Father's will before He went to the cross demonstrates this submission of His own personal self-will:

"Then cometh Jesus with them unto a place called Gethsemane, and saith unto the disciples, 'Sit ye here, while I go and pray yonder.' And he took with him Peter and the two sons of Zebedee, and began to be sorrowful and very heavy. Then saith he unto them, 'My soul is exceeding sorrowful, even unto death: tarry ye here, and watch with me.' And he went a little farther, and fell on his face, and prayed, saying, 'O my Father, if it be possible, let this cup pass from me: nevertheless not as I will but as thou wilt.' And he cometh unto the disciples, and findeth them asleep, and saith unto Peter, 'What, could ye not watch with me one hour? Watch and pray, that ye enter not into temptation: the spirit indeed is willing, but the flesh is weak.' He went away again the second time, and prayed, saying, 'O my Father, if this cup may not pass away from me, except I drink it, thy will be done.' And he came and found them asleep again: for their eyes were heavy. And he left them, and went away again, and prayed the third time, saying the same words. Then cometh he to his disciples, and saith unto them, 'Sleep on now, and take your rest: behold, the hour is at hand, and the Son of man is betrayed into the hands of sinners. Rise, let us be going: behold, he is at hand that doth betray me.' And while he yet spake, lo, Judas, one of the twelve, came, and with him a great multitude with swords and staves, from the chief priests and elders of the people. Now he that betrayed him gave them a sign, saying, 'Whomsoever I shall kiss, that same is he: hold him fast.' " (Matthew 26:36-48).

Here we see that, in His human self, Jesus did not want to suffer the experience of the cross. His divine nature desired the cross as the will of the Father who sent Him, but it was not so with His human nature.

Every leader in God's kingdom must lay down his plans and desires to fulfill God's will, even as Jesus did. Only as we lay down our own fleshly and carnal ambitions can God use each of us as a vessel for His glory.

VISION TEST

Definition. The Vision Test occurs when contrary people and circumstances besiege a leader's spiritual insight into the purposes of God. Natural and physical vision is not enough for a leader of God's people. He must also have spiritual eyes of faith to see God's will and desire for His people. The spiritual Vision Test asks two main questions: "Can you see the spiritual needs and answers of the people of God?" and, "Can you resist opposition and adversity, and tenaciously hold the vision that God has given you as a leader?"

Purposes. The Vision Test shows a leader how shallow his spiritual insight really is. Every leader feels he has a measure of insight into God and His people, otherwise he could not serve the Lord in a ministry capacity. All leaders are tempted to think that their present education, insight, knowledge and wisdom is totally sufficient to meet the challenges of Church life. "After all," many exclaim, "wasn't I fully trained in the seminary or Bible college for this ministry?"

The plain answer is: No! No leader receives full training for the ministry in a seminary or a Bible college. God desires to keep His leaders constantly dependent on Him and His Spirit, and not dependent solely on their abilities, past training or experience. At this point, unfortunately, many who are called to a ministry fail. When they begin to see what it actually takes to walk by faith and minister by the power of the Holy Spirit, they cannot be so humbled!

Many of their friends had told them, "Oh, you will make such a good minister. You will really be able to do a lot for God because you have so many talents and abilities!" The school textbooks told them, "Now this is the way to run a service; and this is the way to preach a sermon; and this is the way to save souls; and this is the way to cause the church to grow." But when those called of God graduate from formal education and get away from their friends, everything changes. They find that the true spiritual success of their ministries depends on different criteria than their friends or textbooks told them! What do they do then? They either drop or desperately call on God. Only the latter make it.

The Vision Test also ensures that the glory for success goes to God. A vision from the Lord may seem to die once, or even twice, so that its final fulfillment gives God much more glory than an uninterrupted march to success. God receives much glory when a vision is fulfilled supernaturally and in God's way.

Biblical Illustration: Nehemiah (Nehemiah 1,2,4). The story of Nehemiah's Vision Test, and its fulfillment, has two major elements. First, Nehemiah had spiritual eyes of faith to see the needs and answers of God's people in Jerusalem after the Babylonian captivity. Nehemiah describes the scene:

"The words of Nehemiah, the son of Hachaliah. And it came to pass in the month Chisleu, in the twentieth year, as I was in Shushan the palace, that Hanani, one of my brethren, came, he and certain men of Judah; and I asked them concerning the Jews that had escaped, which were left of the captivity, and concerning Jerusalem. And they said unto me, 'The remnant that are left of the captivity there in the province are in great affliction and reproach: the wall of Jerusalem also is broken down, and the gates thereof are burned with fire.' And it came to pass, when I heard these words, that I sat down and wept, and mourned certain days and fasted and prayed before the God of heaven, and said, 'I beseech thee, O Lord God of heaven, the great and terrible God, that keepeth covenant and mercy for them that

love him and observe his commandments: let thine ear now be attentive, and thine eyes open, that thou mayest hear the prayer of thy servant, which I pray before thee now, day and night, for the children of Israel thy servants, and confess the sins of the children of Israel which we have sinned. We have dealt very corruptly against thee, and have not kept thy commandments, nor thy statutes, nor thy judgments, which thou commandedst thy servant Moses. Remember, I beseech thee, the word that thou commandedst thy servant Moses, saying, 'If ye transgress, I will scatter you abroad among the nations: but, if ye turn unto me, and keep my commandments, and do them; though there were of you cast out unto the uttermost part of the heaven, yet will I gather thee from thence, and will bring thee unto the place that I have chosen to set my name there! Now these are thy servants and thy people, whom thou hast redeemed by thy great power, and by thy strong hand. O Lord, I beseech thee, let now thine ear be attentive to the prayer of thy servant, and to the prayer of thy servants, who desire to fear thy name: and prosper, I pray thee, thy servant this day, and grant him mercy in the sight of this man.' For I was the king's cupbearer. And it came to pass in the month Nisan, in the twentieth year of Artaxerxes, the king, that wine was before him: and I took up the wine, and gave it unto the king. Now I had not been beforetime sad in his presence. Wherefore, the king said unto me, 'Why is thy countenance sad, seeing thou art not sick? This is nothing else but sorrow of heart.' Then I was very sore afraid, and said unto the king, 'Let the king live forever: why should not my countenance be sad, when the city, the place of my fathers' sepulchres, lieth waste and the gates thereof are consumed with fire?' Then the king said unto me, 'For what dost thou make request?' So I prayed to the God of heaven. And I said unto the king, 'If it please the king, and if thy servant have found favour in thy sight, that thou wouldest send me unto Judah, unto the city of my fathers' sepulchres, that I may build it.' And the king said unto me, (the queen also sitting by him) 'For how long shall thy journey be? and when wilt thou return?' So it pleased the king to send me; and I set him a time" (Nehemiah 1:1-2:6).

Nehemiah knew that the Jews could not serve the Lord without their city, walls and temple being rebuilt. He desired God to use him to restore the ways that his people would use to worship God. He spiritually recognized that his people had sinned against God's law (Nehemiah 1:7-9) and had thus incurred God's judgment upon them. This should be the spiritual vision of every true leader. Each must see where the Church has sinned against God, and then help to regain God's blessing through repentance, faith, and obedience to His Word.

Second, Nehemiah's commitment to his spiritual vision from the Lord did not buckle under adverse circumstances. Note what this leader did in time of opposition:

"So, built we the wall; and all the wall was joined together unto the half thereof; for the people had a mind to work. But it came to pass, that when Sanballat, and Tobiah, and the Arabians, and the Ammonites, and the Ashdodites, heard that the walls of Jerusalem were made up, and that the breeches began to be stopped, then they were very wroth, and conspired all of them together to come and to fight against Jerusalem, and to hinder it. Nevertheless, we made our prayer unto our God, and set a watch against them day and night, because of them. And Judah said, 'The strength of the bearers of burdens is decayed, and there is much rubbish, so that we are not able to build the wall' " (Nehemiah 4:6-10)

Nehemiah did not allow the enemies of Judah to discourage him in his vision. Instead, he gave himself to prayer. Similarly, every leader should never allow negative people or circumstances to cause him to lose the vision that God has given him for the Church.

USAGE TEST

Definition. A leader undergoes the Usage Test in his life or ministry preparation when he cannot find the need, demand, opportunity, invitation, results or expected occasion to exercise his ministry. "Put on the shelf" is a common description for this situation.

Purposes. God may put a leader "on the shelf" temporarily for several reasons.

First, God may desire to show the leader that he depends too heavily on his actual service or activity, rather than upon the Lord Himself, for his joy and spiritual fulfillment. Being "on the shelf" may stimulate the leader to develop his personal prayer and life in the Word far more than ministry success would.

God may desire to humble the leader. A leader who is greatly used of God may become proud and self-sufficient. He may need to lose part or all of his active or public ministry to see that his own power or ability are not the true cause of his accomplishments in the kingdom. God is more inclined to use a man's weakness for His glory, than to use his strengths. It is simply human nature to credit men for being the source of their strengths, especially their obvious ones.

The Usage Test also gives God an opportunity to purify the motives of His leaders. What causes a leader to act or speak the way he does? Why does he do the things that he does? Many times a leader's motivation will turn from pure ministry service to building a personal kingdom. The name of Jesus Christ, saving souls, and edifying the Church may take the back seat to highlighting the leader's ministry and reputation. God must set this kind of leader on the shelf to purify his motives. Otherwise, this leader will take many into spiritual destruction with himself.

The Usage Test may also deepen the message of the leader. Many leaders live on their past sermons and messages wtihout getting fresh words or experiences from God. Some leaders stay so busy that they either do not have, or do not take the time to deepen their messages. But the flock of God cannot constantly feed from the same pasture of sermons without growing thin and hungry for more. God must sometimes put a ministry out of public commission for awhile so that he will be motivated to deepen his understanding of the Word of God. After a leader's messages deepen, he can return to give the sheep a much more enriching diet.

Biblical Illustration: John the Baptist (Matthew 3; Mark 1; Luke 1,3; John 1). John was born (c. 7 B.C.) to Zacharias and Elizabeth, and was raised and called to the prophetic ministry in the wilderness of Judea (Luke 1:80 and 3:2). He was the forerunner of the Messiah, and the last and greatest member of the prophetic guild before the kingdom of God was proclaimed. For a man whom Jesus Himself highly honored, he had a very humble attitude. But he had a rather brief period of ministry.

John's humble attitude is shown by the words which he said to Christ when the Messiah came to him for baptism: *"I have need to be baptized by You, and do You come to me?"* (Matthew 3:14). His lowly attitude also appears when he preached about Christ, *"After me comes one who is mightier than I, and I am not even fit to stoop down and untie the thongs of his sandals"* (Mark 1:7). John recognized that although he held an important place in God's economy, it was his purpose to lead men to Jesus Christ, even his own disciples (John 1:35-37). Every leader in the Church must know that the entire purpose of his service to God is in leading men to know and to serve the Savior.

John was also willing to accept a longer time of preparation than his actual period of ministry. Luke 1:80 states, *"And the child* (John) *continued to grow, and to become strong in spirit, and he lived in the deserts until the day of his public appearance to Israel."* This preparation time in the desert was probably much longer than the duration of his active ministry. This is a definite part of the Usage Test. Sometimes a leader's service is so unique in kind or timing that God extends his preparation for reasons known only to Himself.

How many leaders would complain if they had to spend thirty years in preparation for a three and a half year ministry, as our Lord did? Most leaders are so service-minded that they think they would be doing their best for God if they spent only three and a half years in preparation for a thirty year ministry! Every leader, however, must accept God's full time of preparation for his ministry. The length of preparation differs for every leader. It will depend upon God's call on his life, his cooperation with the dealings of God, and the future extent of his ministry. God must be trusted wholeheartedly in the fulfillment of all of the details of a leader's ministry, including the timing.

John the Baptist, also, was willing to be used of God only as long as God sovereignly intended to use him. John condemned Herod the tetrarch for many evil things, including marriage to Herodias, his brother's wife. For this Herod had John imprisoned and beheaded. What an inglorious death for one of the greatest eschatological prophets of all time — a short ministry, ending in decapitation! John was totally submitted to the will of God and to God's Usage Test. He did not complain in prison about "being on the shelf," but submitted to God's timing for the end of his ministry.

In the same way, every leader should have a light "grip" on his gift and ministry. He or she must allow God to remove these at any time without complaining, doubting or grumbling. May every leader submit all of the aspects of his ministry to God, especially its timing and usage, throughout all its stages. May all leaders keep their hearts so humble and dependent upon the Lord that He may approve their total patience and trust in Him, even through the Usage Test.

Conclusion

The tests of ministry preparation described in this chapter may come especially during the early stages of a leader's ministry. But they can come at any time — as they did for the men we used for biblical illustrations. Governmental ministries face what may be a "hotter" refiner's fire. God takes all Christians through these tests to refine their faith, however. Because God's imagination is limitless, so are His ways of bringing His children into maturity. This chapter has developed only the more common tests that appear throughout Scripture.

For some, the last test in our series is the hardest. The next chapter, "The Test of Promotion," takes a clear look at the test that God will use to bring your ministry to its full potential. Because God will use this test wisely and lovingly, you can receive it in the same way that you receive God Himself--with open arms.

CHAPTER 12

THE TEST OF PROMOTION

If you want to grow as a Christian, if you want an effective ministry, if you want to extend the kingdom of God, you want to go through the Test of Promotion.

In our age, fear of failure is very strong. Unless a person is walking in the Spirit, he may unconsciously sabotage the success of his Christian walk or his ministry. Deep in his inner man, he may believe that he does not deserve promotion. Or he may fear that success brings with it a standard of faith and practice that he cannot sustain for long. Or he may simply fear failure so strongly that he focuses on trying to avoid failure, rather than trying to succeed in serving God and His Church.

Beloved, be encouraged. God uses the small things of this world to confound the great, and the foolish things to confound the wise. He knew His purpose in making you, and He made you in harmony with His purpose. *"For we are His workmanship, created in Christ Jesus unto good works, which God hath before ordained that we should walk in them"* (Ephesians 2:10).

God has plans to use you. Welcome Him, welcome His plans, welcome His tests, for they are the *"good, acceptable and perfect will of God"* (Romans 12:2).

We have devoted a special chapter to the Test of Promotion for several reasons. First, all of the other tests directly affect this one. Second, it is one of the most difficult of all tests to pass, especially in large churches with many ministry opportunities. Third, this test is one of the most frequent causes of frustration in younger ministries. Finally, this subject is greatly misunderstood in the Church. In studying this test, therefore, we will develop a sound biblical base. And we will apply to this test the principles that have been applied to the tests we have already studied.

Definition

When a leader finds himself not moving forward in ministry in the Church, as he expects he should, he is in the Test of Promotion. The leader is tempted to become angry and bitter at the lack of enlargement, preference, advancement or influence that is evident in his life and ministry. This test can come into a leader's life at any point in his ministry. The more developed his gift or ministry is, however, the more difficult this test is to endure.

The Institute in Basic Youth Conflicts has pointed out that one of the measures of true spiritual maturity is the length of time a person can wait between achieving a ministry and being recognized for it. Most people expect to be promoted the very minute they achieve the function of a certain gift or ministry. God's timing in promotion, however, may not always be man's timing. In fact, most of the time it is not.

Purposes

Most of the reasons that have previously been given for the other tests also apply here. Some of these are: the development of humility, purifying of motives, deepening of one's message, increase of glory to God, the trying of inner attitudes, submission of one's will to God's will. Though all of these are frequent and legitimate reasons for the promotion test, another biblical reason stands out above them all. Promotion does not come from man but from God, and it comes according to one's unique and divine calling. The verses that so aptly sum up this biblical theme of the test of promotion are found in Psalm 75:

> "I said unto the fools,
> 'Deal not foolishly:' and to the wicked,
> 'Lift not up the horn:
> Lift not up your horn on high:
> speak not with a stiff neck.'
> For promotion cometh neither from the east,
> nor from the west, nor from the south.
> But God is the judge: he putteth down one,
> and setteth up another."
> (Psalm 75:2,5,6,7)

The Parable of Promotion

Judges 9 contains a parable that can easily be called "the parable of promotion," because it uses the word promotion three times (vs. 9,11,13). This parable is found in the midst of a political upheaval that includes a terrible blood bath. The men of Shechem accepted as their king, for a short time, Abimelech, the son of Jerubbal (Gideon) by his Shechemite concubine (Judges 8:31). By recruiting help from his mother's kin, the Shechemites, Abimelech won the family fight among Gideon's seventy sons for rulership over the tribe of Manasseh. The Shechemites, who were mostly Canaanite, gladly conceded to Abimelech because he had more blood ties to them than did the other sons of Gideon.

With the support of the Shechemites, Abimelech went to his father's house at Ophrah and murdered his seventy half brothers upon a single stone. Only Jotham, the youngest, escaped his hand. Jotham, from the safety of Mount Gerizim, screamed out this incisive parable of promotion. He used it to bring division between Abimelech and his followers, and then fled from the scene. Through a series of circumstances, the division did appear, and Abimelech was finally killed. Let us take special note of the promotion parable in its setting. In it we will also see certain principles that illuminate the workings of leadership:

> "And all the men of Shechem gathered together, and all the house of Millo, and went, and made Abimelech king, by the plain of the pillar that was in Shechem. And when they told it to Jotham, he went and stood in the top of mount Gerizim, and lifted up his voice, and

cried, and said unto them, 'Hearken unto me, ye men of Shechem, that God may hearken unto you. The trees went forth on a time to anoint a king over them; and they said unto the olive tree, "Reign thou over us." But the olive tree said unto them, "Should I leave my fatness, wherewith by me they honour God and man, and go to be promoted over the trees?"

'And the trees said to the fig tree, "Come thou, and reign over us." And the vine said unto them, "Should I leave my wine, which cheereth God and man, and go to be promoted over the trees?"

'Then said all the trees unto the bramble, "Come thou, and reign over us." And the bramble said unto the trees, "If in truth ye anoint me king over you, then come and put your trust in my shadow; and if not, let fire come out of the bramble, and devour the cedars of Lebanon."

'Now, therefore, if ye have done truly and sincerely in that ye have made Abimelech king, and if ye have dealt well with Jerubbal and his house, and have done unto him according to the deserving of his hands;

(For my father fought for you, and adventured his life far, and delivered you out of the hand of Midian. And ye are risen up against my father's house this day, and have slain his sons, threescore and ten persons upon one stone, and have made Abimelech, the son of his maidservant, king over the men of Shechem, because he is your brother.)

If ye then have dealt truly and sincerely with Jerubbaal and with his house this day, then rejoice ye in Abimelech, and let him also rejoice in you. But if not, let fire come out from Abimelech, and devour the men of Shechem, and the house of Millo; and let fire come out from the men of Shechem, and from the house of Millo, and devour Abimelech.' And Jotham ran away, and fled, and went to Beer, and dwelt there, for fear of Abimelech, his brother.

When Abimelech had reigned three years over Israel, then God sent an evil spirit between Abimelech and the men of Shechem; and the men of Shechem dealt treacherously with Abimelech: that the cruelty done to the threescore and ten sons of Jerubbaal might come, and their blood be laid upon Abimelech, their brother, which slew them: and upon the men of Schechem, which aided him in the killing of his brethren...

Then went Abimelech to Thebez and encamped against Thebez, and took it. But there was a strong tower within the city, and thither fled all the men and women, and all they of the city, and shut it to them, and gat them up to the top of the tower. And Abimelech came unto the tower, and fought against it, and went hard unto the door of the tower to burn it with fire. And a certain woman cast a piece of a millstone upon Abimelech's head, and all to brake his skull. Then he called hastily unto the young man his armor-bearer, and said unto him, 'Draw thy sword, and slay me, that men say not of me, "A woman slew him".'

And the young man thrust him through, and he died. And when the men of Israel saw that Abimelech was dead, they departed every man unto his place. Thus, God rendered the wickedness of Abimelech, which he did unto his father, in slaying his seventy brethren. And all the evil of the men of Shechem did God render upon their heads: and upon them came the curse of Jotham the son of Jerubbaal." (Judges 9:6-24 and 50-57)

Historical Fulfillment. Historically, Jotham's prophesy came to pass. Since the men of Shechem had not shown respect to the house of Gideon, one of the men of Shechem, Gaal ben Ebed, turned against Abimelech (vs.23-29). Gaal ben Ebed's rebellion failed. But Abimilech was eventually murdered by his own armor-bearer, that he might not be remembered as being killed by a woman when he tried to set fire to the city fortress of Thebez (vs.50-55).

Spiritual Teaching. The "parable of promotion" also demonstrates through nature the spiritual principle that every leader must know his own place of ministry, and stay in it! Jotham's parable describes how all but one tree knew the place that God had given to them in nature, and were content to stay there. The olive tree, the fig tree, and the grape vine showed their acceptance of their place in nature, when they said:

"Shall I leave my fatness with which God and men are honored, and go to wave (be promoted) over the trees?" (olive tree, v.9)

"Shall I leave my sweetness and my good fruit, and go to wave (be promoted) over the trees?" (fig tree, v.11)

"Shall I leave my new wine, which cheers God and men, and go to wave (be promoted) over the trees?" (grape vine, v.13)

The bramble bush, however, expressed its desire to go beyond the realm that God had given to it in nature. It wanted to be promoted over all the other trees, and to upset the natural order of all things around it:

"If in truth you are anointing me as king over you, come and take refuge in my shade but, if not, may fire come out from the bramble and consume the cedars of Lebanon" (v.15).

Upon hearing this audacious claim, some questions logically arise. Really now, what kind of shade does a bramble bush offer? And how could a bramble hope to overshadow or replace the majestic, exalted and ancient cedars of Lebanon? Absurd!

Application. In applying this parable to leadership and promotion, we see that every leader must adopt the attitude of ministry acceptance expressed by the olive, fig and vine. They accepted from God their present and future status in nature. So must every leader accept the place of ministry which God has given him (and from time to time gives him) in His vineyard. Much strife, jealousy and hurt feelings could be avoided if God's leaders would just find their ministries and stay within their boundaries.

A tragic example from recent history illustrates this. William Branham, a prophetic ministry in the 1950s, desired to function beyond the ministries of prophecy, word of knowledge, revelation and healing which God had so obviously given to him. He wanted to be a Bible teacher also. It was at this point, according to international traveling Bible teacher Ern Baxter, that Branham's pride put his ministry off the track. Branham had a great prophetic ministry, yet the end of his life and ministry was tragic. Many have speculated that William Branham could have stayed within the boundaries of his prophetic mantle, and prospered. His example teaches all leaders an obvious lesson: every leader must be satisfied with being only that which God intended him to be.

The Horn: Symbol of Promotion in Scripture

A study of the word "horn" in Scripture demonstrates the principle of ministry promotion coming from God alone. In biblical typology, animal horns have the following values or uses:

As vessels for the anointing oil in the ceremonial anointing of offices (I Samuel 16:1,13; I Kings 1:39)

As a musical trumpet (Joshua 6:5)

As a place of refuge (Leviticus 4:7; I Kings 1:50 and 2:28)

As an illustration of power in the prophecies of Daniel, Zechariah and John (Zechariah 1:18; Daniel 7 and 8; Revelation 13:1,11)

As a symbol of the wicked (Psalm 75:4)

As a symbol of the righteous (Psalm 75:10)

As a symbolic example of a ministry or a servant of the Lord (I Samuel 2:1,10)

In the natural world, the horn is an animal's strength and defense. In relation to a servant of the Lord, the horn represents a leader's anointing, power, strength, speech, fruitfulness and ministry.

Let us now observe the exaltation of four persons' horns (or ministries) in the Bible: Hannah's, David's, the righteous', and Christ's. In all four examples, we will see how God sovereignly exalted some horns and put down others.

Hannah had been barren for many years and felt bitterness of soul because she was childless. She saw in her condition that her horn (life) had not been exalted by God. After God gave her Samuel as a son, however, she felt that her horn had been exalted. She greatly rejoiced in the Lord's victory, not only over her physical barrenness, but also over Eli, her corrupt high priest (I Samuel 3:1ff).

"And Hannah prayed, and said, 'My heart rejoiceth in the Lord, mine horn is exalted in the Lord: my mouth is enlarged over mine enemies; because I rejoice in thy salvation. There is none holy as the Lord: for there is none beside thee: neither is there any rock like our God. Talk no more so exceeding proudly; let not arrogancy come out of your mouth; for the Lord is a God of knowledge, and by him actions are weighed. The bows of the mighty men are broken, and they that stumbled are girded with strength. They that were full have hired out themselves for bread; and they that were hungry ceased: so that the barren hath born seven; and she that hath many children is waxed feeble. The Lord killeth, and maketh alive; he bringeth down to the grave, and bringeth up. The Lord maketh poor, and maketh rich: he bringeth low, and lifteth up. He raiseth up the poor out of the dust, and lifteth up the beggar from the dung-hill, to set them among princes, and to make them inherit the throne of glory: for the pillars of the earth are the Lord's, and he hath set the world upon them. He will keep the feet of his saints, and the wicked shall be silent in darkness; for by strength shall no man prevail. The adversaries of the Lord shall be broken to pieces; out of heaven shall he thunder upon them: the Lord shall judge the ends of the earth; and he shall give strength unto his king, and exalt the horn of his anointed.'." (I Samuel 2:1-10)

Notice how Hannah referred to her horn being exalted (vs.1,10). She applied this two ways: to her own life, and to the ministry of her son. God purposed to exalt Hannah's son over Eli, because the sins of Eli's house had corrupted him before God. God chose the horn of Samuel to replace the horn of Eli.

Exaltation of the Righteous

The following chart shows how Hannah's exclamations about God's power have contrasting applications to Eli and Samuel. Where Scripture does not use direct, contrasting poetic parallelism, the author has added unquoted portions to aid the reader's understanding.

ELI	**SAMUEL**
My heart has grown dull and grossly wicked.	*"My heart rejoices in the Lord."*
My horn is brought low because of my sins.	*"My horn is exalted in the Lord."*
I have become an enemy to God, though a priest, because of my sins.	*"My mouth speaks boldly against my enemies."*

I can no longer rejoice in the Lord.

All holiness has left me.

I cannot escape the Lord's judgment because of my religious position.

I have slipped off of God, my rock, because of my sins.

"Boast no more so very proudly."

"Do not let arrogance come out of your mouth."

"For the Lord is a God of knowledge."

"And with Him actions are weighed."

"The bows of the mighty are shattered."

"Those who were full hire themselves out for bread."

"But she who has many children languishes."

"The Lord kills."

"He brings down to Sheol."

"The Lord makes poor."

"He brings low."

He puts down those who think themselves rich.

He puts the rich into the ash heap.

To make them know that they are but men.

And inherit a seat of dishonor.

For He knows how to remove any man from any office.

And the balance of a man's life is in God's hands.

"But the wicked ones are silenced in darkness."

"For not by might shall a man prevail."

"Those who contend with the Lord shall be shattered."

"Against them will He thunder in the heavens."

"The Lord will judge the ends of the earth."

He will give weakness to the self-appointed king.

He will bring low the horn of those who have lost the anointing through sin.

"I rejoice in thy salvation."

"There is no one holy like the Lord."

"Indeed, there is no one besides thee."

"Nor is there any rock like our God."

The Lord exalts the humble and meek.

I will only confess that glory belongs unto the Lord.

The Lord knows every man's sins and will forgive them only as he confesses them.

God will evaluate every action of His leaders.

"But the feeble gird on strength."

"But those who were hungry cease to hunger."

"Even the barren gives birth to seven."

"The Lord makes alive."

"He brings up."

"The Lord makes rich."

"He also exalts."

"He raises the poor from the dust."

"He lifts the needy from the ash heap."

"To make them sit with nobles."

"And inherit a seat of honor."

"For the pillars of the earth are the Lord's."

"And He set the world on them."

He keeps the feet of His godly ones.

For only by God's will and a righteous life shall a man prevail.

Those who cooperate with the Lord shall be blessed.

For them will He work all things for good.

The Lord will judge even His chosen leaders.

"He will give strength to His king."

"He will exalt the horn of his anointed" (see also Isiah 54:1-17).

Every leader must realize that he, like Eli, can bring down God's judgment upon his life out of sin. No matter what a person's religious or spiritual position is in the Church, he still must obey all of God's moral and ethical laws.

Only God Can Promote the Righteous

We must also remember that the prophet Samuel did nothing to exalt himself to the position of prophet-judge in Israel. As you read through the columns below, evaluate the application of this principle to your own life and ministry.

SAMUEL

Samuel was chosen by God before birth for his ministry.

Samuel was dedicated to ministry in the temple by his parents.

Samuel ministered before the Lord as a child.

Samuel ministered unto the Lord under Eli's leadership.

Samuel was sleeping when God first called him by His Spirit.

Samuel became a servant in the temple, and was in charge of opening and closing its doors.

Samuel did not try to exalt himself by freely proclaiming to everyone the prophecy that he had received about his future exaltation.

TODAY'S CHRISTIAN LEADER

Do I sense a real divine call and destiny upon my life?

Do I realize that my divine calling may have much to do with the way my parents or others prayed for me before I was born, or when I was a young child?

Am I willing to believe that God has so ordained my life that He can and will (if I ask Him) use all of the things in my younger years for His glory in my ministry?

Am I striving to make a better position for myself, or do I submit, as unto the Lord, when those over me in the Lord make a decision with which I disagree?

Am I so rested and content in my present ministry that God could call me, as out of a sleep, to do the next thing He wants me to do?

Am I willing to do menial service in the house of the Lord, though I feel a higher calling upon my life?

Do I tell everyone how great is God's calling on my life, or do I wait for the Lord to bring it to pass in His timing and in His way?

From the points above, we can see Samuel did nothing to exalt his own ministry. May it be the same for all of God's leaders. If someone has a call of God upon his or her life, God will exalt that person in His due season.

God's Appointed Leader

We can also see the principle of God exalting a ministry in the life of David. Saul is in stark contrast to the true Spirit-anointed king of Israel. Saul was not God's appointed ruler; instead, the authority of Saul's kingship came from the people themselves. The following brief list contrasts the man-appointed leader, Saul, with the God-appointed leader, David.

SAUL

Saul was anointed with a human instrument, a vial or bowl (I Samuel 10:1), indicating a human anointing.

Saul was approved by the popular vote of the people.

Saul became proud and was brought low by God.

DAVID

David was anointed with what was always considered a divine instrument, a horn (I Samuel 16:3), indicating a divine anointing.

David was chosen by the leading of the Spirit of God (Psalm 89:17-24).

David remained humble and was lifted up by God (Psalm 92:10 and 132:17,18).

God Exalts Only the Called

As this book mentioned earlier, the Church has too many man-appointed leaders today. Some are chosen just because they finished a prescribed seminary training. They may be attractive because they are good businessmen, or because they want to give their lives to the profession of "being a minister." These kinds of men fail in the ministry if they do not also have a divine call upon their lives. God calls and exalts leaders; man does not.

Many denominational pastors say that the only reason for the growth of some charismatic churches is their focus on a leader with a charismatic personality. This may tend to be true in some cases, but the criticisms on this point still miss the mark. A man must have a divine call and a divine, charismatic ability to preach or teach before he can succeed in ministry.

Those who chose the ministry purely for logical or altruistic reasons might as well resign today. Both they and their churches would be better off if they did resign, if they only want to help people, do the world some good, please their parents or take new psychologies to the people. Only God can call a person into the ministry. And if God has called, a person's gift will be recognized and he will not have to strive or struggle to gain notice.

God's principles for exalting a ministry are evident in the horns of the righteous being exalted (Psalm 75:4,5,10). God promises to exalt the horn of the righteous, but the horn of the wicked He will bring low. God promises to bless those who do His will and keep His commandments. In contrast to the righteous, the wicked do not obey God's commandments. The wicked are described as "fools" before the Lord. The words "fool" or "foolish" mean:

To shine forth as a bright light or star that would attempt to shine more brightly than the others.

To make a show of oneself.

To stand out by giving a sharp sound or a loud noise.

A fool always tries to gain the center of attention, to make a name for himself. This should never be the attitude of a man or a woman of God.

The Prerequisite of Righteousness

We see a great contrast between the wicked or foolish, and the righteous, in the way God treats their horns (i.e., their lives and strengths).

DOWNFALL OF THE WICKED	EXALTATION OF THE RIGHTEOUS
Lift not up your horn.	God lifts up the horn of the righteous.
Lift not up your horn on high.	God lifts up the righteous on high.
Promotion comes not from the north, south, east or west, but from the Lord.	God promotes the righteous as they seek him.
God puts down the wicked.	God exalts the righteous (Psalm 112:9 and 148:14).

The above list illustrates the truth that every leader should seek first the kingdom of God, and His righteousness (and character), and all good things (ministry included) will be added to him (Matthew 6:33). A man of God does not need to declare his abilities to other people. Others will be able to see them clearly by themselves. A leader should seek no position except one of humility before the face of the Lord. Neither should a man who is called by God try to anoint himself, or to speak when God has not given him a word. All must realize that the world is not eagerly waiting for a manifestation of one's "great" ministry! All leaders should keep in mind this excellent definition of contentment, "not seeking a ministry but the fruit of a disciplined life" (Institute in Basic Youth Conflicts).

A true leader need never fear that God has forgotten him. He can be assured that as he gives himself to character development, God will expand his ministry.

Samuel gave himself to being a servant in the temple, having the righteousness of God, ministering to God in prayer and temple service, and serving those who were over him in the Lord. God brought to pass his ministry as prophet to the people.

David gave himself to serving Saul, seeking after God's own heart in prayer and praise, and true penitence for all of his sins. God brought to pass his ministry as a prophet, priest and king in Israel.

Elisha gave himself to serving Elijah, the great prophet who gave up his all to follow the Lord, and who lived a righteous life. God brought to pass Elisha's ministry as a double-portion prophet.

In the same way, every leader can develop a servant's heart, a righteous life and a broken spirit before the Lord--and then trust the Lord to fulfill the ministry to which He called him.

Jesus — the Ultimate Exaltation

All of our study on the exaltation of horns finds its fulfillment in the Lord Jesus Christ. Jesus is the ultimate example of how God exalts one who humbles himself and goes the route of death. Paul wrote of Jesus:

"Let this mind (attitude) *be in you, which was also in Christ Jesus: who, being in the form of God, thought it not robbery to be equal with God; but made himself of no reputation, and took upon him the form of a servant, and was made in the likeness of men: and being found in fashion as a man, he humbled himself, and became obedient even unto death, the death of the cross. Wherefore, God also hath highly exalted him, and gave him a name which is above every name: that at the name of Jesus every knee should bow, of things in heaven, and things in earth, and things under the earth. And that every tongue should confess that Jesus Christ is the Lord, to the glory of God the Father. Wherefore, my beloved, as ye have always obeyed, not as in my presence only, but now much more in my absence, work out your own salvation with fear and trembling: for it is God which worketh in you both to will and to do of his good pleasure. Do all things without murmurings and disputings; that ye may be blameless and harmless, the sons of God, without rebuke, in the midst of a crooked and perverse nation, among whom ye shine as lights in the world; holding forth the word of life; that I may rejoice in the day of Christ, that I have not run in vain, neither laboured in vain."* (Philippians 2:5-16)

Jesus Christ humbled Himself, therefore God highly exalted Him. He stripped Himself of all exercise of His eternal sonship and power independent of the Father while He was on the earth, therefore God gave Him a name above all other names. He made Himself of no reputation, thus God gave Him an eternal reputation. Christ's exaltation came through His humiliation, death, servant's heart, perfect sinlessness, and by the will and timing of the Father. So shall it be with every God-ordained leader in the kingdom. As a leader truly humbles himself, with no ulterior motives for recognition, God will exalt him in due season.

In exact contrast to Jesus, Satan tried to exalt himself and his own will. Satan arrogantly declared his own self-will in the following words:

"I will ascend to heaven."

"I will raise my throne above the stars of God."

"I will sit on the mount of assembly in the recesses of the north."

"I will ascend above the heights of the clouds."

"I will make myself like the Most High."

(Isaiah 14:13,14)

Here, five times, Satan says "I will." Self-will is the basic root of all sin. It is men doing or saying exactly as they will, with no thought for God's will. Self-will and sin is the reason why Jesus had to die on the cross, as God willed, to bring man's proud and independent nature back to God. The following diagram contrasts man's self-exaltation with God's way of exaltation.

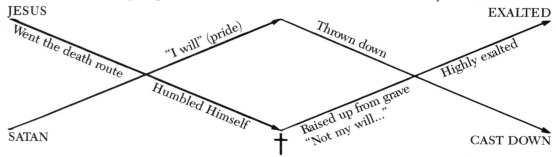

"Not my will, but Thy will be done" (Matthew 26:39; see also 19:30). *"And hath raised up a horn of salvation for us in the house of His servant David"* (Luke 1:69).

God exalts ministry at the proper time. May all leaders, with trust and contentment in God, wait patiently for God to bring His will to pass in their lives and ministries.

Conclusion

Up to this point, we have studied Christian leadership in a perspective that could be described as "from the outside in." We have looked at leadership in its larger context in the Body of Christ. We have studied the calling, the requirements, the preparation and the tests of leadership. In short, we have studied leadership as one might consider the many facets of an important decision. Because we live in a consumer society, we may find it useful to draw on the analogy of a major purchase decision.

Once the decision is made, the perspective changes. A person no longer studies the item of purchase as an object. Now he wants to know about the use of it, how to have its full value. So it is with leadership in the Church. Once a person has bought it with his prayers, his service, his warfare and his tears, he wants to know how to use it to accomplish God's goal--to build the kingdom of heaven.

In the chapters ahead, we will attempt to lay a foundation to explain how leadership operates. We will not borrow from secular disciplines, however. We examine the Bible's teaching on "The Law of Reproduction in Leadership" in Chapter Thirteen. And in the following chapters, we will study the disciplines of the Spirit as developed in the Psalms.

As we have said frequently throughout this book, we repeat now: these principles apply to your own life, no matter what gift and ministry God has given you. Come study leadership, from the perspective of a leader.

CHAPTER 13
THE LAW OF REPRODUCTION
IN LEADERSHIP

The law of reproduction is simply stated: in nature and among men, one kind reproduces its own kind. Trees reproduce trees, flowers reproduce flowers, and trees do not reproduce flowers nor do flowers bring forth trees. God has set an order in which plants propogate what they themselves are. The following scriptures demonstrate this point in relation to the plants as well as to the animals and to God's creation of man:

Genesis 1:11	*"Fruit tree yielding fruit after its kind, whose seed is in itself."*
1:21	*"Waters brought forth abundantly, after their kind. Every winged fowl after his kind."*
1:24	*"Earth brought forth living creatures after his kind. Cattle, creeping things, and beasts of earth, after his kind."*
1:25	*"Beast after his kind . . . Cattle after their kind . . . Every thing that creepeth upon the earth after his kind."*
1:26	*"God said, 'Let us make man in our image, after our likeness'."*
1:27	*"So God created man in his own image (after his kind)."*
1:28	*"God said to man, 'Be fruitful and multiply; and fill the earth; and subdue it; and rule over the fish of the sea'."*

Here we see that every kind reproduces its own kind. This law of reproduction is very obvious, but deserves detailed consideration in relation to leadership. Every leader must realize that he is going to reproduce himself in those under him. He must remember that not only his strengths, but also his weaknesses, will be reproduced in those to whom he ministers. This fact is not meant to put the ministry into a bondage of over-conscientiousness. But it should cause all leaders to examine their own lives very carefully.

To illustrate the law of reproduction in man, let us look at two lines of descent in the Bible. Cain's descent presents a negative example, and Seth's descent presents a positive one.

Cain, the first-born son of Adam and Eve, murdered his younger brother Abel. God set a curse upon Cain, and his lineage ever after reproduced only his own kind. The following diagram traces the story in brief, as the Bible tells it through the meanings of the names of the descendants of Cain and Seth. It is a striking illustration that like produces like, spiritually, as men reproduce after their own kind.

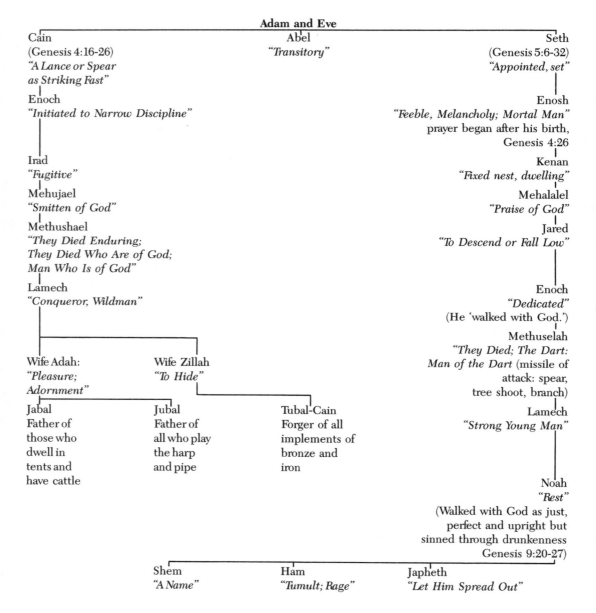

Adam and Eve

Cain
(Genesis 4:16-26)
*"A Lance or Spear
as Striking Fast"*

Abel
"Transitory"

Seth
(Genesis 5:6-32)
"Appointed, set"

Enoch
"Initiated to Narrow Discipline"

Enosh
"Feeble, Melancholy; Mortal Man"
prayer began after his birth,
Genesis 4:26

Irad
"Fugitive"

Kenan
"Fixed nest, dwelling"

Mehujael
"Smitten of God"

Mehalalel
"Praise of God"

Methushael
*"They Died Enduring;
They Died Who Are of God;
Man Who Is of God"*

Jared
"To Descend or Fall Low"

Lamech
"Conqueror, Wildman"

Enoch
"Dedicated"
(He 'walked with God.')

Methuselah
*"They Died; The Dart:
Man of the Dart* (missile of
attack: spear,
tree shoot, branch)

Wife Adah:
*"Pleasure;
Adornment"*

Wife Zillah
"To Hide"

Lamech
"Strong Young Man"

Jabal
Father of
those who
dwell in
tents and
have cattle

Jubal
Father of
all who play
the harp
and pipe

Tubal-Cain
Forger of all
implements of
bronze and
iron

Noah
"Rest"
(Walked with God as just,
perfect and upright but
sinned through drunkenness
Genesis 9:20-27)

Shem
"A Name"

Ham
"Tumult; Rage"

Japheth
"Let Him Spread Out"

As we can see for the most part, Cain reproduced a line whose names had negative meanings, whereas Seth produced offspring who had positive meanings to their names. We see occasional exceptions to this: Methushael, "Man Who Is of God" on Cain's side; Ham, "Tumult; Rage" on Seth's side. But the majority of generations show each man reproducing after his own kind.

In the New Testament, Jude draws on this theme of reproduction by describing certain apostates with the words, *"Woe unto them; for they have gone in the way of Cain"* (Jude 11). Jude is saying here that just as Cain was a murderer and wanderer who attempted to offer an inferior sacrifice to God, so many apostates of the faith have followed his bad spiritual example.

The following diagram illustrates how the apostates described in Jude 11-16,19 followed the way and spirit of Cain.

CAIN (Genesis 4)

Cain hid his anger toward his brother Abel until the day that he slew him (v.8).

Cain did not fear to kill his brother Abel (v.8).

Cain cared only for himself; he could not stand his brother to please God more than he did (vs.4,5,9).

As the older brother to Abel, Cain offered the promise of setting the good example, but did not.

Cain was carried by the winds of his own anger (vs.6,7).

Cain did not offer to God the right kind of fruit for his offering (v.3; Hebrews 11:4).

Cain was twice dead; he both offered the wrong offering to God, and killed his brother (vs.3,8).

Cain, uprooted from his place, became a wanderer (v.12).

Cain's rage and anger made him a wild wave of the sea (v.5).

Cain made his shameful anger and jealousy obvious by killing his brother (v.8).

Cain was cursed by God and given a mark (vs.11,15).

Cain rejected the blood sacrifice of his brother in an ungodly way (vs.3,4).

Cain grumbled at God's judgment--"My punishment is too great to bear" (v.13).

Cain found fault with Abel's offering being more acceptable in God's sight than his own (vs.4,5).

Cain followed after his own lust by declaring, "Am I my brother's keeper?" (v.9)

Cain spoke arrogantly to God--"I do not know (where my brother is). Am I my brother's keeper?" (v.9)

Cain may very well have flattered himself in thinking that God would accept his bloodless offering as He accepted Abel's blood sacrifice.

THE APOSTATES (Jude)

"These men are hidden reefs in your love feasts" (v.12).

"They feast with you without fear" (v.12).

"They care for themselves" (v.12).

They are *"clouds without water"* (v.12).

They are *"carried along by winds"* (v.12).

They are *"autumn trees without fruit"* (v.12).

They are *"doubly dead"* (v.12).

They are *"uprooted"* (v.12).

They are *"wild waves of the sea"* (v.13).

They *"cast up their own shame like foam"* (v.13).

They have *"the black darkness"* reserved forever for them (v.13).

They have sinned *"in an ungodly way"* (v.15).

They are *"grumblers"* (v.16).

They *"find fault"* (v.16).

They *"follow after their own lusts"* (v.16).

They *"speak arrogantly"* (v.16).

They *"flatter people for the sake of gaining an advantage"* (v.16).

Cain divided his family by killing his brother and declaring that he did not know where he was. And his act of murder divided him from the ground's fruitfulness (v.12).	They "cause divisions" (v.19).
Cain was worldly-minded toward his sacrifice and his brother (vs.3-5,8).	They are "worldly-minded" (v.19).
Cain was totally devoid of the Spirit in his sacrifice and in murdering his brother.	They are "devoid of the Spirit" (v.19).

David — The Warrior Who Reproduced Other Warriors

The Bible teaches us that David was a man of war even before he became king of Israel. When Israel was confronted by the Philistine giant Goliath, the young warrior David cried, *"For who is this uncircumcised Philistine, that he should taunt the armies of the living God? . . . Let no man's heart fail on account of him; your servant will go and fight with the Philistine"* (I Samuel 17:26,32). King Saul questioned David's ability to kill the giant. David answered that he had already killed both a lion and a bear (v.34). Having thus gained Saul's confidence in his ability to slay Goliath, David proceeded to do so (vs.50,51).

No other soldier in the Israelite army had the courage to slay Goliath. Why? Saul probably did not infuse his men with courage. He himself was too much of a coward to go out to defeat the giant. The king merely offered to the man who would slay Goliath a reward of riches, marriage to his daughter, and freedom from taxes and public service (I Samuel 17:25). Saul did not try to defeat the giant himself. The law of reproduction is seen here in a negative way: Saul could not produce fortitude in his army because he lacked it himself.

David, on the other hand, reproduced other giant killers as he himself was a giant killer. The following scripture demonstrates this:

"And it came to pass after this, that there arose war at Gezer with the Philistines; at which time Sibbechai the Hushathite slew Sippai, that was of the children of the giant: and they were subdued. And there was war again with the Philistines; and Elhanan the son of Jair slew Lahmi the brother of Goliath the Gittite, whose spear staff was like a weaver's beam. And yet again there was war at Gath, where was a man of great stature, whose fingers and toes were four and twenty, six on each hand, and six on each foot: and he also was the son of a giant. But when he defied Israel, Jonathan the son of Shimea, David's brother, slew him. These were born unto the giant in Gath; and they fell by the hand of David, and by the hand of his servants" (I Chronicles 20:4-8).

Thus, we can see that because David killed giants and the enemies of Israel, he produced servants who could do the same. In contrast to David, we see king Saul, who did not produce great soldiers because he himself was not a brave commander or fighter.

Another example of how David reproduced good soldiers is found in I Samuel 22:1,2 and II Samuel 23:8-23. When David escaped to the cave of Adullam, he became the captain of approximately four hundred men who were in distress, debt or discontent (I Samuel 22:1,2). No doubt, to produce a mighty army, David had to take the time to train these men with problems (II Samuel 23:8-23). This latter reference recounts the victories of eight of these men of David.

Adino, who slew 800 men with a spear in one battle, v.8.

Eleazar, who struck down Philistines until his hand clung to his sword, vs.9,10.

Shammah, who defended a plot of ground full of lentils from the enemy, vs.11,12.

Three mighty men of the thirty chief men, who broke through the Philistine line and obtained water for David, vs.13-17.

Abishai, who slew 300 of the enemy, vs.18,19.

Benaiah, who killed two sons of Ariel of Moab; a lion in the middle of a pit on a snowy day; and an impressive Egyptian--using the enemy's own spear! vs.20-23.

Because David himself was a mighty warrior, he took weak and cowardly men with problems and turned them into great soldiers. David reproduced himself in these men.

Jesus Christ's Reproduction of Ministries

Jesus Christ also demonstrates the law of reproduction. Only because He Himself was the Apostle, Prophet, Evangelist, Pastor and Teacher of the Body is He able to reproduce these same ministries in the Church (Ephesians 4:11,12. Remember, however, that Christ has fullness in all things, and the Body only a measure.) Jesus Christ, Who had the gifts and fruit of the Holy Spirit in fullness, can reproduce the same in His people (Galatians 5:22).

All born-again believers have the *"seed of the Word of God"* within them (I Peter 1:23). Thus we all have the potential of becoming like the source of that seed, Jesus Christ Himself. Consequently, the Lord Jesus also stands as an example to every leader to guard the contents of his heart, because that will be reproduced in others.

Paul's Reproduction in Timothy

Paul's ministry gives us a positive example of the law of reproduction. Paul wrote to Timothy, *"And the things which you have heard from me in the presence of many witnesses, these entrust to faithful men, who will be able to teach others also"* (II Timothy 2:2). Paul desired to reproduce his life and doctrine in Timothy, so that his son in the faith could then reproduce the same in others.

Paul knew that as he lived in accordance with the teachings of Jesus, he could say to Timothy and others, "Follow me as I follow Christ." Paul deeply desired to reproduce the life of Jesus Christ. He exclaimed, *"Oh, how I travail in labor that Christ be formed in you"* (Galatians 4:19). The apostle desired to reproduce not only his doctrine, but also his lifestyle. He wanted men to live and think like Jesus Christ, in addition to knowing that their savior was God.

In the same way, every leader should order his life so he can reproduce the life of Christ in others.

A leader's co-workers should be like-minded with their leader. They should agree on basic goals and objectives. In addition, co-workers should demonstrate a maturity, a holiness, an ability to do their job, and a faithfulness to those whom God has called them to serve. This will express itself in loyally performing small responsibilities, in working cheerfully with others, and in a righteous lifestyle.

Paul's example of reproduction in Timothy, and through him into other faithful men, is demonstrated in the following diagram:

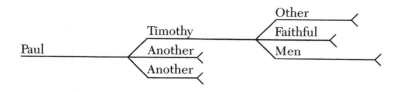

Word of Balance

Though God desires leaders to reproduce the good in their lives into others, He has not ordained that all would be little robots or link sausages in uniformity. Not all of God's people or ministries are exactly the same! God uses his universal principles creatively, in and through the different personalities of His people.

Every leader must remember that by himself, he is insufficient to reproduce all of the maturity or ministry which the Body of Christ needs. Bringing the Body to full maturity requires all of the five-fold ministries (apostles, prophets, evangelists, pastors and teachers). No leader can provide all of these gifts and ministries for all of the people under his care.

Perfection requires the full acceptance and operation of the diverse and unique five-fold ministries upon the Church. God will not use man-made uniformity, or one-man-band ministry, to accomplish His eternal purpose in His people. May every leader continue to recognize the variety of flowers in God's garden.

Reproduction: From Father, Through Son, To Leadership

A servant becomes like his master. A worshipper comes to resemble his object of worship. A son grows into the image of his father. All these illustrate the idea of reproduction. In the following chart, we will see how a trait begins with the Father, is expressed through the Son, and is then reproduced in Christian leadership. As we look at the Son, Who is "the express image of the invisible God," we will take on the image of the Father.

FROM THE FATHER	THROUGH THE SON	TO THE LEADERSHIP
"My Father is working until now" (John 5:17-19).	*"I Myself am working"* (John 5:17 and 9:4 and 10:25,38).	Leaders are to do the work of ministry (Acts 6:4; Ephesians 4:12; I Timothy 3:1).
The Father judges (John 8:16).	*"I judge"* (John 8:16).	Leaders must judge (I Corinthians 6:1-6).
"God is light" (I John 1:5).	*"I am the light of the world"* (John 8:12 and 12:46).	Leaders are light, and are to walk in the light (Matthew 5:14; I John 1:7).
The Father teaches (John 8:28).	The Son teaches (John 8:28; Acts 1:1).	Leaders are teachers (Acts 5:42; I Timothy 3:2 and 4:11).
The Father gave His Son (John 3:16).	The Son gives His life (John 10:11).	Leaders lay down their lives for the sheep (I John 3:16).
The Father loves by sending His only Son.	The Son loves by giving His life as a ransom.	Leaders love by giving their lives for the sheep.
The Father is perfect.	The Son is perfect.	Leadership is commanded to be perfect and set the pattern (II Corinthians 3:18; Colossians 3:10; Matthew 5:48).

FROM THE FATHER	THROUGH THE SON	TO THE LEADERSHIP
The Father is a physician; "He healeth (stitches, cures) *the broken in heart and bindeth up wounds* (Psalm 147:3,4).	*The Son is a physician; "He hath sent me to bind up the broken-hearted."* (Isaiah 61:1,2; Luke 4: 18-23,27)	*Leaders must be physicians* (like the balm of Gilead), to whom God will never say, *"You are all physicians of no value"* (Job 13:4).
The Father is The Image, The Creator, The Everlasting One in Eternity.	The Son manifests Image and the New Man in the flesh with: — Perfect mercy — Perfect kindness — Perfect humility — Perfect meekness — Perfect longsuffering.	The Leadership must put on the New Man and the New Image of The Creator with: — Bowels of Mercy — Kindness — Humility — Meekness — Longsuffering — Forbearance — Love — Bonds of Perfectness.
The Father seeks him that would please Him (John 4:22-24).	The Son pleases the Father by perfect obedience (John 8:26,28).	Leadership pleases the Son by obeying, and feeding the flock (John 21:15-17).
Father God is Spirit (John 4:22-24). The Father is the source of the Anointing. and 10:38).	*"The Spirit of the Lord is upon Me"* (Isaiah 61: 1-3; Luke 4:18; Matthew 3:16,17). *"The Lord hath anointed Me"* (Isaiah 61:1-3; Luke 4:18; Acts 4:27	God's Spirit is upon His leaders (I Corinthians 14:37; II Corinthians 1:21). Leadership must be anointed to preach the Gospel unto the meek (Galatians 1:15,16).
The Father is the source of liberty.	Jesus was to *"proclaim liberty to those who were bound"* (Isaiah 61: 1-3; Luke 4:18).	Leadership should take the message of liberty to the captives (Galatians 5:1).
The Father is the source of power.	Jesus was to *"Open the prison doors to them that are bound, and to set at liberty them that are bruised"* (Isaiah 61: 1-3; Luke 4:18).	Leadership must know how to obtain the key to the prison doors, and know those who are bound, to set them free (esp. those who are bruised in Zion) (Matthew 16:19).
The Father is the God of all comfort (II Corinthians 1:1-5).	Jesus was *"to comfort all them that mourn in Zion"* (Isaiah 61:1-3; Luke 4:18).	Leadership must recognize the sheep who mourn in Zion (the house of God) and must have an eye to comfort them (II Corinthians 1:1-5).

FROM THE FATHER	THROUGH THE SON	TO THE LEADERSHIP
Father God loves to meet needs.	*Jesus meets the needs of the people (Isaiah 61:1-3; Luke 4:18).*	*Leadership must meet the spiritual needs of the people.*
The Father is the source of beauty.	*Jesus was to "Give beauty for ashes"* to those whose lives were ashes (Isaiah 61:1-3; Luke 4:18).	Leadership must adjust, mend and restore mangled lives. It is to give beauty in place of the ashes of wasted lives.
The Father is the source of joy.	Jesus was the oil of joy for those who mourned (Isaiah 61:1-3; Luke 4:18).	Leadership must teach the Church how to rejoice in the Spirit.
The Father is the source of praise.	Jesus went about doing good; healing all manner of sickness and disease; taking away garments of affliction and giving garments of praise for the spirit of heaviness (Isaiah 61:1-3; Luke 4:18).	Leadership must remove the garments of heaviness, affliction, sorrow, sickness, and give the sheep the garments of praise and rejoicing in Jesus Christ.

CHAPTER 14
WARFARE MINISTRIES OF THE LEADER

As we established in the last chapter, God's goal in Christian leadership is to reproduce His life and the life of His Son. Spiritual reproduction produces a measure of the image of God in man.

The Church makes a mistake when she patterns leadership after corporate, government, military, academic or other secular communities. Though these communities have developed disciplines that are occasionally useful, they cannot provide a true foundation for leadership in the Church. Our community is the unique Body of Christ, the only divinely established society on earth. Our example is none other than God Himself, and our source for knowledge of God is the Bible.

The book of Psalms is a very useful study in establishing the traits of God that He wants to reproduce in His leaders. The Psalms, which were written out of intense personal relationship with God, provide a wealth of insight about His personality. We encounter numerous typologies of God in the Psalms that provide us a pattern on which to build the Christian discipline of leadership.

For the next three chapters, we will study nine typologies of God and their reproduction in Christian leadership:

God the Protector	God the Restorer
God the Defender	God the Authority
God the Deliverer	God the Guide
God the Consoler	God the Husbandman
God the Cleanser	

For convenience, we will divide these nine typologies of God into three groups. We will study God the Protector, the Defender and the Deliverer in this chapter, under the unifying principle of "Warfare Ministries of the Leader."

We live in a world where spiritual warfare is the norm. In this chapter, we will study the elements in God's Image that teach us how to minister to God's people in spiritual conflict. May every leader be a student of this information, and may he petition the Most High to reproduce His own Image in the life of His leaders. These functions of Christian leadership are not "extra-credit assignments." They are God's requirements for leading His people.

God the Protector
The Leader as a Refuge
"The Lord shall also be a refuge for the oppressed" Psalm 9:9

The Bible clearly describes God as a refuge and a place of safety for those who trust in Him (Psalm 46:1 and 7:11 and 48:3 and 62:7,8 and 71:7 and 91:2,9 and 94:22 and 142:4,5). We realize that God wants to reproduce these elements of His personality in His leaders:

Lofty cliffs and inaccessible places (secure from spiritual danger and attack)

Shelters

Places of protection

Retreats to which those in need can flee (Hebrews 6:18)

To function as *"a refuge in times of trouble"* (Jeremiah 16:19), the leader must be known and accessible to the troubled person. A leader cannot expect others to flee to him for spiritual help and strength unless they know about him and his ministry. A leader must be accessible to provide help for the oppressed. A leader must not dwell far away from the people. He must dwell in their midst, so they can easily come to him in times of need.

The Latin word we translate as "refuge" means a person, place or thing to which a person flees for help, safety, rescue, succor and relief from distress and affliction. Whenever God's people feel they are oppressed or afflicted by God's enemies, they must be able to come to the leader for help, to regain new strength for oncoming battles.

A leader must realize that as a "refuge" for people, he will have to deal with many human problems, oppressions and sins. These problems require spiritual deliverance. If a leader cannot handle people's problems, he must cry out to God for help. Scripture frequently refers to God as a refuge for those who have very definite needs in their lives (Psalms 9:9 and 14:6 and 57:1 and 59:16; Isaiah 25:4 and 28:15-17).

In the Old Testament, cities of refuge for the unintentional manslayer were easily accessible on either side of the Jordan (Numbers 35:6-32; Deuteronomy 33:27; Job 20:2,3 and 21:13-38; I Chronicles 6:57-67). In the same way, the leader of God must always be available to his people, and ready to deliver them from their sins.

The Leader as a Rock
"Be thou to me a rock of strength" Psalm 31:2

The Hebrew word for "rock" connotes a lofty, craggy stone (probably upon which a sure-footed mountain goat could find protection from its enemies; see Isaiah 33:16). In painting the picture of such an inaccessible place, we should include the psalmist's description of God the Rock. God is an immoveable, all-encompassing foundation for a person's past, present and future life (Isaiah 26:4). The Bible clearly presents God as a strong rock for His people (Psalm 18:2,31 and 27:5 and 31:2 and 61:2 and 78:16). The Bible also prophesies of the Lord Jesus Christ as *"the shadow of a great rock in a weary land"* (Isaiah 32:2). Both God the Father and God the Son are described as rocks of safety and salvation to God's people. The traits of being a rock apply to the Christian leader in these ways:

Just as a rock is made by God (and not man) through natural means, so a man is called and prepared by God Himself for the ministry, and not by man's calling or preparation. As we have said before, a human ordination ceremony does not necessarily indicate the reception of a divine commission from God. A man can be officially ordained and not have a call from God on his life.

As a rock is stable and firm, a leader's character, personality and decision-making ability should be also. A leader should be a source of stability to his people in the sense of giving spiritual direction by wisdom and personal example.

As a rock is strong, so should every leader be spiritually, mentally and emotionally strong in the Spirit of God. When a leader is strong, the people can lean upon him for help, with confidence.

As a rock provides protection from heat and rain, so should a leader be a dependable source of protection from spiritual troubles.

As a rock can be used for a building's foundation, so a leader should be able to ground the people in a firm scriptural foundation in Christ.

As people sometimes used rocks for houses in ancient times, so a leader should bring people to Jesus Christ, Who is the Rock of Ages, and establish them in His house, the Church of the Living God.

A rock is durable, permanent and lasting. A leader should be such a faithful guide to the people of God that they can depend on him always to help them in the things of God.

Rock formations provide the most pleasant and pure water in nature. A leader's life should produce the pure flowing water of the Holy Spirit (see John 7:38,39).

Rock and rock formations produce rich mines of gold and silver. A leader should be a storehouse of the precious truth of God's Word (Job 28:1-3).

A large rock gives a weary traveler shade and refreshing. So should a leader give rest and refreshing through Jesus Christ to weary Christians in their life pilgrimage to heaven.

A rock is many times produced slowly, secretly, under much pressure and in the dark. A leader's ministry will many times be produced line upon line, out of the view of the people, during times of spiritual blackness, and through many spiritual pressures.

The Leader as a Shelter and Strong Habitation

"Thou hast been a shelter for me" Psalm 61:3
"Be thou my strong habitation" Psalm 71:3

It is very important for the leader to be a spiritual habitation for his people. A leader must know the Lord and His Word well, to provide his people a spiritual shelter in which they can dwell in peace and security. Being a habitation for God's people speaks of a leader providing a place of commitment, relationship and communication for the saints.

Hebrew words that relate to "habitation" can describe the leader, in spiritual terms, as a:

Home for rest, beauty and satisfaction
Seat of comfort
Residence for living
Retreat for refreshing
Shepherd's hut for safety
Judgment seat for equity
Wall for defense
Establishment for permanency

All of these descriptions apply to the leader's role in providing a dwelling place for the people of God.

The Bible speaks of God having a habitation (Exodus 15:2; II Chronicles 6:2 and 29:6; Job 5:24; Isaiah 54:2). It also describes the wicked as having a habitation--in destruction (Psalm 69:25; Job 5:3; Isaiah 27:10 and 34:13; Acts 1:20; Jude 6). The enemies of God's people desire to trap Christians in their own houses of evil (pride, envy, hatred, lust; see Revelation 18:2; Genesis 49:5; Psalm 74:20). A leader must provide the following qualities for his people, which the Bible describes as a kind of habitation in which God dwells:

Holiness (Psalm 68:5)
Strength (71:3)
Justice (89:14)
Peace (Isaiah 32:18)
Quietness (Psalm 33:20)
Spirituality (Psalm 33:14; Ephesians 2:22)

In providing these spiritual qualities for God's people, a leader will give them a spiritual habitation.

The Leader as a Covering
"O God, the Lord . . . thou hast covered my head in the day of battle" Psalm 140:7

Today, the Church greatly needs God's leaders to provide coverings of protection. Leaders must guard the Church in this way to protect her from the spirit of deception running rampant throughout the world (Matthew 24:4-26; Mark 13:22). Many people are being led astray into error and falsehood because they lack leadership that is bold enough to direct them into the right ways of God. Paul himself gives many warnings to the Church about not being deceived (II Thessalonians 2:3; Ephesians 5:6,7; Galatians 6:7; I Corinthians 15:33). Even the elect can go astray.

Throughout the Bible, God documents the true necessity for spiritual covering. The Bible illustrates spiritual covering in the following ways:

The Tabernacle of Moses had coverings to protect its furniture from the storms and winds of the dry desert life (Exodus 26:7,14 and 35:11,12 and 39:34; Numbers 4:11 and 9:15-16).

The ark of the covenant was covered with the mercy seat and two gold cherubim (Exodus 25:18 and 37:9).

The holy things of the tabernacle were covered to protect them from defilement (Numbers 4:20).

The bronze altar of the tabernacle had a covering (Numbers 16:38,39).

The holy vessels of the tabernacle were covered (Numbers 19:15).

The priests who ministered in the tabernacle had garment coverings (Exodus 28:42).

The righteous are covered with the robe of righteousness (Isaiah 61:10) and the hand of God (Psalm 51:16; Exodus 33:22) and God's feathers (Psalm 91:4) and God's strength (Psalm 140:7).

The natural and spiritual house is to be covered through proper authority structure (Ephesians 5:21-25; I Corinthians 11:3).

The Church is to be covered with the Lord Jesus and His ministries (Ephesians 4:11-13; Hebrews 13:7,17). See also the two women in I Corinthians 11:10 and Genesis 3:1-15; also Psalm 91:1-4,9-11; Matthew 18:10; the passover houses in Exodus 12:2-30; and the cities of refuge in Numbers 35:11-28.

From these scriptural examples, we can see that God desires to cover His holy people with His love through the leaders He appoints over them. God appoints leaders over his people not for cruel domination, but for loving protection from the many deceptions that are growing in the world today. These deceptions are growing out of many evil root attitudes. Some of these root attitudes are:

Pride (to be lifted up in a fog) Proverbs 6:17 and 8:13 and 11:2 and 15:25.

Foolishness (to despise the sound judgments of wisdom) Proverbs 1:22 and 14:16 and 12:15 and 23:9.

Instability (to reject correction or change) Proverbs 14:15.

Individualism (to trust oneself more than God) Proverbs 3:5 and 28:26.

Intellectualism (to think that the mere accumulation of knowledge is going to lead to truth) Genesis 3:6,24; Isaiah 47:10; Romans 1:22; II Timothy 3:7; Colossians 2:8.

Unchangeableness (to have a hard heart and mind toward God and His Word) Exodus 7:15-22; Deuteronomy 2:30; Proverbs 28:14; John 12:40; Hebrews 3:13.

Rebelliousness (to insist constantly on having one's own way) I Samuel 15:23; Psalm 66:7 and 68:6; Jeremiah 5:23.

Immorality (to delight in the lusts of the flesh) II Samuel 11:1-17; Romans 1:18-32.

Because of these and similar attitudes, God's ministries must become better guides to the people of the Lord. If any one of these attitudes remains in the heart of a Christian, that Christian will soon fall away from faith in Jesus Christ. To help guard the people from deceptions, a leader must:

Guard his own heart and the heart of his people from all evil attitudes.

Stay submitted to other holy men of God.

Maintain his position as the covering over his own home.

Maintain his first-love relationship with Jesus through an intense devotional life.

Stay where God has planted him and not roam aimlessly.

Teach his people to maintain their commitments to their families and their local church.

The Leader as a Watchman
"Set a watch, O Lord, before my mouth" Psalm 141:3

Every leader is a certain type of spiritual watchman. Being a watchman over the flock of God is one of the most awesome responsibilities of a leader, because of the way that God looks upon this ministry. God said to Ezekiel, the prophet:

"Son of man, speak to the children of thy people, and say unto them, 'When I bring the sword upon a land, if the people of the land take a man of their coasts, and set him for their watchman: If when he seeth the sword come upon the land, he blow the trumpet and warn the people; Then whosoever heareth the sound of the trumpet, and taketh not warning; if the sword come, and take him away, his blood shall be upon his own head, He heard the sound of the trumpet, and took not warning; his blood shall be upon him. He that taketh warning shall deliver his soul. But if the watchman see the sword come, and blow not the trumpet, and the people be not warned; if the sword come and take any person from among them, he is taken away in his iniquity; but his blood will I require at the watchman's hand.' So thou, O son of man, I have set thee as a watchman unto the house of Israel; therefore

thou shalt hear the word at thy mouth, and warn them from me. When I say unto the wicked, 'O wicked man, thou shalt surely die;' if thou dost not speak to warn the wicked from his way, that wicked man shall die in his iniquity; but his blood will I require at thine hand. Nevertheless, if thou warn the wicked of his way to turn from it; if he dost not turn from his way, he shall die in his iniquity; but thou hast delivered thy soul. Therefore, O thou son of man speak unto the house of Israel." Ezekiel 33:2-10

Here we see the grave accountability on the shoulders of the watchman. He must cry out against the sins that he sees; otherwise, God will make him guilty of blood. The more that the Lord has revealed, or the more of God's vineyard that is under his responsibility, the more he must speak forth.

The Hebrew word for "watchman" means to lean forward; to peer into the distance; to observe; to await; to hedge about as with thorns; to guard, to protect; to attend to.

One of the largest aspects of the watchman's ministry that emerges is to take initiative to look into the distance (the future). He must see where the present attitudes and actions of the people of God are going to take them. Through years of experience, a watchman can discern good or bad consequences of certain actions. He knows from his own walk with God that a person reaps what he sows (Galatians 6:7). God thus requires him to warn His people of His judgments upon sin in their lives.

God also speaks of the ministry of the watchman in the New Testament. "Obey those who have rule over you, for they watch over your souls (for they are constantly keeping watch over your souls and guiding your spiritual welfare)" (Hebrews 13:17, Amplified Bible; see also Luke 12:37 and Ephesians 6:18). Thus, the leaders under the New Covenant are also challenged constantly to watch for the spiritual welfare of the saints in Christ Jesus.

Because this ministry has always been so important to God, the rest of this section will give the New Testament leader some brief applications of the watchman ministry. You can do further study as the Spirit leads to develop each of these important points.

Characteristics of God's Watchman

As the Old Covenant watchman needed good eyesight and perception (II Samuel 18:24), so the New Testament leader must have spiritual sight and insight to see the future consequences of his and his people's attitudes and actions before the Lord.

Old Covenant watchmen had to be faithful to God and man, to clearly communicate from the city wall what he saw coming (II Samuel 18:24-27; Isaiah 21:12). The New Testament leader must also keep faith in performing the ministry of oversight which God has entrusted to him.

The Old Covenant watchman was a messenger for the king (II Kings 9:17-20). The New Testament leader must also be a messenger of the King above all Kings, the Lord Jesus Christ.

The Old Covenant watchman needed a good relationship with the king of the city which he served (Psalm 127:1). The New Covenant leader must have a healthy spiritual relationship with Jesus Christ, King over His Church and over the city of the living God (Hebrews 12:22).

The Old Covenant watchman was set in his place of service by the Lord Himself (Isaiah 21:6). The New Covenant leader must also be placed in his ministry by the Lord's call, and not by a human system.

The Old Covenant watchman had to warn the people with the sound of the trumpet (Ezekiel 33:3; Jeremiah 6:17; Joel 2:1). The New Covenant leader must teach and preach the Word of God with power from on high.

The Old Covenant watchman accepted the Lord's judgment if he failed to sound the trumpet to warn of approaching trouble (Ezekiel 33:6,7). God will hold the New Covenant leader accountable if he does not warn the Church about approaching spiritual danger.

The Old Covenant watchman had to communicate to the people exactly the message he had received from the Lord (Ezekiel 33:7,8). The New Covenant leader must clearly communicate God's specific word to him, without adding to or reducing from its contents.

The Old Covenant watchman had to tell the people the Word of the Lord (Ezekiel 33:9). The New Covenant leader must communicate on the level of the people, so they can understand the Word of the Lord.

The Old Covenant watchman lifted up his voice with other watchmen in song (Isaiah 52:8), showing a spirit of unity and rejoicing. The New Covenant leader must pursue spiritual unity with other leaders of the Body of Christ, by coming together with them to sing and praise the Lord.

The Old Covenant watchman saw eye to eye with other watchmen in their day of visitation (Isaiah 52:8). The New Covenant leader must flow in cooperation with other leaders during his day of spiritual visitation.

The Old Covenant leader had to be clear of character deficiencies (Isaiah 56:10-12). Like him, the New Covenant leader must also be clear of these deficiencies:
— Blindness (as dogs that cannot see)
— Ignorance (as dogs that do not know)
— Speechlessness (as dogs that cannot bark)
— Laziness (as dogs that often sleep)
— Greediness (as dogs never satisfied with their portion)
— Imperceptiveness (as dogs untrainable by their masters)
— Selfishness (as dogs who pursue only their own gain)
— Nearsightedness (as dogs who cannot see down the road)

The Old Covenant watchman made mention of the name of the Lord all day and all night, not remaining quiet (Psalm 63:6 and 90:3,4 and 119:148 and 130:6; Isaiah 62:6). The New Covenant leader must constantly call on the name of the Lord Jesus Christ for power, strength and wisdom in his ministry.

The Old Covenant watchman had to proclaim a prophetic word to the people during a time of visitation (Jeremiah 31:6; Micah 7:4). The New Covenant leader must sense the presence of the Lord, and the prophetic mantle, during today's visitations.

The Old Covenant watchman hoped in the Lord and watched for Him; especially during times of judgment (Lamentations 4:17). The New Covenant leader must hope in Jesus Christ, his Lord, and watch for displays of truth and mercy during His time of judgment and visitation.

The Old Covenant watchman performed his specific service of watching for the enemy (Nehemiah 7:3 and 12:9). The New Covenant leader must know his specific calling in God, and be faithful to function in it.

The Old Covenant watchman protected and guarded the house of the Lord, as a soldier guarded the house of the king in the day of battle (II Kings 11:4-8; II Chronicles 23:6-8). The New Covenant leader must be willing and able to respond to the cry of the people of God at any time of day or night.

The Old Covenant watchman was in the hand of the Lord to give the people their needs, rather than their wants (a rebuke, rather than a compliment; Jeremiah 31:28). The New Covenant leader must both edify and correct God's people.

The ancient watchman continually watched and prayed (Mark 13:33). So the leader of the Church must continually watch and pray today.

The apostle Paul admonished the early Church to watch, to stand fast in the faith and to be strong (I Corinthians 16:13). Today's Church leader must do the same.

The apostle Paul encouraged the early Church to watch and pray with thanksgiving (Colossians 4:2). The leaders of the Church today should keep thankful and joyful hearts before the Lord.

The apostle Paul exhorted the early Church to watch with an attitude of seriousness, and not to sleep (I Thessalonians 5:6). The leader of the Church today must soberly face his spiritual responsibility to the Lord as watchman over God's people, realizing that the eternal destinies of souls are in his hands.

God the Defender
The Leader as a Shield and Buckler
"But thou, O Lord art a shield about me" Psalm 3:3a
"He is the buckler to all those that trust in him" Psalm 18:30

Scripture many times refers to God as a shield (Psalm 3:3 and 5:12 and 18:35 and 28:7 and 33:20 and 47:9 and 59:11 and 84:9,11 and 91:4 and 115:9-11 and 119:114 and 144:2). Let us look at how God's leaders can be shields to the people of God.

The shield is one of the oldest forms of defense. In ancient times, shields were of a tough crocodile hide, formed into the shape of an oval or a door. Shields protected ancient army troops from the spears, swords, rocks and arrows of the enemy.

The Bible clearly speaks of God being a shield to some, but not to others. God protects those who obey Him, but does not guard those who disobey His voice. Thus, God is described as a shield to Abraham (Genesis 15:1), to the nation of Israel (Deuteronomy 33:28,29; Psalm 115:9,10) and to David (II Samuel 22:3). God was not a shield to the disobedient king, Saul (II Samuel 1:21). To further specify this truth, the Bible clearly states whom God will shield:

Those who serve Him (Psalm 33:20).
Those who reverence Him (115:11).
Those who walk in His truth (91:4).
Those who are anointed with His Spirit (84:9).
Those who trust in Him (Proverbs 30:5).
Those who hold up their shield of faith (Ephesians 6:16).

When all of these things operate in a leader's life, God will shield him. Furthermore, if these qualities operate in the people's lives, and in a balanced way toward their leaders also, their leaders can be true shields to them as well. Just as God protects only the submitted, obedient, humble and covenanted believers, however, the leader can only be a true shield to those who exercise these qualities. The Lord and His leaders want to protect all people from the wiles of the devil. But the people must allow them to be protectors, so that they can function as true spiritual shields.

A leader is a spiritual shield to those who will submit to him through his spiritual teaching and counseling. In the days of Christ, shepherds of the flocks were sometimes literally the doors to the sheepfolds, because they laid their bodies down in the sheepfold's opening. This is true of today's spiritual shepherds as well. They will, at times, literally lay aside their own life's interests for the spiritual interests of the sheep.

The buckler closely resembles the shield in its role in defense. The buckler was a light, round shield, usually held in the hand or strapped to the wrist of a soldier or bowman. The soldier carried not only a large shield (see I Samuel 17:7), but also a small buckler. The buckler was the best quick defense against fiery darts, stones and blazing torches that were hurled down from the wall of a besieged city. The buckler was usually made of wood, overlaid with leather, and anointed with oil to protect it from drying and cracking.

The Lord Himself is described as a buckler to those who trust in Him (II Samuel 22:3,31; Psalm 18:2,30 and 35:1,2 and 91:4; Proverbs 2:7; Jeremiah 46:3). The Psalmist, David, knew the value of having a small, mobile buckler at his side. He spent many weeks in and out of cities and caves, eluding the hand of Saul who was out to kill him. David had to be ready to defend himself, instantly, against any enemies that might come unexpectedly from Saul or his army. In these experiences, David found the Lord to be his real buckler of protection. The Lord was always there to help him just as quickly as the Psalmist would call upon His name for help.

In the same way, God's leaders must be bucklers to the people, who trust in them to be their emergency help in time of need.

As a true door (shield or buckler) to the flock of God, a leader must demonstrate the following character qualities:

Stability in the Lord	Grounded spiritually	Zeal
Love	Loyalty	Strength
Resiliency	Trustworthiness	Availability
Steadfastness	Dedication	Flexibility

The Leader as a Fortress and High Tower

"The Lord is . . . the horn of my salvation and my high tower" Psalm 18:2

The leader also must be a fortress and a high tower to the people of God. These two figures are linked; a city fortress had a high tower in each corner, and some ancient vineyards (see Isaiah 5:2; Matthew 21:33) had towers in the center of a fortress. The broad Hebrew definition for the word "fortress" is: a net to capture, a fastness, a fortification, a castle, a fortified city, a defense. As a fortress for God's people, a leader provides them safety and security from the attacks of the enemy (see II Samuel 22:2; Psalm 18:2 and 31:3 and 71:3 and 91:2 and 144:2; Isaiah 17:3 and 25:12 and 34:13; Jeremiah 6:27 and 10:17 and 16:19; Amos 5:9; Micah 7:12; Hosea 10:14).

A leader should also be a high tower for the people. "The name of the Lord is a high tower and the righteous run into it and are safe" (Proverbs 18:10). In the natural realm, the high tower many times protected the outside wall of the city. It was used as a place from which arrows and stones could be hurled upon the enemy. In the countryside, towers were erected to protect flocks, herds and even roadways (II Kings 17:9; II Chronicles 26;10 and 27:4). A leader can fulfill all of these needs by doing the following:

Defending the people of God by watching for the coming adversary, the devil.

Casting the Word, the Spirit, the Name and prayers in the Spirit down at the devil, to stop him.

Protecting God's flocks and herds--His people--from the enemies' tactics to divide them.

Safeguarding all of the spiritual highways of God (including the "highway of holiness") that the people of God may walk unhindered to the City of God.

Guarding against the devil's attempts to rob God's vineyard (His people) from the fruit of the vine (the fruit of the Holy Spirit--love, joy and peace) in their lives.

The Leader as a Defender

"For the Lord is our defense" Psalm 89:18

The Bible declares that God is the defender of His people (Job 22:25; Psalm 7:10 and 59:9,16,17 and 62:2 and 89:18 and 94:22; Zechariah 9:15). God offers His people safety in the proclamation of His name over His possession, all of creation (Psalm 20:1). If God defends His people, His leaders must do the same.

To defend God's people, a leader must match his actions and attitudes with the biblical sense of "defense" and "defend." A leader must:

Be a shade and shadow to God's people, protecting them from the sun's harsh rays.

Be as a bird who hovers over its nestlings.

Be as a hedge to hem in a portion of the garden of God.

Be a fortress of protection from attack.

Be a shield to the people, warding off the fiery darts of the enemy.

Be a canopy or chamber in which the people can find security and rest.

Be as a governor who punishes the wicked but rewards the righteous.

Give an honest account of himself to God and the people.

Make a (legal) plea for the rights of his people before God and man.

Be a peacemaker, who clears difficulties for other people.

How does a leader become a good defense for his people? The Bible shows that God certainly desires a leader to be that defense. In both the Old Testament judges and the New Testament apostle Paul, His leaders are defenders of the faith and of the faithful (Judges 10:11; II Kings 19:34 and 20:6; II Samuel 23:12; Philippians 1:7,17).

First, a leader must be a man of wisdom. Wisely applying the spiritual principles of the kingdom, a leader will defend his people from the adversary. He will know the enemy's tactics (Ecclesiastes 7:12).

Second, a leader must keep his own family in order and in unity. In this, he will mount a stronger defense for the families of the church against the attacks of the devil (II Chronicles 11:5; Psalm 31:2).

Third, a leader should take pains to maintain a strong commitment to the house of the Lord. The house of the Lord will be a sure defense against the foe.

Fourth, a leader must stay in the presence of the Lord. God's presence (or glory) is a defense for the people of God, as it was for Israel in the wilderness (Isaiah 4:5).

Fifth, a leader should realize that every time he prepares something for the good of God's people, he is defending them (see Nahum 2:5).

Finally, a leader will defend God's people well if he remembers that he will defend the same people that God Himself has defended throughout history: the poor and the fatherless (I Samuel 31:5; Psalm 5:9-11 and 82:3). May every leader feel his duty to help, protect and defend those who are spiritually poor and without a personal knowledge of their heavenly Father. If he does, he will lead them to Jesus Christ, who is the greatest defender the Church will ever have.

God the Deliverer

The Leader as a Deliverer

"Thou art my help and my deliverer, O Lord" Psalm 70:5

A deliverer causes others to slip out of trouble or escape from the hold of death. When Israel came out of Egypt, God delivered them by causing the Red Sea to open for their passage, and closing it down upon the pursuing Egyptians. When the nation entered Canaan, God delivered them by enabling them to defeat armies, peoples and cities that were larger and stronger than themselves. When God operated as a deliverer for His people, He moved in the area of the miraculous.

In the same way, every leader should believe the Lord to make him a powerful deliverer of God's people. Not every leader will have the gift of faith, miracles or healings. But each leader can believe God to answer his prayers for God's people to be delivered from the snares of sin.

After the war with the Philistines and Goliath's kin, David declared, *"The Lord is my rock, my fortress, my deliverer, my shield, the horn of my salvation, my high tower, and my refuge"* (Palm 18:2). In response to this same time of deliverance, David also wrote,

"I called upon the Lord, who is worthy to be praised,
And I am saved from my enemies.
The cords of death encompassed me,
And the torrents of ungodliness terrified me.
The cords of Sheol surrounded me;
The snares of death confronted me.
In my distress I called upon the Lord, And cried to my God for help;
He heard my voice out of His temple,
And my cry for help before Him came into His ears"

Psalm 18:4-6

God delivered David out of deep troubles, even from the very snares of death itself. In the same way, every leader should believe God to enable him to deliver God's people out of the snares of unbelief, depression, purposelessness, fruitlessness, and all sin. This happens by the power of the Holy Spirit and the Word of God. One of the keys in this warfare: the leader himself must have experienced God's deliverance. This will give him both the confidence and the ability to set others free in the name of the Lord Jesus Christ.

The Leader Who Looses and Redeems the Prisoner

"O Lord, truly . . . Thou hast loosed my bonds" Psalm 116:16

A Christian leader is one of God's main instruments to deliver the spiritual prisoner. The leader must be equipped with the keys of the kingdom of God to open the doors of people's bondages through the power of the Holy Spirit.

Scripture presents Joseph and Sampson as two illustrations of how people can become spiritually bound in an area of his life. Joseph was in prison due to the dealings of God in his life (Genesis 39:20-23 and 40:3-5 and 42:16-19). By contrast, Sampson was behind prison doors due to disobedience to God's Word (Judges 16:21-25).

A leader must discern why a person is in prison. Is God dealing with him, and trying to change some area of his life? Or is he in prison because he disobeyed God? A leader must counsel these two situations very differently. In the final outcome, God released Joseph from prison and exalted him in Egypt, but Sampson's continued disobedience meant his own destruction. In Joseph's case, God acted as the scriptural deliverer who looses the prisoner (see Psalm 79:11 and 102:20 and 146:7; II Kings 25:27-29).

When we refer to a leader and the loosing of the prisoner, we refer to a spiritual loosing from spiritual captivity. This can apply in many different realms, but we are referring here to David's cry in Psalm 142:1-7

"I cried unto the Lord with my voice: with my voice unto the Lord did I make my supplication. I poured out my complaint before him; I shewed before him my trouble. When my spirit was overwhelmed within me, then thou knewest my path. In the way wherein I walked have they privily laid a snare for me. I looked on my right hand, and behold, but there was no man that would know me: refuge failed me; no man cared for my soul. I cried unto thee, O Lord: I said, 'Thou art my refuge and my portion in the land of the living.' Attend unto my cry; for I am brought very low; deliver me from my persecutors; for they are stronger than I. Bring my soul out of prison, that I may praise thy name: the righteous shall encompass me about; for thou shalt deal bountifully with me."

In this passage, the meaning of being a prisoner in one's soul has a progressively bolder expression. Sometimes being a prisoner means being without friends. Sometimes it means persecution for the sake of the Gospel. It may mean that one's soul is overwhelmed. In each of his own cases, David knew that God would deliver him out of his prison experience.

Every leader is to deliver people from being snared in the devil's prison house of pride, anger, unbelief, witchcraft and deception. He is to loose prisoners into the kingdom of God, where they can be a prisoner and love-slave of the Lord Jesus Christ (see Ephesians 3:1 and 4:1).

Redemption is directly related to setting prisoners free. Redemption has various meanings, but its central idea is to deliver or set free from evil by payment of a price. In Bible days, both slaves and prisoners were redeemed or ransomed by the payment of a price. In biblical thought, the concept of redemption also has the following elements:

To purchase or buy back an estate which had been sold

To pay what has been vowed or is otherwise due to God

To break loose by rending; to pull or rescue out of the hands of an enemy

To the Christian leader, every one of these points finds its fulfillment in Jesus Christ. Through the death and resurrection of Jesus Christ, men are redeemed back to God, in the full sense of the word. Boaz, an Old Testament kinsman-redeemer, was both willing and able to redeem Ruth, a Moabitess. In the same way, Jesus Christ became a man so that He might redeem His Church back to God. The Bible clearly describes God as a redeemer of men (see Psalm 19:14 and 107:2; Job 19:25). This description also fits the leader. Every leader helps to redeem people back to God by presenting the claims of Christ to them.

But from what things, through the power of the Spirit, is the leader to deliver the people of God? He must help to deliver them from many of the same things from which God delivers them. Some of these:

All of their troubles (Psalm 25:22)
Deceit (Psalm 72:14)
All iniquity (Titus 2:14)
The house of the bondman (Deuteronomy 7:8)
All adversity (II Samuel 4:9)
All distress (II Kings 1:29)
Their enemies (Psalm 136:24)
The house of servants (Micah 6:4)
The curse of the Law (Galatians 3:13)
Spiritual and physical destruction (Psalm 103:4)

Each of these ten points of deliverance has spiritual application in the lives of the people of God. Through Jesus Christ, the souls and the lives of the people of God need to be redeemed (Psalm 49:8,15 and 69:18); Lamentations 3:58). God will hold His leaders accountable for both the temporal and eternal destinies of many people, because He sometimes puts it within the power of His leaders to help redeem a soul or a life from destruction.

In redeeming souls through Christ, the leader must:

Share the redeeming power of Jesus Christ with an emphasis on God's mercy (Psalm 26:11 and 44:26)

Take the initiative to share the redemption of Christ with others, not waiting for them to come to him or to a church service, because God redeemed Israel with an outstretched arm (Exodus 6:6)

Pay special attention to those already in the family of God who need to experience a further dimension of God's redemption, even in practical ways (see Leviticus 25:25-49)

Fully trust in the might and power of God to redeem someone. God is surpassingly great to fully redeem any person who truly desires redemption (Deuteronomy 9:26)

Reject all diversions from the spiritual and incorruptible truths of God's redeeming power; reject a focus on the changeable and temporal (I Peter 1:18)

Remember that every person needs to be redeemed, and that each is equally precious and costly in the sight of God (Psalm 49:8)

In applying these insights to his life, a leader will be equipped to help the Lord loose and redeem the spiritual prisoner from his prison-house of sin.

The Leader as an Opener of Blind Eyes

"The Lord openeth the eyes of the blind" Psalm 146:8

When we speak of a leader being a divine influence in a person's life to open the eyes of the blind, we are not limiting ourselves to the ability of the Lord Jesus Christ to work through him to heal physical eyes of natural blindness (Isaiah 43:8). Physical healing does and should occur. But we are now referring primarily to the healing of spiritual blindness (Matthew 4:16). The devil has *"blinded the minds"* of the unbelieving in this world (II Corinthians 3:14 and 4:4; I John 2:11). Therefore, it is a part of every leader's spiritual warfare to open blinded hearts and minds.

Scripture makes it obvious that God and His Son open the eyes of the blind both naturally and spiritually (Psalm 146:8; Matthew 11:5; Luke 4:18). The first step of spiritual healing happens when the Lord opens someone's spiritual eyes to see Jesus as Lord and Savior in a new spiritual birth experience (John 3:1-16). In this, the saying of Job is fulfilled: *"I was eyes to the blind"* (Job 29:15).

Jesus Christ anointed the natural eyes of the blind man so that he could physically see (John 9:6). He also anoints the spiritual eyes of a person with the Holy Spirit when he receives the Lord Jesus by faith. No longer is the born-again Christian to walk as a blind man who stumbles in darkness (see Zephaniah 1:17 and I Thessalonians 5:1-11). God has promised that *"the eyes of the blind shall be opened"* (Isaiah 35:5), and the leader can put his confidence in this.

It is a tragedy that the very people God wants to use to cure spiritual blindness can themselves be spiritually blind. This happened in the day of the prophet Isaiah (Isaiah 56:10) as well as in the day of Christ (Matthew 15:14 and 23:16,24,26; Luke 6:39) and of Paul (Romans 2:19). In all of these cases, the religious leaders themselves were spiritually blind.

Many things can cause spiritual blindness in God's leaders, but three must be remembered.

Character Deficiencies. These can render a leader unable to walk in the light (II Peter 1:5-11). A leader will be spiritually blind and short-sighted in life without the qualities of diligence, faith, moral excellence, knowledge, self-control, perseverance, godliness, brotherly kindness and love.

Pharisees certainly did not manifest the character quality of brotherly kindness in their proud, self-righteous attitudes toward the common folk of Jesus' day. A leader should "welcome as a friend" any dealings of God that help these character qualities grow in his life.

Spiritual Bribery. Christian leaders can become spiritually blind, also, when the Church associates too closely with the educational, economic or political segments of the world system. The problem takes the form of a specialized type of bribery. Deuteronomy 16:19 wisely declares that even a wise man can be blinded through bribery: "A gift doth blind the eyes of the wise."

The word "bribe" comes from a Middle French word that means "bread given to a beggar." The idea here is that a starving beggar will do anything for the person who gives him a scrap of bread. A bribe today is understood as money or favor bestowed on or promised to a person in a position of trust to prevent his judgment or corrupt his conduct. A bribe is money or favor that serves to induce or influence another person in a certain direction. Throughout the history of the Church, her leaders have been bribed in various ways and by various means. Church leaders have been spiritually bribed, and still can be, by various inducements:

Financially: when the devil offers financial gain to leaders for using their spiritual gifts and ministries.

Educationally: when the State offers funds in support of a Church, but in turn demands certain curriculum, teacher and enrollment requirements.

Politically: when the State offers to support the Church's facilities if the State can ordain certain men into the ministry and use the Church's facilities for anything it desires.

Spiritually: when the devil offers leaders a life of power, pride and position in his kingdom, tempting them away from serving the people of God.

Morally: when the lusts of the flesh offer them momentary pleasures instead of self-control and faithfulness to their wives and families.

Ecclesiastically: when leaders' denominational deacon boards or headquarters offer them a higher position and salary in the organization if the leader will only deny their experience of the Baptism of the Holy Spirit with speaking in tongues.

A leader must never compromise the Word of God for any bribe, be it as blatant as money or as subtle as the approval of men.

Personal Sin. A third cause for spiritual blindness in leaders is an unrighteous lifestyle. Sin and immorality always lead to spiritual blindness. In this regard, note the following scriptural principles:

A leader continues to see light by staying in God's light (Psalm 36:9).

A leader must continually ask God for His light and His truth (Psalm 43:3).

A leader must live a righteous life in every way to be able to receive God's light (Psalm 97:11 and 112:4; Proverbs 4:18).

Every leader should remember that in the beginning, God separated the light from the darkness (Genesis 1:3-5). This is a natural principle and cycle in nature, but is also a spiritual reminder that those who are *"of the day"* are His people and should stay out of the darkness of this world (I Thessalonians 5:1-11).

May every leader realize that he is also to avoid the different levels of blindness that can come upon his people. Some deceptions are deeper and blacker than others. But any darkness whatsoever he should shun. The Lord led the children of Israel in the wilderness by a pillar of fire at night and constant lamps upon their golden lampstand (Exodus 35:14; Numbers 8:2). In the same way, let every leader continue to *"walk in the light of the Lord"* (Isaiah 2:5). By setting a good example for his people, a leader can rejoice in his heart as he sees the spiritual light grow in his people's eyes (Proverbs 15:30).

Conclusion

Joshua first led the children of Israel in the office of a warrior-general. In the same way, the Christian leader today must take on his responsibilities to lead the Church in its war against the enemy. He must seek the reproduction of God's own image in his personality, to function as protecter, defender and deliverer of God's people. He does this out of compassion for God's people. And he accepts this role because God has ordained this fallen world, and even the enemy himself, as tools to prepare the Bride of Christ.

The Christian leader is a man of war. In this function, he paves the way for the ministries we will study in Chapter Fifteen, "Restoration Ministries of the Leader."

CHAPTER 15
RESTORATION MINISTRIES
OF THE LEADER

In these ministries, the leader seeks God to reproduce His personality as consoler, cleanser and restorer in the leader's own life. In these functions, the Christian leader binds up the wounds of God's people. He prepares them to receive their calling and become functioning, healthy members of the Body of Christ.

God the Consoler

The Leader as a Comforter

"Thy rod and thy staff, they comfort me" Psalm 23:4.

The leader of God's people must stay within the boundaries of the ministry that God has given to him. A leader must not dominate the people's faith, but be a "helper of their joy" in the Lord, even as was Paul the apostle.

To comfort means to be bright, to share faith, to make cheerful, to enliven, to revive, to refresh the heart, to strengthen, to console and to support another person. Every leader treasures the times of God's comforting in his own life. He should thus be motivated to comfort the people under him. He must comfort the people by reviving their faith in Jesus Christ, brightening their countenance with the Joy of the Holy Spirit, and strengthening them in the Lord.

But how does a leader go about comforting the people of God? He must remember and use the principles in the Word that comfort people. Comfort comes to God's people in the following ways:

God's rod and staff (His Word and Spirit in discipline) Psalm 23:4

God's Word (comforts in affliction) Psalm 119:50; Romans 15:4

God's mercy and kindness (which relieve the people's fear of accusation before the Lord) Psalm 119:76

God's presence (maintained in the congregation's life through repentance, prayer and worship)

Isaiah 51:3 and 61:2; II Corinthians 1:3

God's Holy Spirit (in prayer through the Spirit-filled believer using a heavenly language) John 14:16,18,26 and 15:26; Acts 9:31

The memory of God's past comfortings (which can help us identify with the needs of others) II Corinthians 1:4

God's love (which comforts and heals) Philippians 2:1

Fellow Christians (who should constantly comfort and support one another in fellowship) I Thessalonians 4:18 and 5:11

A leader should use all of these scriptural means to bring comfort to his people. People are always looking for comforters. Unfortunately, like David, they are not always finding them (Psalm 69:20).

A person can be a good comforter or a poor one, depending on how he uses wisdom, love and the Word of God when he tries to comfort another. Job lambasted all of his friends who were attempting to comfort him: *"unmerciful comforters are ye all"* (Job 16:2). God wants His leaders to be good comforters, and people who see deeply into the real heart of a person's problems. It is unwise to quickly equate bad problems or circumstances with sin, as Job's "friends" did.

Sometimes, a person finds himself in afflictions and distress, and simply needs the comfort of the Holy Spirit through some willing channel (Psalm 71:21). God commands His leaders to comfort His people with His Word (Isaiah 40:1), whether they feel like it or not. Leaders must realize, however that they need comfort, too (Psalm 69:20; Lamentations 1:21). If they do not give it out, they may notice a lack of any coming back.

As leaders make a special effort to comfort their people's faith, hearts and particularly the weak and feeble-minded, they will also find personal comfort from God. (See I Thessalonians 3:2 and 5:14; II Thessalonians 2:17)

The Leader as an Obliger

One of the character qualities of Jesus that will make a leader respected and attractive to people is his graciousness and kindness. Proverbs 19:22 states, *"What is desirable in a man is his kindness."* A leader can be full of power and truth, but without *"the law of kindness"* (Proverbs 31:26) in his mouth, his ministry is not going to be very effective. The Bible connects kindness and love with righteousness and truth (II Samuel 2:6; Psalm 116:5 and 141:5; Genesis 24:49 and 47:29; Joshua 2:14). If they are not connected, flattery occurs. However, honesty does not require a leader to forsake the graciousness and kindness; he must never do this.

Graciousness and kindness are closely associated, and are characteristic of God (II Kings 13:23; Amos 5:15; Jonah 4:2), even from eternity (Isaiah 54:8). God is kind and gracious to man. God has given to men His own undeserved favor and kindness through Jesus Christ (Ephesians 2:7), with no condescension because of His superiority over men.

Similarly, God challenges every leader to give his life to the undeserving and even unthankful (Luke 6:35). In doing so, a leader practices the very way of blessing that God has shown to him. Just as God has promised His people that His kindness would never depart (Isaiah 54:10; Exodus 33:19), so a leader's kindness should never depart from the people God has given him. God has received us graciously (Hosea 14:2) into His family through the blood of Jesus Christ. In the same way, a leader should continuously cause his people not only to understand God's graciousness, but to truly experience and taste it in their daily lives (I Peter 2:3).

In the New Testament, the word "kindness" has the connotation of moral excellence in character and behavior. Mercy and compassion, two of God's moral attributes, can be closely compared to kindness. The Bible demonstrates their closeness very clearly (Exodus 34:6; II Chronicles 30:9; Nehemiah 9:17,31; Psalm 86:15 and 103:8 and 111:4 and 112:4 and 145:8). As a leader allows the Lord to develop kindness in his life, he should know that the formation of mercy and compassion are also a part of the same process. The New Testament clearly connects kindness with love:

"Charity suffereth long and is kind" (I Corinthians 13:4).

"Put on a heart of compassion, kindness, humility, gentleness and patience" (Colossians 3:12).

"But when the kindness of God our Savior and His love for mankind appeared, he saved us" (Titus 3:4,5a).

"And in your godliness, (supply) brotherly kindness, and in your brotherly kindness, Christian love" (II Peter 1:7).

The ultimate expression of graciousness and kindness in a leader's life is his love for the unlovely. May each leader believe God for such a heart of compassion and kindness in his ministry. Every leader should believe God for close relationships with people in the family of God. Our example is Joseph's words to his younger brother Benjamin: *"God be gracious unto thee, my son"* (Genesis 43:29-30). There is a depth of feeling and relationship in these words of Joseph to his younger brother, particularly as one reads the entire context of the previous family conflict.

A leader must not allow the various conflicts in his church to become a source of division in his affections. Instead, they provide him opportunities to grow closer to those over whom God has given him spiritual charge. It may seem at times that God has forgotten to be gracious to a leader, in light of the many conflicts that confront him (see Psalm 77:9). But if a leader will ask the Lord to extend His mercy and kindness in a situation, God will respond (Exodus 22:27).

A leader must remember, moreover that the Lord is *"slow to anger"* (Joel 2:13). Every leader should follow His example and control his temper. Ideally, every leader should so grow through God's dealings that he eventually finds nothing inside of him that responds in anger to any provocation, save a righteous indignation at sin (see Hebrews 1:8,9).

God will continue to cause every leader to experience His kindness in his life (Psalm 31:21 and 117:2), for personal spiritual comfort (Psalm 119:76). He will continue to exhort every leader, as all Christians (Romans 12:10; Ephesians 4:32), to be kind to others. The leader must set an example of kindness for others to follow. If a leader keeps in mind the following keys to being gracious and kind, he will be blessed by the Lord in many ways:

With kindness, a leader retains the honor of his position, but with unkindness, he forfeits that honor (Proverbs 11:16).

As a leader applies his heart to spiritual wisdom of the Lord, the Holy Spirit will make his words gracious (Ecclesiastes 10:12).

As God gives His Word to His people graciously, so should a leader realize that God's people desire this in his own ministry of the Word, too (Psalm 119:29).

The more a leader dwells on the Lord's graciousness to him, even from the time of his youth, the more he will be kind to those to whom he ministers (Jeremiah 2:2).

It is as important for a man of God to minister by kindness, as it is for him to minister by the Holy Spirit's power (II Corinthians 6:6).

The Leader as a Long-sufferer

"But Thou, O Lord, art a God full of . . . patience" Psalm 86:15.

The Bible clearly describes the patience and long-suffering of God (I Timothy 1:16; I Peter 3:2; II Peter 3:9,15; James 5:7; Revelation 1:9). Consequently, every leader should seek the reproduction of these character qualities in his or her own life. Long-suffering and patience are closely related in meaning. "Long-suffering" comes from the picture of a person breathing very hard and elongating his face in an effort to endure pain. Patience is:

Bearing pains or trials calmly and without complaint.

Manifesting forbearance under provocation or strain.

Remaining steadfast despite opposition, difficulty or adversity.

A leader must be patient, in the three ways above, in waiting for Christ (I Thessalonians 1:3; II Thessalonians 3:5). He must also be patient in relation to difficult circumstances or provoking people (see Romans 9:22 and God's attitude). Some leaders overcome difficult circumstances easily, but have trouble dealing with obtrusive people. Other leaders have a built-in understanding for "problem people" but go into a rage if they sense a situation or circumstance turn against them. We all know our strong and weak points, and we all have a need for more patience (Hebrews 10:36).

In addition to being connected with graciousness and kindness (Exodus 34:6; II Corinthians 6:6), patience is also related to other qualities in Scripture:

Mercy (Numbers 14:18)
Goodness (Romans 2:4; Galatians 5:22)
Forbearance (Romans 2:4; Ephesians 4:2)
Love (Galatians 5:22; II Timothy 3:10; Titus 2:2)
Joy (Galatians 5:22; Colossians 1:11)
Peace (Galatians 5:22)
Meekness (Galatians 5:22; Colossians 3:12)
Temperance (Galatians 5:22)
Faithfulness (Galatians 5:22)
Self-control (Galatians 5:22)
Humility (Colossians 3:12)
Consolation (Romans 15:5)

To be truly patient in his inner spirit (Ecclesiastes 7:8), in all situations, a leader must have the Holy Spirit develop the above qualities in his life as well. It is not enough for a leader to exhort in doctrine, he must also exhort with patience (II Timothy 4:2).

Patience is not an option for the man or woman of God. This quality is a requirement for eldership (I Timothy 33; II Corinthians 6:4 and 12:12). Key to a leader's patience is his ability to dissolve all of his own expectations and wait for the Lord's will and plan to come to pass (see Psalm 37:7 and 40:1). Only with patience and faith in God working together can a leader inherit God's blessings and promises (II Thessalonians 1:4; Hebrews 6:12; Titus 2:2). Hebrews 12:1 so aptly describes the process: *"Let us run with patience the race that is set before us."*

As a leader runs the race of his own life and ministry, he will increase in the necessary patience of the Lord as his faith is tested (James 1:3). God let's patience do her perfecting work in the leader's heart and life (James 1:4). Though a leader may grow "weary in well-doing," Paul exhorts him to continue (Romans 2:7). He is to continue in well-doing not only toward some men, but to all (I Thessalonians 5:14). Through patience, a leader will not only establish his heart firmly in the Lord (James 5:8), but he will be able to establish others' hearts as well. As he lives his life and ministry with patience (even as Job did; see also James 5:11 and Romans 15:4), he will find that he will become even more acceptable to God (I Peter 2:20).

Finally, the leader who not only experiences God's patience (Psalm 86:15), but also shows that same patience to others, will find these results in his life and ministry:

He will bring forth more spiritual fruit unto God (Luke 8:15).

He will better possess his soul, and the souls of others (Luke 21:19).

He will increase his spiritual experience and proven character (Romans 5:3,4).

May every leader effectively grasp his spiritual inheritance by developing the quality of patience.

The Leader as a Listener

"I cried unto the Lord with my voice, and he heard me out of his holy hill" Psalm 3:4.

Only because God Himself is a good listener can the leader be challenged in this vital key to communication and ministry. The Psalmist knew that the Lord was a good listener, because he declared many times, *"I cried unto the Lord and he heard my prayer"* (see Psalm 4:1-3 and 10:17 and 13:3 and 17:1,6 and 20:1-7 and 27:7 and 28:2 and 30:10 and 54:2 and 55:2,7,19).

A leader must listen to people in the same way that he expects the Lord to listen to him. He should be an example of how good a listener the Lord really is. Moreover, the leader should set the example for others in the way that he listens to God. A leader must learn how to develop a listening ear so that he can minister effectively and with sensitivity. James 1:9 says, *"Be swift to hear and slow to speak."*

The leader should set a high priority on developing a listening ear. Roughly 45 percent of a pastor's communication each day is spent in listening (the balance, roughly: speaking 30 percent, reading 16 percent, writing 9 percent). Of his total day, about 80 percent is spent in some form of communication. Improvements in his communication can dramatically improve his overall effectiveness.

To listen means to make a conscious effort to hear, to attend closely, to give earnest heed to what someone is trying to communicate. Listening is the attempt to attach meaning to oral symbols. It is the reception and evaluation of sounds and their comprehension. To truly listen, one must accurately and seriously decode the encoded message of the speaker. The very heart of the meaning of the word "listen" or hear is expressed in the definition of the related Hebrew word. It means to hear intelligently, to hear correctly, to give careful and diligent attention to the possible hidden meaning. Listening was very important to the nation of Israel, since speaking and listening was God's major form of communicating to the nation and its leaders.

Ecclesiastes 1:8 states *"The ear is not filled* (or satisfied) *with hearing."* Some things are good to hear, some not, for Jesus said *"Take heed what ye hear"* (Mark 4:24). But He also said *"Take heed how ye hear"* (Luke 8:18). Christian leaders should thus filter what they hear through correct content and correct method. The Christian leader's correct content is the Word of God. Romans 10:17 says *"Faith comes by hearing and hearing by the Word of God."* Thus, leaders should cause themselves and their people to be hearers of the Word.

But there is also a certain way or method in which a Christian leader should hear. Christian leaders can grow dull of hearing (Hebrews 5:11) and hear only with their natural ears, without their spiritual ears (Matthew 13:13). In short, a leader must teach himself as well as his people the key to listening and hearing the Lord: a pure heart. It is through a Christian's pure heart and spirit that he hears God (Malachi 3:16; Matthew 7:24-26; Luke 6:47-49). May every leader keep his heart and spirit pure before the Lord so that he can be a good example to the people of hearing the Lord.

There are, more specifically, some pracitcal hints that will help a leader become a better listener. To clarify what works — and what doesn't — we have developed the characteristics of both in opposing columns.

A POOR LISTENER

Tunes out subjects that he finds uninteresting or boring.

Judges the speaker by his outward appearance or manner.

Grows over-stimulated by one thought of the speaker, so he cannot concentrate on the rest of what he has to share.

Uses only one style of note-taking no matter who the speaker is.

Expends little or no energy or concentration upon the one who is sharing.

Avoids new challenges and does not appreciate the unfamiliar areas the speaker is relating.

Operates with a closed mind; allows emotional words to interfere with a careful evaluation of the situation.

A GOOD LISTENER

Searches for information to acquire additional insights on how to help a person.

Judges by the content of what is said, rather than the speaker or his manner or method.

Withholds his emotional reactions until he comprehends the whole idea that the speaker is sharing.

Stays flexible in note-taking, adapting to each speaker.

Expends much energy on the communicator, and works hard at listening.

Minimizes and ignores possible distractions whenever he can.

Listens to all material in its variety, and attempts to see some significance in all of it.

The Leader as a Feeder

The Lord *"giveth food to the hungry"* Psalm 146:7

Before any outpouring of the Holy Spirit, there is generally a great spiritual hunger for more experience and knowledge of the Lord. The movement of the Spirit in the "Jesus Movement" of the Sixties and Seventies was preceeded by many years of fasting, prayer and hungering after God. This spiritual hunger continues through divine visitations as well. Believers grew hungry for the anointed Word of God by special teaching ministries during the Jesus Movement, which was scarce when the movement began.

This hunger continues today. A leader of the Church who has any insight can easily observe the spiritual hunger and thirst in God's people for more truth. It is also true that, in spite of the current fad of belittling fallen Christian leaders, unbelievers are hungry for the Lord as well. Our time is a time of spiritual hunger. Every leader can thank the Lord that He has promised to feed the hungry with good spiritual food (Psalm 146:7; see also Genesis 2:9).

Every leader can be confident that God desires to feed those who hunger and thirst after Him. A leader can trust the Lord to help him feed the multitudes, just as Jesus multiplied the five loaves and two fishes that the disciples brought from the little boy (Matthew 14:17), so the Holy Spirit will use and increase what a leader already has in order to feed the people.

We are now talking about spiritual hunger and not soup kitchens. A Christian should not neglect these physical needs (Matthew 25:35-44; Isaiah 58:7; Job 22:7). But a Christian leader should never place physical feeding as a sole or primary priority in his ministry.

Many evangelical Christians are doing this today and missing the most important "meat" Jesus Christ spoke about--doing the will of God. Jesus identified the most important meat and food in His life when He declared, *"My meat is to do the will of Him who sent me and to finish His work"* (John 4:34). He spoke this in a context of showing the superiority of the spiritual water, Himself, over the natural water of Jacob's well (John 4:1-40). Jesus stated, furthermore, *"He who comes to me shall never hunger"* (John 6:35). Job also showed that he had the same understanding when he said, *"I love the words of your* (God's) *mouth more than my necessary food"* (Job 23:12).

Consequently, a leader's first priority is to minister the spiritual food of God's Word to people and thus build up God's spiritual house (see Acts 6:1-6 for the balancing of natural and spiritual feeding). God is raising up many teaching ministries today, because God's people so greatly need it. God always moves to meet needs. Note how the Lord always has a special place for those who admit their spiritual need of God.

"Blessed (happy) *are they who hunger and thirst after righteousness for they shall be filled"* (Matthew 5:6).

"He fills the hungry soul with goodness" (Psalm 107:9).

"There (near the springs of water) *He makes the hungry to dwell"* (Psalm 107:36).

God always has a special desire to meet the needs of the spiritually hungry and thirsty. In Jesus' day, the religious leaders were not hungry after God. It was mostly the common and uneducated classes who gladly received Jesus as their Messiah. This principle has held true throughout Church history, in relation to the revelation of God's truth. Too many times, the proud, intellectual, critical people reject what God is doing. They think they have no spiritual need. But God greatly criticizes this kind of self-sufficient attitude of the Pharisees, Sadducees, scribes, priests and lawyers--and in their counterparts today (see Revelation 3:17).

God responds to the leaders and the people who are spiritually hungry and thirsty because they appreciate what God gives them. Others, who believe that they themselves are sufficient to meet their own needs, do not give God thanks for everything. Or they do it with a smug attitude that says "I know that I really did it." Proverbs 27:7 states this very clearly: *"The full soul loathes a honeycomb, but to the hungry soul, every bitter thing is sweet."* A hungry and humble leader even appreciates the bitter things that God brings into his life because he sees the spiritual good in them.

People are spiritually hungry today because they ate of the tree of the knowledge and evil, and were left very unsatisfied (see Genesis 3:6). When Adam and Eve ate of this forbidden tree, they realized that they were naked, having lost the Shekinah light of God's glory that had probably clothed their innocent lives up until that time.

When people today eat of the tree of knowledge of good and evil, or even just the tree of knowledge, they come away empty spiritually. This tree is not rooted in the Holy Spirit. The spiritual hunger of people will be satisfied only when they eat and drink of the Word of God and the Tree of Life, which is the Lord Jesus Himself. And only the leaders of the Church can show them how to do this. Jesus is the Tree of Life that satisfies the mental, emotional and spiritual hunger in every person.

The leader is responsible to lead people to the Tree of Life. As he does so, he will see Isaiah's declaration fulfilled in his ministry: *"If thou draw out thy soul to the hungry and satisfy the afflicted, then shall thy light rise in obscurity"* (Isaiah 58:10). For those leaders who believe that God desires to give them a greater influence in His kingdom, this truth is a key. As a leader proves that he can satisfy the thirsting soul, God will increase his ministry. God does not increase a ministry in order to flatter or glorify a man. He does so to meet the spiritual needs of more people. A leader can expect more demand for his ministry as he successfully meets people's spiritual needs. A leader should not seek more influence or a greater position. He should seek to meet the spiritual needs of those whom God has already given him.

Finally, every leader should keep in mind the following principles concerning spiritually feeding the people of God:

A leader must spend much time in prayer, meditation and study in order to feed people spiritually.

A leader should take full advantage of every opportunity that he has to grow in spiritual understanding (even like Joseph, who stored wheat in barns during times of plenty; see also Proverbs 6:8).

A leader should learn to discern the spiritual level of his hearers, to feed milk to babes, meat to the mature (Hebrews 5:11-6:2) bread to the eater, and seed to the sower (Isaiah 55:10,11). A leader should remember that giving a piece of tenderloin steak to a baby is a risky proposition.

A leader should be totally willing to give out all that he has to feed others, knowing that this is God's purpose for him (see Ecclesiastes 11:1).

A leader should give his spiritual food to those who admit their need and hunger and thirst after the Lord, not to the smug or self-satisfied.

A leader must feed people with a meek, humble, sincere and teachable spirit and attitude, rather than a proud and domineering one. Always demonstrate the truth of the Word by example.

The Leader as a Beautifier of the Meek

"He will beautify the meek with salvation" Psalm 149:4

Those who have grown to be truly meek have a special place in the Bible. Meekness is strength under control, patience, mildness, submissiveness, and not being inclined to anger or resentment. The Lord Himself promises to beautify this kind of person (Psalm 149:4b). God states that He would adorn, deck with jewels, embellish and add even more beauty to those who are meek. Peter tells us that God cherishes a meek and quiet spirit (I Peter 3:4).

The Lord Jesus Himself was a man with meekness (Matthew 11:29), and Christians are exhorted to come to the house of the Lord to observe His beauty (Psalm 27:4 and 96:6). As they observe the beauty of God's meekness, God beautifies His people with the same quality (see Psalm 29:2 and 50:2; Isaiah 60:13). This is why Zephaniah the prophet exhorted the people of God to *"seek meekness"* (Zephaniah 2:3; see also Ephesians 4:2; Colossians 3:12; I Timothy 6:11; II Timothy 2:25; Titus 3:2 James 1:21 and 3:13; I Peter 3:15). Paul, as an example leader, demonstrated the importance of a meek spirit as he ministered to a Corinthian church with many charismatic problems (I Corinthians 4:21; II Corinthians 10:1).

To help God's people grow in meekness, every leader should do the following:

See the value of the character quality of meekness in people.

Share God's attitude toward the meek.

Beautify the people in his care with spiritual things, to develop and reward meekness in their lives.

Discern between natural and spiritual beauty, and emphasize spiritual beauty over the natural.

In these ways, a leader will "beautify the meek" in the Lord.

Finally, we should note the many positive results that come from the development of a meek spirit before God. The following list describes some of these blessings. The meek shall:

Eat and be satisfied (Psalm 22:26).

Receive guidance in their judgments and decisions (25:9).

Be taught the ways of God (25:9).

Inherit the earth (37:11).

Be saved (76:9).

Be lifted up (147:6).

Have their joy increased (Isaiah 29:19).

Have the good tidings of the Word of God preached to them (Psalm 61:1).

Be blessed and happy in Jesus Christ (Matthew 5:5).

Be able to restore fallen brethren (Galatians 6:1).

God has promised special blessings and great fruitfulness to the meek. A leader will miss many good and truly spiritual blessings if he does not attempt to "beautify the meek" in his ministry.

God the Cleanser
The Leader as a Refiner and Prover

"For thou, O God hast proved us: thou hast tried (refined) *us, as silver is tried"* Psalm 66:10

One of the less understood aspects of leadership is that of proving the hearts of men. A prover of men's hearts is used by God to test and prove people to see their true motivations and attitudes. A similar word, "refine," means to strain, filter melt, try by fire, purge gold or silver, separate from dross, or examine. God proves or tests His people's faith by allowing adversity to come into their lives.

God also calls upon His leaders to prove the people of God in various ways. Every leader was probably tested for a time before becoming a deacon (I Timothy 3:10) or an elder, thus he should know what it is to be proven before the Lord. Many times in the Old Testament, young leaders were sent to go in and out before the congregation that they might prove themselves and their ministries before the congregation. A leader should not fear that God wants to use him as a prover of men. God Himself proves men (Exodus 20:20; Malachi 3:1-3; Zechariah 13:9; Isaiah 48:10). And Paul exhorts the Church to prove all things (I Thessalonians 5:21), men included.

God Himself sends various kinds of tests into the lives of His people from which a leader can learn basic principles of proving younger ministries. The Church greatly needs older ministries to prove younger ministries. Today, too many younger ministries are falling by the wayside due to pride, because they did not experience a time of humbling and proving before receiving authority and responsibility in the house of the Lord.

Younger ministries are promoted so quickly to positions of authority because the Church greatly needs spiritual leadership. But this does not justify the loss of a young man's ministry, through pride or immorality, because he was promoted too quickly into a temporary pastor's position. Older ministries must allow the Lord to develop a father's heart within them, that they will be willing to test younger ministries before using them. God tests His people by allowing them to go through a dry wilderness experience (Deuteronomy 8:2). An older ministry may also use a spiritual wilderness of no apparent fruit in ministry to test a younger ministry. This helps him to recognize whether the younger is truly in humble submission to the Lord.

Another test is the lack of money and possessions. One of the qualifications for an elder is the freedom from lust for money (I Timothy 3:3). A leader can tell whether a younger ministry has an abnormal desire for money by observing how he reacts to times of financial destitution. Does he center his whole life around money when he is not officially or publicly preaching the Gospel from the pulpit? Does he always desire money for all that he does? Is he able to trust the Lord to supply his financial needs? God sent a test of lacking to Israel in the wilderness when He took away from them the leeks, garlics, cucumbers and meat that they had in Egypt, and gave them manna instead. Israel failed the test. God gave Israel their heart's desire for flesh to eat, until they were overfull. In the same way, He may give money and possessions to younger ministries, to the satisfaction of their wants but the leanness of their souls.

God also tested Israel with a lack of water in the wilderness. Scripture refers to this test, at the campsite of Rephidim, as the proving of the waters at Massah and Meribah (Deuteronomy 33:8; Psalm 81:7). The name Massah means "to test" or "to prove." The name Meribah means "quarreling" or "dissension." It was here at Rephidim that Israel ran out of water and complained to Moses about the possibility of dying in the wilderness. Here Moses disobeyed God when he became angry at the people and twice struck the rock with his rod to bring forth water, rather than merely speaking to the rock, as God had commanded.

In a similar way, older ministries can prove younger ministries by observing what they do during times of spiritual dryness and a lack of anointing. The younger ministries who fall during such times show that they were drawing too much fulfillment and meaning from their activities of ministering, and not enough from the Lord Himself.

A younger ministry who has this problem will be a super-spiritual man of God in the pulpit, but a spiritual flop at home and on the street. Older ministries must prove younger ministries in this area so that they will not fall into this snare. Of course, the main purpose of testing is not craftily to "catch someone in a mistake." It is, rather, to allow God the use of circumstances to reveal a younger ministry's weakness, that they may be healed. Testing may lead to exposure, but exposure should always lead to cleansing and healing. This is the responsibility of the older ministry.

Testing and proving is nothing new to the leaders of the New Testament Church. Paul the apostle, himself, exhorted the brethren about proving. He said:

"I am . . . proving through the earnestness of others the sincerity of your love also" (II Corinthians 8:8).

"Test yourselves to see whether you are in the faith; examine yourselves" (II Corinthians 13:5).

"But let each one examine his own work" (Galatians 6:4).

Paul's apostolic example is worth following. Every leader should learn how to prove men's hearts in love. If done correctly, this spiritual proving will save a young leader from many heartaches down the line (see also Psalm 17:3 and 26:2 and 105:19), and will save many of God's people the repercussions of those failures.

The Leader as a Washer

"Wash me and I shall be whiter than snow" Psalm 51:7.

One of the most beautiful illustrations of the relationship between Jesus Christ and the Church is the picture of the husband-wife relationship. As a husband, Christ "washes" his Church with the *"washing of water by the Word"* (Ephesians 5:25-27). Similarly, every leader should consider himself as a washer of the Church; one who takes the soap of the Word of God and washes away the dirt from off of her garments.

The idea of water and washing is not limited to the application of the Word of God to a Christian's life. It is also seen in the themes listed below, which should all be taught in a minister's "washing" ministry:

The Spirit of God and innocency (Psalm 26:6).

Sanctification of the Holy Spirit (I Corinthians 6:11).

Having a clear conscience before God (Hebrews 10:22).

The saving power of Jesus Christ, which washes away all sin (Titus 3:5; Revelation 1:5).

A leader's function of washing the Body of Christ is obviously connected with cleansing it from the filth of sin. There is no need to wash anything if it is already clean. David declared, *"Wash me thoroughly from my iniquity"* (Psalm 51:2). David desired every sin in his life to be cleansed away by God. This attitude of complete and total cleansing should not only be the attitude of the leader toward his own life, but should also be the attitude of a leader toward the lives of his people.

The Psalmist confidently declared, *"Wash me and I will be whiter than snow"* (Psalm 51:7). A leader must have a confidence and a faith in the spiritual efficacy of the blood of the Lord Jesus Christ. He must really believe that what God has cleansed, no man should call unclean. All legalism and Pharisaical hypocrisy is dismissed at this point (I John 1:9). For example, when the woman came to anoint Jesus' body with ointment, she literally washed his feet with what were probably tears of repentance (Luke 7:44). This is a beautiful picture of the Church, who must humble herself more often at the feet of Jesus Christ and shed true tears of repentance that her daily walk might not bring a reproach to the Body of Christ.

Moreover, Old Testament priests had to have their feet, hands and entire bodies cleansed with water (Exodus 29:4,17 and 30:18,19 and 40:12) while ministering under the old covenant laws. How much more should all New Testament priests (I Peter 2:5-9) have to have their thoughts, motives, attitudes, desires and actions cleansed by the Holy Spirit while ministering under the real substance of spiritual truth!

Even in the Old Testament, however, the idea of total inner cleansing is not absent. The prophet David saw it many years before Jesus Christ came (Psalm 51). But its ultimate reality never came until the time of Jesus Christ's death and resurrection. Since then, men have been able to enter into the very presence of God through the veil (the broken body and shed blood of Christ; see Hebrews 10:20).

In the Old Testament, sacrifices had to be washed (Leviticus 1:9,13 and 6:27), even the inward parts of the animals at times (Leviticus 9:14). How much more should New Testament leaders wash the inner hearts, minds, spirits and consciences of their people before the Lord, as they offer themselves up to Him as *"living sacrifices"* (Romans 12:1,2).

God the Restorer
The Leader as a Shower of Mercy

The Lord *"showeth mercy to his anointed"* Psalm 18:50

The Church is hurting from want of mercy today. Like the intellectual Pharisees of Christ's day, who had minds full of Scripture, many leaders today have forgotten that mercy out of the heart is one of the "weightier matters of the law" (Matthew 23:23).

The Bible clearly calls God the source and *"the father of mercies"* (II Corinthians 1:3; see also Exodus 34:6; Numbers 14:18; Deuteronomy 4:31; Nehemiah 9:17,31; Joel 2:13; Psalm 57:10; Ephesians 2:4). God sends forth His mercy to man (Psalm 57:3), because it endures forever (I Chronicles 16:34,41; Hebrews 2:17). One of the main ways that God sends forth His mercy to the earth is in and through His leaders. He deposits His mercy within them, that they can give it out to others.

Mercy encompasses a large area of meaning. It includes the ideas of: desire or zeal toward a person in a good sense; showing love, kindness, grace and favor to those in misfortune; cherishing or soothing with a gentle emotion; beholding with tender emotion and compassion; helping the wretched; feeling sympathy with the misery of another; having resources adequate to meet someone's needs. All of these can apply to the leader who is to be a source of mercy to others.

The Bible explains that God's mercy is tender (Psalm 25:6 and 77:9 and 79:8 and 103:4) and soft. Thus it should be present in a leader's way of communicating the gospel of Christ to others. Gods mercies were so gracious and gentle to David, that he wrote a song about them (Psalm 89:1). No one writes a song about something or someone who is not dear and precious to their heart.

On the other hand, David also knew that his sins had to be atoned for by the sprinkling of the sacrificial atonement blood on the mercy seat of the ark of the covenant (Exodus 25:17-22; Leviticus 16:2-15). Thus, David knew that mercy without truth was very incomplete (Psalm 25:10 and 57:3 and 85:10 and 89:14; see also Proverbs 3:3 and 16:6). Mercy and truth must go together, for mercy without truth will lead to loose living and truth without mercy will lead to bitterness, legalism and hardness of heart. God wants to keep the heart and spirit of man soft and pliable through both truth and mercy.

For a leader to show mercy adequately, he must:

Be a recipient of God's mercy.

Personally know the God of mercy (II Corinthians 4:1).

Show mercy, but never at the expense of truth (Psalm 25:10).

Be merciful in order to receive mercy from the Lord Jesus (Matthew 5:7; II Samuel 22:26; Psalm 18:25).

Show mercy--and always with cheerfulness and without complaint (Proverbs 15:13 and 17:22; Romans 12:8).

Rejoice in mercy over judgment (James 2:13) and not be like Jonah who was grieved when the Ninevites repented.

Be merciful in order to be an example of God's heart of mercy (Luke 6:36).

Heal the souls of the afflicted and oppressed through the quality of mercy (Psalm 41:4).

Discern the difference between natural pity (which does nothing to help them) and spiritual mercy.

The Leader as a Forgiver

"For thou, Lord, art good, and ready to forgive" Psalm 86:5.

A key to success in a leader's ministry is his ability to forgive other people for their offenses toward him and toward others (especially toward the ones he loves). God's leaders must remember that they are sinners like everyone else, and need to receive God's forgiveness continually (Psalm 32:1-6; James 5:15). If they learn to confess their faults daily, they will minister with a free and clear conscience. If not, something inside will bind up their ministry. Every leader must personally experience that "there is forgiveness with thee that thou mayest be feared" (Psalm 130:4; see also Psalm 25:18 and 85:2 and 86:5 and 103:3; Exodus 34:7; Numbers 14:18; Daniel 9:9; I John 1:9).

What is the actual meaning of "forgiveness?" The Hebrew word for "forgive" generally means to pardon, to be merciful, to be propitious, to show oneself gentle, to cause lightness and a lifting up; to take up or lift up, to raise up or bear (see also Genesis 7:17, in what the flood waters did to the ark). All of these meanings are included when a leader forgives a person for his offense toward him.

The Greek definition of the verb "to forgive" is to do something pleasant or agreeable to one; to do a favor to someone; to gratify; to show oneself gracious, kind and benevolent; to pardon; to send forth something that is near; to set at liberty; to deliver. When a leader truly forgives someone, he pardons his trespass and is kind to him in every way. His showing of sincere outward kindness proves that the leader has inwardly forgiven the offender.

Forgiveness is a matter of the heart, and it affects one's feelings toward others. Every leader should ask the Lord to give him a forgiving spirit which is a daily heart attitude that has already forgiven every offense before it is ever committed. This attitude is what the Bible means when it says, *"Being ready to forgive"* (Psalm 86:5). Such an attitude of spirit, however, is only possible in the heart of a leader if he himself has a broken spirit due to personal confession and repentance from sin. If not, a leader will never be able to forgive another person without that person first externally proving that he had repented of his offense toward the leader.

Moreover, we commonly understand forgiveness as giving up resentment against another, or the desire to punish; to cease to demand a penalty of. Whenever a leader truly forgives another person, all resentment and bitterness toward that person is gone. He no longer desires to see the offender punished or suffer pain. He only desires the offender to be healed, forgiven and restored. The Institute in Basic Youth Conflicts defines forgiveness as "Healing others by using their offenses as a means of expressing Christ's love to them." A mature leader looks upon every offense as an opportunity to demonstrate the love that Jesus Christ desires him to show to all people.

Offenses provide an excuse for revenge or an outlet for anger. The Greek word for forgiveness also brings out the thought of letting go, cancelling, reuniting, discharging, setting free, voluntarily releasing a person over which one has legal or actual control (see also Leviticus 25:27 and Deuteronomy 15:1-9 for the releasing of legal debts in the year of jubilee). In forgiving a person, a leader releases them of all emotional, mental and spiritual debts that the carnal mind would desire someone to owe to him.

Another important point concerning a leader and forgiveness is that a leader's response of forgiveness toward others will affect the way that God responds to him. Matthew 6:12-15 includes a very important phrase about this: *"forgive us our debts as we forgive our debtors"* (Luke 6:37). If a leader cannot forgive others of their debts, then God will not forgive the leader of his. If a leader in this condition believes he is free from sin and indebtedness (through offenses toward others) he is sadly mistaken.

When a leader will not forgive his offender, he will find himself in a prison of bitterness, guilt, hatred, depression, mistrust, criticism and insensitivity; all of which will quench a leader's spiritual effectiveness. What leader wants his life and ministry to be bound up in prison? Let him forgive from his heart (Matthew 18:15-35; Ephesians 4:32; Colossians 3:13). Any leader who cannot forgive freely from his heart has not yet understood the tremendous debt of sin from which Jesus Christ freed him (Luke 4:18).

Joseph was not only rejected by his own brothers, but also sold by them into slavery in Egypt. This man of God had been seriously wronged. But because he had a forgiving spirit, he was able to nourish, comfort and speak kindly to his brothers when they came down to Egypt (Genesis 37-50). Because Joseph had a broken spirit before God, he did not judge or retaliate against his brothers (Genesis 50:19), but had a right attitude and perspective toward those who had offended him (Genesis 50:17-21).

All leaders need the spirit of Joseph, that they may freely forgive from their hearts when their brethren in Christ have offended them.

The Leader as a Provider of Strength

"I will love Thee, O Lord, my strength" Psalm 18:1

Extreme pressures in the accelerating pace of the world today are over-stressing and injuring people, both inside and outside the Church. There are political, environmental, economic, domestic, mental and spiritual pressures coming upon everyone (Proverbs 24:10). Due to these various pressures, God's people must know the strength of the Lord (Psalm 8:2 and 18:2 and 2:7,8 and 37:39) and the strength of their leaders. The Church desperately needs established and responsible leaders. She especially needs leaders who are strong spiritually, domestically, emotionally and morally. We have seen too many negative examples of men with "powerful ministries" who caved in morally because they were spiritually hollow.

God does not want his people to faint in the heat of the battle (Ephesians 3:13). But without solid leaders, the people of God will spiritually faint and fall. When a Christian faints, he loses heart, becomes discouraged, or totally surrenders his objective for fighting. The word "faint," as used in Isaiah 40:25-31, means to be fatigued or worn out. In these verses we see that although men can feel faint, weary and totally discouraged, the Lord is still available as the source of everlasting spiritual vitality for His people:

> *"To whom then will ye liken me, or shall I be equal? saith the holy one. Lift up your eyes on high, and behold who hath created these things, that bringeth out their host by number: he calleth them all by names by the greatness of his might, for that he is strong in power; not one faileth. Why sayest thou, O Jacob and speakest, O Israel 'My way is hid from the Lord, and judgment is passed over from my God?' Hast thou not known? Hast thou not heard that the everlasting God, the Lord, the Creator of the ends of the earth, fainteth not, neither is weary? There is no searching out of his understanding. He giveth power to the faint; and to them that have no might, he increaseth strength. Even the youths shall faint and be weary, and the young men shall utterly fall. But they that wait upon the Lord shall renew their strength; they shall mount up with wings as eagles; they shall run, and not be weary; and they shall walk, and not faint."*

When we say that God and His leaders are the strength of His people, we mean that they are the ability, might, power, substance, force, security, stronghold, victory, wealth, abundance, dominion and cause for their firm establishment in spiritual truths. Without strong leaders, the people will be destroyed. The Bible says, *"Smite the shepherd and the sheep will be scattered."*

Every Christian and leader desperately needs the strength of other members of the Body of Christ. Unfortunately, however, many leaders do not feel that they need the strength of other leaders, let alone other Christians. For this reason, many of these over-confident leaders fall. I Corinthians 10:12 states, *"Let him who thinks that he stands, take heed, lest he fall."* Too many leaders are used to being the one and only "big shot" in their churches, and gain the proud attitude that they can stand alone. This spirit of independence is exactly what allows their destruction.

Leaders who have such an attitude should remember that even David, the king and prophet of Israel, many times felt that he had no strength left in himself (II Samuel 21:15; Psalm 22:14 and 31:10 and 71:9 and 88:4). This is a natural feeling, and should indicate to a leader not only his need for God, but also his need for other Christians. Without realizing his own need for strength for others, he will never be able to provide strength to those who need it from him, because he will not understand the feeling of their need.

A leader must make a firm act of will to be strong in the Lord and for God's people. But in order to be a strong shepherd to God's people, the leader must realize that his own soul (his emotions, will and mind) must be renewed in the Lord's strength. Psalm 138:3 confidently declares, *"God strengthens me with strength in my soul."* Psalm 71:16 states, *"I will go in the strength of the Lord."* Every leader can proclaim that *"The Lord upholds all that fall"* (Psalm 145:14) when he experiences the empowering of the Spirit in his own life. By standing on such promises of God, every leader will be a source of strength to his people. Even when people stumble and have hard times, they need not totally fail. Psalm 37:23-24 states, *"Though he fall, he shall not be utterly cast down, for the Lord upholds him with His hand."*

Some leaders may know times of success in which they experience no weakness in their very busy schedules. Times like these are true blessings from the Lord. At times, the more a leader does in the will of God, the more he is anointed to do for the Lord. The Church at Ephesus knew what it was like to labor for the Lord and not grow weary, for the Lord Jesus spoke to them and said:

> *"I know your deeds, and your toil, and perseverance and that you cannot endure evil men, and you put to the test those who call themselves apostles, and they are not, and you found them to be false: and have perseverance and have endured for my name's sake, and have not grown weary (faint)"* (Revelation 2:2,3)

Yet one of the secrets of strongly leading the people of God is in allowing the Lord to use one's weaknesses for His glory. A weak area is a part of the personality or ability of a person which needs improvement. It is also this very area that God uses, since it is a humble area in a leader's life. God cannot use the area in a leader's life which is lifted up and a source of pride. The Psalmist said, *"They go from strength to strength"* (Psalm 84:7). This meant, in principle, that a leader goes from one revelation of his own human weakness to another, only to find that at each point he is met by God's strength. Thus the scripture is fulfilled, *"They that stumble are girded with strength"* (I Samuel 2:4).

The principle that God does not delight in the strong areas of a man's life is well summarized in Psalm 147:10, *"The Lord delights not in the strength of the horse."* Scripture many times uses the horse as a symbol of the strength of man. God does not enjoy man's strength, because it does not give Him glory. While the *"glory of young men is their strength"* (Proverbs 20:29a), the glory of the older and more mature man of God is in his weakness and frailties.

Note what the apostle Paul said about his own strengths and weaknesses: *"His strength is made perfect in my weakness"* (II Corinthians 12:9) and *"whatever things were gain to me, those things I have counted as loss for the sake of Christ"* (Philippians 3:7). Paul knew the secret of obtaining the power and operation of God as his strength. It was not to obtain a better self-image through "self-improvement" classes. It was voluntarily and verbally exposing all of the weak areas of his life to the grace of the Lord Jesus Christ.

There are several keys in Scripture that can help the leader be a real strength to his people. The leader must:

Be Full of Persevering Faith
Keeping one's eyes on the good results of the end product of God's purposes will help the leader see what God is trying to accomplish in the lives of His people. Galatians 6:9 states, *"We will reap if we faint not."* Through teaching his people to be full of unchangeable faith, a leader can provide strength for them.

Look and Ask for the Goodness of God
A leader needs to get his people to look at the positive things in the will of God and not at negative appearances. This attitude is not the power of "positive thinking." It is a deep belief that God will eventually show a person a spiritual good from something which appeared to have none. David

understood such a need for positive faith, when he declared, *"I would have despaired* (fainted) *unless I had believed that I would see the goodness of the Lord in the land of the living"* (Psalm 27:13).

Keep Yourself Unspotted from the World
Genesis 25:29-30 tells us that when Esau came in from the field he was faint. We know that he subsequently sold his birthright to satisfy a desire of the flesh. This story can be applied to the leader who may become spiritually faint if he dabbles with the sins of this world, for Jesus said, *"The field is the world"* (Matthew 13:38). Anytime a leader is attracted to the lusts of the world, he allows them to wage war against his soul (I Peter 2:11). No leader can continue to minister effectively to his people if he must constantly war in his soul against the lusts of the world system. He will have no more emotional energy left with which to minister. Therefore, every leader must experience total repentance and deliverance in every area of his personal life.

Pray Constantly
Christians lose their spiritual strength when they do not pray, and many of them do not know how to converse with God. This is why a leader must not only pray for himself and pray for his people, but must also teach his people how to pray. Luke 18:1 states, *"Now He* (Jesus) *was telling them a parable to show at all times that they ought to pray and not to lose heart* (faint).*"* Through learning how to pray (and get results) a leader's people will not grow faint in the battle.

Receive the Mercy of God
Paul said, *"Therefore, since we have this ministry, as we received mercy, we do not faint, but we have renounced the hidden things* (of darkness) *because of* (their) *shame"* (II Corinthians 4:1. It is very important for a leader to teach his people how to continually receive the mercy of God in their lives. They must come to understand the process of confession of sin, total repentance and faith in God's cleansing power. In this way, a leader's people will be equipped to maintain their spiritual strength during times of failure.

Consider the Sufferings of Jesus
A leader must continually remind his people that their present contradictions or sufferings are really nothing in comparison to Christ's. Hebrews 12:3 states, *"For consider him who has endured such hostility of sinners against himself, so that you may not grow weary and faint in your minds."* The more a leader reminds his people of the intense sufferings of the Savior, the more they will hold on to their strength during times of testing.

Allow the Daily Renewal of the Inner Man
A Christian's spiritual vitality comes from the activity of the Holy Spirit in his innermost being or spirit. When his spirit experiences the touch of God's Spirit, new life is created within him. This spiritual rejuvenation power is not necessarily dependent on the Christian's physical or outward health. It is dependent on the spiritual health of his inner man. Paul recognized this when he wrote, *"Therefore we do not faint, but though our outer man is decaying, yet our inner man is being renewed day by day"* (II Corinthians 4:16). As the leader teaches his people to rely upon the renewal of their inner man through prayer and the Word, their spiritual enthusiasm will continue to grow and show real strength.

The Leader as a Binder of Wounds and Healer of Breaches
"I will love Thee, O Lord, my strength" Psalm 18:1

"Thou hast made the earth to tremble: thou hast broken it: heal the breaches thereof" Psalm 60:2

Psalm 147:1-3 contains these beautiful words about the nature of God: *"He gatheregh together the outcasts of Israel. He healeth the broken in heart, and bindeth up their wounds"* (see also Jeremiah 30:17; Job 24:12). Isaiah 30:26 also says, *"The Lord is the one who binds up the breach and heals the wounds."* Because God's nature includes a desire to bind and heal the wounds of both large nations and individuals, this aspect of His character should also be included in the character of one of God's leaders. A leader should be a healer of the wounds of God's people.

But what are the "wounds" and "breaches" in peoples' lives? Wounds and breaches are those areas in a person's mind, spirit or emotions that have been crushed under great pressue. They are those feelings that have been thrust through, pierced, stabbed, or hammered (Proverbs 18:8 and 26:22). Wounds are the areas of a person's life in which they feel bruised, overly sensitive or greatly pained. In these feelings, there have been deep penetrations of sorrow (possibly due to bitter disappointments) resulting in unhealthy brokenness of a person's personality and emotions (Job 16:12-14). These wounds and breaches could have come from persons, places, situations or things. But all caused deep sorrow in the human spirit.

Moreover, the Bible also speaks of a person being broken. David said, *"I am like a broken vessel"* (Psalm 31:12 and 34:18 and 51:17 and 147:3; Proverbs 15:13 and 17:22; Hosea 5:11). In describing himself as a broken vessel, we can be certain that David had many wounds and breaches that he needed God to heal. In reality, God was the healer of his wounds and his breaches. David was a man of God and a prophet. He understood, at least partly, the spiritual meaning of the words that Christ would one day speak about the source of healing, *"This is my body which was broken for you"* (I Corinthians 11:24). God was and still is the healer of people's wounds and breaches, and it is to this source that the leader must direct his people.

Wounds and breaches have several causes. Some may originate with the Lord. David declared, *"Thou hast smitten, and thou hast wounded"* (Psalm 69:26 and 64:7; Deuteronomy 32:39; Job 5:18; Hosea 6:1). This is usually directed by God to the wicked and those who constantly rebel against His Word.

The words of a tale-bearer (or gossip) also cause wounds (Proverbs 18:8 and 26:22 and 18:14). How many times do the people of the Lord come to their leadership because they have been hurt by gossipers! A leader must teach against gossip and show his people how wrong words can wound people (see Job 6:254 and 8:2 and 19:2; Psalm 12:6 and 19:14 and 55:21; Proverbs 15:1,26 and 16:24; Ecclesiastes 12:11).

A faithful friend may cause wounds, but these are wounds (or rebukes) for the betterment of his friend (Proverbs 27:6). May every leader be a faithful friend and cause good wounds that lead to healing of his people. God also does this to make us return to Him when our spirits and affections stray (Isaiah 28:28 and 42:3 and 53:5).

A person's liberty can also cause wounds in other Christians' weak consciences (I Corinthians 8:12). Every leader needs to teach his people that they must always avoid offending their brothers' consciences in Christ. Paul said that if eating meat caused his brother in Christ to stumble, he would never eat it again (I Corinthians 8:13). This is the kind of sensitivity that leaders must have toward the weak of the flock, for they are to set the godly example.

Leaders are needed to "bind up" the wounds and breaches of their people. In order to do this, they must understand the process. To bind up is to wrap on or about (as a head band or turban), to put together, to heal up a wound, to act as a physician who restores a broken limb in a body, to wrap with and bandage, and to make to stick together. The Lord Jesus came to *"bind up the broken-hearted"* (Isaiah 61:1 and 30:26; Job 5:18 and 28:11; Ezekiel 34:4,16; Hosea 6:1; Luke 10:34). This is also the ministry of every leader in bring every person to the cross of Jesus Christ, who was the Bruised One.

To effectively bind up the wounds of others, a leader must:

Be healed himself, and free of a wounded spirit.

Have the people at heart, which is the heart of God.

Remember his miserable condition before God healed his own wounds, lest he become impatient and angry with the people.

Have a large heart that identifies with the wounded and broken.

Discern the areas in peoples lives that need to be healed (spirit, mind or body) (Luke 10:34; I Corinthians 12:28-30).

The Leader as a Healer of the Brokenhearted

"He healeth the broken in heart" Psalm 147:3.

Brokenheartedness is a deep state of the affliction of the mind, emotions or spirit of a person. This state can result from the dealings of God (which eventually cause health) or by the negative circumstances of life (which produce bad results without God's grace).

The Hebrew meaning of the word "broken" carries the idea of bursting (literally or figuratively) and can be described in terms of something breaking down, breaking off, breaking in pieces, or breaking up. The word can also mean a crushing, destruction, hurting or an extinguishing of someone's life or feelings. A brokenhearted person is crushed by grief or despair. Psalm 109:16 states, *"The wicked persecute the poor and needy man that he might even slay the broken in heart."*

Sadly, many Christians and non-Christians today have broken hearts, emotions, thoughts and lives. It happens through wrong response to tragedies; mental break-ups; family disappointments; criticism; rejection and not turning one's entire life over to God. Many lives are in disarray. Psalm 69:20 states, *"Reproach* (disgrace or shame) *will break the heart."* Since sin brings disgrace, shame and destructive guilt to a man's life, it will eventually cause a man's heart to break.

Proverbs 15:13 states, *"By sorrow of heart is the spirit broken."* So many people are also in the depths of sorrow today because they have not made Jesus Christ the master of every area of their life. This sorrow is bringing many to the point of a totally broken spirit. One of the biggest problems with a broken heart is that it also causes a person physical problems. Proverbs 17:22 states, *"A broken heart drieth the bones."* Without Jesus to heal his heart, a person is open to many spiritual and physical problems.

Brokenheartedness also has a positive side. The heart of Jeremiah the prophet was broken over the influence that the false prophets of his day had on the people of God (Jeremiah 23:9). This had positive results, because it includes a godly sorrow for sin and a desire to release the grace of God. This kind of a broken heart has some positive advantages.

First, the presence of God is near to the person who has a broken heart in a godly way. Psalm 34:18 says *"The Lord is nigh them that are of a broken heart."*

Second, a person that has a broken heart for a godly reason can offer to God a true and spiritual sacrifice. Psalm 51:17 describes such a true and spiritual sacrifice: *"The sacrifices of God are a broken heart, a broken and contrite heart thou wilt not despise."*

Thus, for those who deeply sorrow over other's sins (similar to God's own heart about sin), an abundance of God's healing grace and mercy is available. But to those who have broken hearts through their own selfishness and lack of trust in Jesus, there is only grief upon grief. To those who seem broken beyond repair, God promises, *"I will heal the broken heart and bind up their wounds"* (Psalm 147:3). Those who really need a mental, spiritual or emotional healing in their life receive God's promise of wholeness through His son.

This situation creates a great responsibility for God's leaders. God's leaders must be the ones to lead men to the healing power of God. In the past, when the leader's of God's people did not heal them, they received a strict indictment (Ezekiel 34:4). This same judgment is upon every one of God's leaders who does not help to heal the brokenhearted. God the Great Shepherd has promised to bind up the wounded (Ezekiel 34:16). Since the same Holy Spirit that was upon Jesus Christ to bind and heal the bruised (Isaiah 61:1; Luke 4:18) is now upon His leaders, they must minister in this way to the needy.

The following list contrasts the unhealthy and the healthy broken heart:

THE NEGATIVE	THE POSITIVE
Sin breaking the heart results in:	God breaking the heart results in:
Bruising	Restoration
Grief	Joy
Crushing	Humility
Bursting	Gentleness
Destruction	Protection
Hurt	Meekness
Quenching	A Contrite Spirit
Strickening	Consolation
Wounding	Healing
Breaking	Building up
Shattering	Fortifying
Tearing	Soothing
Subjugation	Submission
Crumbling	Constructing
Weakening	Strengthening
Hatred	Love
Discouragement	Encouragement
Reduction	Increase

Every leader must remember that it was after the breaking of the alabaster box of ointment that a sweet fragrance filled the room (Matthew 26:7; Mark 14:3; Luke 7:37,38). It was after the bread was broken that it fed the multitudes (Matthew 14:19 and 15:36 and 26:26). In leading people through brokenheartedness, may every leader note that to be broken by God leads to life, but to be broken by sin leads only to death. May every leader bring people through brokenheartedness to the healing love and forgiveness of Jesus Christ.

CHAPTER 16
GROWTH MINISTRIES OF THE LEADER

In our study of God's personality as reproduced in the lives of His leaders, we now come to an area that is very dear to the hearts of most Christian leaders: the ministries that support growth. It is the exercise of these ministries, through the moving and power of the Holy Spirit, that releases the Church to her full potential for fruitfulness.

The Psalmist intimately knew and understood God as his Authority, his Guide and his Husbandman. God exalted David from leading sheep to leading His people. During David's reign, Israel was established as one of the greatest powers in the world, a great and prosperous kingdom that showed forth a measure of the glory of God. As with the other areas of ministry function, we will base our studies in growth ministries on the personality of God, as described in Psalms.

Before we proceed into our study, we must interject a brief note about the reproduction of God's personality in His leaders. While the leader of God's people need not and cannot "be God" for his people, he is responsible to ardently pursue the character of God in his own life. The Christian leader is one of the believer's most important resources in maintaining his personal relationship with God. Father God sent His Son in the form of human flesh, because only this way could He truly reach us. To a lesser degree, with a measure of the fullness of the Spirit, the Christian leader functions in a similar capacity.

God the Authority
The Leader as a King

"Save, O Lord, let the king hear us when we call" Psalm 20:9.

We hesitate even to include this section in our study, because the leader's function as a "king" has been so misunderstood and abused in the past. In many churches, the pastor has been the virtual king in a very unscriptural way. This section should not encourage a leader to be a fierce and domineering fleecer of the sheep. We include this function in our study to provide a scriptural balance of gentle rulership and spiritual protection.

The Psalms describe God as a king, reigning over heaven and earth, and over His people (Psalm 47:2 and 93:1 and 96:10 and 97:1 and 99:1). Similarly, every leader is responsible to exercise spiritual rulership in Christ over the evil principalities and powers in the spiritual realm.

God the King demonstrates the attributes of holiness (Psalm 2:6), wisdom (Psalm 2:10) and humility (Psalm 5:2). Every leader must demonstrate these same qualities in the exercise of his mantle of government and responsibility. In Hebrew, the word for king means to reign, to ascend to the throne, and to induct into royalty. By implication, it also means to take counsel. Therefore, any leader must exercise his governmental ministry with the people of God in gentleness, wisdom and humility. Continually listening to God's counsel and the spiritual wisdom from those He sends is an important part of the exercise of spiritual "kingship."

The Leader as a Judge

"For God is judge himself" Psalm 50:5.

Many scriptures declare that God, Jesus Christ and the Church are all judges. (God: Psalm 7:8 and 9:8 and 10:18 and 26:1; Proverbs 31:9; Isaiah 1:17. Jesus: John 5:30 and 7:24 and 8:15,16; Acts 17:31; II Timothy 4:8. The Church: I Corinthians 6:3).

A judge brings punishment or justice to one who is accused of a crime. God is the judge of all men through His Son, Jesus Christ, due to man's crime of sinning against God's commandments. The Church will eventually judge even angels, because to her has been imputed the righteousness of God through Jesus Christ.

Before that final day of judgment, however, God uses His leaders to vindicate His people and preach repentance to the wicked. God has entrusted His leaders with the gospel of Jesus Christ, through which men can be delivered from their death sentence.

God has also given the Church a promise through the prophet Isaiah, who declared, *"I will restore judges to you as at the first"* (Isaiah 1:26). In this prophetic promise, the Church can trust that God will raise up leaders in this day who can execute judgement like some of the leaders of the early Church. Leaders, too, can have confidence that God will work to form within them the positive characteristics of a Biblical judge, to which we will now refer. The scriptures below describe the True Judge and the False Judge, as contrasted in different areas of function and personality. Every leader should allow God to develop the positive attributes of the True Judge in his own life and ministry, and forsake the negative attributes of the False Judge.

THE TRUE JUDGE

Chosen: true judges will be appointed by God and the people: *"You shall appoint for yourself judges and officers in all your towns which the Lord your God is giving you"* (Deuteronomy 16:18).

Responsible: true judges will be appointed over certain areas of responsibility: *"You shall appoint for yourself judges . . . according to your tribes"* (Deut. 16:18, see also II Chronicles 19:5).

Righteous: true judges will judge with righteous and just judgment: *"You shall appoint for yourself judges . . . and they shall judge the people with righteous judgment"* (Deut. 16:18).

THE FALSE JUDGE

Unchosen: false judges rule by their own power: *"An appalling and horrible thing has happened in the land . . . the priests rule on their own authority"* (Jeremiah 5:30,31b).

Irresponsible: false judges will be so irresponsible that they lead God's people astray: *"Thus saith the Lord concerning the prophets who lead My people astray"* (Micah 3:5).

Unrighteous: false judges will be unrighteous: *"Hear now, heads of Jacob and rulers of the house of Israel . . . You who hate good and love evil"* (Micah 3:1,2).

Sound: true judges will not twist their judgments: *"You shall appoint for yourself judges . . . (who) shall not distort justice"* (Deut. 16:19).

Impartial: true judges will not be partial in their decisions: *"You shall appoint for yourself judges . . . (who) shall not be partial"* (literally, regard persons) (Deut. 16:19).

Honest: true judges will not fall for financial gifts: *"You shall appoint for yourself judges . . . (who) shall not take a bribe, for a bribe blinds the eyes of the wise and perverts the words of the righteous"* (Deut. 16:19).

Just: true judges will only pursue the proper discernment: *"You shall appoint for yourself judges . . . (who shall pursue) justice and only justice that you may live and possess the land which the Lord your God is giving you"* (Deut. 16:20).

Decisive: true judges will bring spiritual decisions over controversies in the Church: *"If there is a dispute between men and they go to court . . . the judges (shall) decide their case"* (Deut. 25:1).

Loyal: true judges will stand up for the person who is right: *"If there is a dispute between men and they go to court . . . they (shall) justify the righteous"* (Deut. 25:1).

Courageous: true judges will not stand up for the person who is in the wrong: *"If there is a dispute between men and they go to court, and the judges decide their case . . . they shall condemn the wicked"* (Deut. 25:1).

Objective: true judges will punish the guilty according to the Word of the Lord: *"Then it shall be if the wicked man deserves to be beaten, the judge shall make him lie down and be beaten in his presence with the number of stripes according to his guilt"* (Deut. 25:2).

Fair: true judges will not overextend their sentence of judgment against the guilty party: *"He may test him 40 times but no more, lest he beat him with many more stripes than these, and your brother be degraded in your eyes"* (Deut. 25:3).

Unsound: false judges will not be sound: *"An appalling and horrible thing has happened in the land: the prophets prophesy falsely"* (Jer. 5:30,31).

Partial: false judges put financial and emotional bribes above the Lord: *"His (Samuel's) sons, however, did not walk in his ways, but turned aside after dishonest gain and took bribes, and perverted justice"* (I Samuel 8:3).

Dishonest: false judges will profit from the abuse of their gifts and ministries: *"Her priests instruct for a price, and her prophets divine for money"* (Micah 3:11).

Unjust: false judges will be unjust: *"Hear now, heads of Jacob and rulers of the house of Israel. Is it not for you to know justice . . . who build Zion with violent injustice?"* (Micah 3:1,10).

Indecisive: false judges will waver after they hear the word of God, rather than sticking to it: *"And God said to Balaam, 'Do not go with them: you shall not curse the people; for they are blessed' . . . and Balaam answered and said to the servants of Balak . . . 'And now please, you also stay here tonight, and I will find out what else the Lord will speak to me'."* (Numbers 22:12,18,19).

Disloyal: false judges will take advantage of God's people: *"Hear now, heads of Jacob and rulers of the house of Israel . . . who tear off the skin of them (my people) and their flesh from their bones, and who eat the flesh of my people, and strip off their skin from them"* (Micah 3:1-3).

Fearful: false judges will fear people's disagreements and say what pleases those who meet their financial or political desires: *"Her leaders pronounce judgment for a bribe"* (Micah 3:11).

Subjective: false judges will not be able to make correct decisions according to God's Word: *"Now hear this, heads of the house of Jacob . . . who . . . twist everything that is straight"* (Micah 3:9).

Unfair: false judges will be selfish and unfair to the people of God: *"He (Saul) will take your sons and place them for himself in his chariots . . . some to do his plowing and to reap his harvest and to make his weapons of war . . . also your daughters for perfumers and cooks and bakers . . . And he will take the best of your fields . . .*

Understanding: true judges will have a heart that hears the true cries of the people: "*So give thy servant an understanding heart to judge thy people*" (I Kings 3:9).

Discerning: true judges will know the difference between right and wrong: "*So give thy servant an understanding heart to judge thy people to discern between good and evil*" (I Kings 3:9).

Humble: true judges will recognize their inability to judge the people properly by their own abilities: "*So give thy servant an understanding heart to judge thy people . . . for who is able to judge this great people of thine?* (I Kings 3:9).

Wise: true judges desire God to give them wisdom that they might be a good example to the people of God: "*Give me now wisdom . . . that I may go out and come in before this people*" (II Chronicles 1:10).

Knowing: true judges will desire God to give them knowledge that they might be a good example to the flock: "*Give me now . . . knowledge . . . that I may go out and come in before this people*" (II Chron. 1:10).

Watchful: true judges will be careful about their ministries: "*And he* (king Jehoshaphat) *said to the judges, 'Consider what you are doing'* (II Chron. 19:6).

Aware: true judges will be aware of their tremendous responsibility to the Lord: "*And he* (king Jehoshaphat) *said to the judges, 'Consider what you are doing, for you do not judge for man but for the Lord who is with you when you render judgments' "*(II Chron. 19:6).

Reverential: true judges deeply respect the Lord more than anyone else in life: "*Now let the fear of the Lord be upon you*" (II Chron. 19:7).

vineyards, and your olive groves, and give them to his servants" (I Samuel 8:11-14).

Misunderstanding: false judges will not comprehend what God is doing because they will have no divine communication: "*The sun will go down on the prophets, and the day will become dark over them. The seers will be ashamed and the diviners will be embarassed. Indeed, they will all cover their mouths because there is no answer from God*" (Micah 3:6,7).

Undiscerning: false judges follow the enemy, and do not discern right from wrong: "*When they have something to bite with their teeth, they cry, 'Peace'* (like the Baal worshippers who bit olives, the symbol of peace, around their idolatrous altars). *But against him who puts nothing in their mouths* (like the follower of the Lord) *they declare holy war*" Micah 3:5).

Proud: false judges may become proud after obtaining a reputation: "*For he* (king Uzziah) *was marvelously helped until he became strong. But when he became strong, his heart was so proud that he acted corruptly . . . for the entered the temple of the Lord to burn incense on the altar of incense*" (II Chronicles 26:15,16).

Unwise: proud judges will grow unwise because they do not trust in the Lord: "*Let not the wise man glory in his might, let not the rich man glory in his riches: But let him who glories, glory in this: that he knows me*" (Jeremiah 9:23,24.

Unknowing: false judges will not know the way of the Lord because God will give them darkness: "*Therefore it will be night for you without vision, and darkness for you without divination*" (Micah 3:6)

Unwatchful: false judges will not watch to see what falsities the people fall into: "*An appalling and horrible thing has happened in the land: the prophets prophesy falsely and the priests rule by their own authority, and my people love it so*" (Jer. 5:30,31).

Unaware: false judges are unwatchful over the state of God's people: "*But if the watchman sees the sword coming and does not blow the trumpet, nad the people are not warned, and a sword comes and takes a person from them . . . his blood will I require from the watchman's hand*" (Ezekiel 33:6).

Violent: false judges will not respect the Lord or anyone else, but will live violently: "*Now hear this, heads of the house of Jacob . . . who build Zion with bloodshed and Jerusalem with violent*

Circumspect: true judges desire to be a good witness for the Lord at all times: *"Be very careful what you do, for the Lord will have no part in unrighteousness"* (II Chron. 19:7).

Faithful: true judges will be faithful: *"Then he* (Jehoshaphat) *charged them saying, 'Thus you shall do in the fear of the Lord, faithfully . . .'."* (II Chron. 19:9).

Wholehearted: true judges will be wholehearted in their work: *"Then he* (Jehoshaphat) *said to them, 'Thus you shall do in the fear of the Lord . . . wholeheartedly"* (II Chron. 19:6).

Admonishing: true judges will warn the people: *"And whenever any dispute comes to you from your brethren . . . you shall warn them that they may not be guilty before the Lord"* (II Chron. 19:10).

Submissive: true judges will be submitted to other men spiritually and politically: *"And behold Amariah, the chief priest, will be over you in all that pertains to the Lord: and Zebadiah . . . in all that pertains to the king:* (II Chron. 19:11).

Respected: true judges will be respected: *"Also, the Levites shall be officers before you"* (II Chron. 19:11).

Resolute: true judges will be resolute: *"Act resolutely, and the Lord be with the upright"* (II Chron. 19:11).

injustice" (Micah 3:9,10).

Presumptuous: false judges will live in sin and presume that God is still with them: *"Her leaders pronounce judgment for a bribe . . . Yet they lean on the Lord saying 'Is not the Lord in our midst? Calamity will not come upon us"* (Micah 3:11).

Unfaithful: false judges will be unfaithful to God's people by taking away their strength: *"Hear now, heads of Jacob and rulers of the house of Israel . . . (who) break their* (My people's) *bones and chop them up as for the pot and as meat in a kettle"* (Micah 3:1,3).

Zeal Without Knowledge: false judges sometimes have zeal, but not according to knowledge: *"For I bear them record that they have a zeal of God but not according to knowledge. For they, being ignorant of God's righteousness, and going about to establish their own righteousness, have not submitted themselves unto the righteousness of God"* (Roman 10:2,23).

Apathetic: false judges are too lazy to warn the people about their sins: *"When . . . you do not speak to warn the wicked from his way, that wicked man shall die in his iniquity, but his blood I will require from your hand"* (Ezekiel 33:8).

Unsubmissive: false judges will not submit and walk in the ways that their spiritual fathers have walked: *"His* (Samuel's) *sons, however, did not walk in his ways"* (I Samuel 8:3).

Unrespected: false judges do not gain the people's respect, because the Lord does not respect them due to their sins: *"Then they* (the judges) *will cry out to the Lord, but he will not answer them. Instead, he will hide his face from them that practiced evil deeds"* (Micah 3:4).

Backsliding: false judges will not cling to the Lord diligently, but will fall away and thereby cause others to do the same: *"For those who guide this people are leading them astray; and those who are guided by them are brought to confusion"* (Isaiah 9:16).

The Leader as a Father of the Fatherless
"Like as a father pitieth his children, so the Lord pitieth them that fear him" Psalm 103:13.

It is not strange that Israel's laws would include statutes to protect and guide the fatherless and the widow (Exodus 22:22; Deuteronomy 10:18 and 14:29 and 16:11-14 and 27:19). The Psalmist also perceived God's protective heart toward the orphan and the widow (Psalm 82:3 and 94:6 and 109:9 and 146:9). *"God is the helper of the fatherless"* it states in Psalm 10:14,18.

Other related scriptures bring out the idea of God taking up (Isaiah 22:21), defending, relieving, delivering, visiting, guiding (Jeremiah 3:4) and bringing justice to the widow and the orphan (Psalm 68:5). God is obviously concerned about the widow and the orphan because He desires all to have a safe, happy and secure life in Him. Since God has ordained this through the institution of the family, He takes special measures to protect people when the family structure breaks down.

If God is so concerned about the widow and the orphan, so should every spiritual leader be full of care for the spiritual widows and orphans in the world today. Although the apostle James stated that visiting the natural widow and orphan in their affliction was *"pure religion and undefiled"* (James 1:27), God is even more greatly concerned about the spiritually fatherless.

God wants His leaders to have a heart for those people today who are not yet His children by faith in Jesus Christ. Leaders need to have a burden for those who are spiritually alienated from God's family. By default, these people have Satan as their spiritual father (John 8:44). A leader must have a heart for the lost souls that know God only as their earthly Creator, but not as their heavenly Father.

God's leaders must also enter another aspect in ministering to the spiritually "fatherless." This is a burden for those who are born again by faith in Jesus Christ, but who are not set into local church families where they can be protected and fed. These are Christian widows and orphans, who have no earthly spiritual parents to help them grow in their new faith in Christ. They may have God as their spiritual Father, but no other spiritual parents in the family of God. A leader must realize that just as natural parents guide and protect the affairs of the home, so the elders and deacons guide the house of God as its spiritual parents. May the Lord work into the heart of every leader the heart of a father of the fatherless.

The Leader as a Teacher

"He teacheth my hands to war" Psalm 18:34.

The leader is commonly regarded as a teacher of the people. It is not surprising that God has set teachers into His Body, because God Himself is intimately involved in teaching His ways and truths (Psalm 45:4) to His leaders (Psalm 105:22) and His people. God greatly desires to teach His people about Himself and about His present kingdom (Psalm 32:8).

God's people often have a problem obeying what He teaches. But if Christians live humbly and righteously before the Lord, the promise in Proverbs 9:9 will be their experience: *"Teach a just man, and he will increase."* A just man will increase bringing his entire life into line with the Word of God as he is being instructed in it. When people do not want to respond to God's teaching, they usually have not responded to the last truth that God desired them to obey. People stifle their own spiritual growth by not responding to the Lord's teaching. But a just man will hear and increase, because he puts into practice all that he hears.

The Church can rejoice that God has been prophetically fulfilling Isaiah 30:20 in this generation: *"Your teachers shall not be removed into a corner any longer, but your eyes shall see your teachers."* This scripture had a measure of fulfillment in relation to natural Israel's instruction in the law of the Lord by their teachers, after their return from the Babylonian captivity. It also applies spiritually to the Church, which has a dire need of teachers who know the Bible and who also know the Lord. Through an emphasis on healings, miracles and mass evangelism in the Church, God has been restoring the teaching ministry. God is now emphasizing the importance of teaching and anointed leadership. His people are now learning how to live a practical Christian life in their homes and neighborhoods. Christ's witness is not only going out through the mass media, but also in a local and personal way through individual Christians.

Just as God teaches, so the leader is to instruct the people with a gentle, humble, obedient and loving spirit. What are the principles for teaching that enable the leader to teach his people wisely? Here are some ways and keys for the leader:

Teach the people only as much as they are ready to understand, receive and put into action.

Use natural illustrations to show them spiritual truths (Romans 1:20).

Teach them how to meditate and study the Word of God for themselves, so individuals and families can be continually fed the Word during the week.

Use repetion to bring truths back into their memory.

Give them practical applications that help them put the Word into action in their lives.

Teach them how to teach others.

Teach the teachers how to teach their age groups.

Teach new converts the foundational truths of Christianity and their families the principles of family life.

Teach them how to become involved in the house of the Lord according to their age group and gift from the Lord.

Teach them how to win souls to Christ and how to lead them into the Baptism of the Holy Spirit.

Teach them by example, always doing first what you want them to do.

On a theological level, note the following things that God teaches His people. These are the same things that a leader is responsible to teach his people as well. God teaches:

His ways (not just His truths or facts) Psalm 25:4 and 27:4.

His truth (the only thing that will set the captive free) Psalm 25:5.

Submission (how to truly obey Him) Psalm 25:8.

Meekness (the meak are humble and hungry for His Word) Psalm 25:9.

The fear of the Lord (through which men depart from evil) Psalm 34:11.

Spiritual priorities (which helps people to *"number their days"* in wise use of time) Psalm 90:12.

His statutes (so that the people clearly know His specific boundaries) Psalm 119:12.

His judgments (so the people will not think that Grace is a license to sin) Psalm 119:66.

His knowledge (which He desires to balance with character in a person's life) Psalm 119:66.

His will (which is always according to His Word) Psalm 143:10.

Spiritual warfare (with the spiritual armor of Ephesians 6:10-20 and not carnal weapons) Psalm 18:34 and 144:1.

All of these principles and keys will help the leader teach the people over whose spiritual lives God Himself has given him charge.

The Leader as a Disciplinarian

"But unto the wicked God saith, 'What has thou to do to declare my statutes, or that thou shouldest take my covenant in thy mouth? Seeing thou hatest instruction (discipline), *and castest my words behind thee?' "* Psalm 50:16,17.

Many leaders do not like to correct or discipline their people. This is not only unbiblical, but also gives Satan the opportunity to spiritually ruin the lives of many of God's people. Satan loves an undisciplined house (whether natural or spiritual). In such an environment, he can easily cause loose and compromising living that spreads to all family members. In contrast, God loves discipline and correction. Psalm 39:11 states about God, *"With reproofs thou dost chasten a man for iniquity."* Because God does not hesitate to discipline and correct (see Psalm 118:18), neither should the godly leader.

Leaders are afraid to discipline members of their congregations for various reasons. Some of these reasons are:

If he has undisciplined children in his own home, he may feel he cannot discipline others.

He may have unconfessed sin in his own life.

He may not know the Word well enough to identify areas that need correction.

He may desire to please man more than God, because he has impure motives in his heart.

His wife may constantly correct him at home, and he desires not to sound like her.

He may not be truly called to be a shepherd or watchman of the flock.

He may be reading and believing some worldly philosophies about discipline, instead of making God's Word his rule for conduct.

He may not have the general respect and cooperation of his people when he tries to discipline them.

He may be insecure in his own spiritual position and/or authority.

He may think that godly discipline is relatively unimportant in the Church, that the main purposes are healings, miracles or evangelism.

He may never have allowed anyone else to correct him (perhaps not even the Lord Himself).

He may fear — wrongly — that he will lose his good reputation or his many good friends if he corrects anyone.

He may have his hands tied by the deacon board of his local church, or by some denominational and external authority.

Whatever a leader's excuses, God clearly wants His leaders to apply godly discipline to those whom God has entrusted to him. It is his spiritual responsibility before God to *"watch for their souls"* (Hebrews 13:17), knowing that this, at times, will involve discipline. Young children are happier and more secure when they know the boundaries their parents have set. In the same way, the children of God need a sense of boundary from their spiritual parents in the Lord. Such boundaries should always be scriptural, for the Word of God is the staff with which a shepherd disciplines the sheep of God (II Timothy 3:16). When done in love (Proverbs 3:12; Revelation 3:19) discipline will always lead to a person's spiritual benefit, and ultimately, happiness (Job 5:17).

Though chastisement is not pleasant to the flesh, it is pleasant to the spirit. And it is the spiritual life of a person that is most important to God. A leader must remember that God often sacrifices elements of a person's natural and external life, so his spirit may become disciplined and mature (I Corinthians 5:5). The Bible exhorts believers not to be weary of God's correction (Proverbs 3:11; Job 5:17; Hebrews 12:5-11). It also exhorts leaders not to neglect disciplining their own children, but to use their natural family for an example (Proverbs 23:13). Words are not always sufficient in correcting someone; at times actions are needed (Proverbs 29:19).

To correct a person is to show what is wrong, to reprove, to rebuke, to punish, to instruct or to admonish. Many shepherds consider themselves "teachers," but do not realize that office requires them to warn and discipline. To be true teachers, leaders must set a good example to the flock, and they also must lovingly correct the flock when necessary.

A leader's relationship to a member of his spiritual family is similar to the Lord's relationship to His people, or father to his son. Deuteronomy 8:5 states: *"As a man chasteneth his son, so the Lord chasteneth thee."* When a leader is chastened by the Lord Himself, he knows the spiritual value of such correction. He knows that God's dealings will not totally kill him physically (II Corinthians 6:9). Such a leader knows that God wants to correct the spirit and soul of a man, not his outward person (Psalm 69:10). A leader who has been corrected by God knows that no chastening seems good during the time that he is receiving it, but that it afterwards builds godly integrity and character into his life and ministry (Hebrews 12:5-11).

A man of God lovingly and tenderly corrects his people with the Word of God for their own good. He knows that he must minister the Word of God to them while there is still hope for them to learn and change (Proverbs 19:18). He knows he must show them the right ways of God without anger (Psalm 6:1 and 38:1). Too many parents correct their children in anger. A wise leader knows that with love, gentleness and firmness, his people will grow when they are corrected.

God the Guide
The Leader as a Guide

"For this God is our God forever and ever: he will be our guide even unto death" Psalm 48:14.

Most Christians believe that God guides His people. But many do not believe that He uses the leaders, who are walking with Him, to do so. Some Christians have adopted the rebellion and independence in our society, taking orders from no one — at times not even from God!

The Church today desperately needs true spiritual guides, but not dictators. In many cases, blind leaders are leading blind people, and both are falling into the ditch (Matthew 23:16,24). This section will attempt to motivate leaders to make themselves available to God, so God can guide His people through their lives and ministries. A leader must realize that God reserves a severe judgment for those who lead God's people in the wrong direction (see the case of Jeroboam in I Kings 16:2,19,26).

God has promised to guide those who follow Him, from the time of their youth (Jeremiah 3:4) even to the time of their death (Psalm 48:14). The trouble comes in when Christians who are walking away from the Lord still expect God to guide them. God will not directly guide any Christian, church or leader who is deliberately violating His Word. The only place to which God will guide those who are walking out of His ways is to a place of repentance and change.

God will directly guide a person only after he personally submits totally to the lordship of Jesus Christ. The goal of Christian leadership is not to tell Christians what they should do and where they should go. The goal is for both leader and Christian to put themselves in the very center of God's will by complete obedience to God's Word. From there, God can begin to guide them both.

Whenever we move away from God and His Word, we know we are not following the Holy Spirit. Once a Christian or a leader places himself in God's perfect will by obeying all that he knows God is telling him to do from His Word, then they can claim the promise: *"The Lord shall guide thee continually"* (Isaiah 58:11).

God guides His people and His leaders by His Holy Spirit through His Word. God does this because He greatly desires His people to enter into His spiritual truth. He also desires to guard the reputation of His name as the Head of the Church (see Psalm 31:3). God leads His people so that the world cannot say, "Where is the God of Israel?" Micah the prophet reiterated the fact of God's people depending upon their God to guide them when he said, *"Trust not in a friend, and put ye not confidence in a guide"* (Micah 7:5).

As God uses His leaders to guide and direct His people, He has several things in mind. Some of them are expressed in the meanings of the Hebrew word for guidance:

A leader should consider himself to be the spiritual head (underneath Christ, of course) of a spiritual family or tribe. He unites and guides them in their Christian walk.

A leader should not think of his ministry of guidance as only that of precedency or rule over the people, but of fellowship and mutual confidence as well.

A leader should guide His people only in the straight path of the Lord, His Word and His ways.

A leader should give correct and godly counsel to his people as an essential part of guiding them, instead of sending them off to a secular psychiatrist for treatment.

A leader can only guide and lead as he is gentle and soft with the people whom God has given him.

A leader must base all of his guidance to the people upon the Spirit and the Word of God.

In doing these things, a leader will live up to the meaning of the word "guide."

In guiding God's people, a leader should realize that God's overall purpose is two-fold: first, to have his people enter into all truth (John 16:13), and second, to develop Christ-like character within them (Luke 1:79). A leader should not overemphasize either one of these aspects of in his ministry. Truth and character should not be at odds, but must be balanced by the leader as he applies biblical principles to his people.

How is a leader to guide the people whom God has given to him? The following is a list of some of the functions of guidance:

Closely observe the flock for needs and problems (Psalm 32:8).

Look to the Holy Spirit as the ultimate counselor (Psalm 23:2).

Share principles of Christian growth and spiritual strength with the people (Exodus 15:13), so that they can learn to fight the fight of faith for themselves.

Relate how God has helped in certain areas of his own life.

Ask God what spiritual principles of His Word He may be trying to teach someone through the specific dealings or tests that they are undergoing.

Demonstrate proper Christian principles through his own words and actions, as God guided Israel through the skillfulness of His own hands and words (see Psalm 78:72).

God the Husbandman
The Leader as Rain and Showers to God's People

"(God) shall come down like rain upon the mown grass . . . He shall come down . . . as showers that water the earth" Psalm 72:6.

Throughout the Bible, God is considered as the source of rain for His people (Genesis 2:5 and 7:4 and 8:2; I Samuel 12:17). It is God who controls the rain for His own purposes (Revelation 11:6). Jeremiah aptly asked, *"Are there any among the idols of the nations who give rain? Or can the heavens grant showers? Is it not Thou, O Lord, our God? Therefore we hope in thee, for thou art the one who hast done all these things"* (Jeremiah 14:22).

The prophet Amos also described God's sovereignty in relation to rain in the words, *"Then I would send rain on one city, and on another city I would not send rain; one part would be rained on, while the part not rained on would be dry"* (Amos 4:7). Israel had to learn to trust in God for their rain, rather than in the irrigation systems of Egypt or the other methods of other nations.

The land of Palestine is a very rocky and dry land in most places. The people of Israel had to store the water that fell in the form of rain in clay vessels and cisterns. Living in such a dry land, Israel had to trust the Lord for rain. This needy condition made them very dependent upon God through faith and obedience. Deuteronomy 11:11 describes the land as a person, so thirsty that it would "drink" in the rain water that falls upon it.

Similarly, the world today is in dire need of the spiritual rain of God. But one of the means through which people receive the growth and provision of spiritual rain (Hebrews 6:7,8; Exodus 16:4) is through God's appointed leadership. God declared that He will come to His people *"as the rain"* (Hosea 6:3). God desires to use His leaders to bring spiritual refreshing to His people. Today there is a great spiritual famine in the land because of a lack of people entering into the outpouring of God's Spirit. Therefore, God needs His leaders to understand the principles that cause rain to fall upon His people. This understanding will then be communicated to God's people through those whom He has chosen to be His leaders.

Though rains of various sorts sometimes meant judgment in Scripture (Exodus 9:18; Psalm 11:6), they were often associated with blessing (Ezekiel 34:26), gladness (Acts 14:17), mercy (Matthew 5:45), righteousness (Hosea 10:12), patience (Job 29:23), expectancy and doctrine (Deuteronomy 32:2). These are all important principles which every leader should teach in order to receive the rain of God.

Probably one of the most important aspects of teaching for the provision of rain is the breaking up of the dry ground of people's hearts through prayer and repentance from sins (Jeremiah 4:3; Hosea 10:12). God pours down His rain upon the mown grass (Psalm 72:6), those hearts that are made low and humble before Him. There are certain special reasons for rain even in the spiritual realm (Leviticus 26:4; Psalm 147:8; Jeremiah 3:3), such special times of the Holy Spirit's visitation (I Kings 18:41). But at all times, God will pour out His Spirit upon those who seek Him with their whole hearts.

A leader must be as a refreshing rain to God's people in his preaching, teaching and counseling. He must learn the principles that cause the rain of God to be outpoured upon the Chuch. Then he can cause his people to experience, in both their individual and corporate lives, the Lord Jesus Himself as the rain from heaven.

The Leader as a Vineyard-Planter and Husbandman

"His hands formed the dry land" Psalm 95:5.

A leader is to do more than sow seeds. He is also to be a planter of vineyards. He must be a good spiritual farmer who provides fresh water, fertile soil, and an observing eye for his crops and vineyards. He must be aware of the spiritual east winds, locusts, worms, thieves, birds and fires that can destroy the plantings of the Lord (Isaiah 61:3). As a planter of vineyards, the leader must be concerned about what happens to the seed after it is sown. A leader must watch over every plant which God has planted. He must nurse it through starting as a sprout of faith in Christ, and find a safe vineyard where it can continue to grow and bear much fruit.

There is a time, eventually, to root up what has been planted (Ecclesiastes 3:2). But every new plant in God's vineyard needs time for its roots to go down deeply into the soil and become strong. Unfortunately, many times after God plants a vineyard, the leaders of the vineyard do not tend it to produce healthy fruit. Jesus applied this analogy to the Jewish nation in Matthew 21:33.

It seems that Scripture emphasises the spiritual regarding the planting of vineyards. As a husbandman of God's people, the leader must:

Keep his people from mixing themselves with the vine strips of other gods (Isaiah 17:10).

Convince his people that just as surely as God has planted the heavens and the earth, so He has chosen His Church to cause the universe to know of the Lord Jesus Christ (Isaiah 51:16).

Teach his people to follow the example of Jesus Christ who grew up before the Lord as a tender shoot (Isaiah 53:2).

Make it clear to his people that just because they have had a good beginning in the Lord, they are not guaranteed a good ending unless they continue to obey Him (see the failure of the nation of Israel in Jeremiah 2:21 and Ezekiel 17:1-24).

Realize that God desires to establish His Church forever.

Realize that every tree (person) that has not been planted by the Lord will be uprooted (Matthew 15:13). Therefore, he must make sure that all of his people have affirmed their salvation in Christ.

Teach his people that the counsel of the ungodly will disrupt them from meditating day and night in the law of the Lord, which will plant them firmly as trees of righteousness by the rivers of God's Spirit (Psalm 1:1-3).

Take care that all of the plants of the Lord are planted in a house of the Lord (Psalm 92:11-13).

Realize that in water baptism, all of the plants of the Lord are *planted in his likeness* (Romans 6:5), and encourage them to build from this foundation.

It is true that a leader must sow the seed of God's Word. He must also care about what happens to that seed after it takes root in a person's heart. May every leader learn how to be a better husbandman of God's vineyard. (Further scriptures on the leader as a husbandman: II Chronicles 26:10; Jeremiah 31:24; Joel 1:11; John 15:1ff; II Timothy 2:6; James 5:7).

The Leader as Field-Sower

"Sow the fields . . . which may yield fruits of increase" Psalm 107:37.

God is pictured as a sower in Scripture. He sowed the nation of Israel in the land of Palestine for blessing (Hosea 2:23). He sowed the nations of the earth for cursing (Zechariah 10:9). In the same way, a leader is the one through whom Jesus Christ sows the seed of His Word (Luke 8:11). One of the strong admonitions of the Law of Moses, however, was that Israel was not to sow her field with more than one kind of seed. Otherwise, she would harvest a mixture of fruit (Deuteronomy 22:9; see also Proverbs 11:30 and 12:12).

A Christian leader should take this principle to heart. He must realize that he will produce pure and healthy spiritual fruit before God only if he sows exclusively the seed of God's Word in the souls and hearts of his hearers. Otherwise, he may cause a mixture of the godly and the ungodly in the kingdom. God challenges every leader to trust in His Word and His Spirit alone (Isaiah 30:23) to bring forth kingdom fruit (Ecclesiastes 11:6 and Matthew 6:26). Other seeds are prohibited. In this way, no flesh is glorified or allowed to cause compromise in the hearts of God's people.

A leader must remember the following principles in his ministry of sowing the seed of God's Word:

Disobedience to God's will in a leader's life will be as useless as sowing seed in the rain

(Leviticus 26:16; Micah 6:15).

Though a leader sows the seed with many tears, he can still have the confidence that God will cause him to reap the fruit of that seed in joy (Psalm 126:5).

If a leader looks upon the faces of his hearers or the external circumstances of the situation, and not to the Lord, he will probably not sow the seed (Ecclesiastes 11:4).

A leader who sows the seed to many people and nations will be blessed by the Lord (Isaiah 32:20).

A leader is advised not to sow the seed among the thorns (Jeremiah 4:3; Matthew 13:22).

A leader is to sow the seed for the purpose of producing a harvest of righteousness in people's lives (Hosea 10:12; Proverbs 11:18).

A leader must realize that some ministries in the Word furnish seed to the sowers (Isaiah 55:10; II Corinthians 9:10).

A leader must realize that the Church is God's cultivated portion of the field of the world (Matthew 13:38; John 4:35; I Corinthians 3:9).

A leader must realize that many times that sown seed seems to die before it brings forth fruit (I Corinthians 15:36,37).

A leader should guard against sowing trouble (Job 4:8), discord (Proverbs 6:14), strife (Prov. 16:28), or iniquity (Prov. 22:8).

A leader must remember that he will reap what he sows (Prov. 1:31; Galatians 6:7,7). If he sows sparingly, he will reap sparingly (II Corinthians 9:6).

A leader should note that both sowing and reaping ministries are equal before God, and should rejoice together before the Lord (I Corinthians 3:6-8; John 4:36,37).

A leader should produce in his ministry the fruit of holiness (Leviticus 19:23,24), tithing (Lev. 27:30), strength in old age (Psalm 92:14), good works (Psalm 104:13; Proverbs 31:31; Jeremiah 17:10; Colossians 1:10), the Holy Spirit (Galatians 5:22), goodness (Ephesians 5:9), one's lips speaking thanks to God (Hebrews 13:15), righteousness (Proverbs 12:12), good works (Prov. 12:15), good thoughts (Jeremiah 6:19), humility (Isaiah 10:12 in contrast), and spiritual growth in Jesus Christ (Jeremiah 12:2).

All of these principles will help a leader to more effectively sow the Word of God in the hearts of hungry and open people. If a leader sows, but the enemy scatters the fruit thereof (Job 31:8), he can know that God is judging his ministry for some reason. However, if a leader follows the foundational principles of sowing and reaping he should see a harvest of righteousness and faith from the seeds that he has sown.

CHAPTER 17
THE FUNCTION OF LEADERSHIP

Our study of leadership has reached the stage of "nuts and bolts." This chapter will explore the functions of leadership, the actual performance of ministry to God's people. We will look closely at the life of three anointed ministries: Elisha the prophet; Nehemiah, who lead in the rebuilding of Jerusalem's walls after the Babylonian captivity; and the apostle Paul, an example leader for the New Testament Church.

The Function of Leadership: Elisha the Prophet

After Elisha received the mantle of Elijah, his life and ministry demonstrated many principles of ministry function. In the left-hand column below, the chronological progress of Elisha's ministry is continued from the previous section on the preparation of Elisha. In the right-hand column, the principles behind the ministry of Elisha are applied to today's Christian leader.

In the first set of columns below, we will study Elisha's entry into ministry. Several important character traits that he relied upon during this stage of his ministry are important to today's Christian leader as well. God desires to bless the ministry of His servants abundantly. That requires of each leader a quality of character that gives God a vessel of honor to fill with His Spirit and His working. Indeed, the more God plans to bless a ministry, the more he or she must take great care to give him an appropriate vessel, by pursuing godly character qualities.

ELISHA'S MINISTRY

Inheriting the Mantle

After Elijah's translation to heaven, Elisha took up the prophet's mantle (II Kings 2:13).

After receiving Elijah's prophetic mantle, Elisha turned back and smote the Jordan River, then passed over it as Elijah did (II Kings 2:13,14).

APPLICATION FOR LEADERSHIP

Entering Ministry

Only as God Himself makes a way for a leader's ministry, at His proper time, will it produce fruit for the kingdom of God.

A leader must trust God to provide all of the necessary outward confirmations to his ministry.

This repetition of Elijah's miracle confirmed to others Elisha's succession into Elijah's office.

After Elisha's first miracle at the Jordan, the sons of the prophets openly recognized that the spirit of Elijah was upon him (II Kings 2:15), and even bowed to him (3:12,13).

"A man's gift makes room for him": a leader's ministry will be recognized and respected by other Christian leaders.

The sons of the prophets looked for Elijah in case the Spirit had cast him upon some mountain or valley. Elisha, however, discouraged them (II Kings 2:16) because he knew what God had done with Elijah.

A leader must never allow the pressure of fellow Christian leaders, even though they have great respect for him, to cause him to doubt the know-ledge or faithfulness of God.

Nevertheless, the sons of the prophets insisted on searching for Elijah, but did not find him, just as Elisha had said (II Kings 2:17,18).

A leader knows that people will sometimes insist on returning to old ways of doing things, not accepting counsel of the new leadership that God has raised up. In such cases, a new leader still gives his own spiritual judgment, and if it is of God, waits for it to come to pass as he declared.

Elisha next performed his second miracle of putting salt into the bitter waters and healing them (II Kings 2:19-22).

Only as God uses His leaders to place Christians (the salt of the earth) into strategic places in the world will the world be healed of its spiritual blindness and bitterness.

Elisha's behavior in the following set of events demonstrates a strong sense of honor. His assertive behavior may surprise some people. Is this the way a humble man of God behaves? The answer is yes, because Elisha's sense of dignity shows his strong respect for the hand and purposes of God upon his life. In the same way, today's Christian leader needs to have the character traits of a truly humble personality, that respects above all else God and His purposes.

A Prophet's Honor

Because the little children mocked him as a worth-less fellow, Elisha cursed them with a bear (II Kings 2:23,24). Even in India today, calling someone a "bald head" implies general worth-lessness, and not just baldness.

Functioning in the Office of Ministry

God demands respect for his ministries, and may judge those who curse His called leaders.

Jehoshaphat, king of Judah (c. 873-849 B.C.) was told about Elisha the prophet, who had "poured water on the hands of Elijah." Since eating utensils were not used in that day, a servant did the menial task of washing his master's hands with water (II Kings 3:1-11).

A leader must have a servant's heart, willing to do even menial tasks for his teachers and for others.

When Jehoshaphat inquired for a word from the Lord through Elisha, the prophet asked for a minstrel to come and play before him. The Spirit of God came upon him and he prophesied his third miracle, the filling of ditches with water, which was fulfilled (II Kings 4:1-7).

A leader will obtain a full release of the Spirit in his life and ministry only as he functions in praise and worship before the Lord.

Elisha followed the example of his master. He asked the indebted widow, "What shall I do for you?" just as Elijah had asked him before the master was translated (II Kings 4:1-7).

A leader must learn to observe the many good qualities of his master in order to emulate him.

Elisha aided the divine sovereignty of God in filling the widow's borrowed vessels of oil to her own pot of oil (II Kings 4:1-7).

A leader must teach his people how to combine God's resources with their own to reach a life of spiritual anointing and fruitfulness.

Elisha's respect for the purpose of God was balanced by his respect for the position and the needs of the people around him. This was reflected in his discrete behavior, which models several important character traits for today's Christian leader.

A Prophet's Discretion

Elisha received bread, a bed, a table, a chair and a lamp from a prominent Shunnamite woman (II Kings 4:8-11).

Elisha attempted to return the Shunammite woman's generosity. "What can I do for you?" he asked, and declared that she would have a son at the same time next season (II Kings 4:12-17).

Elisha spoke to the Shunammite woman indirectly, through his servant Gehazi, because it was not proper or customary at that time for a woman to visit a man in his private room (II Kings 4:12-14).

Elisha did not ask the Shunammite woman why she had not come to him during the traditional season for people to visit holy men in pilgrimage. (even her own husband asked, "Why will you go to him (Elisha) today? It is neither new moon nor Sabbath") II Kings 4:23-26).

Elisha did not insist on his servant Gehazi giving the customary long and elaborate greetings of the day to those he passed by as he was going to meet the woman's needs (II Kings 4:29).

As the Shunammite approached, Elisha admitted that the Lord had not yet revealed her need to him (II Kings 4:27,29,33-35).

Elisha acted in a traditional and normal way in his emergency request, by asking Gehazi to lay his staff on the face of the Shunammite's dead son before he received the more specific mind of the Lord through prayer (II Kings 4:29,31-35).

In Gilgal, Elisha put some meal in a pot of food that the sons of the prophets had contaminated with wild gourds from the field (II Kings 4:38-41).

Proper Ministry Behavior

A leader must humbly receive gifts and provisions of the Lord through others.

A leader must learn how to return thanks and gifts to others who have blessed him.

A leader must exercise proper discretion and etiquette at all times.

A leader must never become like a Pharisee who puts things before the needs of people.

A leader must learn that meeting the needs of people comes before custom or tradition.

A leader must be humble enough to admit when God does speak to him about something, and when He does not. A leader should never let self-confidence lead him into presuming the mind of the Lord. He must always pray to receive the specific mind of God for every situation, and wait for revelation.

In emergencies, a leader should do what God has taught him through past experience and wisdom. But he must never solely rely upon it. He must turn to God in fresh prayer as soon as possible. Relying on tradition, without the reception of the mind of the Spirit and without seeing positive results, will only lead to coninued death.

A leader must be able to use the Word of God to bring healing to the spiritual food he serves his younger ministries, when it might be contami-

As was the custom, Elisha's disciples sat before him, probably repeating his words, in a student-teacher relationship.

Elisha told a man from Baalshalisha ("lord of the third part") to distribute the food that he brought to Elisha to the people, and that they would have plenty left over (II Kings 4:42-44). 15:32-38).

nated by one of them through mixture of the worldly.

A leader must learn to use and give out what he presently has to meet the needs of the people, and then believe God by faith to multiply it to meet everyone's needs (see Matthew 14:16-21 and

As Elisha's ministry grew toward maturity, he became involved in works of service that affected the entire nation of Israel. This required great discernment in his own personality, and the ability to listen carefully to God for instructions regarding His will. In this, he modeled this character trait for all leaders who wish to become vessels fit for all of the Lord's uses.

A Prophet's Discernment

Elisha maintained his own spiritual dignity and respect, though Naaman, the captain of the Syrian army, came with a military fanfare to obtain a healing from him. The prophet maintained his own dignity by refusing to go out to meet Naaman, and instead sent his messenger to him (II Kings 5:9,10).

Elisha did not accept Naaman's gifts, though this Syrian captain declared that he believed in the God of Israel (II Kings 5:15,16,26).

Elisha judged Naaman's heart motives as being pure, instead of judging him only by outward appearances when the Syrian captain asked him for some of Israel's soil. Though Naaman had to continue to take his master to the pagan temple, he himself would not offer worship, but would offer sacrifices upon the bit of Israel's soil (II Kings 5:17-19).

Elisha told Naaman the leper to dip in the Jordan River seven times, and he would be healed. From Naaman's reaction to such a humbling request, we can assume the prophet was sensitively challenging his pride. Furthermore, Elisha did not use the same method here as he did for the healing of the Shunammite woman's son (II Kings 5:1-19).

Elisha showed great spiritual discernment and sensitivity to the motives of his servant Gehazi, who ran after Naaman to obtain gifts for his healing by the prophet. Gehazi was smitten with the

Functioning With Discernment

A leader must always maintain his dignity and respect as a servant of the most high God, even though politically or educationally prestigious people flaunt their positions before him, with motives of personal benefit.

A leader must never be tempted by a bribe. He must always discern the motive behind a gift. Is it for selfish purposes? Every leader should remember that no one is past "being blinded" through gifts. Every man of God must guard his heart from coveting material possessions, and must always put his spiritual purpose and ministry first.

A leader must not judge people only by externals. He must always discern the basic attitude and motives of an individual. Jesus condemned the Pharisees for judging by externals, and Paul exhorted Christians not to judge their brothers harshly on less important matters.

A leader must seek the specific mind of God for every situation, according to the specific attitudes of the person's heart. God has general principles, but He also deals with His people individually, according to their own particular problems, motives or needs.

A leader should ask the Lord for spiritual discernment into the inner motives and attitudes of all of his people. What appears on the outside is not always what is on the inside. Moreover, a leader leprosy of Naaman for his covetous spirit (II Kings 5:20-27) and slander of Elisha's reputation by giving Naaman the impression that the prophet had changed his mind about receiving Naaman's gift.

should never retaliate with a spirit of defensiveness when even one of his closest friends slanders his reputation in some way. Rather, he should allow God to vindicate him.

As Elisha progressed in ministry, he became a man who could trust God to do the miraculous in his life. He showed character traits of faithfulness--he was a man whom God could trust. Some of the most delightful miracles of his career of service to God happened in the section we are studying next. If the Christian leader wants to see God do miracles that build the kingdom of heaven, he must cultivate similar traits of faithfulness.

A Prophet's Miracles

Through the supernatural power of God, Elisha helped one of the sons of the prophets to find his submerged and borrowed axe head. After the axe head was found, however, he told the man, "Take it up for yourself." Here Elisha demonstrated a balance between divine sovereignty and human responsibility (II Kings 6:1-7).

By divine revelation, Elisha told the king of Israel, who was fighting against the king of Syria, just where the enemy would attack the next time (II Kings 6:8-13).

Elisha had spiritual insight to see the heavenly armies of God surrounding them as the enemy approached. He prayed for Gehazi that he, too, might see the victorious heavenly armies (II Kings 6:14-19).

Elisha led the blinded Syrians into Samaria, the capital of Israel. There he told the king not to kill them, even though they were his enemies. Historically, Israel's kings had a reputation for mercy with captives (despite a few exceptions). Elisha probably wanted them to continue to live up to that reputation (II Kings 6:20-23). As a consequence, the enemy did not invade Israel again.

Elisha was given a word of knowledge by the Lord about an assassin who was coming to kill him (II Kings 6:23-33).

Functioning in the Miraculous

A leader should always be willing to help someone who is training for the ministry. However, a true leader does not constantly do all the work himself. He eventually gives increasing responsibility to those whom he is training. He teaches young ministries how to find their lost or undeveloped ministry potential both through divine sovereignty and human responsibility.

A leader should trust the Lord for spiritual insight to recognize spiritual problems in people's lives before they erupt into major catastrophes.

A leader should have the spiritual insight to see that the heavenly power of Jesus Christ is greater than any obstacle or difficulty. A leader must also have the compassion to pray for others that they, too, might have a spiritual understanding of the Church's victorious position in God.

A leader must exemplify a spiritual balance between truth and mercy. He must realize that God's ultimate intention in disciplining someone is always to restore him to health. In showing mercy with his truth, a leader will find that the enemy may not invade again (v.23).

A leader can believe God for revelation of the Spirit about the kinds of attacks that the enemy would bring against him and his ministry, to be more prepared to overcome them.

Just as Elisha's honor was balanced by his discretion, his ability to move in the miraculous power of God was balanced by his concern for individual needs and concerns. If the man or woman of God cannot care for the needs of individuals, neither can he or she effectively lead many people. In his kindness, Elisha is a model of the character qualities that constitute true godly leadership.

A Prophet's Kindness

Elisha sent the Shunammite woman and her family into Philistia during the seven years of famine, that God had showed to the prophet were coming upon the land. Moreover, upon the woman's return to Israel after the famine, the king restored to her all that she had before she left (II Kings 8:1-6).

Elisha trusted God to bless the Shunammite woman when he found himself stopped from doing so. God did this by arranging it so that Gehazi related the good things of Elisha's ministry to the king at exactly the same time that the Shunammite requested the return of her land (II Kings 4:13 and 8:1-6).

Elisha wept over the terrible cruelty that Hazael of Syria would inflict on Israel. Though this future was given him by revelation, he was not so captivated by this process that he forgot about the sadness that would come upon Israel (II Kings 8:7-15).

Meeting Practical Needs

A leader must care about the practical aspects of people's lives, as well as the spiritual.

A leader must trust the Lord to bless those whom he is unable to bless. Many times a leader will feel "the weight of the world" on his shoulders. This is too much for any man to bear. Every leader must bless and help as many people as the Lord brings to him, but leave the rest to the sovereign Spirit of God and to other ministries.

A leader should guard himself from becoming so taken by God's movements in power that he forgets either the joys or the sorrows of the people involved in a certain situation. A leader should keep his eyes on the Lord and the people, not just on spiritual gifts and processes.

Nehemiah: A Leader in Action

In the year 530 B.C., after the seventy-year Babylonian captivity, Persia defeated Babylon. The king of Persia then ecouraged the Jews to leave Babylon and go back to Jerusalem to rebuild their temple. Ezra chapter 1-6 records their rebuilding of the temple, and chapters 7-10 record their restoration of worship sixty years later. The events in the book of Esther occurred between Ezra 1-6 and Ezra 7-10.

During the Jews' first return to Jerusalem in 537 B.C., Zerubbabel brought 50,000 Jews back to the holy city and laid the foundation of the temple (Ezra 3). Because the Jews became discouraged after building this foundation, God sent the prophets Haggai and Zecharia sixteen years later to encourage them to continue their work. Sixty years after Zerubbabel brought his group of Jews back to Jerusalem, Ezra the priestly scribe began to instruct the people in the law of the Lord. It was, moreover, another thirty years before Nehemiah came to Jerusalem to help reconstruct the walls of the city (Nehemiah 1-6) and reinstruct the people (chapters 7-13).

The book of Nehemiah, therefore, is called the book of the "Reconstruction of the House" and the "Reinstruction of the People." The book of Esther, similarly, is called the book of Restoration. Both of these books are prophetic of the day of restoration in which we are now living. God is restoring, rebuilding and reinstructing His people. Let us now note in the book of Nehemiah some of the spiritual principles associated with the building of the house of the Lord.

Ministry's Burden to Rebuild the Church

Ministry must have a burden to build up the broken walls of the Church. In Nehemiah 1:3,4, we see a specific order in which Nehemiah (who represents the ministry) responded to the broken walls and burned gates of the city because of the burden he had to reconstruct them.

First, Nehemiah wept over the problem (v.4). Sitting down can represent a good reaction of ministry to problems in the Church. Whenever a leader becomes aware of a problem in his local church, he should not throw together a new church program. He should avoid nervous reactions and sit down to pray, think and study God's Word. He should seek the Lord through the Word for answers to the problems.

Next, Nehemiah wept over the problem (v.4). The poor condition of Jerusalem and God's people so moved this man inwardly that he expressed his concern outwardly. Leaders need to feel the needs of the Body of Christ. They must pour out their souls before the Lord in an emotional and heart-felt way. Heart-felt prayers are the only kind that God listens to.

David was a "man after God's own heart" because he took his relationship with his heavenly Father as a serious covenant that involved his emotions. David cried, *"The zeal of thine house hath eaten me up . . . I wept and chastened my soul"* (Psalm 69:9,10). Sometimes God allows us to enter into a captivity or a bondage of some sort before we cry out to Him in tears and supplications. God lead Judah into the Babylonian exile for this purpose. *"By the rivers of Babylon, there we sat down, yea, we wept when we remembered Zion"* (Psalm 137:1) was Judah's response.

Jesus, too, wept before the Lord over the city of Jerusalem (Luke 19:41-44). In the same way, every Church leader must pour out his heart to God in weeping and tears. There is nothing unspiritual about crying. As a matter of fact, the Church would be farther along spiritually if more leaders would do it.

Following this weeping, Nehemiah mourned (v.4). The word for "mourn" here means to bewail, to cut, or to beat. It also means the mourner beating his breast or head in mourning and sorrow for the death of a loved one. Nehemiah's mourning can speak of the need of every leader to have a deeply repentant attitude over the house of the Lord. Leaders should mourn and bewail the weak condition of God's people today. They should be involved so strongly as to be one with the people in this; they should go through *"a time to mourn"* (Ecclesiastes 3:4) as if it were their own sin. The following scriptures illustrate the importance of mourning before the Lord.

"Give ear to my prayer . . . I mourn in my complaint and make a noise" (Psalm 55:1,2).

"The priests, the Lord's ministers, do mourn" (because of the poor condition of God's temple)(Joel 1:9).

"Blessed are they who mourn, for they shall be comforted" (Matthew 5:4).

"Be afflicted, and mourn, and weep, let your laughter be turned to mourning and your joy to heaviness" (James 4:9).

Every leader should be so able to identify with the people of God, that he mourns over their sins and spiritual poverty.

Next, Nehemiah fasted (v.4). He denied himself food to humble himself so that he might seek the Lord. In the same way, a ministry must also fast and seek God. The following scriptures show that fasting is a Bible principle to be obeyed:

David fasted and wept (II Samuel 12:16-17).

"Is this not the fast that I have chosen: to loose . . . to undo . . . to let go . . . to break every yoke?" (Isaiah 58:3-6).

"Sanctify ye a fast, call a solemn assembly" (Joel 1:14).

Jesus fasted forty days (Matthew 4:2).

"Moreover when ye fast, be not as the hypocrites" (Matthew 6:16-18).

The apostles fasted and prayed (Acts 13:2,3).

After Nehemiah fasted, and even during his fast, this leader prayed. A time of trouble in the local church is always a time to seek the Lord. During difficulties, leaders should not quickly blame themselves or others, but they should quickly pray. When walls are broken down or gates burned, it is time not to seek guidance from ourselves or even from others. It is time to seek guidance from the Lord.

True prayer is not dependent on its volume, length, posture or formality. It is simply an attitude of heart being expressed to God in faith. Every leader needs to learn how to pour out his deepest thoughts and feelings to the Lord, even as David did in the Psalms.

Prayer, too, must become a habit. Several scriptures tell how men of God sought the Lord early in the morning (Psalm 57:8 and 63:1 and 108:2 and Proverbs 8:17). A good habit for the ministry and the people: pray at least thirty minutes before each service. This gives an opportunity of spiritually cleansing their hearts before they enter into God's presence.

Finally, God can answer our prayers in one of four ways: "yes," or "no," or "wait," or "do it yourself." When leaders pray, they must be aware of these four possible answers from God. If Jesus, the Son of God, had to pray much, how much more do undershepherds need to do so!

Ministry Must Identify With the Problem at Hand

In Nehemiah 1:6-11, Nehemiah admits, *"We have sinned against thee, both I and my father's house have sinned."* Nehemiah identified himself with the problem, to the extent that he confessed his sin along with the peoples'. He did not say, "You people must repent for you have sinned." Leaders must not blame the people for all of the problems in the Church. They, too, must take a share of the responsibility and admit their sins and mistakes. If there is confusion in the Church, it is many times primarily the minister's fault. A leader's teaching without demonstration makes his ministry ineffective. All leaders must take their share of responsibility for the needs that still prevail in the house of the Lord.

The main reason for the Church's spiritual needs is a lack of biblical teaching and practice in those areas of need. Any need represents evidence of a lack of teaching and obedience in a given area. A leader can ask himself, "What area of Bible teaching have I been missing that would meet this need?" A leader should not expect his people to enter into certain areas of truth without first receiving proper scriptural teaching on that truth. Faith and obedience to enter into areas of truth spring out of first hearing the taught Word of God. Teaching precedes walking. Isaiah wrote, *"He will teach us his ways, and we will walk in his paths"* (Isaiah 2:3; Micah 4:2).

The teaching ministry is very important in a leader's life. The following list of scriptures shows the importance of teaching and walking in the Bible:

Teach them the good way wherein they should walk (Exodus 18:20).

"For Ezra had prepared his heart to seek the law of the Lord, and to do it, and to teach in Israel statutes and judgments" (Ezra 7:10).

Teach them the good way wherein they should walk (I Kings 8:36).

Heavenly rain comes when you teach them the way they should walk (II Chronicles 6:26,27).

"And Jesus came and spake unto them saying, 'All power is given unto me in heaven and in earth. Go ye therefore, and teach all nations, baptizing them in the name of the Father, and of the Son, and of the Holy Ghost: Teaching them to observe all things whatsoever I have commanded you: and lo, I am with you always, even unto the end of the world' " (Matthew 28:18-20).

Teaching is of utmost necessity in the ministry of every governmental minister of God. If a man of God is not especially gifted in the area of teaching, he should either learn how to teach, or bring in teachers who can instruct the people. Every leader must remember that people can obey a truth only after being taught that truth. It has been said, "If the student is not learning, the teacher is not teaching."

Some leaders fail to assume the responsibility to teach. They say, "If the saints would only get with it, then I would have a good church." A leader must realize that those in his congregation whom he calls "rebels" will most probably leave the church when good, specific teaching begins. The pastor should not worry about people who fit into this category. Instead, he should concern himself with the true, hungry sheep that desire the sincere milk and meat of the Word. Basically speaking, most of God's people are sincere and open to teaching when it is presented properly.

Ministry Must Initiate Problem-Solving

Nehemiah 2:11-16 shows how Nehemiah initiated his problem-solving:

"So I came to Jerusalem, and was there three days. And I arose in the night, I and some few men with me; neither told I any man what my God had put in my heart to do at Jerusalem: neither was there any beast with me, save the beast that I rode upon. And I went out by night by the gate of the valley, even before the dragon well, and to the dung port, and viewed the walls of Jerusalem, which were broken down, and the gates thereof were consumed with fire. Then I went on to the gate of the fountain, and to the king's pool: but there was no place for the beast that was under me to pass. Then went I up in the night by the brook, and viewed the wall, and turned back, and entered by the gate of the valley, and so returned. And the rulers knew not whither I went, or what I did; neither had I as yet told it to the Jews, nor to the priests, nor to the nobles, nor to the rulers, nor to the rest that did the work."

Here, Nehemiah took the initiative to study the problems in Jerusalem. Many leaders are too afraid to observe and face the problems in their own congregations. But Nehemiah sets a good example for all to follow.

Nehemiah did not tell all of the nation what he was going to do at Jerusalem. Similarly, neither should the shepherd tell the entire congregation all of his plans or all of the problems in the church. Instead, he should first take any plans and problems to the Lord, the elders and the deacons.

Every leader should ask the Lord, "What areas in our church need attention and repair? What are the waste places? Where are the broken-down walls?" These questions will sometimes be answered by the Lord in the most down-to-earth ways. For example, the Lord may ask a pastor, "Is your church building clean? Does it have an offensive odor?"

Examples of other questions a leader may use to evaluate the health of his church:

Do the young people enter into worship in the services? How many young people do we have?

Do our families have a lot of marriage problems? Do both the wives and husbands come to church?

Do all age levels of the church have sufficient times of fellowship together?

Are there musicians in the church?

Are there teachers for all age levels?

Do just as many people come out for the mid-week and Sunday evening services as come for Sunday morning?

Who are the counselors in our church? Are they adequately trained?

What kind of follow-up program do we have to help new converts?

Do the people receive variety in their spiritual diet from the pulpit?

How do we minister to the unmarried in our congregation?

Every leader should try to spot problems in early stages, before they grow or fester. A shepherd must continually watch over the sheep and search out areas which need help and healing.

Let us use three other illustrations to make this point. A leader must be like the quarryman who digs out the lively stones, squares them, and fits them into the House of the Lord. The leader must be like the farmer who harvests wheat, mills it, and bakes it into a nice loaf of bread. The leader is like the lumberman who cuts down trees, saws them into lumber, and nails them into God's building.

Although the quarryman's digging is dirty and dangerous, and his fitting challenging, he does them. It comes with the job. Although the farmer's harvesting takes proper timing and his milling a tender touch, and his baking some experience, he does them. Although the lumberman's cutting requires future planning about where to fell trees, a careful eye with a saw, and a firm hand for nailing boards, he nonetheless accomplishes the task because he sees the goal ahead of him.

In the same way, a leader must face the messy parts of his own job if he is ever to see the stones of God's temple, the wheat of God's bread or the lumber of God's house fit into place. Every leader must learn to face the church's problems head-on and seek a solution from the Lord.

Ministry Restores God's House in a Certain Order.

In Nehemiah 3, we have an illustration of the order of spiritual truths in the city of God, through the order of the restoration of the gates of Jerusalem. Let us see how this order can apply to the Church.

The Sheep Gate (v.1): Ministry to God's People. The first gate to be rebuilt in the time of Nehemiah was the sheep gate. The sheep gate speaks to us of the necessity of first ministering to God's people, His sheep, in the Church (Psalm 100:3). The sheep need feeding, not evangelizing. Merely preaching repentance, faith, salvation and deliverance to the sheep will not feed them. A shepherd, bishop and pastor must feed the sheep. If a leader cannot feed the sheep, he is missing a primary requirement of his ministry.

Another important requirement is compassion, which Jesus had for the people in His day who were like *"sheep without a shepherd"* (Matthew 9:36-38). Jesus felt pity for the needy people, and so must every leader.

Sheep feed best when they know the shepherd is near to feed them. This makes them secure enough (John 10:2,3) to lie down. The word "ruling" actually means feeding. It has been said, "Ruling is compassionate leadership first by example and then by careful instructions in Scripture." The New Testament exhorts every leader to feed the flock of God (I Timothy 5:17; I Peter 5:2; Acts 20:28).

Shepherding is giving to the needs of the sheep. The shepherd must not be concerned only for himself. God exhorts him to feed, not fleece. But if a pastor's first concern is for himself, it will manifest itself in one of two ways. It will show up in a love of money (pastoring only to obtain financial support), or in a lust for power (exercising influence over people's lives in a way he could not do in the secular world). To prevent such motivations from becoming a part of the ministry, no leader should ever be given the oversight of the flock of God through pressure, force or mere circumstances. God must be the one to place a man into the ministry of shepherding (I Corinthians 9:16,17; John 10:12,13).

Sheep need many things from the shepherd. They need protection from attacks by wild animals, and from unhealthy influences of wandering sheep. Like sheep, people must be protected from false ministries.

Sheep also need a personal touch from the shepherd. John 10:3,4 states, *"He calleth his own sheep by name."* The pastoral ministry is far more than just preaching or teaching the Word. A pastor can preach or teach with great zeal and unction, but unless he relates to the sheep, he will not have an effective shepherding ministry.

A shepherd should be a counselor. He must spend time with individuals as Jesus did. It is not abnormal for a sheep to expect his shepherd to help him grow spiritually.

Pastors have varying attitudes, however, toward immature sheep. The following list of questions allows the pastor and leader to check his own heart in this area:

Do I tell myself that these are just not the kind of sheep that can learn or grasp truth?

Do I blame, scold or beat the sheep for areas of immaturity that I have in my own life?

Do I realize that immaturity is a normal thing with babes in Christ?

Do I understand and accept that I must first preach for some results in the sheep before I get them, just as a seed reproduces after its own kind (Genesis 1:11)?

Do I have a firm trust that God will watch over His Word and bring it to pass (Mark 16:20)?

Do I believe that the sheep really do not want to be eaten by wolves?

Do I notice the many sick sheep who need to be nursed back to health?

The Fish Gate (v.3): Ministry to the Unsaved. The next gate to be restored was the fish gate. This gate was built after the sheep gate was constructed. The spiritual principle here is that it is only after the people of God are strong and mature that souls can be brought into the kingdom properly. Jesus told the disciples that they were going to be *"fishers of men"* (Matthew 4:19). To use the previous analogy of the sheep gate, we can see that god's sheep can bear healthy lambs only as they are healthy and well-tended. The shepherd does not bear lambs. He only tends and guides the lambs that the sheep naturally bear! Healthy sheep will always produce healthy lambs, just as a healthy family produces healthy children.

One of the five-fold ministries in Ephesians 4:11,12 is the evangelist. In verse 12 it says that all of these ministries are for the *"equipping of the saints for the work of their ministries."* The evangelist's ministry is not just to go forth and attempt to win the world for Christ on his own. The evangelist's ministry must include the function of training and equipping the saints so that they can go out and win the lost for Christ! The sheep gate must be restored before the fish gate. God's sheep must first become healthy before they can reproduce healthy lambs.

The Old Gate (v.6): Restoration of Foundational Doctrines. The next gate to be restored was the old gate. The old gate speaks to us of the foundational principles of the Chruch found in Hebrews 6:1-3 and Acts 2:41,42. These foundational principles are the old truths, as deposited by Jesus Christ and the apostles in the early Church, that never change from generation to generation. After souls (the fish gate) are brought into the kingdom, they must be established on a Christian foundation (the old gate). Proverbs 22:28 states, *"Remove not the ancient landmark which thy fathers have set"* (see also Proverbs 23:10). Similarly, the Church is not to remove the ancient truths that the fathers or founders of the Church have established.

New truths will never directly contradict these old truths. As a matter of fact, to retain her balance the Church must hold on to the former truths while receiving new truths. "New" truths are not new to the Bible, but "new" to the experience and understanding of the Church. In a seeming paradox, Matthew 13:52 states, *"Therefore every scribe which is instructed unto the kingdom of heaven is like unto a man that is an householder, which bringeth forth out of his treasure things new and old."* A scribe of the kingdom teaches both new and old truths from Scripture.

The Valley Gate (v.13): the Ministry of Compassion. The next gate to be restored was the valley gate. The valley gate can speak to us of the experience of meeting another's needs. The meaning of the name of Hanun, one of the men who helped to rebuild this gate, very significantly illustrates this. Hanun means, "to bend or stoop in kindness to another." It takes a ministry of kindness and compassion to build the valley gate. After people are firmly established in the first principles of the Christian life (the old gate), they should begin to reach out to others in need. Galatians 6:1 says, *"When a brother is taken in a fault, you who are spiritual restore such a one in the spirit of meekness."*

Restoring a fallen brother or ministering to a spiritual need must be done by someone who has experienced the grace of God in that area. A baby cannot help an older man to walk. Neither can an immature Christian help another child of God in an area in which he is still immature.

People go through different types of valleys. Some are spiritual, mental or emotional. Others are marital, domestic or financial. One of the valleys through which God takes all Christians is the valley of death (death to the old, fleshly man). But even there, God comforts and guides (Psalm 23:4).

Another valley is the valley of decision (Joel 3:14). Here people need to break away from double-mindedness, which only causes them frustration, insecurity and depression. They must decide with a whole heart fo follow the Lord Jesus Christ in every area of their lives.

No matter what kind of valley experience a person is undergoing, he can look in faith to the Lord and find his valley of troubles turning into a valley of springs and fountains (Deuteronomy 8:7 and 11:11; Isaiah 41:18; Psalm 104:10). Jesus said, *"But whosoever drinketh of the water that I shall give him shall never thirst, but the water that I shall give him shall be in him a well of water springing up into everlasting life"* (John 4:14).

The restoration of the valley gate is the restoration of those ministries of the Lord who will provide a way out for those who are in need. Finally, it is through such a ministry of valleys of need being filled, and mountains of pride being brought low, that the glory of Jesus will be seen by the world on the King's Highway (Isaiah 40:4,5)!

The Dung Gate (v.14): the Ministry of Cleansing. The next gate to be restored was the dung gate. The purpose of the dung gate was to provide the inhabitants of the city a means of disposing of their waste and garbage.

This gate can speak to us of the purging and refining ministry of the Holy Spirit (that is also presently happening in the Church today). The Holy Spirit is cleansing the Church today of sin and corruption. Though this sometimes leads to sad displays of sin, even among her leaders, the Church can welcome this necessary ministry. The Church must rebuild this gate and allow all of the cleansing ministries of the Holy Spirit (the preaching of the Word and the counseling ministry) to take full sway in her midst.

The Fountain Gate (v.15): the Ministry of Refreshing. The next gate that was restored was the fountain gate. This speaks to us of the ministry of the Holy Spirit in spiritual refreshing and restoration. After people come through the dung gate and throw out all of the garbage from their lives, they must come through the fountain gate where the Word and Spirit can change them. More specifically, when a person puts off one bad habit, he must put on a new and good spiritual habit to take its place in his life.

The following scriptures illustrate that God wants to cause the flow of His Spirit in the life of every believer:

"Out of your belly shall flow rivers of living water. This spoke he concerning the Spirit" (John 7:37-39).

"When the times of refreshing shall come from the presence of the Lord" (Acts 3:19-21).

"And he showed me a pure river of the water of life, clear as crystal proceeding out of the throne of God" (Revelation 22:1,2).

"And ye shall ask for rain in the time of the latter rain" (Zechariah 10:1).

"And he will come unto us like the rain" (Hosea 6:3).

Since now is the time of the Latter Rain, the Church should be asking for that rain and looking for the complete restoration of the fountain gate.

To obtain such a rain and restoration, however, we must not use human methods. We must follow divine principles and let the rain come down. The Lord said that Canaan would not receive rain like the land of Egypt, which was watered with human irrigation systems, representing human methods. The Lord promised that Canaan was going to drink in the rain from heaven.

God will pour out His Spirit on His people only under certain conditions, however. This depends on the amounts of prayer and praise that His people send up to Him. Job 36:27,28 illustrates this principle by telling us that the clouds drop down dew according to the amount of vapors that ascend into the sky. Just as natural vapors are formed by changes in temperature from one extreme to another, so should the Church offer praises to God even when she finds herself under the extreme pressures and temperatures of God's dealings. God puts the pressure on the Church to cause her to pray and praise. The rains of blessing descend as the vapors of praise ascend.

The Water Gate (v.26): Ministry of God's Word. The next gate that was restored was the water gate. This gate can speak to us of the restoration of the water of the Word. Ephesians 5:26 states that the Lord will cleanse the Church through *"the washing of water by the Word."* Numbers 8:7 refers to the *"water of purifying"* for the cleansing of the Old Testament Levitical priesthood. Ephesians 5:26 can be applied to the cleansing of the New Testament priesthood. As water cleanses in the natural realm, so God's Word cleanses in the spiritual realm.

After people came through the fountain gate of God's Spirit, they must experience the water gate of God's Word. The Word gives direction and parameters to the moving of the Spirit. The Word and the Spirit must always go together (like the water from the rock in Numbers 31:23 and 33:9; Deuteronomy 8:15; I Corinthians 10:4).

The Horse Gate (v.28): Lifting of the Burden of Flesh. The horse gate was next to be restored. The horse gate speaks to us of two related truths. First is the truth of the restoration of burden bearers to the House of the Lord. Horses bear heavy burdens, too heavy for men to carry. In the same way, God is rebuilding ministries who can listen, empathize and counsel those with weighty problems and needs in their lives.

Second, the horse gate speaks to us of the restoration of holines, and death to the self-life, that the Spirit is doing today. In Scripture, the horse often represented carnal life and willful strength of man (Exodus 15:1,21; Psalm 147:10; Jeremiah 51:21). As the Church walks through the horse gate, she must lay aside all of her self-life and be conformed to the image of Jesus. She must put off her own human strength and take up God's spiritual strength.

The East Gate (v.29): the Perfection of the Bride of Christ. The next gate to be considered here is the east gate. This can speak to us of the final restoration of the Church and the return of Jesus Christ to the earth for His perfected bride. Three wise men came from the east to worship the infant Christ (Matthew 2:1,2,9). So shall the Wise Man, Jesus, come from the east. Matthew 24:27 states, *"For as the lightning cometh out of the east, and shineth even unto the west; so shall also the coming of the son of man be"* (see also Revelation 7:2 and 16:12).

As the Church allows God to rebuild all of these gates, in their spiritual sense, to the Church, she can be assured that Jesus Christ will come back for *"a glorious Church without spot or wrinkle"* (Ephesians 5:27).

Establishment of Personal Responsibility in the Church

Once Nehemiah had established the proper order in rebuilding the broken walls of Jerusalem, he equipped his people for the project. The ministry must teach the people about their personal responsibilities in the Church. Just as Moses gave some of the mantle of his responsibility to those under him, so must every leader learn how to distribute responsibility to different church members. Nehemiah 4 gives us three areas in which every leader must equip his people: tools for work, weapons for war, an ear for the Spirit.

Tools for Work. Every leader must see to it that each of his members is equipped with a tool with which he can work. Nehemiah 4:17 states, *"They which builded on the wall, and they that bear burdens, with those that laded, every one with one of his hands wrought in the work."* Every one who built the wall or bore a burden had a certain tool with which he worked on the wall. Each had a different type of tool so that together they could accomplish their task. In the Church, the leaders are responsible for helping every member find his spiritual tool (gift or ministry).

The following list shows the three different aspects of the spiritual tools in the Church today.

Spiritual Offices: the apostle, prophet, evangelist, pastor and teacher are the five ruling offices that Jesus Himself gave to the Church to build it up (Ephesians 4:11,12).

Spiritual Gifts: the Holy Spirit distributes one or more of His nine gifts to different members of the Body so they can be used to build it up (I Corinthians 12:1-10).

Spiritual Ministries: God gives to various members of the body different realms of service used to build up the Body of Christ (Romans 12:6-8; I Corinthians 12:28-30).

Every leader must recognize, equip and release every one of his members in the spiritual offices, gifts or ministries which the Holy Spirit has laid upon them. With every citizen in the City of God building on the wall with a specific and sharp tool, the walls will be restored.

Weapons for War. Next, every leader must see to it that each of his members is equipped with spiritual weapons. Nehemiah 4:16-18 states,

"And it came to pass from that time forth, that the half of my servants wrought in the work, and the other half of them held both the spears, the shields and the bows, and the habergeons; and the rulers were behind all the house of Judah. They which builded on the wall, and they that bare burdens, with those that laded, every one with one of his hands wrought in the work, and with the other hand held a weapon. For the builders, every one had his sword girded by his side, and so builded."

Nehemiah's men carried a variety of different weapons: spears, shields, bows, habergeons and swords. It was not enough for the builders on the wall to have only a tool. Neither is it enough for every Christian in the Church to have only a spiritual gift or ministry. Every Christian must also know how to use spiritual weapons for either offensive or devensive spiritual fighting. Every leader is responsible to teach every member of his congregation how to war.

Christian warare is of a spiritual nature, not a carnal one. A Christian's weapons are spiritual. Paul states:

> *"For though we walk in the flesh, we do not war after the flesh: (For the weapons of our warfare are not carnal, but mighty through God to the pulling down of strong holds;) Casting down imaginations, and every high thing that exalteth itself against the knowledge of God, and bringing into captivity every thought to the obedience of Christ"* (II Corinthians 10:3-5).

In another epistle, Paul enumerates some of a Christian's weaponry and armament. He declares:

> *"Finally, my brethren, be strong in the Lord, and in the power of his might. Put on the whole armour of God, that ye may be able to stand against the wiles of the devil. For we wrestle not against flesh and blood, but against principalities, against powers, against the rulers of the darkness of this world, against spiritual wickedness in high places. Wherefore, take unto you the whole armour of God, that ye may be able to withstand in the evil day, and having done all, to stand. Stand, therefore, having your loins girt about with truth, and having on the breastplate of righteousness; And your feet shod with the preparation of the gospel of peace. Above all, taking the shield of faith, wherewith ye shall be able to quench all the fiery darts of the wicked. And take the helmet of salvation, and the sword of the Spirit, and watching thereunto with all perseverance and supplication for all saints"* (Ephesians 6:10-18)

These are the weapons a Christian must learn to use to fight the enemy: truth, righteousness, the gospel, faith, fellowship, salvation, the Word, and prayer.

A Christian must also learn how to use the weapon of praise. Isaiah 40:31 says, *"But they that wait upon the Lord shall renew their strength; they shall mount up with wings as eagles; they shall run and not be weary; and they shall walk, and not faint."* The Lord promises Christians in this verse that if they will wait ("give service" in the Hebrew) on Him, He will renew their strength. Every warrior needs strength to win the battle. But from where does strength come? In the tabernacle of David in the Old Testament, it was the service of priests to praise and worship the Lord. Just as their service of praising God gave them strength, so it does for every Christian today.

Throughout the Bible, praise is associated with strength and victory. The following list provides some of those instances:

PRAISE	STRENGTH
Man Doing The Possible	God Doing The Impossible
"Out of the mouths of babes and sucklings thou hast perfected praise" (Matthew 21:16)	*"Out of the mouths of babes and sucklings thou hast ordained strength to still the enemy"* (Psalm 8:2)
The name of Judah means "praise" in Hebrew.	*"Thy hand (Judah) shall be on the neck of thy enemies"* (Genesis 49:8).
The men of Judah gave a great shout (II Chronicles 13:15)	God smote Jeroboam (the enemy) (II Chronicles 13:15)
Israel began to sing and to praise the Lord (II Chronicles 20:20-22)	God set ambushments against the children of Ammon (II Chronicles 20:20-22).
Paul and Silas sang praises at midnight (Acts 16:25)	God sent an earthquake that opened the prison doors (Acts 16:26)
The children of Israel marched, shouted and blew the trumpets around Jericho (Joshua 6:12-17,20)	God caused the walls of Jericho to crumble (Joshua 6:20)

Ear for the Spirit. Finally, every leader must equip every member of his congregation with a spiritual ear to hear the voice of God's Spirit. Nehemiah spoke to his people with these words: *"In what place therefore ye hear the sound of the trumpet, resort ye thither unto us: our God shall fight for us"* (Nehemiah 4:20). Nehemiah exhorted Judah to gather to the place on the wall that had the most trouble defending itself against the enemy, whenever the trumpet sounded. Every man had to have an open ear, even though he might be fighting, to listen for the sound of the trumpet.

Likewise, all Christians need to have ears to hear what the Holy Spirit says to the Church. Christians can become so involved in defending the city that they lose their ability to hear the voice of God. The voice of God to natural Israel had been sounded through the different trumpets for many years (Numbers 10:1-10; Proverbs 20:12 and 25:12; Psalm 40:6; Leviticus 25:9). Each different trumpet sound meant something different to God's people. The New Testament also emphasizes the importance of the church having spiritual ears to hear God's voice. The following list of scriptures shows us this importance.

"Take heed, therefore, how ye hear" (Luke 8:18).

"My sheep know (hear, follow) *my voice and they will not follow the voice of a stranger"* (John 10:27).

"The things of God knoweth no man except the Spirit of God, for they are spiritually discerned" (I Corinthians 2:11-14).

"If the trumpet gives an uncertain sound who will prepare himself for the battle?" (I Corinthians 14:7,8).

"They will gather to themselves teachers, having itching ears, who will turn their ears away from the truth" (II Timothy 4:3).

"I was in the Spirit on the Lord's day, and I heard behind me a great voice, as the sound of a trumpet" (Revelation 1:10).

"He that hath ears to hear, let him hear what the Spirit saith unto the churches" (Revelation 2:7).

Every church leader is responsible to train his people to hear what the Holy Spirit is saying to the Church today.

With a tool, a weapon and an ear, every Christian will be able to do his part to make the City of God — the Church — what God intends it to be.

The Apostle Paul: A Pattern Leader For the New Testament Church

One of Paul's richest epistles concerning ministry and leadership principles is his second letter to the church at Corinth. Written approximately 58 or 60 A.D. on Paul's third missionary journey, this epistle was probably written from a city in Macedonia. Macedonia is a beautiful piece of land on the plains of the gulf of Thessalonia, which was famous for wood and precious metal products.

Paul's attitude in writing this letter could be expressed with the words that it was "written with a pen dipped in tears." II Corinthians is an impassioned self-defense of a wounded spirit to some of his own spiritual children who were erring and ungrateful. Consequently, this letter is the most personal and emotional of all of Paul's writings. One can see some of the deep emotions in Paul, expressed through key words in this letter: gift, sorrow, glory, gospel, ministry, suffering, affliction, flesh, and comfort.

Unique to this epistle are the following historical facts about Paul: his escape from Damascus in a basket (11:32,33); his being caught up into the third heaven (12:1-4); his thorn in the flesh (12:7); and some of his different sufferings (11:23-27).

In looking at both I and II Corinthians we can see a unique contrast between them. The following shows the various contrasts between these two letters of Paul:

First Corinthians	Second Corinthians
Very objective in content and character	Very subjective in content and character
Very practical in approach	Very personal in its approach
Gives insights into the character and ministry of an early church	Gives new insights into the character and ministry of an apostle--Paul
Gives deliberate church instruction	Gives a more personal life and experience instruction
Deals with the problems of a local church	Deals with the problems of an individual ministry
Disciplines as a father	Disciplines as an apostle
Demonstrates church principles	Demonstrates ministry principles

This second epistle also deals with certain problems to which Paul makes special reference. These specific problems are the following:

Accusations Against Ministry (1:13-17 and 10:9-11)
Restoration After Discipline (2:6-11)
Ungratefulness (4:8-13 and 6:1-10 and 11:7-9)
Being Unequally Yoked (6:13-18)
Impurity (7:1-10 and 11:1-3)
Insincerity (8:1-10)
Comparing With One Another (10:12,13)
Deception (11:1-4)
Disguised Ministries (11:13-16)
Glorying After the Flesh (11:18)
Debates, Envying and Wrath (12:20)
Strifes and Backbitings (12:20)
Unrepentance (12:21)
Reprobates (13:5)
Receiving Apostolic Correction (13:6-12)

Each of these fifteen problems is a study in itself. Our goal here, however, is to view a thread of truth that runs through all of them: the Corinthians' rejection of Paul as an apostle of Jesus Christ and pattern leader (one copied by others). It is very obvious throughout his letter that Paul is defending his apostolic ministry and authority against false accusations and false ministries (1:6,12,17,23; and 2:4,17 and 3:6,12 and 4:1,3,5,8 and 5:14,21).

The Corinthians expressed their mistrust of Paul as an apostle and a pattern leader in various ways. They accused him of lightness and indecision, of purposing at one time to visit them and then of having changed his mind (1:10-19). They charged him with pride and domination (1:24). They also suggested that he was deceitfully cunning in his conduct (12:16) and, therefore, denied his apostolic authority (12:11-12). Finally, some of Paul's own spiritual children said that his outward appearance was base and his speech very contemptible (10:1-10).

To say the least, this church made Paul very sad in his spirit. Though the signs of an apostle were wrought among the Corinthian Christians, they did not accept Paul's apostolic authority as a pattern leader for all leaders in the Body of Christ to follow. Paul, however, was ordained by God Himself to be an apostle of the Lord Jesus Christ (Romans 1:1; I Corinthians 1:1; II Corinthians 1:1; Galatians 1:1,11-024; Ephesians 1:1; Colossians 1:1). It is understandable that Satan would desire to challenge any such fact, in an attempt to protect his various realms of spiritual darkness. The following verses demonstrate that Paul was and is a pattern leader to be followed:

"But thanks be to God that though you were slaves of sin, you became obedient from the heart to that form (pattern) *of teaching to which you were committed* (by me)" (Romans 6:17).

"I (Paul) *exhort you to be imitators* (patterns) *of me"* (I Cor. 4:16).

"Be imitators (patterns) *of me, just as I also am of Christ"* (II Cor. 11:1).

"I (Paul) *urged Titus to go, and sent the brother with him. Titus did not take any advantage of you, did he? Did we not conduct ourselves in the same spirit and in the same steps* (pattern)?" (II Cor. 12:18).

"Brethren, join in following my (Paul's) *example* (pattern), and observe those who walk according to the pattern that you have in us" (Philippians 3:17).

"You also became imitators (patterns) of us and of the Lord (I Thessalonians 1:6).

"So that you became an example (pattern) to all the believers in Macedonia and Achaia" (II Cor. 1:7).

"For you yourselves know how you ought to follow our example (pattern), *because we did not act in an undisciplined way among you"* (II Thessalonians 3:7).

"Not because we do not have the right to do this, but in order to offer ourselves as a model (pattern) *for you, that you might follow our example* (pattern) (II Cor. 3:9).

These scriptures clearly indicate to us that Paul is a pattern leader for all Christians, and especially for all leaders, to imitate and to follow. Every leader should spiritually blend the principles of leadership from the lives of all of the leaders in the Bible, particularly Jesus Christ and Paul, in their preparations for positions of responsibility in God's kingdom.

Leadership Principles of Paul

The final part of this section lists the many different principles of leadership from II Corinthians. Every leader can use this list also to discern how he measures up to Paul, the pattern leader. We encourage every leader to expand each one of these points for his own understanding and ministry. By the guidance of these leadership principles, leaders should:

1. Serve in the place to which God has called them (II Cor. 1:1; Galatians 1:1; Acts 13:2).
2. Comfort those in trouble with the same comfort they have received from the Lord (II Cor. 1:4-6).
3. Be dependent upon prayer (1:11).
4. Be people of integrity in their dealings with the world and in their dealings with the Church (1:12; Acts 6:3; I Timothy 3:7).
5. Have the interest of others at heart (1:13-23 and 7:12).
6. Be anointed by the Spirit (1:21,22).
7. Not be interested in having dominion over other believers (1:24; Luke 22:24-27).

8. Work the principle of forgiveness, so Satan cannot acquire a foothold among the people of the Lord (2:10,11).
9. Be triumphant in Christ (2:14).
10. Be a sweet savour (good fragrance) unto the Lord (2:15).
11. Find their sufficiency in God (3:5).
12. Remember that they are made into able ministers by the Lord Himself (3:6).
13. Use plain (open, bold, confident, outspoken, free, blunt) speech.
14. Be personally experiencing change from glory to glory (3:18).
15. Show forth the glory of the Lord (4:1,2) by doing these things:
    Renounce hidden and shameful things;
    Not walk in craftiness;
    Not adulterate the Word of God;
    Manifest forth the truth in their lives;
    Commend themselves to every man's conscience in the sight of God.
16. Minister the Word by the power of God and not by the strength of man (4:7; I Cor. 2:1-5).
17. Realize that the glory is in earthen (human) vessels (4:7).
18. Encounter affliction, but not be crushed by it (4:8).
19. Be in perplexity, but despair not (4:8).
20. Encounter persecution, but never feel forsaken (4:8).
21. Be cast down with discouragement, but not destroyed by it (4:9; II Timothy 2:3,4; Psalm 116:10).
22. Be determined to fulfill their charge before the Lord (4:1,10).
23. Cause men to relate to Christ and not to themselves (4:5).
24. Have a vision for the things of the Lord (5:7-9).
25. Have a motivation acceptable to the Lord (5:9).
26. Remember that they will be judged for their actions both now and in the future judgment (5:10).
27. Conduct their lives so the people of the Lord can be encouraged (5:11-13).
28. Be motivated by the love of God to lay down their lives for the sheep (5:14).
29. See the people of God as the Lord sees them (5:16,17).
30. Have a ministry of reconciliation (5:18).
31. Be representatives for the Lord in an obvious way (5:20).
32. Give no offense in any way, so that the ministry will not be corrupted or blamed (6:1-3).
33. Prove their ministries (6:4,5) by exhibiting patience in the midst of great trials:
    afflictions
    necessities
    distresses
    stripes
    imprisonments
    tumults
    labors
    watchings
    fastings
34. Prove their ministries (6:6-8) with the qualities or presence of:
    pureness
    knowledge
    long-suffering
    kindness
    the Holy Ghost

    love unfeigned
    the word of truth
    the power of God
    the armor of righteousness
    honor above dishonor
    evil report overcome by good report

35. Prove their ministries (6:8-10) by enduring as:
    deceivers yet true
    unknown yet well known
    dying yet living
    chastened yet not killed
    sorrowful yet always rejoicing
    poor yet making many rich
    having nothing yet possessing all things

36. Speak openly to those they minister to and enlarge their hearts unto them (6:11).

37. Cleanse themselves in flesh and in spirit in the fear of God to perfect holiness (II CJor. 7:1).

38. Be honest and truthful so that accusers will have nothing to say (7:2).

39. Do not condemn, but edify the people of the Lord, through the channels of relationship and love (7:3).

40. Give themselves to and for the people (7:3).

41. Experience what the people experience (7:3).

42. Be open to the people of God (7:2-4).

43. Be free to share experiences back and forth with the people of God (7:2-4).

44. Support (comfort) the people of God, and receive the same in return (7:5-7).

45. Esteem themselves as lowly persons (7:6).

46. Be comforted with the fruit of their labor, which is the positive response of the people to their instructions and reproof (7:5-7).

47. Chasten the flock as a father, bringing them to godly sorrow, and not worldly sorrow; correction in love brings life, but correction in any other manner brings death (7:8-13).

48. Work godly sorrow into the people by loving rebukes (Cor. 7:11), which brings:
    carefulness in the sheep's walk
    clearing of self (repentance unto good works)
    indignation towards evil
    the fear of God
    vehement desire for God
    zeal for God
    revenge against sin
    comfort to the leaders

49. Reveal their care and concern for the flock, even if they have to show it to them by rebuke (7:12).

50. Exhort the sheep to do good works even when they notice them already doing good works (7:13).

51. Remember that when they reveal truth to the Body, the Body wil reveal that truth to others (7:14).

52. Be open to comforting by the people as well as by God (7:6,13).

53. Have confidence in the sheep, as well as confidence in themselves, but trusting mainly in God (7:16).

54. Have perseverance in trials with joy (8:2).

55. Be willing to sacrifice (8:4).

56. Be willing to "let go and let God" (8:6).

57. Exhort in love and diligence (8:7).

58. Be willing to serve, and be able to put that into the action of brotherly love (8:9).

59. Include mutual helpfulness (8:14).
60. Be able to give wise counsel (8:14).
61. Look to God as the source of their supply, though God may use many different instruments to meet needs (8:15).
62. Be thankful (8:16).
63. Be zealous for the Lord (8:17).
64. Have integrity and blamelessness (8:20).
65. Be honest in the sight of God and man (8:21).
66. Be good messengers (8:23).
67. Realize that they are not alone, but also have fathers in the faith (8:23).
68. Challenge the people to demonstrate their faith and ministry (8:24).
69. Have hearts that are birthed in love (8:24).
70. Often use repetition in teaching the people of the Lord (9:1).
71. Encourage a positive focus in the people of the Lord (9:2).
72. Sometimes remind people of their own words (9:3,4).
73. Collect money regularly before it is coveted by the givers (9:5).
74. Receive from the Lord (9:6-11).
75. Remind the people that giving blesses both the receiver and the giver (9:13).
76. Teach the people that giving is comparable to praising God in spiritual sacrifices (9:12).
77. Boast of the good in their people so that the people will try and live up to it (9:13,14).
78. Move in the boldness of the Spirit and not in the boldness of the flesh (which manifests itself in elevating the leader above the people)(10:2,3).
79. Look on the inward root of rebellion and disobedience and not focus on outward appearances (10:5-7).
80. Exercise authority for the edification of the flock, and not for its destruction (10:8).
81. Live what they speak, and not compare themselves with others (10:12).
82. Operate with what the Lord has given them, and not try to impress the people with religious jargon (10:13,14).
83. Bring those who are under them to perfection, as they themselves grow in the Lord (10:15,16).
84. Boast only in what the Lord has given them, and not boast in the knowledge of their own hearts (10:17,18).
85. Always protect those under their charge, and not flee from trouble, as the hireling does (11:1-3).
86. Always demonstrate a servant spirit and not be a burden to those to whom they minister (11:5-9).
87. Provide their own needs when necessary, and not expect the people always to do so (11:7-9).
88. Warn the flock against false ministries, and be alert to the ways of the adversary (11:12-15).
89. Always be motivated by the love of the Lord (11:11).
90. Boast only in their infirmities and in their weaknesses and not make themselves greater than other ministries (11:21-22,30-33 and 12:5).
91. Suffer hardships in life along with persecutions often times more than other people (11:23-29).
92. Always bear the responsibilities of their position, and not delegate them just to get out of a job (11:28-29).
93. Keep a clear conscience before the Lord (11:31).
94. Remain humble in time of great revelation (12:1-4).
95. Understand God's purposes in His dealings in their lives ((12:5-7).
96. Remember that they are given grace in their weaknesses (12:8,9).
97. Be content in their weaknesses (12:10).
98. Recognize God's strength in their weaknesses (12:9).

99. See their limitations, yet see themselves as God sees them (12:11).
100. Not think too highly of themselves, or have false humility (12:11).
101. Learn to admit when they are wrong (12:13).
102. Live a life of sacrifice for the sheep (12:14).
103. Give without expecting return (12:15).
104. Walk uprightly before the Lord and His people (12:18).
105. Not feel defensive concerning the call of God upon their lives (12:19).
106. Be able to mourn over the sins of the people (12:21).
107. Have the confirmation of two or three witnesses in the things that they say (13:1).
108. Exercise spiritual authority and maintain church discipline (13:2).
109. Have in them the power of God (13:4).
110. Examine themselves in the sight of the Lord (13:5).
111. Know their position in the Lord (13:6).
112. Shun evil (13:7).
113. Not be selfish, but have a pure love for the Body of Christ (13:9).
114. Build up the Body which will produce love, comfort, peace and unity (13:11).

CHAPTER 18
TEAM MINISTRY

We have nearly reached the end of our leadership study. If you are (or want to be) a young ministry asking God for release into service, this chapter was written for you. It is also for the older ministry who wants to move into team ministry.

Team Ministry as a Biblical Pattern

Many leaders in the Church today do not appreciate the truth and importance of team ministry. In team ministry, two or more leaders work together to accomplish a single spiritual task. It is a group of men or women of God who are knit together in spirit and purpose for God's kingdom.

Unfortunately, many leaders have never cooperated with others in a team effort. For many years, the Church has been dominated by "one-man-bands," that is, one person carrying all the responsibility and doing all of the work himself. God never intended for one man to carry all of the pressure or responsibility for a local church or major ministry. Many men have collapsed physically, mentally, morally or emotionally under such a load. For this practical reason, as well as moral, doctrinal and spiritual reasons, God has ordained ministry to work in teams.

Team ministry is a scriptural pattern. The list below provides some examples of team ministry in the New Testament:

Jesus and His apostles (the Gospels).
Peter and John (Acts).
Philip and then Peter and John (Acts 8).
Peter and certain brethren (Acts 10).
Paul and Barnabas (Acts 13,14).
  (Acts 13:13 refers to Paul and his company.)
Judas and Silas join Paul and Barnabas (Acts 15).
Barnabas and John Mark travel together and Silas goes with Paul (Acts 15).
Timothy joins Paul and Silas (Acts 16).
Paul takes Priscilla and Aquila with him (Acts 18).
Timothy and Erastus are sent to Macedonia (Acts 19).

Going into Asia, Paul was accompanied by Sopater, Aristarchus, Secundus, Gaius, Timothy, Tychicus and Trophimus (Acts 20).

The Purpose and Advantage of Team Ministry

Team ministry provides a living demonstration of the principle of body ministry (I Corinthians 12).

In teaching present day truth, more than one voice speaking the same thing makes a better impact (Deuteronomy 17:6; Matthew 18:16; II Corinthians 13:1).

A team can more effectively find the mind of the Lord for a meeting or series of meetings and pray towards the fulfillment of God's will (Matthew 18:19).

Team ministry will be much more effective and will produce greater results (Ecclesiastes 4:9-12).

Team ministry provides a greater possibility for safety and balance in ministry (Proverbs 11:14).

Team ministry helps guard against the immoral traps set by the enemy, which have snared so many individual ministries.

Team ministry provides strength and encouragement for the ministries themselves (Exodus 17:12). Ministering with others provides a sense of inspiration and spiritual growth. The great fellowship involved provides great strength.

When less experienced ministries can accompany more mature ones, the process of discipleship and training is strengthened.

The Principles and Practice of Team Ministry

The very first key to the success of team ministry is being teamed up with the Lord (Mark 16:20). If the Lord is not in an endeavor, it will certainly fail, or at least, will dissipate with only a small measure of success. Before all else, then, each member must earnestly seek the mind of the Lord, and all must be convinced that the venture is His will. This should also include the vision or goal for the ministry. Only then is it appropriate to form a team.

The second key to the success of team ministry is commitment. The measure of success will correspond with the measure of commitment from each individual member. The team should give itself without reservation to fulfilling God's purpose for it, without allowing anything to hinder or distract. Also, each member must commit himself to the others, for that will be the foundation of his growing love for them.

Another key to success is both the individual and corporate devotional life of the team members. Ministry to the Lord will gauge the ministry to the people. A consistent, earnest and lively prayer life is of vital importance to team ministry. "The team that prays together will minister together."

The principle of leadership must be recognized in team ministry. Though no member is more important than another, for the sake of order and efficiency, one must take the leadership and have the final responsibility. To fail to recognize and apply this principle is to head toward disaster.

Closely connected to the previous principle is a tremendous key to the actual functioning of a team: the principle of submission (Ephesians 5:21). Time after time, true submission is required of a team member, and unless he has a submissive spirit, he will find it very difficult to function in the team. Just one member deciding to go his own way without regard for the other members can greatly disrupt a team effort and spirit.

Success in the development of strong personal relationships is vital to team ministry. Unity is a must. Many team efforts have been squelched by breakdowns in this area. The principles of communication are of great benefit in this realm, and one should alertly guard against jealousies, rivalries, bitterness, a critical spirit and complaining.

Each member must constantly remind himself that he is a team member by the will of God, and as such, he must surrender his own personal rights and do all that he can to support and help the other ministries in the team.

Scripture supports the fact that God wants all Christian leaders to be involved in some form of team ministry in their work. What form of team ministry can each leader say that he is a part of now? With the restoration of team ministry to the local church and major ministries, the Church can function more safely and effectively in meeting the needs of God's people.

Moving an Existing Ministry into Team Ministry

In the case of young ministries, the faith venture of team ministry may well involve the beginning of a new ministry. Sometimes, however, a leader may be functioning in an established ministry, and desire to move into team ministry. At this point, he will go through the process of choosing co-laborers. This is an important transition, and must happen in a measured, orderly fashion to avoid confusion and enemy attacks against the ministry.

The following questions can help the leader evaluate his potential co-laborers, their contributions, and the nature of the team working relationships. These questions are an initial resource for a process that will take much time and prayer. The leader must develop a detailed understanding of his ministry team before actively moving into this form of ministry.

How Should A Shepherd Choose His Co-laborers?

By the character and not just the ability of the person.

After much prayer and seeking God.

After examining others' feelings about the individual(s).

By their dedication to Jesus Christ.

By their specific ministry and calling.

By their love for lost souls.

By their love for God's people.

By their willingness to serve when unnoticed.

By their unity in spirit.

How Should A Shepherd Not Choose Co-laborers?

On their ability and not character.

When under pressure to fill a position in the church.

When he must compromise his own standards or the standards of the Word of God.

Because the co-laborer will give a lot of money to the church.

Because they have the most academic education.

Because they are young, with much talent and energy.

Because they threaten to leave the church if you do not use them immediately.

Because they have a competitive nature in other areas.

How Should A Shepherd Train His Co-laborers?

By giving them direction, not confusion.

By giving them encouragement, not condemnation.

By giving them service, not servitude.

By giving them inspiration, not negation.

By giving them discipline, not disconcern.

By giving them channel, not control.

By giving them release, not bondage.

By giving them hope not despair.

How Should A Shepherd Work With His Co-laborers?

By recognizing his own ministry strengths.

By recognizing his own ministry limitations and weaknesses.

By recognizing other team members' strengths.

By maintaining a servant's heart and spirit.

By having interpersonal involvement with one another.

By maintaining a family spirit in the team.

By cultivating loyalty and trust in the team.

By maintaining and encouraging a forgiving spirit.

By cultivating an honest and open attitude with the team.

By maintaining a teachable spirit.

By maintaining good communications.

CHAPTER 19
THE ANOINTING OF THE HOLY SPIRIT

A leader's success in ministry depends heavily on the Holy Spirit's anointing on his life. Without God's anointing on a leader's ministry, it will not produce any lasting fruit for the kingdom of God. Without the spiritual quickening which only God can provide, a leader's ministry will be dead and lifeless. The external, professional look of a leader is not a primary issue, but the Spirit's ability to use his life to bring change into the lives and characters of others is a primary issue. As Paul said, *"For the kingdom of God does not consist in words, but in power"* (I Corinthians 4:20; see also 2:4,5).

The Church today desperately needs to operate under the anointing of the Holy Spirit. This need is heightened by the Church's tendency to go the other way--to rely on operating practices of the professions. The Church obviously needs something divine to create its success. A spiritual lethargy that has come upon churches today demonstrates this need. Because the kingdom of God is a spiritual kingdom, it must operate under spiritual principles and spiritual power.

Improper Sources of Anointing

Unfortunately, Church leaders today that are trained in secular institutions or highly academic seminaries know virtually nothing about God's supernatural anointing power. Yet some seminary graduates are made to feel that they have learned most of the "how-to's" of local church success. They graduate with confidence, having studied such areas as: How to Prepare a Sermon, How to Preach, How to Baptize, How to Serve Communion, How to Hold a Church Service, How to Hold a Revival Meeting, How to Make the Church Grow. Obviously, these are all important to Church ministry, but they must have the life of the Spirit.

When graduates enter their ministries, some encounter much trouble in making these "how-to's" work. Little professional pastor's kits are essentially the average equipment of many beginning leaders today. When the kits don't work, these leaders experience extreme frustration.

One problem immediately appears. Many of the principles learned in secular colleges and some seminaries are not based on the Word of God. I thank God for those seminaries that are deeply committed to the Word of God, and instill firm biblical convictions into their graduates.

Unfortunately, some seminaries don't provide this, instead offering dry academics (often filled with humanistic content and "higher critical" studies) that quench the Spirit. How can four to eight years of dwelling in this kind of environment fail to affect a man or woman's spiritual life? Too many seminaries use the Bible as a secondary reference. To answer the Church's needs, they look primarily to psychology, philosophy, sociology, anthropology, social psychology, secular history, business management, etc. All of these subjects have a wealth of practical tips and observations on life. But when they become the focus of a leader's study life, they can dry up his anointing in the Spirit.

Why? Because God will not let any flesh glory in His presence (I Corinthians 1,2). The holy anointing oil cannot rest upon the things of the flesh. It can only rest upon that which has experienced the death and cleansing of the blood of Jesus Christ. When a leader insists on ministering intellectually from his mind, rather than from his spirit under the hand of God, he will produce Christians with full heads and empty hands--much knowledge, but no power. As in every past spiritual visitation of the Holy Spirit, God is again emphasizing the things He uses to build His kingdom: prayer, the Word, holiness, fasting, obedience and a dependence upon the anointing of His Spirit.

What the Anointing Is Not

Before we move into defining the anointing of the Spirit, let us define what it is not. The anointing of God is not:

Mere natural ability or talent

Professionalism

External show

Mere fancy oratory

Famous preaching styles mimicked

Formal homiletics courses

Ecclesiastical position or authority

Recognition by an organization

Good speaking techniques

The direct result of a good education

External religious forms

Nice-sounding, aesthetic music

Mere emotionalism

Following a simple "how to . . ." list

A quiet religious meeting

None of the above can ensure God's anointed presence on a life, a leader or a church service. The anointing is born from a humble and broken heart before God.

Anointing Defined

To make a general, conceptual definition of God's anointing on a ministry, we must first view the basic Hebrew and Greek words the Bible translates as "anointing" or "anoint."

Hebrew Words:

"Balal": a primary root, meaning to overflow (especially with oil, and by implication, meaning to mix.

"Dashen": a primary root, meaning to be fat or, transitively, to fatten or regard as fat. It means, especially, to anoint, or figuratively, to satisfy.

"Yitshar": a noun for oil, as used to produce light or figuratively to anoint.

"Mimshach": comes from a primary root which means to rub with oil, in the sense of expansion and outspreading (by extension, do this with outstretched wings).

"Mashach": a primary root, meaning to rub with oil, to anoint. By implication, it means to consecrate. Also, to paint.

"Mashiyach": usually refers to a consecrated person (king, priest or saint) and especially to the Messiah.

"Cuwk": a primary root, meaning to smear over with oil, to anoint.

"Shemen": a form of grease, especially liquid (as from the olive) which is often perfumed. Figuratively, this word means richness.

New Testament Greek Words:

"Aleipho": to oil (usually with perfume).

"Egchrio": to rub in (oil), to besmear.

"Epichrio": to smear over or upon.

"Murizo": to apply (perfumed) unguent to something.

"Chrio": to smear or rub with oil; by implication, to consecrate to an office or religious service.

Related English Words:

Anoint: to rub over with oil or an oily substance: to apply oil to something as part of a sacred rite, especially for purposes of conserving.

Anointed: a person who is consecrated to God.

Ointment: a salve or unguent applied to the skin, often mixed with some form of medication, for healing or beautification purposes.

Quickening: to make alive, to come to life, to revive spiritually, to cause to be spiritually stimulated or kindled, to cause to burn more intensely, to hasten or accelerate, to enter into a stage of active growth and development, to shine more brightly.

Consecrated: dedicated to God for His purposes; made holy in character and, thus, fit for spiritual use and a setting apart for God's service.

General Definition of Anointing. Let us now combine the meanings of these Hebrew, Greek and English words into one general and conceptual definition of anointing. This will provide some spiritual understanding of the anointing of God's Spirit:

The anointing of God's Spirit is the overflowing of the Messiah's divine life of holiness into a human life which has been consecrated to God through personal cross of Christ experiences which make it spiritually rich and thus able to impart effectively the light and fragrance of God's Word into the lives of others, producing in them deep spiritual satisfaction and obvious Christian fruitfulness.

For personal studies, the reader can expound more fully on each of these phrases in relation to the subject of the anointing.

Illustrations of the Anointing. To make this compact definition more practical at this point, however, we offer the following items as both further definitions and illustrations of God's anointing in the life of a teacher. The anointing of the Spirit is in evidence:

When God goes beyond the natural abilities of a leader and gives him supernatural ability to preach, teach or counsel.

When a leader preaches an entire message spontaneously, as quickened by the Spirit, totally discarding his planned message, and the congregation is moved spiritually in a special way. (If you have ever seen this attempted without the moving of the Holy Spirit, however, you can remember that it was obviously non-productive!)

When the conscious sense of God's abiding and moving presence appears.

When a leader's message brings spiritual results in the lives of his hearers, even though it might not follow the rules of grammar, homiletics, organization or professional presentation. (This does not negate the need for these speaking skills, however. They are greatly needed!)

When a leader senses God very near to him after he is broken or repents of some sin, and then he ministers to his people in the same spirit.

The power of the Spirit in the ministry of a leader when God heals the sick, delivers sinners, and shows His power through His yielded vessel.

When some Christian song or music has the touch of God's presence and power upon it, even though all the singers or musicians are not professional.

When a singer or a musician sings or plays a song spontaneously unto the Lord, which spiritually edifies the congregation.

When a leader is lifted up in spirit and ministers the Word of God by prophetic illumination and speaks directly to the needs of the people present.

When a spirit of prayer and intercession comes upon a congregation and all pray, in turn, spontaneously as God puts particular burdens on different individuals' hearts.

When God through the Lord Jesus Christ gives spiritual authority to demonstrate the character and/or gift of a leader.

When the practical ministry of true healing, which happens through love, understanding and prayer, helps one whose heart is broken or wounded.

When a person's whole being (spirit, mind, will, emotions and body) responds positively to the wooing of the Holy Spirit.

When a person is sensitive and obedient to the inward leadings of the Holy Spirit, which never contradict the Word of God.

When a leader inwardly senses through the Spirit the specific spiritual or physical needs of a congregation in a church service, and ministers to them.

We could state more of these descriptions, because God moves mightily in so many ways. The essence of all descriptions would focus on spontaneously following the leading of the Spirit, which always glorifies Jesus Christ and exposes (for healing) the spiritual condition of people. We should add here that a leader can function in the anointing by following previously made plans, previously outlined sermons, etc., provided that they were originated or quickened for that occasion by the Holy Spirit. The anointing of the Holy Spirit does not negate the importance of discipline and organization in leadership. The anointing does not make void the mind of man. It uses the mind of a leader as a vessel for transmitting the heart and spirit of God into each particular occasion, as the leader flows with the moving of the Spirit.

We therefore ask the reader not to over-react to our emphasis on the Holy Spirit at this point.

In fact, the anointing requires great effort and discipline to exercise spiritual gifts. It requires discipline in pursuing a deep prayer life, and in true spiritual meditation on the Word of God. It also requires a leader to diligently focus his spiritual ear on God at each service or event, and to be prepared to change his "game plan" to shift to another way of releasing God's provision for the people at that specific time. The Spirit will release further understanding of the anointing to leaders who do these things.

The subject of the anointing is truly a delicate one. It is a totally mystical (spiritual) thing, and yet relates directly to practical application in specific situations. One important key to moving in the anointing: keep a humble heart, and realize that God has not used any of us yet as fully as He would desire. Another key: remain open to the specific and different ways the Spirit may lead us to save souls, edify the Church, and release the presence and power of Jesus Christ in meetings. God's Word provides the balance, the "safety-check" and the principles that can help us understand the leading of the Spirit.

Words for Further Study. The student will be interested in key synonyms he can study to develop further understanding of the anointing. Each word adds a new dimension of insight. Further English synomyms for the student are: power, empowering, dynamic, unction, oil, moving, prophecy, spirit and mantle. For deeper study with full library resource, you may want to "mine" these words: charisma, charismatic, preaching (power in), communication, prophet(s), prophecy, prophetic mantle, ecstacy, pentecostalism and gifts of the Holy Spirit. Finally, here are some key biblical words to unfold the meaning and the typologies in anointing: oil, the various symbols of the Holy Spirit (fire, water, wind, fruit, dove, ointment), Spirit, quicken, make alive, move upon, perfume, fragrance, sweet smelling savour, fat, consecrate, olive (oil, tree, branch), overflow, flow, Messiah (the Anointed One), prophecy, prophet, mantle and fat(ness).

Detailed Studies on Anointing

As an example of how even a little study of these words can be a great asset in understanding the anointing, let us look at two biblical words: mantle and olive tree.

Mantle. In the Bible, a mantle is normally an outer garment to protect the body against the elements. In common use, the word has the idea of a covering that is ample (large and wide enough) to cover what it is supposed to protect. Figuratively, the mantle is most significant of the power, anointing and ministry of the Holy Spirit upon the life of the person wearing it. The best scriptural example of this is the prophets Elisha and Elijah (II Kings 2:12-15).

These two powerful prophets of Israel performed many signs and wonders in an attempt to turn back to God the corrupt people of their day. This demonstration of power is connected with Elijah's mantle which Elisha inherited (I Kings 19:16). In I Kings 19:13, Elijah wrapped his face in his mantle to hear the voice of God. In II Kings 2:8-14, Elijah divided the Jordan River with his mantle as he and Elisha set out to cross it. After they crossed, Elisha said, *"I pray thee, let a double portion of thy spirit* (mantle) *be upon me."* Thus, when Elijah is subsequently translated into heaven in chariots of fire, Elisha received this double portion of the prophet's spirit and anointing. But not without Elijah's mantle. He picked the mantle up and used it to divide again the river, and crossed over, as Elijah had done. The mantle was the anointing.

Olive Tree. The second example that we will use to illustrate the richness in detailed studie' in anointing is the olive branch or olive tree. In the scriptures, the olive branch is genera' significant of that which receives or contains the anointing of God, because of its natural content of oil and fruitfulness.

More specifically, the olive branch (or branch of olive oil) represents peace (Genesis 8:11); the righteous (Psalm 52:8); natural Israel (Hosea 14:5,6; Jeremiah 11:16); the Church (Romans 11:16-24); and God's two anointed witnesses (Zechariah 4:11-014; Revelation 11:3,4). Each of these subjects demonstrates something that has had or presently possesses the anointing or blessing of God upon it. Certainly those who are righteous through the blood of the Lamb, and thus are a part of the Church, have received an anointing from the Lord. If the Church in general has received a unique anointing of the Holy Spirit, how much more does God want to put His unction upon His leaders!

To the ancient Hebrews, the olive was the most important of trees. It was even called the king of all trees (Judges 9:8,9). The cultivated olive tree grows to approximately twenty feet in height and has a very twisted trunk with many branches. The tree grows very slowly. It must be maintained very diligently, and if it is, it can grow huge crops of oil-rich olives for centuries. The fruit of a wild olive tree, however, is useless, and can bear usable fruit only by in-grafting a portion of a cultivated tree.

Olives ripened in the early autumn. They were gathered in through shaking and beating the branches with long poles, at the end of November. After harvesting, olives were gathered together into a shallow rock cistern where they were crushed with a large, upright millstone (normally preferred over crushing by foot). The crushing would release the rich oil from the olives, which then sat, allowing foreign matter to settle out. After impurities were removed, the rich oil was then stored in earthen vessels or rock cisterns.

The facts of harvesting olives and producing olive oil contain many spiritual truths that can be applied to the anointing of the Holy Spirit in the life of the leader. Fact: the rich oil of the olives could come forth only after crushing by a millstone. Spiritual application: only as a leader's life is crushed by God can His holy anointing oil begin to flow through the leader's life. For this reason, leaders should never question the Lord's crushing in their lives or ministries, for God is only trying to enlarge and make their ministry more effective and anointed with His holy oil.

A second parallel between the olive and the leader's life involves the removal of impurities from olive oil. When a leader feels himself to be "on the shelf" (not openly and publicly flowing in the ministry to which he believes God has called him), it is for the purpose of removing spiritual impurities from his life, so that he will be a purer vessel for the Master's use. A leader should not complain when he is "on the shelf." Rather, he should seek the Lord even more diligently to find what areas of his life the Lord may desire to change for his own benefit.

Both the mantle and the olive tree illustrate the depth of spiritual application available through studies on biblical words and synonyms related to the anointing. We encourage every leader to do further study in this area, to increase his own understanding and personal experience of the Spirit's power in his life and ministry.

Uses of the Anointing

In the Old Testament, the anointing oil was a symbol for prosperity (Deuteronomy 32:13), spiritual tithing (12:17), and a means of financial payments (I Kings 5:11). In addition, one of the main uses of the anointing oil was its addition to some of Israel's various sacrifices and offerings.

The unleavened cake wafers used to consecrate Aaron and his sons to God were spread with oil (Exodus 29:1,2). This has significant applications to today's leaders for two reasons. First, to be anointed by the Holy Spirit, a leader must have sin (leaven) removed from his life and only sincerity and truth in his attitude and motivation (see I Corinthians 5:1-13). Second, all leaders must be anointed to be consecrated to God's service, as were Aaron and his sons (Exodus 29:1,23; Leviticus 6:20-22; Numbers 6:13-15).

The fact that the fine flour was offered with a lamb offering both morning and night--and was mixed with oil (Exodus 29:2,7,40)--has two spiritual applications today. A leader must be aware that his anointing must be renewed continually (morning and night). When a leader offers sacrifices to God (a lamb in the Old Testament), he can know that an ointing (the oil) will come along with it. It pays for every leader to makes sacrifices to God. In return for a leader's sacrifices, God gives a richer anointing to his life and ministry.

The grain offerings that were baked in the oven or cooked on the griddle were mixed with oil (Leviticus 2:4,5; see also 2:1,2,6,7 and 7:10,12 and 9:4 and 14:10,21 and 23:10-13). In application, this signifies that God will give a leader the anointing of His Spirit no matter what tests and trials (the oven or the griddle) through which He causes a leader to pass. Every leader should be able to confess with confidence, *"All things work together for the good of my life and ministry, because I love God and am called to minister according to His purpose"* (derived from Romans 8:28).

The peace offerings that we offered with thanksgiving were also mixed with oil (Leviticus 7:12). This expresses the spiritual truth that God will pour his anointing upon the leader who "makes peace" (as it were) with all of his troubling circumstances (welcoming them as friends, as in James 1:1-3). As a leader thanks the Lord for the spiritual good in every circumstance, he will experience ever greater release of the Holy Spirit in his life.

The burnt offering of the male lamb that was offered on the same day as the sheaf of first fruits after Israel entered the land was also mixed with oil (Leviticus 23:10-13). This indicates that the Lord will anoint the leader with more of His Spirit's unction as he enters into a new truth from the Lord (a new part of the land), along with the necessary sacrifices (burnt offerings) so that he can hold claim to that truth. Entering into truth always demands some form of sacrifice from a leader (family misunderstanding, church rejection, loss of friends). God will always honor such sacrifices.

The unleavened cakes which were a part of the offering for the Nazarite were mixed and spread with oil (Numbers 6:15). This signifies that God will always give His anointing to those who seriously separate themselves (as the Nazarites did) wholly unto the Lord. God anoints a leader with His holy ointment in a greater way every time a leader further separates himself from involvements with the world system (the lust of the flesh, the lust of the eyes, the pride of life, bitterness, hatred, anger). Every leader must embrace repentance as a lifestyle (not a one-time event), for both he and his family, as they set the example for their people.

The offerings of the leader's silver dishes which were filled with fine flour also included oil (Numbers 7). This signifies that only through the anointing of the Holy Spirit (God's oil) can a leader fully enter into all of the promises and provisions inherent in the Lord Jesus Christ's full redemption (whose color is silver). Only the Holy Spirit can make the truths of God's redemptive work in Jesus Christ real, practical and experiential to a leader.

The offering for the cleansing of the Levites for their priestly service included the addition of oil (Numbers 8:6,8). A New Testament priest (I Peter 2:5,9) must be cleansed by the Holy Spirit, revealing and then working out of him all of the impurities in his life. This is true for all Christian believers (who are all New Covenant priests), but particularly applies to everyone who must lead God's people into truth.

The breast of the wave offering and the thigh of the heave offerings (from the peace offerings for Aaron and his sons) were considered to be their anointed portions (Leviticus 7:34,35). This can signify to every leader that the two most important parts of his life, his heart affections (the breast) and his strengths (the strong thigh) must be given totally to God in order for the Spirit to anoint his life. What is done with the area of a leader's heart affections and strengths can mean either the total success or the complete failure of his ministry. May every leader give his spiritual "breast" and "thigh" to God.

The sacrifices that the prince and the people offered for sabbath and new moon observances were mixed with oil (Ezekiel 46:1-12). This signifies a truth of utmost importance: Church leaders (princes) and the people (the congregation) totally depend on the Holy Spirit for peace (sabbath) with one another, and for entering into all of the new truth (new moon) that God has for the Church.

Anointing oil was used to consecrate Moses' tabernacle and Solomon's temple, along with all of their parts (Exodus 40:9; Numbers 7:1,10,84,88). This list of the different parts of the tabernacle, and the references where they were anointed with the holy oil for service, also includes spiritual applications to a leader.

Anointing of the brass altar (Exodus 29:36 and 30:25,28 and 40:11) encourages every leader that the place of sacrifice to God is the place of the anointing of the Spirit.

Anointing of the brass laver (30:25,28 and 40:11) encourages every leader that the place of cleansing by the Word (Ephesians 5:25-27) is the place of the anointing of the Spirit.

Daily anointing the golden candlestick and all of its utensils (30:25,27b) speaks to a leader of the importance of daily filling his vessel (life) with the Spirit of God.

Anointing of the showbread table (the table of His Presence) and all of its utensils (30:25,27a) challenges a leader to pray for more illumination and understanding on the communion table of the Lord, so the Church can experience more of God's Spirit here.

Anointing of the golden altar of incense (30:25,27c) signifies to the leader that the more deeply he enters into the ministry of prayer (Revelation 5:8 and 8:4) and worship unto the Lord, the more he will experience God's anointing.

Anointing of the golden ark of the covenant (30:25,26b) speaks to the leader that the more he enters into the presence of God through the blood of Jesus Christ, the more he will experience the anointing of the Lord upon him (the two anointed cherubim over the ark and the doors of the inner sanctuary in Solomon's temple being made of olive wood, I Kings 6:23,31-35).

Anointing to Prophecy

All of these spiritual applications of the anointing point to one ultimate prophetical application for the anointing of God. That is to anoint the Church of Jesus Christ to go out and witness with power for Christ (Acts 1:8; II Corinthians 1:21,22). One of the Old Testament types of the Holy Spirit's anointing coming down upon the Church is that of Jacob (the third of the three main patriarchal fathers).

JACOB   poured oil and a drink offering
                             (the Holy Spirit)

                    upon the stone pillar
                    (the Church, I Timothy 3:15)

              where he had the revelation of the heavenly ladder
        (Jesus Christ, John 1:51; Genesis 28:18 and 31:13 and 35:14)

The oil came upon the stone pillar just as the Spirit has and will come upon the Church, which is the pillar and ground of the truth. In the New Testament as well, the anointing of the physical body of Jesus Christ (Mark 14:3,8 and 16:1) becomes prophetic of the anointing that was to come to His Body, the Church (I Corinthians 12:12-27).

More specifically, the New Testament very clearly teaches the importance of receiving the sight, insight and illumination of the Holy Spirit. John wrote to the Church of Laodicea about their need of this anointing: *"I advise you to buy from Me . . . eyesalve to anoint your eyes that you may see"* (Revelation 3:18). Today, leaders of the Church need to see, with the help of the Spirit, God's eternal purpose and use of His Spirit. He uses the Spirit to anoint His Body, the Church, with His glory and power. Because Jesus Christ Himself was anointed by God (Acts 4:27 and 10:38; Hebrews 1:9), so shall His Church be clothed with His power from on high (Luke 24:49).

In connection with the area of God's anointing coming upon His Body, we can note another spiritual truth for the leader. In ancient Israel, both priests and kings received the anointing upon their heads and garments (I Samuel 9:16 and 10:1 and 12:3,5 and 15:17 and 16:3,12,13). The anointing oil would also drip down from their heads upon their garments. When Aaron and his sons were anointed, Exodus 28:41 states, *"And you shall put them* (the tunics, sashes and caps) *on Aaron our brother and on his sons with him and you shall anoint and ordain them and consecrate them."* Here the anointing oil is connected with the donning of clean, priestly garments (Leviticus 8:30). Furthermore, Exodus 29:7 says, *"Then thou shall take the anointing oil and pour it on his head and anoint him"* (Exodus 30:30 and 40:13,15; Leviticus 8:12 and 21:10; Numbers 3:3 and 35:25).

Why did holders of two of the most important offices in Israel receive the anointing oil upon their heads? It was certainly prophetic of the necessity of the sight, insight and illumination of the Holy Spirit in the minds of the Church leaders.

All of God's leaders must have minds and thoughts (heads) totally consecrated to God in order to be the leaders that they are meant to be. David realized this even as a lowly Shepherd, when he wrote, *"Thou anointest my head with oil"* (Psalm 23:5). David was referring to the oil that he, as a shepherd, would apply to the heads of his sheep to protect them from the pestilent springtime flies. But he was also referring to his desire to place his head under total control of his Lord, that his entire life might consecrated to God. Similarly, a woman broke a vial of precious ointment over the head of Jesus, recognizing Him as Lord, in Mark 14:3. May every leader realize that God uses His anointing to keep His leaders totally controlled through His Spirit and His Word.

Anointing Tied to Character

Anointing oil was also used figuratively in the Bible to portray different character qualities that would receive the blessing of God. Christian leaders should see that God is interested in more than developing in them the gifts of the Spirit. Also, and more importantly, God wants to develop in them the fruit of the Spirit. As stated before in this book, God desires a balance between character (integrity) and ability (power) in every leader's ministry. Some of the most important character qualities which the Bible connects with receiving the anointing of the Spirit:

Concern. *"Thou anointest my head* (David, a shepherd concerned for the sheeps' welfare) *with oil"* (Psalm 23:5b).

Giving. *"The liberal* (giving) *person shall be made fat* (filled with oil)*"* (Proverbs 11:25).

Diligence. *"The soul of the diligent shall be made fat* (filled with oil)*"* (Proverbs 13:4).

Trust. *"He who trusts in the Lord shall prosper* (be made fat with oil)*"* (Proverbs 28:25).

Responsibility. *"About this time tomorrow I will send you* (Samuel) *a man* (Saul) . . . *and you shall anoint him to be prince over my people Israel"* (I Samuel 9:16).

Righteousness. *"Thou hast loved righteousness and hated iniquity, therefore God, even thy God, has anointed thee with the oil of gladness above thy fellows"* (Psalm 45:7).

Purity. *"Wash yourself, therefore, and anoint yourself* (Ruth) *and put on your best clothes and go down to the threshing floor"* (Ruth 3:3).

Courage. *"They* (the enemy) *set the table, they spread out the cloth, they eat, they drink; 'Rise up, captains, oil the shields,' for thus saith the Lord to me, 'Go station the sentry' "* (Isaiah 21:5,6).

Obedience. *"O mountains of Gilboa, let not dew nor rain be on you, nor fields of offerings. For the shield of the mighty was defiled, the field of Saul, not anointed with oil"* (II Samuel 1:21; I Samuel 15:22).

Submissiveness. *"This is the law of the leper* (a type of the sinner) *in the day of his cleansing. Now he shall be brought in to the priest* . . . *then the priest shall take* . . . *the log of oil* . . . *and present them as a wave offering before the Lord"* (Leviticus 14:2,12; see also oil in vs. 10,14-18,21,24,26-29).

Unity. *"Behold how good and how pleasant it is for brothers to dwell together in unity! It is like the precious oil upon the head"* (Psalm 133:1,2).

Joy. *"The Spirit of the Lord God is upon me because the Lord has anointed me* . . . *to grant those who mourn in Zion* . . . *the oil of gladness"* (Isaiah 61:3).

Humility and Brokenness. *"And behold there was a woman in the city who was* . . . *standing behind Him at His feet, weeping* . . . *kissing His feet, and anointing them with the perfume"* (Luke 7:36-50).

These are some of the most essential character qualities in a leader's life. With their development, a leader can believe God for a greater anointing.

Finally, several other uses of oil also have certain spiritual truths for a leader of God's people. These can be commonly categorized as social uses.

Oil was used in the preparation of food (I Kings 17:12-16). The spiritual food that a leader feeds his people through teaching and preaching the Word must be quickened by the Holy Spirit to be digested.

Oil was used as fuel for domestic and other kinds of lamps (Matthew 25:1-13; see also wicks of flax in Isaiah 42:3). Every leader must accept part of the responsibility to fill the lamps of his people's lives with the oil of the Spirit, that they might truly be what Jesus Christ Himself said they would be: the light of the world' (Matthew 5:14).

Oil was used in various medicines (Isaiah 1:6; Mark 6:13; Luke 10:34). Every leader must be a clean channel through which the Holy Spirit can heal the minds and lives of the spiritually wounded.

Oil was included in some cosmetic ointments (II Samuel 14:2; Ruth 3:3; Psalm 104:15). Every leader must use the Spirit's anointing upon the Church so that she might show forth the image and countenance of Jesus Christ.

Oil was customarily used to anoint and refresh guests in one's home (Luke 7:46). Evey leader's spirit of hospitality (I Timothy 3:2) should minister spiritual refreshing to everyone who enters his home.

Oil was used in combination with myrrh to anoint the dead (Mark 14:8; Luke 23:55,56). The anointing of the Spirit of God should be so blended together with a leader's experience of the cross of Jesus Christ (myrrh), that he will be able to bring spiritual life to those who are dead in trespasses and sins.

Purposes of the Anointing

Purposes of the anointing oil are very similar to its uses. But we have listed here several that should add to our understanding. Each can be applied to the New Testament leader. Some of the major purposes of the anointing (oil) were:

1. To enable God's leaders to defeat their enemies (as when the Spirit of the Lord came upon judges of Israel for this purpose: Judges 3:10 and 6:34 and 11:29 and 13:25 and 14:6,19 and 15:4).
2. To consecrate things and people to God and His service (Exodus 28:41 and 29:29).
3. To enable people to perform their ministries unto the Lord.
4. To bring good news to the afflicted (Isaiah 61:1).
5. To bind up the broken-hearted (Isaiah 61:1).
6. To proclaim liberty to the captives (Isaiah 61:1).
7. To proclaim freedom for the prisoners (Isaiah 61:1).
8. To proclaim the favorable and acceptable year of the Lord (Isaiah 61:1,2).
9. To proclaim the day of God's vengeance (Isaiah 61:1,2).
10. To comfort all who mourn (Isaiah 61:1,2).
11. To grant a garland of beauty instead of ashes to those who mourn in Zion (Isaiah 61:1,3).
12. To give the oil of gladness to those who mourn in Zion (Isaiah 61:1,3).
13. To give a garment of praise, instead of a spirit of fainting, to those who mourn (Isaiah 61:1,3).
14. To cause those who mourn to be called oaks of righteousness and the planting of the Lord (Isaiah 61:1,3).
15. To glorify the Lord and not man (Isaiah 61:1,3).
16. To qualify Aaron's sons for their ministries (Exodus 40:15).
17. To qualify Aaron for his ministry of the offerings (Numbers 18:8).
18. To moisten the fine flour in the offerings (Ezekiel 46:13-15).
19. To be an essential part of the daily burnt offering (Ezekiel 46:13-15).
20. To make blind eyes see (John 9:6).
21. To empower the Christian with the gifts and ministries of the Lord (I Corinthians 12; Ephesians 4:11,12).

All of these purposes seek their spiritual fulfillment in the life and ministry of a leader. Probably the most important of all these purposes in the list above are 3, 16 and 17, in light of our purpose of helping leaders function in the anointing. Succinctly, these purposes are to enable people to perform their ministries unto the Lord, and to qualify them for their offices.

As we have already stated, one of the greatest controversies in Christianity has always been: "Who is qualified for the ministry? Who is able to speak with authority in the name of the Lord? What qualifies a person for a certain ministry?" These questions are still debated today, but the purposes of the anointing we have just singled out (3, 16 and 17) lead us to part of the answer to these questions.

One side of qualification for ministry is character and integrity (I Timothy 3:2-7), and no one should deny this. Whenever a person steps beyond scriptural guidelines for moral character and conduct, he disqualifies himself from ministry. But ministry also requires more than character. A man may be a very honest and virtuous plumber, but if he can't fix a leaky sink, how much good is he to a person with a leaky sink? Similarly, a person needs God's anointing (ability), in addition to character, to perform a specific ministry. A person must have the power and ability in the Lord to perform that ministry effectively.

God chose Bezaleel and Oholiab (Exodus 31:2 and 35:30 and 36:1,2 and 37:1 and 38:22; see also II Chronicles 2:14) to build the pieces of furniture for the tabernacle in the wilderness. God did not choose them just because they had integrity and fine moral virtues. He chose them because He was going to anoint them by His Spirit. He was going to put the enabling of His Spirit on their naturally developed talents to make them uniquely equipped for a specific purpose.

When David chose singers and musicians to minister before the ark in God's tabernacle, he did not choose people just because they had certain spiritual traits. He chose them also because he knew that they would be able to sing and play skillfully before the Lord (I Chronicles 15:22 and 28:21; II Chronicles 34:12 and Psalm 33: and 78:72). When God chose a man to write thirteen books of the New Testament, He did not choose Peter the fisherman. He chose a very able Pharisee of the Law of Moses--Paul.

Therefore, it is not just character that qualifies people for a ministry. It is also the anointing of the Spirit that God has given to them. True, it is not always natural abilities or skills that are used by the Lord. Even certain abilities must experience the cross before they can be resurrected to give God glory. But the point here is that God gives each person a certain anointing which enables him to perform his ministry effectively. Leaders, however, must be careful not to enter into the spirit of professionalism which glorifies men's abilities. The anointing may or may not fall on a natural talent; the anointing is the important matter here, not the talent. God will sometimes take weakness, lack of talents or abilities, and needs in people, and then supernaturally anoint them for a task.

It is also interesting to note the ingredients of the holy anointing oil. The holy anointing oil was comprised of the finest of spices (Exodus 30:23-25). These fine spices were: myrrh, cinnamon, calamus (or cane), cassin and olive oil. Anointing oil contained nothing inferior or degenerate. This fact speaks of God's desire to provide His leaders with only the best graces in his particular ministry. To receive this anointing, however, a leader must give his time and energy to the good things of God's Spirit, and not the things of this world. God will anoint every one of His leaders. But He desires to anoint the leader's best gifts and abilities, and He will anoint nothing of the devil's kingdom.

Divine Typology in Anointing Oil

The anointing oil also provides a typological understanding of the Godhead. The following diagram demonstrates how the individual spices represent the members of the Godhead. First, we see how the myrrh, cinnamon and calamus represent the fullness of the Godhead bodily in the Lord Jesus Christ.

SPICE	MEMBER OF GODHEAD	EXPLANATION
500 shekels of pure MYRRH	Lord Jesus Christ	Myrrh has a pleasant smell, but a bitter taste. It was given to Jesus at His birth, and His crucifixion. These experiences were a sweet aroma in God's nostrils.

250 shekels of sweet CINNAMON	Lord Jesus Christ	Like the precious spice of cinnamon, so the birth, life, death and resurrection of Jesus Christ were precious to God and the Church.
250 shekels of sweet CALAMUS (or Cane)	Lord Jesus Christ	Calamus was a rare and costly spice, and so was the life, death and resurrection of Christ.
500 shekels of CASSIA	Father God	As Cassia changed form in being ground to a powder from strips of bark, so the Father, as the divine and ultimate Spirit, fully expressed Himself in the bodily form of the Lord Jesus Christ.
One hin of OLIVE OIL	The Holy Spirit	As olive oil was used to anoint the kings and the priests, the Holy Spirit anoints all Christians as kings and priests unto God.

Because all of these spices were fragrant, they can speak to us of the *"sweet-smelling fragrance"* that the Lord Jesus Christ was to the Father (Ephesians 5:2) when He came to earth to perform the work of redemption with the holy anointing oil of God's Spirit upon Him. The fact that the anointing oil was compressed of five separate ingredients can speak to us of the grace of God that is evident in God's anointing.

Traits of Anointing Oil

The Bible uses the following words to describe the anointing oil:

Beaten (Exodus 29:40)
The anointing oil in the Old Testament was beaten from olives. The anointing of the Holy Spirit in the life of a leader of God comes through the hard and deep dealings of God (which release the life of the Holy Spirit within him).

Fresh (Psalm 92:10)
The holy anointing oil had to be fresh and new for use. No leader can depend on past anointings to serve him today. Every leader must obtain a fresh anointing, daily, in the Lord.

Holy (Ex. 30:25,31,32; Psalm 89:20)
The anointing oil was holy. The Holy Spirit enters the life of a leader to make him holy, but will flow through him to others only as the leader himself embraces this holiness.

Perfumed (Ex. 30:25)
The holy anointing oil was a perfumed mixture. The Holy Spirit performs in the life of a leader that which releases a pleasing, perfumed fragrance unto God.

Mixed (Ex. 30:25)
The holy anointing oil was a mixture of spices. The life of the Holy Spirit in the ministry of a leader will be developed and expressed in and through a mixture of various spiritual principles and experiences.

Handcrafted (Ex. 30:25)
The holy anointing oil was a handcrafted work. The Holy Spirit in the life of a leader will work and labor to form him into God's perfect will.

Olive (Ex. 27:20; 30:24)
The holy anointing oil came from the mashing of the olive. The anointing of the Holy Spirit comes upon a leader to develop the fruit of the Holy Spirit in his life (Galatians 5:21,22), and in response to the presence of those fruit.

Pure (Ex. 27:20; I Kings 5:11)
The holy anointing oil was pure. The Holy Spirit will flow through a leader's life only as he is pure before the Lord (morally, emotionally and spiritually).

Anointed (Ex. 37:29)

The holy oil was set aside for the purpose of anointing certain ministries. Every leader has been called to cooperate with the discerning power of the Spirit, that he can be used to set in and anoint certain ministries into the Body of Christ.

Precious (Proverbs 21:20)

Anointing oil was very precious. Every leader should guard and protect the Holy Spirit's precious anointing in his life, as he considers it to be the most valuable possession in his ministry.

Prescribed (Ezekiel 45:13,14)

The anointing oil was specified by God for use in certain prescribed proportions in Israel's offerings. The Holy Spirit will require different levels of sacrifice to be made, according to the degree of the anointing that He gives.

Quality (Amos 6:6; Ex. 30:23; Numbers 18:12)

Only the finest oils in Israel were used in the anointing oil. Every leader should realize that the fine quality of the work of the Holy Spirit, in and through his life, is more important than the quantity of that work.

Costly (Mark 14:3)

Anointing oil required very expensive ingredients. Every leader must realize that for every new depth of spiritual anointing he desires to experience, he must give up precious and costly things to God. The anointing costs the leader something. It cost Jesus Christ His entire life.

Restrictions on Use of Anointing Oil

Not to Be Poured Out Indiscriminately. The anointing oil was not to be poured out on the flesh or the body of just any person (Exodus 30:32). It was only to be poured out upon those whom God had designated to fill certain ministry positions before Him. In application, a leader can see that God's spiritual anointing is not for the uncorrected. Only those who have repented from their sins and received the cleansing of the blood of Jesus Christ can receive the anointing of the Holy Spirit. The blood of Christ must come before His oil. Furthermore, a leader should see that the Lord will not anoint any area of his life that still partakes of his old, fleshly nature. No work of the flesh is blessed by God's anointing oil, only the people and the things which He has cleansed and ordained.

Not to Be Imitated. Israel was not to duplicate the holy anointing oil for private use (Exodus 30:32). Israel was not to mix another mixture of anointing oil by using the same proportion of ingredients. This indicates that, though there may be spiritual counterfeits of the Holy Spirit's anointing, God's true anointing cannot be duplicated because it is uniquely from God. No leader or church organization should try to use games, gimmicks or professionalism to reproduce the work and fruit of God's Spirit. Many do try to do this, but it never brings God's desired results. May every leader depend only on God's true anointing.

Not to Be Made in a Different Way. Israel was commanded by God to use only the divinely given pattern for making the holy anointing oil, and to use no other. Exodus 31:11 states, *"the anointing oil also . . . they are to make them according to all that I have commanded you"* (see also Exodus 35:10-19).

As we have already seen, God gave Israel certain ingredients and proportions by which He wanted His oil to be made for His service. Spiritually, God has not changed. He still requires His people (and especially His leaders) to receive the anointing of His Spirit in His own prescribed ways.

Many people do not enter into further dimensions of God's anointing because they will not humble themselves sufficiently. In the early Church, speaking in tongues was a regular experience with the baptism of the Holy Spirit (Acts 2:4 and 9:17/I Corinthians 14:18; Acts 10:46 and 19:6), but it does not happen so regularly today. Humility is one of the greatest keys to the anointing of the Spirit. If a leader cannot humble himself to receive the baptism of the Holy Spirit with the sign of speaking in tongues, how can he expect to humble himself even further for God to anoint him in other ways? The anointing of God truly includes the baptism of the Holy Spirit.

God has established other means by which His anointing is released, all of which are recorded for us in God's Word, the only authority on the subject. Some of the biblical keys to anointing are: heart brokenness, a spirit of sacrifice, weakness, dependency on God, prayer, fasting, faith in the Word, and obedience to God. These are only some of the valuable principles in the Word that release God's anointing. They are most effective when done simultaneously, as a constant and sincere lifestyle. Only that method which God has ordained will truly release His precious Spirit through a leader's life. The unction of God must come directly from His Spirit, just as Bezaleel was the one ordained to make the tabernacle anointing oil (Exodus 37).

Not to Be Used Unsupervised. After Bezaleel made the holy anointing oil, he brought it to Moses for close examination (Exodus 39:32-43). If Moses found that the oil had been made according to God's divine prescriptions, then he was free to bless it. But if he found it to be inferior, he would withhold his blessing. Five key words stand out in relation to this examination of the holy anointing oil. The oil was to be:

Completed (Exodus 39:32)
Delivered to Moses (Ex. 39:33)
Examined by Moses (Ex. 39:43)
Approved by Moses (Ex. 39:43)
Blessed by Moses (Ex. 39:43)

In the same way, God will bless a leader only if that leader's anointing has passed the inspection of the Lord Jesus Christ and the written Word of God. The oil was brought to Moses, just as a leader's ministry and anointing must be brought to Jesus Christ and the written Word for thorough comparison and examination, before God can bless it any further.

Not to Leave the Holy Place of Ministry. Priests who were anointed with the holy oil were not to leave the holy place of the tent of meeting while the oil was on them (Leviticus 10:1-7 and 21:10,12). They were to continue ministering unto the Lord all the time that the oil was on them. As they were consecrated with the oil, they were to serve the Lord. While the oil was on the priests, they were to fill the lamps on the lamp stand, fix the bread on the table of showbread, and burn holy incense unto the Lord on the golden altar.

Similarly, every leader must perform his ministries while the anointing of the Spirit is upon him. This includes ministry of the Word of God (Psalm 119:105), the communion table (the table of His presence), and prayer and praise (Revelation 5:8 and 8:4) to the Church (the lamp stand, Revelation 1:20). In this way, he will be abiding in the "holy place" while the oil of God is upon him. God's oil will flow while His leaders obey His word in ministering to Him and to His people.

Not a Substitute for a Holy Life. Some leaders believe they have a license to behave and speak in any way they want, due to the Holy Spirit's anointing on their lives, and the experience of some of God's power. This mentality is false. It is the pentecostal counterpart to the Roman Catholic idea that the Pope can speak infallibly in all matters of faith and morals. Both of these concepts are wrong, deceptive and dangerous. Only the written Word of God can provide an infallible guide to the Church in all matters of faith and morals.

Tragically, many pentecostal ministries who have experienced the power of God through their service have ended up in moral shipwreck. These many examples stand as a warning to all leaders to guard their moral life as much as they guard their anointing. The power of God can never substitute for a holy life. In the day of the prophet Micah, when Israel was living in sin, he declared:

"Does the Lord take delight in thousands of rams, in 10,000 rivers of oil? Shall I present my first born for my rebellious acts; the fruit of my body for the sin of my soul? . . . you will tread the olive but will not anoint thyself with oil" (Micah 6:7,15; compare with Haggai 2:12).

When Israel continued in iniquity, not even thousands of sacrifices and rivers of oil could atone for her sins. In the same way, no leader can expect God to continue anointing his ministry or gift if he continues doing things that are contrary to God's Word. May no leader allow himself to become so proud or over-confident in his ministry that he lets his anointing become a substitute for a holy life.

Other Prohibitions. We would like to conclude these thoughts on the restrictions upon the anointing by noting some specific prohibitions that God gave to the priests and the high priests in the Old Testament. They are highly significant for today's Christian leaders, because God directly ties these prohibitions to the priestly anointing (see Leviticus 21:10).

Aaron's Sons (Exodus 29:29)
Aaron's sons were to be anointed with holy oil only while they were wearing their father's priestly garments. The sons of the heavenly Aaron (Jesus Christ, as in Hebrews 5:4 and 7:11) must wear the spiritual garments of righteousness, salvation and praise to be continually anointed by the Holy Spirit.

Aaron's Pattern (Ex. 40:15)
Aarons sons were anointed with oil in the same way that Aaron was. Christ's leaders will only be anointed with the Holy Spirit in the same way that Jesus Christ was anointed--through sufferings and temptations (Matthew 3:16,17 and 4:1; Luke 4:1,2,14).

Aaron's Head Band (Leviticus 21:10)
Aaron was not to remove his head band (with "Holiness Unto The Lord" written upon it). A Church leader must ever keep his mind and life consecrated to Jesus Christ and Christ-like living.

Aaron's Clothes (Lev. 21:10)
Aaron could not tear his clothes for any reason. Today, every leader must protect the spiritual garments of salvation, righteousness and praise that God has given him.

Aaron's Associations (Lev. 21:11)
Aaron could not approach (and certainly not touch!) any dead person. So every leader must never touch any part of the dead fleshly body of sin of his old, unregenerate man.

Aaron's Parents (Lev. 21:10-11)
Aaron could not disobey the Word of the Lord, even if his own parents asked him to. Every leader today must obey God and His Word over and above men, no matter how close they are to him (see Luke 2:49).

Aaron's Sanctuary (Lev. 21:10-12)
Aaron could not defile the sanctuary of God in the wilderness in any way. Every leader must not corrupt through sin the sanctuary of his own life or that of the people of God, which is where God dwells (Ephesians 1:22 and 2:21,22).

Aaron's Bride (Lev. 21:11,13)
Aaron was not to marry a widow, divorcee or harlot. Every leader must marry only a woman who knows and loves the Lord Jesus Christ, a spiritual virgin. He must continually keep himself and his people from having any other lover or husband than God (the entire book of Hosea is devoted to this analogy).

Requirements for the Anointing of the Holy Spirit

Directly related to the restrictions on use of the anointing oil are the different spiritual principles upon which the anointing of the Holy Spirit depends. Many of the following points refer to the oil, rain or temple in natural Israel. These became prophetic of the Holy Spirit's anointing in spiritual Israel, the Church. The natural points to the spiritual.

The anointing of the Holy Spirit (as it applies to a Christian leader) depends upon:

A leader obeying (and teaching his people to obey) the Word of God (Deuteronomy 7:12,13 and 11:13,14 and 28:1-68).

A leader entering into the outpouring of the Holy Spirit (Deut. 11:13,14; Joel 2:23,24).

A leader actively building up the house of the Lord, the Church (Haggai 1:7-11).

A leader recognizing that God (and not himself) is the source of supply for his spiritual anointing and prosperity (Hosea 2:8,9).

A leader using his spiritual anointing and prosperity for the Lord and not the devil (Hosea 2:8,9).

A leader not glorifying his spiritual anointing and prosperity more than God (Hosea 2:8,9).

A leader giving himself voluntarily and freely (and teaching the people to do so, too) to the construction of the house of the Lord, the Church (Exodus 35:20-29).

A leader appreciating and guarding the anointing in his life (and in the lives of his people (Numbers 4:9,16; Proverbs 21:20).

Fruit Resulting From the Anointing

What promises has God given to those who have been anointed by His Spirit? What are some of the good effects from following the Spirit's anointing? Each one of these reference points can be developed for further study by the leader. Some of the major results of the anointing of the Holy Spirit are:

God's help (Psalm 89:19)
Exaltation and authority (Psalm 89:19,24,27,29)
Being called a servant of the Lord (Ps. 89:20)
God's hand being with you (Ps. 89:21)
God's strength (Ps. 89:21)
Freedom from deception (Ps. 89:22)
Freedom from affliction by the wicked (Ps. 89:22)
God's victory over one's enemies (Ps. 89:23)
God's faithfulness and loving kindness (Ps. 89:24,28)
Influence over the nations ("the seas" in Ps. 89:25)
A father-son relationship (Ps. 89:26)
God's saving power (Ps. 89:26)
Partaking in God's everlasting covenant (Ps. 89:28,30-37)
Membership in the Church of the first-born (Ps. 89:27)
Establishment of one's descendants forever (Ps. 89:29)
A glistening countenance (Ps. 104:15)
A breaking of the yoke of bondage (Isaiah 10:27)
Physical healing of the body (Mark 6:13)
The whole house (church, too) being filled with the fragrance of the ointment (John 12:1-3)
Spiritual sight and insight (Revelation 3:18)

The power of God (Acts 10:38)
Ability to go forth and do good (Acts 10:38)
Ability to heal all who are oppressed by the devil (Acts 10:38)
The presence of God (Acts 10:38)
Surpassing joy (Hebrews 1:9)
Continuing in the truth, by unmasking deception (I John 2:26-29)
Continuing in might and strength, from the time of its reception (I Samuel 16:13)
Recognition in the midst of one's family (I Samuel 16:13)
The spirit of prophecy (I Samuel 19:18-24)
The office of a prophet (II Samuel 23:1-7)
Spiritual fruitfulness (Numbers 17:1-11)

The anointing, power and presence are among the greatest needs in the Church today. Many leaders and churches lack the anointing in their activities. Consequently, leaders must enter into a lifestyle that leads into the anointing of God's power, and must teach the people to do the same. Only in this way will we see the huge harvest of souls which God desires in our day.

CHAPTER 20
CHRIST, THE ANOINTED LEADER

If the Church is to grow beyond "Hollywood Christianity," she must seek again the true foundation of Christian leadership. How many times must the Church suffer the wounds of unfaithful, uncalled, ungodly leaders? She will suffer this as often as she fails to pursue the true anointing of the Holy Spirit. This anointing must come not only upon her leaders, but upon all who are given a gift and ministry in the Church--every believer.

Christ stands at the center of the Bible's teaching about the anointing of the Holy Spirit. He is our forerunner, our example, and the tutor of our faith in discovering and functioning in the anointing of the Holy Spirit. Many of God's dealings in calling and preparing leadership vary from person to person. But the anointing of the Holy Spirit is essential in every believer's life. And without it, a believer has no true and lasting ministry. As we study the anointing of the Holy Spirit on Christ, we will discover how we ourselves are to come under the anointing.

The Anointing of Christ

We find a focused account of Christ's anointing in Luke 3:21-4:20. It shows that the believer's anointing, like His, will come in a series of ever-deepening involvement with the work of the Holy Spirit.

Coming of the Spirit. In the first stage, the Spirit came upon Christ (Luke 3:21,22).

"Now when all the people were baptized, it came to pass, that Jesus also being baptized, and praying, the heaven was opened, and the Holy Ghost descended in a bodily shape like a dove upon him, and a voice came from heaven, which said, 'Thou art my beloved Son; in thee I am well pleased.' "

Filling of the Spirit. In the second stage, the Spirit filled Christ (Lk. 4:1).

"And Jesus being full of the Holy Ghost returned from Jordan and was led by the Spirit into the wilderness."

Power of the Spirit. In the third stage, after Christ endured temptations in the wilderness and held a true faith, the Spirit moved powerfully in Christ (Lk.4:14).

"And Jesus returned in the power of the Spirit into Galilee: and there went out a fame of him through all the region round about."

Anointing of the Spirit. In the final stage, which Christ faithfully maintained until the end of His earthly ministry, the Spirit anointed Christ to function in a specific ministry (Lk. 4:15-21).

"And he taught in their synagogues, being glorified of all. And he came to Nazareth, where he had been brought up: and, as his custom was, he went into the synagogue on the sabbath day, and stood up for to read. And there was delivered unto him the book of the prophet Esaias. And when he had opened the book, he found the place where it was written, 'The Spirit of the Lord is upon me, because he hath anointed me to preach the gospel to the poor; he hath sent me to heal the broken-hearted, to preach deliverance to the captives, and recovering of sight to the blind, to set at liberty them that are bruised, To preach the acceptable year of the Lord.' And he closed the book, and he gave it again to the minister, and sat down. And the eyes of all them that were in the synagogue were fastened on him. And he began to say unto them, 'This day is this scripture fulfilled in your ears'."

We have already studied the language roots of the concept of anointing in detail, in the last chapter. It is worth reiterating a few foundational points about the anointing here.

1. To anoint someone was to commission him for a certain purpose, and often involved induction into a major office, such as king, priest or prophet.

2. Anointing was accompanied by a special divine enablement to carry out the mission for which one was commissioned.

3. The anointing set aside an object or person for God's use, as a sacred vessel.

4. In the New Testament, the anointing process focused on a function of the Spirit in every believer's life. The anointing is the "dunamis" (power of God--see Romans 1:16) in action, the strength and might to take dominion over the enemy, to exercise authority in any situation, to establish God's rule and build His Church.

Nature of the Anointing

Tragically, the Church sometimes misunderstands the anointing when she tries to understand it with a carnal mind.

Some believers feel the anointing is given primarily for our joy. This is selfish and unbiblical. This attitude is at the root of the "Hollywood Christianity" that has resulted recently in tragic leadership failures. The part of the Church that maintains a pentecostal faith appears to be most vulnerable to this delusion, yet it can be found anywhere in the Church.

Some believers feel the anointing is given primarily to a limited number of individuals, to establish pastoral ministry. While this confusion may not seem as pernicious as the first, it is just as wrong.

To answer the two confusions above, we re-state two foundational principles of the anointing of the Holy Spirit: the anointing is given to accomplish a purpose in God's Church; and it is given to all believers, because all receive a related gift and ministry that they are to exercise to the building of God's Church.

Purposes of the Anointing

In the life of Christ, we see fifteen specific purposes of the anointing. Christ was annointed to:

Create zeal, the passion of the Spirit (John 2:13-17).
Destroy the works of the devil (I John 3:8).

Serve unselfishly and sacrificially (Mark 10:45; John 13:3-4).

Preach Good News of hope to the hopeless (Luke 4:18).

Heal those with crushed hearts and shattered emotions (Lk. 4:18).

Release captives from satanic prisons (Lk. 4:18).

Set at liberty the bitter-hearted (Lk. 4:18).

Give beauty in place of the ashes of ruined lives (Isaiah 61:3).

Give the garment of praise in place of the spirit of heaviness (Isaiah 61:3).

Make us oaks of righteousness, planted securely (Isaiah 61:3).

Minister healing power to the sick (James 5:14; Mark 6:13)

Take a leadership position and lead (I Samuel 2:10,35 and 10:1 and 15:17; II Corinthians 1:21-22).

Equip for warfare, and give power to do battle (Isaiah 21:5; Psalm 20:6 and 28:8).

Comprehend the truth given by the Spirit (I John 2:27).

Balance authority with joyful expression of ministry (Hebrews 1:9).

For the balance of this chapter, we will study two of the specific purposes on this list: zeal, and sacrificial service.

The Anointing Creates Zeal

Without the anointing of the Holy Spirit, the Church becomes dull, flaccid, listless and lifeless.

Perhaps you have heard of the discovery of a frozen ship in the Arctic Ocean, which happened over a century ago. The ship's captain froze as he was making his last entry in the logbook. The date of his entry showed that the ship, with her frozen crew scattered icily in hammocks and cabins, had wandered among the icebergs for thirteen years before her rediscovery. A drifting sepulchre, manned by a frozen crew. How frightening to realize that some churches today fit this description all too well.

For a dramatic and exciting contrast, we can see what the Bible says about zeal in the Church.

In various translations, John 2:17 says:

"Zeal of thine house shall eat me up"
"Concern for God's house will be my undoing"
"Jealousy for the honor of thy house shall burn in me"

Various translations of Psalm 69:9 say:
"I am on fire with passion for your house"
"Enthusiasm for your house has devoured me"
"My zeal for God and his work burns hot within me"

And hear Isaiah 59:17:
"For he put on righteousness as a breastplate, and an helmet of salvation upon his head; and he put on the garments of vengeance for clothing, and was clad with zeal as a cloak."
(Remember the biblical typology: a mantle or a cloak is a symbol of God's anointing, which entails some protection for its wearer.)

Defining the Zeal of God

Let us now take a closer look at the word "zeal." What does this word mean to us? What are its biblical roots?

The Hebrew word for zeal means to burn with strong feelings of good or bad, as in jealousy or anger. The word was most often used in the context of describing idolatry.

The Greek word, "zeelos," is used 17 times in the New Testament. It has numerous, related meanings: capacity or state of passionate committal to a person or cause; forces which motivate;

in classical Greek, it refers to a warlike spirit; passion; enthusiasm, to boil hot; fervent; to concern oneself with something so as to take up responsibility for the matter, to make it a goal and strive after it energetically.

In common usage today, zeal is understood to involve passionate ardor in the pursuit of something. Zeal is an eagerness or desire to accomplish or obtain some object. In short, zeal burns passionately within a person, is expressed in much concerted activity, and is directed with great focus toward something beyond the person. May we all be able to describe our own Christian walks toward God in just such a way!

The Enemy of Zeal

There are many enemies of zeal. We are focusing now on the deadliest of all, a condition that can swallow even zeal (quite a task!) if it is allowed to spread.

Lukewarmness is the surest evidence that a person is living more in the flesh than in the Spirit. The indictment against the lukewarmness of the Laodicean church in Revelation 3:16 is this: *"So then because thou art lukewarm, and neither cold nor hot, I will spew thee out of my mouth."*

The following verse explains how the Church in Laodicea reached that deplorable state. An attitude was at the root of the problem, an attitude based on a carnal, materialistic lifestyle. *"Because thou sayest, 'I am rich, and increased with goods, and have need of nothing;' and knowest not that thou art wretched, and miserable, and poor, and blind, and naked . . ."* (Rev. 3:17).

Lukewarmness, then, is indifference, coldness, lack of heat. Spiritually, it consists in placing oneself at the center of the universe; from this position, one has no responsibilities, no desires. Lukewarmness causes:

Spiritual paralysis.
Surrender of the first-love relationship with Christ.
Profession of faith without its substance.
Mediocrity in service to Christ and the Church.
Indifferent, ineffectual prayer.
Complacency and idleness.
Extreme reluctance to sacrifice anything.
Burdenless attitude toward the suffering of others.
Passionless attitude toward all good things.
Neglect of spiritual activities and responsibilities.
Spiritual deception about one's actual status as a believer.

The Focus of Zeal

Throughout Scripture, healthy zeal is most often focused on the house of God. The zeal and fervency of the Spirit was concentrated on God's purpose, which had its apex as the tabernacle in the wilderness, or the temple in Jerusalem. In the New Testament, we are also anointed with this same anointing of zeal for the house of God.

Jesus exemplifies this zeal in John 2:13-17:

"And the Jews' passover was at hand, and Jesus went up to Jerusalem, And found in the temple those that sold oxen and sheep and doves, and the changers of money sitting: And when he had made a scourge of small cords, he drove them all out of the temple, and the sheep, and the oxen; and poured out the changers' money, and overthrew the tables; and said unto them that sold doves, 'Take these things hence; make not my Father's house an house of merchandise.' And his disciples remembered that it was written, 'The zeal of thine house hath eaten me up'."

When Jesus saw the abuse of His Father's house, He became irate. He became hot, his ministry was performed in radical actions, he was so zealous about the house of God that he attacked and cast out anything that threatened it. An Old Testament counterpart to Jesus is the priest Phinehas, who slew an Israelite who was an offense to God and a cause of plague to the people because he had joined himself to a Moabite woman.

(Other important verses about zeal in this context are Isaiah 9:6,7; Romans 10:2; II Corinthians 7:11; Philippians 3:6.)

Zeal in Loving God's House. Numerous verses express the zeal of the Holy Spirit through a focused love of God's house, activities to build and beautify it, and to meet the needs of others through it.

Psalm 26:8	*"Lord, I have loved the habitation of thy house."*
Psalm 132:13-18	*"For the Lord hath chosen Zion; he hath desired it for his habitation. This is my rest for ever: here will I dwell; for I have desired it. I will abundantly bless her provision: I will satisfy her poor with bread. I will also clothe her priests with salvation: and her saints shall shout aloud for joy. There will I make the horn of David to bud: I have ordained a lamp for mine anointed. His enemies will I clothe with shame: but upon himself shall his crown flourish."*

In the New Testament, love of God's house is expressed in loving and beautifying the Bride of Christ, the Church. In II Corinthians 4:7-12, notice the provision for needs and beautification that parallels similar content from the above-quoted passage in Psalm 132.

"But we have this treasure in earthen vessels, that the excellency of the power may be of God, and not of us. We are troubled on every side, yet not distressed; we are perplexed, but not in despair; persecuted, but not forsaken; cast down, but not destroyed; always bearing about in the body the dying of the Lord Jesus, that the life also of Jesus might be made manifest in our body. For we which live are always delivered unto death for Jesus' sake, that the life also of Jesus might be made manifest in our mortal flesh. So then death worketh in us, but life in you."

Another New Testament passage that illustrates the love and beautification of the Bride of Christ is Ephesians 5:25-30.

"Husbands, love your wives, even as Christ also loved the church and gave himself for it; that he might sanctify and cleanse it with the washing of water by the word, that he might present it to himself a glorious church, not having spot, or wrinkle, or any such thing; but that it should be holy and without blemish . . . For no man ever yet hated his own flesh; but nourisheth and cherisheth it, even as the Lord the church: For we are members of his body, of his flesh, and of his bones."

Going to the House of God. Zeal is also expressed often, in the Bible, in the joy of going to the house of God, and the importance of doing so.

Psalm 27:4	*"One thing have I desired of the Lord, that will I seek after; that I may dwell in the house of the Lord all the days of my life, to behold the beauty of the Lord, and to enquire in his temple."*
Psalm 42:4	*"I had gone with the multitude, I went with them to the house of God, with the voice of joy and praise, with a multitude that kept holyday."*
Psalm 55:14	*"We took sweet counsel together, and walked unto the house of God in company."*
Psalm 122:1	*"I was glad when they said unto me, 'Let us go unto the house of the Lord.'"*
Isaiah 2:2,3	*"And it shall come to pass in the last days, that the mountain of the Lord's house shall be established in the top of the mountains, and shall be exalted above the hills; and all nations shall flow unto it. And many people shall go and say, 'Come ye, and let us go up to the mountain of the Lord, to the house of the God of Jacob; and he will teach us of his ways, and we will walk in his paths: for out of Zion shall go forth the law, and the word of the Lord from Jerusalem'."*

Hebrews 10:24,25   *"And let us consider one another to provoke unto love and to good works: Not for-saking the assembling of ourselves together, as the manner of some is; but exhorting one another; and so much the more, as ye see the day approaching."*

Building Up God's House, Not Tearing It Down. True zeal, as produced by the anointing of the Holy Spirit, is more than mere intensity. It is a commitment to doing that which builds the house of God, and to avoiding that which tears down the house of God. In this, true zeal that comes from the anointing of the Holy Spirit embraces wisdom to pursue its goals, even if zeal is not always associated with wisdom.

Proverbs 14:1   *"Every wise woman buildeth her house: but the foolish plucketh it down with her hands."*

Proverbs 24:4   *"Through wisdom is an house builded; and by understanding it is established."*

Psalm 127:1   *"Except the Lord build the house, they labor in vain that build it: except the Lord keep the city, the watchman waketh but in vain."*

In the New Testament, the requirement of zeal to build wisely is expressed in a need to balance intense spirituality with careful attention to appropriate goals.

Corinthians 14:12   *"Even so ye, forasmuch as ye are zealous of spiritual gifts, seek that ye may excel to the edifying of the church."*

As we mentioned in Chapter Seventeen, most of II Corinthians provides instruction on true zeal and spirituality.

Finding Satisfaction in God's House. Zeal produces action that brings satisfaction; your level of commitment will determine your level of satisfaction. (This is expressed in analogy form in the rising waters of Ezekiel 47:2-6). True zeal, that comes from the anointing of the Holy Spirit, functions in a continuous cycle of zeal-action-satisfaction. Revolutionaries and others like them may be able to generate zeal from other sources. But this zeal does not create a complete cycle that perpetuates itself. Thus, only the zeal of the Holy Spirit is an enduring zeal that continues to produce directed effort to a desired goal.

Observe the pursuit of satisfaction evident in these verses that speak directly and indirectly about zeal.

Psalm 36:8   *"They shall be abundantly satisfied with the fatness of thy house; and thou shalt make them drink of the river of thy pleasures."*

Psalm 42:1,2   *"As the hart panteth after the water brooks, so panteth my soul after thee, O God. My soul thirsteth for God, for the living God: when shall I come and appear before God?"*

Psalm 63:1-5   *"O God, thou art my God; early will I seek thee: my soul thirsteth for thee, my flesh longeth for thee in a dry and thirsty land, where no water is; to see thy power and thy glory, so as I have seen thee in the sanctuary. Because thy loving kindness is better than life, my lips shall praise thee. Thus will I bless thee while I live: I will lift up my hands in thy name. My soul shall be satisfied as with marrow and fatness; and my mouth shall praise thee with joyful lips."*

Psalm 87:7   *"All the dwellers of Zion shall say . . . All my springs, my sources of life and joy*
(Amplified Bible)   *. . . are in you, o city of God!"*

Colossians 3:1-3   *"If ye then be risen with Christ, seek those things which are above, where Christ sitteth on the right hand of God. Set your affection on the things above, not on things on the earth. For ye are dead, and your life is hid with Christ in God."*

Being Planted/Rooted in God's House. The true zeal that is produced by the anointing of the

Holy Spirit does not lead to self-destruction. On the contrary, it produces a love of the house of God that leads a person into becoming rooted in God's house. *"Those that be planted in the house of the Lord shall flourish in the courts of our God. They shall still bring forth fruit in old age; they shall be fat and flourishing"* (Psalm 92:13,14).

This verse creates a marvelous picture. Imagine a palm tree, flourishing with growth and life and victory. It is a mature tree, which continually bears fruit, and is full of sap--vigorous and sturdy. The palm tree, with its deep roots and flexible trunk, can withstand storms that bend it literally to the ground.

"For a day in thy courts is better than a thousand. I had rather be a doorkeeper in the house of my God, than to dwell in the tents of wickedness" (Psalm 84:10).

Keeping Unity in God's House. True zeal joins people together in united effort, in mind, in purpose, in sacrifices. Because it comes by the anointing of the Holy Spirit, it includes (as a person matures) the willingness to re-assess personal goals, desires and "needs" to see if they support the pursuit of the over-riding, shared goal. Psalm 133 describes the fruit of this kind of effort:

> *"Behold, how good and how pleasant it is for brethren to dwell together in unity! It is like the precious ointment upon the head, that ran down upon the beard, even Aaron's beard: that went down to the skirts of his garments; as the dew of Hermon, and as the dew that descended upon the mountains of Zion: for there the Lord commanded the blessing, even life for evermore."*

Unity is compared to the holy anointing oil for preciousness (it is also shown to be an outcome of the Holy Spirit's anointing).

Unity is also compared to the dew. In Palestine, the morning dew is what ensures the survival of all vegetation. Even crops depend heavily on dew; dew alone can sustain a flourishing vineyard. In the hot desert, dew will fall only when no wind is stirring. By analogy, unity can happen only when all parties to a group maintain a peaceful, non-combative approach to solving problems and pursuing goals.

Ephesians 4:1-3, implies that *"endeavoring to keep the unity of the Spirit in the bond of peace"* will play a primary role in helping a believer *"walk worthy of the vocation wherewith ye are called."* Matthew 18:18,19 states that the unity of two Christians in prayer moves God to act.

A brief study of unity in the early Church during its first days reveals constant unity, which plays a primary role in releasing constant growth. In Acts 1:14, the believers were all *"with one accord in prayer"* just before the events of Pentecost, and they were in a single large meeting on the very day (Acts 2:1). They continued *"with one accord"* after Pentecost, and the Church grew daily, and was "having favour with all the people" in Jerusalem. Their unity reached the point of dissolving personal ownership of land, items and money into a corporate pool of resources (Acts 4:32). Signs and wonders were worked by the apostles, and multitudes of men and women joined the Church--all in the context of united public meetings on Solomon's Porch of the Temple.

Zeal and Balance

Because zeal involves intensity and passion, it requires wisdom and maturity to be spiritually zealous without injuring other elements of one's life.

Think of the athlete, who not only trains and competes, but who also has to do many things to protect his physical body from injury and keep a keen mental edge. The athletes who have had the longest, most remarkable careers have learned how to balance their zeal in competition with the other needs in their lives.

A life of zeal has potential problems of which the man and woman of God must be aware.

Burnout (an emotional state)
Worn out (physical deterioration from neglecting the body)
Discouraged (from neglecting recreation and simple joys)
Family/Marital Problems (from neglecting family relationships)
Financial Problems (from failing to develop a healthy career and work life)
Isolation (from neglecting friendships)

Many secular psychology and self-help books contain wisdom on these subjects. Unfortunately, much of the advice in these books comes from an ungodly or a "value neutral" standpoint. The Christian may occasionally find some value in these books. We advise, however, to apply principles from these books only after comparing them with biblical principles. You should first be confident that a principle fits into your own lifestyle of faith and service, and does not violate any scriptural principles.

One encouraging word regarding the process of balancing spiritual zeal with other elements in a person's life: quality time is more valuable, and more needed, than quantity time. "Quality time," however, should not be an excuse for inconsistent or haphazard attempts at balancing one's life. Quality time in any area of life requires commitment, discipline and energy. Making the most of family time, for example, does not happen by "just relaxing" and watching a television show with the kids. Quality family time should involve real personal interaction, without distraction.

Living a lifestyle of zeal for ministry requires zeal in balancing other areas of life, as well.

The Anointing Creates A Servant Spirit

Christ the servant was someone who gave, without taking. What a far cry this is from the kind of self-serving, self-glorying ministry that so many of our Christian "leaders" have developed! If the Church is to rebuild a healthy leadership, she must reject "Hollywood Christianity" and get back to the basics of serving as Christ served. This is especially crucial in these latter days, when the Bible says that the Church will be under great attack, and her work will be accomplished under the most trying circumstances. In these times, the Church must not be led by men or women who "fleece" the sheep, and lead them astray.

Christ the Servant. Christ spoke very clearly on the centrality and necessity of servant-leadership.

Leadership Position   **Required Service**

Matthew 20:28
"The Son of Man came . . . . *not to be ministered unto but to minister and to give his life a ransom for many."*

Matthew 23:11,12
"He that is greatest . . . . *shall be your servant."*
"Who . . . shall exalt himself . . . . *shall be abased."*
"humble himself . . . . *shall be exalted."*

Mark 10:43,44
"Whosoever will be great . . . . *shall be your minister."*
". . . will be the chiefest . . . . *shall be servant of all."*
(a willing slave)

Luke 22:26,27
"*He that is greatest* .... *as the younger.*"
"*He that is chief* .... *as he that doth serve.*"
John 13:1-20
"*Your lord and master* .... *have washed your feet.*"

The Gentile Spirit. In Mark 10:42, Jesus describes the Gentile spirit that afflicts many parts of the Church today. In essence, it is being a Christian and serving with some expectation of repayment. It is being a member of the household of faith for what one can get, rather than for what one wants to give to Christ and His Church.

In this section in Mark (as we discussed in this book's Introduction), the disciples are squabbling over who will be given the highest position once Christ becomes a political ruler and the spoils of success start rolling in. They were entirely mistaken both about the nature of the kingdom of heaven, and about greatness in the kingdom.

Once the issue was defined, Jesus didn't take long to straighten them out. He described the Gentile spirit. "*Ye know that they which are accounted to rule over the Gentiles exercise lordship over them; and their great ones exercise authority upon them.*"

The typical Gentile ruler maintains his high position above his subjects by asserting his authority over them. Only thus can they achieve the height of lordship and greatness available in the world, and that they feel they deserve. This spirit is evident in any unredeemed man who is unable to serve unselfishly, but who must create his ego, his position and his image. Serving others makes him feel too "small," and he can't cope with that. He finds his security and fulfillment from maintaining his position of authority, not from serving.

The Christ-like Spirit. Christ then went on to explain to His disciples how the kingdom of heaven really operates. In effect, it totally overturns the Gentile notion of authority. The Gentile ruler sits atop the apex of a pyramid. The Christian ruler is in that same position, with one overwhelming difference: the pyramid has been inverted, so that the pointed apex is at the base! Rather than indolently sitting atop the labors of others, the Christian leader is beneath others in a supporting role, to do all he can to help them realize their full ministry fruitfulness.

Greatness in the kingdom of heaven, then, is measured by readiness and amount of blessed sacrificial service to the people of God. Whether the Christian leader is rewarded and exalted by the people for this service makes no difference. Christ came to serve without position, to give without thought of repayment. It could have been no other way. Christ knew He would have to take the lowliest position to reach the lowliest people, and that His work could never be repaid.

Definition of Serving/Giving

Hebrew Meanings. The Old Testament uses the Hebrew word "abad" to signify intensive labor to serve another, to perform tasks according to his will and direction. By extension, it means the performance of a joyful service to the Lord.

The book of Isaiah devotes much time to messianic prophecies that describe the activities of Christ the servant, Who:

42:1-9	Walks humbly among the bruised and worthless.
49:1-16	Has been shaped by God for a destiny.
50:4-10	Is obedient, to the point of suffering.
52:13	Will be exalted through His death and suffering.
53	Will undergo spite and rejection as a sacrificial offering.

An ideal servant desires to serve and please God with a humble stance before others. He or she is committed to helping others, and is willing to pay the price in personal suffering to do this, knowing how to draw strength to continue from God alone, Who promises to uphold the servant.

New Testament Greek Meanings. The Greek word "diakoneo" connotes a slave who gives his life for others, either figuratively in service to even the smallest need of another, or literally, as for example someone manning the oars in a galley who might be worked to death.

In Greek thought, this type of service was shameful. The first duty of the Greek citizen was to himself, to achieve his full potential for excellence (do any of those words sound familiar in today's culture?). To be forced to subject his will to another, or to surrender his time and efforts for others, was intensely distasteful and humiliating to a Greek.

The New Testament drives home Christ's message of service by using these very words for service, that are so distasteful to the Greeks, as the standard of Christian service. Jesus Himself set the pattern for a transformed value system. In Christ, serving is the highway to greatness. We achieve our full potential by giving to Christ and His Church, not by grasping!

A love-slave was someone who had chosen a lifetime of service to another person, not out of obligation, but out of desire to continue to serve. The love-slave had a hole punched through the ear lobe as a mark of his status. The apostle Paul described himself in most of his epistles as a love-slave or bond-servant of Christ.

In Christ the servant/giver, we see the ultimate servanthood of someone who surrendered His life for our sakes, in a free and uncoerced choice, placing our good above His own. As our ransom, Christ voluntarily, totally and sacrificially gave everything necessary to release the slaves of sin. Christ illustrated His teachings for us with His own life. He proved that greatness is not a goal to be sought, but a by-product of learning to serve others. To achieve true greatness, we must first discard our own ideas of what it is.

Obstacles to True Serving

Confusing Man's Ways With God's Ways. The Bible clearly teaches us that learning how to serve God and the Church will require us to overcome the natural man's instincts. It tells us that we must plan to die, as a grain of wheat dies before it can bear fruit in the ground (John 12:24,25). It tells us that God's thoughts and His ways are too high for us to understand naturally (Isaiah 55:10,11). It tells us that we must resist conformity to the world, and seek God's transformation in the very way we think, if we are to serve God as He deserves (Romans 12:1,2). The chart below illustrates the conflicts between the natural man and the spiritual man when it comes to service.

MAN'S WAY TO GREATNESS	GOD'S WAY TO GREATNESS
Focus on power	Focus on submission
Emphasize freedom	Emphasize responsibility
Concern for gain	Concern for giving
Desire immediate fulfillment	Desire lasting achievement
Yearn for the praise of men	Yearn for the approval of God
Aspire to be served	Aspire to serve others
Long for self-gratification	Long for self-control
Need to push ahead	Need for patience
Strive to lead men	Strive to follow God
Desire to compete	Desire to cooperate

Self-Centered Living. "*Let nothing be done through strife or vainglory; but in lowliness of mind let each esteem other better than themselves. Look not every man on his own things, but every man also on the things of others"* (Philippians 2:3,4). Another translation uses the words "stop acting from motives of selfish strife or petty ambition."

How foreign that sounds to the "Me Generation"! Some of the most popular wisdom in our culture today: feather your own nest, and take care of number one. Advertising has latched onto this spirit with a vengeance. You are told you can "Have it your way," that you should "Do yourself a favor," that "You owe it to yourself," that "You deserve a break today" and that you should "Please yourself."

This is actually nothing new, however, as this list of strong cultural influences from different cultures shows us.

CULTURE	STATEMENT
Greece	Be wise, know yourself
Rome	Be strong, discipline yourself
Epicureanism	Be sensuous, enjoy yourself
Education	Be resourceful, expand yourself
Psychology	Be confident, assert yourself
Materialism	Be satisfied, please yourself
Humanism	Be capable, believe in yourself

But Jesus came with a totally different agenda. Jesus said, *"Be a servant, give yourself and deny yourself."* True Christianity has never been popular, though true Christians have occasionally enjoyed public favor. (This usually does not last for long, however.)

The New Testament in thirteen places uses the Greek word for deny, "aparneomai." This word has the meaning of denying utterly, to the point of disowning, abstaining from, renouncing.

Jesus said, *"If any man will come after me, let him deny himself, and take up his cross, and follow me"* (Matthew 16:24). He refers to the death of our own will, that we may serve God's will. This is a death to self. We are also told that *"ye are dead, and your life is hid with Christ in God"* (Colossians 3:3). And *"ye are not your own . . . ye are bought with a price"* (I Corinthians 6:19,20).

Clearly, the way of Christian service runs totally contrary to the way of the "freedom" that modern Western culture espouses. True Christian service is not only undesirable, but actually impossible to the "Me Generation." True service requires a strong self-image and real self-knowledge, both of which are generally lacking. When Jesus washed His disciples' feet after their last Passover feast (John 13:1-16), He showed them how resolutely they would have to strive to overcome self-centeredness to become true servants.

"Quick Fix" Mentality. The phrase "the American way" has gradually come to include some not-so-positive meanings. It sometimes means a short-sighted desire for immediate results, that leads to using the quickest, cheapest, easiest way to accomplish anything. American manufacturing is legendary for being unable or unwilling to invest to maintain an edge in product quality. It has therefore lost huge portions of the lucrative American marketplace to foreign competitors.

This "quick fix" attitude is even more harmful in the spiritual warfare between the Church and Satan, because the outcome of this warfare is eternal. Christ told the disciples that He came to serve, and that in His service He would pay the ultimate price of giving his life as *"a ransom for many"* (Mark 10:45).

The principle of sacrifice has always been God's way, but never man's. In its very nature, sacrifice causes the flesh to recoil instinctively in fearful attempts at self-preservation. Sacrifice involves paying the high cost of surrendering, destroying or suffering the loss of something precious in order to obtain something of greater importance.

Sacrifice in Salvation History. Salvation history is based on sacrifice. The chart below shows a shortened outline of key points in salvation history, revealing a striking focus on sacrifice.

LOCATION	SACRIFICE
Mt. Moriah	God commands Abraham to sacrifice his son Isaac, who was to be the vessel for the fulfillment of all of God's promises to Abraham. The angel of the Lord called to Abraham out of heaven to prevent the sacrifice, and God provided a ram for sacrifice, only after Abraham's heart was given the ultimate test of faith (Genesis 22).
Mt. Moriah	David builds an altar and makes an offering to God to turn back the angel of death. He will not accept the offer of Araunah the Jebusite to use his oxen and yoke for free, but pays full price for all. "Neither will I offer burnt offerings unto the Lord my God of that which cost me nothing," David said (II Samuel 24:18-25).
Mt. Moriah	Solomon builds the Temple of Jerusalem on Mount Moriah, the same site which his father David bought for making a sacrifice to God. This site becomes the one place where Israel is commanded to offer sacrifices to God, the one place of God's holiest presence in Israel, and the place to which all of Israel turns their faces in captivity when seeking God to forgive their sins and return them to their ancestral possession (II Chronicles 5,6).
Golgotha	Christ, the only begotten son of God, is crucified on a hill very near Mount Moriah, as a sacrifice to turn away the wrath of God from the sins of all mankind. Throughout the events of the crucifixion, it becomes apparent in the fulfillment of many prophecies that Christ's sacrifice is the central focus of all God's workings through history.
Spiritual Golgotha	Christians are commanded to "present your bodies a living sacrifice" as our reasonable service of worship and obedience to God. In practical terms, this means that whenever my will conflicts with the will of God, my will must be crucified (Romans 12:1,2).

Conclusion

Christ set a clear pattern for all to follow, for receiving the anointing of the Holy Spirit. He was anointed to serve as a slave, to the point of death. We are to die to self if we are to serve, to make the needed sacrifices required for functioning under the anointing of the Holy Spirit.

Christ's priority was and is people. He lived to serve people, not to serve and build His own position. His ministry and His purpose was totally focused on obedience to God and service to people. The Scribes and Pharisees criticized His people-centered ministry for eating with sinners, failure to fast in an obvious way, traveling on the Sabbath and healing on the Sabbath.

Christ paid the price to serve. He sacrificed daily, without complaint over the personal price and inconvenience. He paid the final, ultimate price of His life to complete His ministry. Like Christ, we must learn sacrificial living. We must break free from serving ourselves and living in the middle of a self-centered universe. We must push forward into God-centered living.

This is the calling of every believer. It will be accomplished only through the anointing of the Holy Spirit. And it is the only thing that can restore Church leadership to the true authority it must have to lead the Church in her assault on the gates of hell.

CHAPTER 21
NEW TESTAMENT WARNINGS

The New Testament is very specific about the things that Christians (especially Christian leaders) should beware of and take heed to that they might succeed in their lives and ministries. The following is a list of these major admonitions in the New Testament. Every leader should use them as guidelines in his own life and ministry. Each of these points represents a significant area in which a leader can digress from the will of God.

Ostentatiousness	*"Take heed that ye do not your alms before men, to be seen of them"* (Matthew 6:1).
Legalism	*"Take heed and beware of the leaven* (doctrine, Matthew 16:12) *of the Pharisees and of the Sadducees"* (Matthew 16:6; Mark 8:15).
A Child-Rejecting Spirit	*"Take heed that ye despise not one of these little"* (Matthew 18:10).
Being Deceived By Men	*"Take heed that no man deceive you"* (Matthew 7:15 and 24:4; Mark 13:5; Luke 21:8).
Not Hearing God's Word	*"Take heed what ye hear"* (Mark 4:24).
Personal Sloppiness	*"Take heed to yourselves"* (Mark 13:9; Luke 17:3; Acts 20:28; I Timothy 4:16).
Hearing the Word Incorrectly	*"Take heed, therefore, how ye hear"* (Luke 8:18).
One's Light Turning To Darkness	*"Take heed, therefore, that the light which is in thee be not darkness"* (Luke 11:35).
A Covetous Spirit	*"Take heed . . . beware of covetousness"* (Luke 12:15).
Overwhelmed Spirit	*"And take heed to yourselves, lest at any time your hearts be overcharged with surfeiting, and drunkenness and the cares of this life, and so that day come upon you unawares"* (Luke 21:34).
Overlooking the Flock	*"Take heed therefore unto . . . all the flock over the which the Holy Ghost hath made you overseers, to feed the church of God"* (Acts 20:28).
Presuming upon God's Grace	*"For if God spared not the natural branches, take heed lest he also spare not thee"* (Romans 11:21).

Building One's Life Improperly	*"But let every man take heed how he buildeth thereupon"* (I Corinthians 3:10).
Stumbling Another Through One's Freedom	*"But take heed lest by any means this liberty of yours become a stumblingblock to them that are weak"* (I Corinthians 8:9).
Thinking That One Could Never Fall	*"Wherefore let him that thinketh he standeth take heed lest he fall"* (I Corinthians 10:12).
Devouring One Another	*"But, if ye bite and devour one another, take heed that ye be not consumed one of another"* (Galatians 5:15).
Not Fulfilling One's Ministry	*"Take heed to the ministry which thou hast received in the Lord, that thou fulfill it"* (Colossians 4:17).
Listening to Worthless Things	*"Neither give heed to fables and endless geneologies which minister questions, rather than godly edifying which is in faith"* (I Timothy 1:4; Titus 1:14).
Listening to Seducing Spirits and Doctrines	*"In the latter times, men shall depart from the faith, giving heed to seducing spirits and doctrines of devils"* (I Timothy 4:1).
Forsaking Christian Doctrine	*"Take heed unto thyself, and unto thy doctrine; continue in them: for in doing this, thou shalt save both thyself and them that hear thee"* (I Timothy 4:16).
Letting Slip What We Have Learned in Christ	*"Therefore we ought to give the more earnest heed to the things which we have heard, lest at any time we should let them slip"* (Hebrews 2:1).
Having an Evil Heart of Unbelief	*"Take heed . . . lest there be in any of you an evil heart of unbelief, in departing from the living God"* (Hebrews 3:12).
Rejecting Prophecy About Christ	*"We also have a more sure word of prophecy; whereunto ye do well that ye take heed . . . knowing that no prophecy of the scripture is of any private interpretation. For the prophecy came not in old time by the will of man: but holy men of God spake as they were moved by the Holy Ghost"* (II Peter 1:19-21).
Trusting in Pretentiousness	*"Beware of the scribes, which love to go in long clothing . . . and for a pretense make long prayers . . ."* (Mark 12:38,40).
Glorying in the Praise of Men	*"Beware of the scribes which . . . love salutations in the marketplaces, and chief seats in the synagogues, and the uppermost rooms at feasts"* (Mark 12:38,39).
Following Ceremony Rather Than Christ	*"Beware of dogs, beware of evil workers, beware of the concision (false circumcision)"* (Philippians 3:2).
Accepting Vain Philosophies	*"Beware lest any man spoil you through philosophy and vain deceit, after the tradition of men, after the rudiments of the world, and not after Christ"* (Colossians 2:8).
Casting Off Commitment to Christ	*"Ye therefore, beloved, seeing ye know these things before, beware lest ye also, being led away with the error of the wicked, fall from your own steadfastness"* (II Peter 3:17).

Progress and Setbacks in Leadership

Many questions arise along a leader's way to the fulfillment of God's will for his life. A leader may have different questions at different times in his life and ministry. Most men and women of God, however, will be challenged at some point with some of the following questions.

What is my ultimate place in the Church?

How do I find opportunities for ministry?

How do I know that I am being properly prepared?
What do I do when I feel jealous over another's success?
How do I get started in a ministry?
How will my presbytery prophecies be fulfilled?
What role does time play in the development of my ministry?
Why doesn't anyone recognize my ministry?
What must I do to minister successfully?

This chapter will lay some of the scriptural foundations for explaining how ministries can progress or digress in their ultimate calling in God. In doing so, it will answer many of the above questions. Some leaders begin well but fall by the wayside (Samson, Saul and Solomon). Others do not begin as well as they finish. In any case, every leader not only wants to know God's will for his life, but wants to know how to stay dead center in it for all of his years. Church leadership today does too much swerving in and out of the pathway of the Lord. This chapter will point out not only the main pitfalls along the way, but also the positive steps that help a man or a woman of God reach their goal in the Lord. This section focuses on the following diagram:

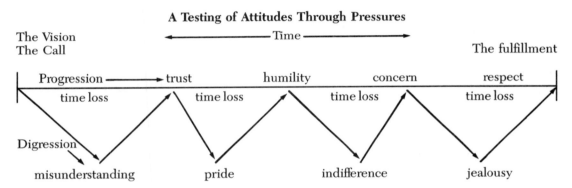

A Testing of Attitudes Through Pressures

The Vision
The Call
←————— Time —————→
The fulfillment

Progression ——→ trust   humility   concern   respect
        time loss   time loss   time loss   time loss

Digression
    misunderstanding   pride   indifference   jealousy

Attitude Testing Through Pressures

The main horizontal line in this diagram represents the time line of a leader's life. To the far left, at the beginning of the diagram, is the point at which a man or woman of God receives a call and vision for the ministry. To the far right, at the end of the chart, is the point at which a leader's call and vision for the ministry is fulfilled. The space between these two points represents the time in which God sovereignly tests a leader's attitudes.

A leader's attitudes (his mental and internal dispositions toward life and the ministry) will help to determine his success or failure in ministry. If a leader cooperates with God in developing godly attitudes in his life, he will succeed. If, however, a leader allows the roots of ungodly attitudes to grow within him, he will fail in performing what God has asked him to do. On the chart, for example, you can see that the attitude of "misunderstanding" has caused the life of this leader to take a digression from the perfect will of God. But when the leader instead allows "trust" to be his inner attitude, his progress continues. The rest of the diagram follows this pattern: "indifference" caused a digression, but "concern" released progress. So it is in the life of every leader. When God convicts a leader of a sinful attitude, his best response is immediate repentence and prayer for cleansing.

Attitudes That Cause Progress or Setbacks

We will now list some of the major causes of ministerial and spiritual digression in a leader's life. The left-hand column lists attitudes that will cause a leader to progress. The right-hand column lists attitudes that will cause a leader to digress.

PROGRESSION

A teachable attitude keeps a leader open to following God's wisdom and understanding (Proverbs 2:1-5).

A patient attitude endures hardship and allows God to accomplish His perfect will through the circumstances.

A forgiving attitude allows a leader to be emotionally free toward every person who hurts him (Matthew 6:14; Mark 11:25; Luke 17:4; Ephesians 4:32).

A blameless character and attitude allows a leader to move forward in the will of God (II Corinthians 3:18).

A single eye prevents a leader from swerving from his goal of serving God in the ministry (Matthew 6:22).

A persistent attitude enables a leader to rise again and again after falling.

A confident attitude toward the ministry of others opens a leader's heart to receive much from others.

A cooperative attitude toward others' ministries opens a leader's heart to receive much from others.

A diligent attitude enables a leader to accomplish twice as much as he thought he could in the first place.

A loving attitude grants a leader to be free from selfish frustration, as he gives himself freely to helping others.

A healing and forgiving attitude allows a leader to forgive and forget the past failures of himself and others.

An understanding attitude allows a leader to see God's eternal purposes in everything that happens to him in life.

A trusting, submissive attitude permits a leader to benefit from other leaders' counsel as he yields to their wisdom.

DIGRESSION

A hardened attitude in a leader prevents him from feeling the conviction of the Holy Spirit. Being too rigid and unyielding stops a leader's growth (Mark 8:17).

An impatient attitude causes a leader to make unreasonable demands on God in a selfish way.

A critical attitude puts a leader into such a bondage of negativism and unbelief that a root of bitterness can easily be developed.

A defective character or attitude eventually causes a leader to stumble and fall.

A double-minded leader will be unstable in all his ways and not able to lead the people clearly.

A discouraged attitude causes a leader to think, self-centeredly, that he is the only one in the kingdom suffering such terrible problems.

A doubtful attitude about a leader's call and place in the kingdom leads him to think that everyone else can do his task better than he can.

A competitive attitude toward others' ministries closes a leader's heart from receiving anything from them.

A slothful attitude makes a leader waste a lot of the precious time that God has given to him as a steward.

An unloving attitude permits a leader's life to close in around him and makes him bitter, angry, selfish and frustrated.

A recollecting attitude puts a leader in bondage by constantly bringing to his mind his past failures as well as others.

A non-discerning attitude leads a man of God to inaccurate interpretations of the facts of his life.

An over-confident attitude will isolate a ministry from his brethren and may cause him to fall into error with few counselors to help him (Proverbs 15:22).

A patient attitude in a leader enables him to rest in the Lord, since he chooses not to try to force God to move on his behalf.

A disciplined attitude in the study, prayer and scheduling habits of a leader allows him to produce much fruit for the kingdom.

A positive attitude causes a leader to look for the good in other people and spiritually revolutionizes all of his attitudes toward people.

A faithful attitude enables a leader to be loyal to God and others, even in the face of adversity. God will reward!

A transparent attitude enables a leader to rid his life of bad habits (such as backbiting, procrastination, tardiness, etc.), enabling a man of God to grow consistently in his spiritual walk.

A sensitive attitude enables a leader to discern the true feelings of those around him, giving him more effectiveness in ministering to the needs of others.

A concerned attitude equips the leader to pay close attention to whatever happens around him, causing people to respond to him more genuinely and more frequently.

A humble attitude, with a realistic and modest sense of one's own abilities and importance, enables a leader to hear from the Lord (Matthew 5:5; Philippians 2:3; I Peter 5:6).

A realistic attitude senses when a goal is possible and practical, balancing out the idealism of many leaders' visions.

A spiritual attitude, which causes a leader to keep growing in his personal relationship with the Lord, also enables him to broaden and deepen his ministry because he has something worth sharing from his own life.

A friendly attitude takes the initiative to meet new people and make new friends, and opens others' hearts to such a leader.

A respectful attitude desires to follow the good example of godly people, and raises people's esteem for a leader; they see that he does not think he is perfect in himself.

A believing attitude trusts the Lord, His Word and His work to be right. This enables a leader to go from one level of faith to a deeper one, since God responds to him as he shows faith in God.

An impatient attitude in a leader makes him blind to the value of time delays and causes him to miss valuable insights that God has for him during such times.

An undisciplined attitude leads a man of God to waste his time, money and energy on less valuable activities.

A negative, critical attitude causes a leader to look for the bad in other people, binding his spirit so the Love of God cannot flow through him.

An inconsistent attitude causes a leader to quit when things get rough, and spreads in every area of his life until he is no longer a dependable person even in the less important areas of life.

A covert attitude permits a leader to hide all of his bad habits with self-justifications, thus not allowing him to consistently mature in the Lord.

An insensitive attitude causes a leader to be aware of only his own thoughts and feelings, and not those of others. This decreases his effectiveness in ministering to the needs of others.

An indifferent attitude causes a leader to be uncaring about people or work, and short-circuits his effectiveness in ministry.

A proud attitude of overestimating his own abilities and importance closes a leader off from hearing the Lord's voice, and others will not listen to him (Proverbs 6:16,17 and 8:13).

An unrealistic attitude centers on things that are not truthfully realizable, causing a leader to be constantly frustrated because he never makes progress on his goals.

A non-spiritual attitude, satisfied with one's present relationship with the Lord, lessens a leader's ability to reach others because he demonstrates no depth in his own spiritual experience with the Lord.

An unfriendly attitude, which does not care about anyone else except itself and its own clique of friends, closes peoples' hearts to such a leader.

A disrespectful attitude does not value the attitudes or lifestyle of any other leader, and isolates a person from others because he thinks that he has sufficient character in himself.

An unbelieving attitude with no confidence in God, His Word or His work degenerates a leader's faith so that he may actually see himself digressing.

A non-comparing attitude accepts oneself and others as they presently are in God, and frees a leader from envy, jealousy and resentment because he does not lust after someone else's lot.

A meek attitude recognizes the extent and limitations of one's own ministry and gifts, enabling a leader to know his need for other brethren because he does not think that he is a "one-man-band" ministry.

A sonship attitude openly recognizes a leader's occasional need for correction by God, and keeps a leader in an open and free relationship with his heavenly Father (Hebrews 12:1-13).

A visionary attitude sees by faith beyond the present circumstances to the good that God will accomplish in the future, keeping a leader following the Lord with a strong faith.

An open attitude realizes one's need for counsel from the brethren, increases a leader's wisdom and understanding because he is making himself available to learn from others.

A trainable attitude sees the need of relating to mature people in the ministry, and broadens a leader's perspective on people and ministry.

An organized attitude properly schedules one's time, increasing a leader's time for serving the Lord.

A balanced attitude, recognizing the proper place of the various activities which God has given a leader to do, enables him to lead a happy and fulfilled life.

A listening attitude hears what people are saying, and also what they are not and cannot say, enabling a leader to counsel more effectively to people who have deep wounds.

A restrained attitude allows a leader to speak in wisdom, propriety and edification, earning respect for the man of God who controls his tongue (James 3:1,2; I Timothy 3:8; Matthew 20:25,26; Philippians 1:15).

An objective attitude puts the clear standards of the Word of God above a leader's personal feelings, causing a person to live an upright life and set a good example for others to follow (Genesis 22:1-13; Psalm 32:8).

A sober attitude recognizes the difference between healthy humor and jesting, and causes a leader to know how to properly relate to people on

A comparing attitude sizes up what one leader has or does with that of another. This leads a man of God into envy and bitterness, because he is never content with what he has and never thanks God for what He has given to another.

A presumptuous attitude does not recognize weakness or limits to one's abilities in God, and isolates a leader from his brethren because he believes that God has given him everything.

A non-sonship attitude makes a leader refuse to accept correction from anyone because he is a leader, closing off his relationship to God as his father.

A non-visionary attitude takes on the feelings of a fatalist: "What will be, will be," and decreases a leader's ability to see beyond the present to what God wants to do in the Church in the future.

A closed attitude thinks that one does not need anyone else's counsel, and decreases a leader's wisdom and understanding, because he is not trying to learn from others.

An untrainable attitude feels that a leader does not need to be linked with older ministries, and cuts him off from valuable insights.

A disorganized attitude puts no framework on the use of time, and wastes many opportunities to help people and serve the Lord.

An imbalanced attitude does not prioritize a leader's responsibilities, causing him to be frustrated and unfulfilled by not allowing God to develop him in a well-rounded way: spirit, mind, emotions and body.

A deaf attitude does not take the time to listen to anyone's problems or joys, cutting a leader's effectiveness in ministry to others, because others do not feel he is genuinely interested in them.

An unrestrained attitude, which permits a leader to say anything he wants to say at any time, decreases the people's respect for him and his counsel (Ecclesiastes 5:3).

A subjective attitude places a leader's personal whims above the mandates of the Word of God, causing a man of God to fall into unbiblical behavior (Numbers 22:9-20).

A jesting attitude, a spirit of constant teasing, sarcasm and cynicism toward the character or unchangeable parts of a person's life, causes all levels.

A motivated attitude enables a leader to be a self-starter and initiate spiritual projects, accomplishing good goals for the kingdom.

A resilient attitude withstands the emotional jarring of criticism and disagreement, enabling a leader to stay strong and yet tender before the Lord and people.

A followable attitude in a leader enables people to follow him for different reasons, which allows him to guide them where God wants them to go.

A modest attitude views things in this world only as means to the end of building God's kingdom, enabling a leader to give his life (without a sign of covetousness) to building the kingdom of God.

A discreet attitude govern's a leader's life through scriptural priorities, enabling him to build the kingdom of God, and not the kingdom of this world.

A steady attitude causes a leader to go into things at an even pace, not unwisely or too soon, keeping a leader from making unwise decisions he may later regret.

A conscientious attitude obeys the inner promptings of the Holy Spirit in a leader's life, enabling him to keep a pure conscience before God and man.

A decisive attitude enables a leader to make judgments appropriately without waiting too long, enabling a leader to function as a good administrator over the house of the Lord.

A courageous attitude gives a leader strength when opposition or contradiction hit his life, in enabling a leader to continue a firm faith in God through all circumstances.

A studious attitude causes a leader to meditate and study the Scripture, deepening his ministry of feeding the sheep, teaching, preaching and counseling, because he has a better grasp of God's perspective on life.

A free attitude causes a leader to enter into the presence of God with praise and worship, keeps his spirit free from guilt through confession of

people to lose respect for a leader that has such an attitude.

An unmotivated attitude causes a leader to be lazy and slow in all areas of his life, displeasing God and himself due to his lack of spiritual and natural accomplishments.

An overly-sensitive attitude is hurt and/or shocked by criticism or disagreement. It cripples a leader emotionally, mentally and spiritually because he takes personally everything he hears.

A non-followable attitude in a leader causes people, for different reasons, to be unable to follow a leader, thus crippling his ministry to them.

A vain attitude puts its affection on external things of this life, and trips up a leader in his efforts to walk with God spiritually because it bends him to a spirit of materialism and covetousness.

An indiscreet attitude does not maintain scriptural priorities, causing a leader to digress from the will of God.

A hasty attitude uses no wisdom in serving God, causing a leader many hurt feelings, wrong decisions and regrettable memories.

A neglectful attitude postpones obedience to the inner voice of the Holy Spirit in a leader's life, causing him not to be able to follow the Lord closely, or hear what the Spirit is saying to the Church, because his heart is too cluttered with unconfessed sins.

An indecisive attitude waits too long to make important decisions, putting a leader or a church into bondage and fear of making a mistake, causing a lack of knowledge of the Word of God, a fear of man, and a spirit of perfectionism.

A fearful attitude is a painful feeling of apprehension over a possible danger, preventing a leader from obeying God in all things. This may come from a fear of the future, of failure, of persecution, or of meeting God's standards.

An inattentive attitude prevents a leader from spending time and energy in the Word of God, leading a man of God into shallowness in feeding and directing the flock.

A condemned attitude is an inward feeling of being unable to enter preventing a leader from being free in his spirit to minister to the Lord sin and the cleansing of the blood of Jesus Christ.

An established attitude appears in the leader who knows how his daily life measures up with the Word of God, giving him a solid base upon which to rest when trials and temptations come.

An uncompromising attitude helps a leader know where he stands on basic issues in the Word of God, providing a great strength to the people who follow his leadership.

A sacrificing attitude puts every aspect of a leader's life at the disposal of Jesus Christ, enabling him to be greatly used of God in his ministry, because God's Spirit works through brokenness.

and to others.

An unestablished attitude appears in a leader who does not know his place in Jesus Christ as a Christian, causing him to be unstable about basic doctrine, counsel to others, and in his daily walk with God.

A compromising attitude, unsettled on basic Christian issues, gives a terrible feeling of instability and inferiority to the people of God, because they do not know what to believe or why to believe it.

A hypocritical attitude of not submitting every area of a leader's own life to Jesus Christ, but preaching that others should, eventually leads his ministry into hollowness and ineffectiveness, because the real life of the Holy Spirit is not flowing in and through him.

Conclusion

Every leader can use the chart above to evaluate attitudes in his or her own life that can cause progress or digression in ministry. By allowing the Lord Jesus Christ to develop all of these positive character attitudes in his life, every leader should be equipped to successfully follow God's will for his life, and harvest the fruit thereof.

CHAPTER 22

DISCIPLINE AND RESTORATION OF CHURCH LEADERS AND MEMBERS

In this chapter, we want to examine two areas of corrective discipline. First, we want to discuss the discipline of a sinning church member. Second, we want to handle the very important area of the discipline of a sinning leader.

We live in a time when discipline is both misunderstood and used poorly or not at all. We see this in public schools, the typical home, the rebelliousness of teenagers, and in the Church itself. Lack of discipline has allowed the misuse of grace, love and forgiveness. God is a loving and forgiving God. But these virtues are released only after the Principle of the Cross, which requires repentance from sin. The Principle of Discipline, when applied wisely, will foster repentance and release the true, lasting blessings of God.

Corrective Discipline For Church Members

In its full context, discipline is training that molds, corrects or perfects the moral character of an individual. In this chapter, we are looking at discipline in a more limited context of corrective action taken to remedy a specific problem.

Before we proceed any further in this discussion, it is important to make some general comments about the purpose of this kind of discipline.

No pastor or Christian leader rejoices over the need for corrective discipline. It is a duty which must be performed when other, more positive methods to cause growth and maturity have failed. Most pastors would prefer never to need to discipline any Church member. Wherever the fault may lie, the need for corrective discipline is an indication of failure, not of success. The wise leader enters into a corrective discipline situation with compassion and understanding.

But the wise leader also enters into corrective discipline with firm resolve. While the need for such discipline may be tragic, the outcome is at the heart of every leader's purpose. What leader does not want to see individuals cleansed and restored into a protected, united, healthy church? Especially at times of spiritual disease in the Church, God's leaders can be grateful that this important tool is available. The Bible clearly develops this tool for the use of the wise shepherd-leader.

Reasons for Discipline

Church members may need corrective discipline for any number of reasons. When a member enters into sin in a way that threatens his own spiritual life and those around him, he and the Church must be protected. The Church needs wise and decisive action of its leaders in such a case. In addition, other Church members must understand their own role in the process of corrective discipline and restoration. Areas that may require decisive discipline of Church members are:

Unresolved offenses between members
Habitual moral impurity
Covetousness
Idolatry
Railing
Drunkenness
Extortion
Active, aggressive divisiveness

Failure to Discipline. A church's leadership may fail to discipline a sinning member for any of several reasons. It is good to explore them briefly, to know and understand them in advance. When discipline situations occur, a foreknowledge of the difficulties involved can support the resolve and effectiveness of church leadership. Fear and ignorance are the two primary reasons, expressed in several ways:

FEAR
Fear of the congregation's distaste for the process
Fear of the people developing an emotional identification with the problem
Fear of the church receiving a reputation in the community of being hard or legalistic
Fear of angry, bitter or destructive reactions from those under discipline
Fear of wounding the tender spirits of children and young people
Fear of embarassment and damaged ministry or reputation to the ones under discipline

IGNORANCE
Ignorance of the necessity for discipline
Ignorance of the biblical principles of discipline
Ignorance of the process of discipline

Benefits of Church Discipline

1. It has the potential for bringing about change and growth in the individual's life when nothing else will.

2. It evidences a standard of biblical conviction for living that the Christian is commanded to uphold.

3. It prohibits the leavening influence of sin from gaining a foothold in other members of the congregation.

4. It counteracts the spirit of lawlessness of our age.

5. It underscores the value of righteousness as the basis for all relationships in the Body of Christ.

6. It is part of the responsibility of the oversight of the local church.

7. It may save some other pastor or Christian leader the task of disciplining an even worse case later.

8. It helps the individual member deal with sin in himself that by himself he has been unable to eliminate.

9. It can potentially save a congregation from a church split in some cases.

10. Without church discipline there is no clear standard of right and wrong among the congregation.

11. Without church discipline, sinning members go on sinning, destroying their own potential fruitfulness in God.

12. Without church discipline, others may do outwardly what they have only been tempted to do inwardly, because the lack of discipline implies approval of an activity.

13. Without church discipline, the spiritual life of the Body as a whole becomes greatly weakened. Spiritual vitality and life seep out and a progressive spiritual stagnation sets in.

14. Without church discipline, confidence and respect for the church leadership is lost.

Process of Church Discipline

The New Testament contains very clear injunctions about the need for discipline, and its place in Church life. We will now look at important verses describing the process of church discipline.

Confrontation. We begin with the words of Christ in Matthew 18:15-17:

"Moreover, if thy brother shall trespass against thee, go and tell him his fault between thee and him alone: if he shall hear thee, thou hast gained thy brother. But if he will not hear thee, then take with thee one or two more, that in the mouth of two or three witnesses every word may be established. And if he shall neglect to hear them, tell it unto the church: but if he neglect to hear the church, let him be unto thee as a heathen man and a publican" (Matthew 18:15-17).

Exclusion From Fellowship. Discipline, then, may reach a stage of putting a person out of fellowship with the church. This reached a very strong expression in a case at the church at Corinth which the apostle Paul addressed:

"For I verily, as absent in body but present in spirit, have judged already, as though I were present, concerning him that hath so done this deed, in the name of our Lord Jesus Christ, when ye are gathered together, and my spirit, with the power of our Lord Jesus Christ, to deliver such an one unto Satan for the destruction of the flesh, that the spirit may be saved in the day of the Lord Jesus Christ . . . For what have I to do to judge them also that are without (as non-members)? *But them that are without God judgeth. Therefore put away from among yourselves that wicked person"* (I Corinthians 5:3-5,12,13).

Discipline involves clear judgment, to pronounce an opinion of right or wrong, and to separate the unrepentantly guilty. It is exercised as an internal function of the Church, and does not function in regard to non-Christians or people who are not part of a church fellowship.

Godly Shame and Sorrow. The act of separating a person needing discipline involves a good deal more than not allowing someone into fellowship at church group functions. Individual members are commanded to avoid any association with that person on an individual basis as well. This is intended to produce a certain quality of shame in the individual that may move him to repentance. The quality of this shame is such that a person turns upon himself, with no recourse to any other person, and feels an honest, wholesome shame which motivates him to change his conduct.

"Now we command you, brethren in the name of our Lord Jesus Christ, that ye withdraw yourselves from every brother that walketh disorderly, and not after the tradition which he received of us . . . .

And if any man obey not our word by this epistle, note that man, and have no company with him, that he may be ashamed. Yet count him not as an enemy, but admonish him as a brother." (II Thessalonians 3:6,14,15).

The Greek word for "note" in this passage involves a process where the church uses an act or circumstance which has a clear meaning and message to the person under discipline.

God protects the Church from the spiritual attacks of the enemy. In some cases, an unrepentant sinner may take harbor under the protective covering of the Church, and will not fully reap what he has sown. That is why Paul states in I Timothy 1:20, *"Of whom is Hymenaeus and Alexander; whom I have delivered unto Satan, that they may learn not to blaspheme."* When a person is totally removed from fellowship, he is in Satan's domain without protection. The vicious attacks of Satan may be the only thing that break through a spiritually hardened condition to reactivate a person's conscience.

Sin Beyond Repentance. It is possible for a Christian to fall beyond repentance. The Church cannot recover those who have consigned themselves to hell. *"A man that is an heretic after the first and second admonition reject,"* Paul commands in Titus 3:10. A heretic is a sectarian, one who follows his own preferences in a self-willed way, to undermine the Church. In the last days, also, blasphemers would do harm to the work of God, and must be cast out of fellowship irretrievably (II Timothy 3:2).

Protecting the Church. In very severe cases, then, discipline in the Church ceases to be a matter of restoring an individual's soul, and becomes a function of the Church defending itself against the attacks of the enemy. As in all areas of Church discipline, but especially in this one, Church leadership must act in a decisive and timely manner. Discipline may benefit not only the ones disciplined, but the rest of the church as well: *"Them that sin rebuke before all, that others also may fear"* (I Timothy 5:20).

But when a person refuses to recover from sin, the Church must protect itself:

"Now I beseech you, brethren, mark them which cause divisions and offenses contrary to the doctrine which ye have learned; and avoid them. For they that are such serve not our Lord Jesus Christ, but their own belly; and by good words and fair speeches deceive the hearts of the simple" (Romans 16:17,18).

Confession and Cleansing. The Bible gives us clear guidance on the next step of effective discipline that leads to recovery. In this stage, the guilty party is responsible to confess, and God is faithful to cleanse.

"And it shall be, when he shall be guilty in one of these things, that he shall confess that he hath sinned" (Leviticus 5:5).

Acknowledge and confess (Psalm 35:1-5).

"Confess your faults one to another" (James 5:16).

"If we confess our sins, he is faithful and just to forgive us our sins, and to cleanse us from all righteousness" (I John 1:9).

"But if we walk in the light . . . the blood of Jesus Christ his Son cleanseth us from all sin" (I John 1:7).

"He that covereth his sins shall not prosper; whoso confesseth and forsaketh them shall have mercy" (Proverbs 28:13).

Confession must be directed toward two parties: to God, and to the people who have been injured by a sin (Romans 14:7).

Restoration and Reception. In this stage, the Church has a responsibility to its fallen and cleansed member. In II Corinthians 2:1-11, the apostle Paul is speaking to the church about restoring a previously disciplined person to the fellowship of the Body. The goal of discipline has been achieved--this person has repented of his sin. To receive this person back into fellowship, the Church is told to:

Forgive (II Cor. 2:7). To forgive someone is to remove all condemnation and critical attitudes toward a person, to release from your spirit all wrong feelings.

Console (II Cor. 2:7). Speak encouraging words, lift up the hands that hang down.

Love (II Cor. 2:8). The church is to assure the repentant one of their love, to reaffirm their love for him, to restore him to his full place in their affections. This step is critically important! Especially when someone has just been separated, the devil will try to turn that into a permanent division. The church must aggressively step forward to re-incorporate the person into the Body.

Give Satan No Advantage (II Cor. 2:11). It's time for a cautious double-checking now. The church must make certain that it has definitely and effectively performed the first three steps above, and that no wrong spirits have crept into the process anywhere along the line, among any of the people involved in the process. "We don't want Satan to win any victory here!" is the J.B. Philips translation of part of this verse. Satan will use any number of devices, maneuvers, designs, schemings and wiles. The church is forewarned to not be overcome by evil, but to overcome evil with good.

Results of Church Discipline

In another case of discipline in the early church, we are given a detailed picture of the results. This is the case of Ananias and Sapphira in Acts 5. This couple tried to earn a reputation as benefactors of the Church, while secretly withholding part of what they said they were giving to the Church. By a word of knowledge, the apostle Peter uncovered the lie of Ananias. Confronted by Peter, Ananias died on the spot. Soon after, Peter also questioned Sapphira, and she also perished instantly, apparently by the direct moving of the Holy Spirit.

The result of this supernaturally directed process of discipline in the early Church was tremendous:

"Great fear came upon the church" (Acts 5:11).
Power for the performance of other supernatural signs and wonders was also released (5:12).
The Church was united (5:12).
People saw the power in the Church and respected and feared it (5:13).
Multitudes of new believers were added to the Church (5:14).

Corrective Discipline of Church Leaders

One of the most important areas in which corrective discipline protects and heals the Church is when a moral breakdown occurs in Church leadership. The following outline of Scripture policy concerning discipline of Church leaders is derived from I Timothy 3:1-7 and 5:17-25, and Titus 1:5-9. We are not addressing divorce or remarriage, but dealing specifically with immorality which defiles the sanctity of the marriage bed. This is probably the most serious failure which destroys ministries in the Church today. When handled properly, however, redemptive restoration can be achieved, ministries can be resurrected, and the Church can move forward in health.

Effects of Moral Breakdown in a Leader's Life and Ministry

Marital infidelity affects a person, and more especially the ministry, in the following areas of life:

Morally. A minister disqualifies himself from ministry through a moral breakdown. A wife can also disqualify her husband from ministry by immoral conduct.

Domestically. If an elder or a ministry does not have his own house in order, he cannot rule the house of God. This order and rule involves all family relationships. The husband-wife relationship, especially, must be rebuilt and restored for family healing to take place.

Mentally and Emotionally. Damage to relationships and the torment of guilt involve deep mental and emotional wounds that can be healed only through God's working. Cooperating with God's healing requires genuine repentance, confession, and reception of cleansing and renewal. Rationalizations for sin cannot be justified or tolerated. They make healing impossible, and open the leader to even greater deception and sin.

Ethically. Any leader who fails morally should step down from public ministry for a period of time. This is an important visible return to scriptural ethics which aids in the healing process. The time period of this removal from ministry should allow fulfillment of discipline, including healing to all parties involved.

Spiritually. Moral breakdowns especially wreak damage and devastation on a public ministry where the leader is in public view and is held up as an example of godly lifestyle. Spiritual restoration must be sought for the good of all individuals concerned.

Ecclesiastically. Proper and scriptural discipline must be upheld because the ministry, which functions before the "Ecclesia," has a very great area of influence. None of us live to ourselves, we all affect others, and this is most true of Christian leaders. If we fail to uphold scriptural discipline, we set precedents for many other moral breakdowns, and the suffering of the Church is magnified. The leader who sins, whether elder or governmental minister, should be openly rebuked before all so that others may fear. Such failings generally become church (or public) knowledge, and must be dealt with scripturally and decisively. This will cause gossiping and imaginations to cease.

Guidelines for Corrective Discipline of Leaders

Because every circumstance and every individual involved is different from case to case, we do not propose detailed disciplinary measures. Nor does the Bible. Scripture does present some practical, general guidelines, however. Note that the process below must not be pursued in a legalistic or pharisaical, "holier-than-thou" spirit or attitude. When God forgives, He truly forgives. When God restores, He truly restores. The goal of the Church throughout this process is to restore the fallen leader in a *"spirit of meekness, considering thyself, lest thou also be tempted"* (Galatians 6:1).

Confession and Repentance. First, the guilty party must genuinely repent and confess. He or she must make this confession to all appropriate parties, based on whom the sin affected, and the level of private or public knowledge of the sin.

Forgiveness. Second, after true repentance, all parties involved must offer forgiveness. This will involve all people directly affected by the sin, but may also involve people who suffer reproach as a result of the sin--the Lord Himself, family, other church leadership, and the church at large.

Probation. Third, the forgiven party should step down from public ministry. A period of probation should be instituted, for 6-12 months, allowing time for "rebuilding the walls" broken down through immorality in the various areas mentioned just above. This is a time to clear away the damage; truly rebuilding the marriage relationship takes more time than this. God's order of healing is: forgiveness, probation and restoration.

Counseling. Fourth, the leader on probation should have an effective, ongoing counseling relationship with a counselor who can minister redemption in a restorative manner.

Restoration. Fifth, the ministry shall be restored to leadership after a suitable period of probation has given evidence of a sound restoration process. Church leaders must understand, however, that there are times when a sinning leader cannot be restored to a ministry office. Causes for this may be the number of failures, or the depth of deception involved. Wherever genuine repentance occurs, restoration of the individual is always biblical--but this does not always mean restoration of the individual's ministry. This is an area which requires great sensitivity and discernment of a church leader.

Pastoral Correction: Example Letter

Rather than dwell at length on hypothetical situations, we find it more useful to present a pastoral letter to a fallen leader in the midst of correction. We present it with only the most minor changes, to protect privacy. We hope this letter both instructs you, and encourages you that although the process of discipline may be painful, it is worth pursuing wisely and well. It offers hope to the Church at times when no other process can.

At the time of this letter, the elder who had fallen into immorality was not fully responding to biblical rebuke. For that reason, this letter is very forceful. It is not an example of a first communication with an elder who has just been found in sin. Your own personal variation on this letter should be used with much prayer and wisdom.

Dear Elder:

With respect to your letter to me, I would like to (also representing the church eldership) address the same, with some important issues.

1. First of all, it seems that the whole seriousness and heinousness of your sins has not smitten you as yet. You know it so much in your head, but need to acknowledge it within your heart, deeply.

It is not enough to simply say "If I have hurt" someone, meaning your wife, children and others. The Bible is specific that sins needs to be confessed specifically.

"And it shall be, when he shall be guilty on one of these things, that he shall CONFESS THAT HE HAS SINNED IN THAT THING" (Leviticus 5:5).

"If we CONFESS OUR SINS, He is faithful and just to forgive us our sins and to cleanse us from all unrighteousness" (I John 1:9).

As we drew your attention in the first of our talks together, you have, over the months, "added sin to sin" (Isaiah 30:1).

To be more specific:

*DECEPTION for months of yourself, your wife, another man's wife and her husband, your children, the staff, the eldership, the church. And also to the the young marrieds of the church, while you were living in sin.

*LYING--numerous lies to people.

*PRIDE instead of a spirit of humility.

*HYPOCRISY of the worst sort. You taught the course on the Timothy elective--with all the epistle says on godliness, holiness, sound doctrine, qualifications for eldership--you wore the outward mask and stage-play, while within, you were full of hypocrisy and iniquity (Matthew 23:25-28).

*ADULTERY (evil thoughts, lusts, adultery with another man's wife in thought, word and deed, defiling the marriage bed, and violating your vows and marriage covenant. Scriptural grounds for divorce, to say the least, unless the grace of forgiveness abounds in the other partner).

Out of the heart, which is deceitful above all things, and desperately wicked, proceed all these things (Jeremiah 7, with Mark 7:21-23). You don't seem to understand, as God does, the deceitfulness of the human heart.

*SINFUL SELFISHNESS in all its evil forms. Taking what you could get out of this situation, meeting your own needs, lust mistaken for love, rationalizations ("Good friendship that went wrong"). Perhaps it was a "good friendship gone wrong" in the beginning, and you never intended it to go the way of sin.

However, it seems all the more as circumstances unfold that you were the chief initiator and deceiver.

2. We also mentioned the "stone in the water" principle, that none of us live to ourselves. When we sin, and more especially in the moral areas, we drop the stone of sin into the water of life and it spreads its concentric circles out far and wide, in ever-increasing circles of effect. Your sin has cast concentric circles of sin which have widened out into violating practically all of the ten commandments:

*Sin against God, violating His commandments and bringing reproach upon His Name (adultery, lying, stealing, coveting, etc. Exodus 20:14-17; Matthew 5:27-30; Psalm 51).
*Sin against your own body by adultery (principle of I Corinthians 6:18-20).
*Sin against your own covenant wife and the marriage bed and covenant, and also against another woman's husband.
*Sin against your own children.
*Sin against your parents.
*Sin against the honored position and authority of eldership, as administrator, treasurer, elder and teacher of a Sunday School elective. Yet you sat through the teaching series on "Lusts," and other tapes.
*Sin against the church members to whom you made verbal commitments, and thus destroying years of confidence and trust, and violated the eldership.

You have received ample warning. You were warned by the person with whom you sinned, by the oversight committee, by Jane and myself. I asked you not to see the person on this over-familiar basis for 3 months. I warned you about passing notes in the orchestra, about over-familiarity in the playroom, and other problems.
   And you accepted the staff position, yet knowing your sinful lifestyle.

3. It has been brought to our attention that you planned to elope together. Walking out in an adulterous relationship, leaving your wife and children and home. Yet you maintained you "loved them." Love does not seek to elope with another man's wife, and walk out on your own wife and children, leaving them desolate. Any other rationalization is self-deception.

4. We asked you to listen to last Sunday's tape, which was intended partly for your help, together with your family. We understood you did not do this. I want you to listen to that tape. It seems to me that you have missed the whole message and purpose on that tape, and sought in your letter to justify your particular guilt. You missed the whole principle that is in that message, instead of letting God speak to you through it. You need to listen to this tape, accept its message in humility, and not attempt to justify your own circumstances.

5. You talk about being "angry" or "hurt." We wish you would get angry with your sins, and not get angry with your wife, the children, John, myself, the eldership, the church, or anyone else.
   YOU are the one who has sinned! Don't get angry with us and play the "guilt-and-blame-game."
   You talk about your "hurts." What about the hurts of hundreds of people you have hurt?
   You ask "Why?" We ask you "Why?" WHY didn't you think of all this over the last months, when you have been given a chance to repent?

6. You say in your letter that you should be "dealt with as any other sinner," and that you are "excommunicated" almost.
   It is evident you do not understand the real issue on these things. Let me spell them out for you.
   Paul states it clearly in I Corinthians 5:9-13 that if *"any be called a brother"* and is involved in immoral areas, with such a one not to keep company, and not to eat.
   John says, *"If we walk in the light as He is in the light, we have fellowship one with another, and the blood of Jesus Christ, His son, cleanses from all sin."* The converse is also true. If we don't walk in the light as He is in the light, we don't have fellowship with one another, and the blood doesn't cleanse from sin.
   You have been walking in immoral darkness, fellowship has been broken all round, and the blood has not cleansed you from sin (I John 1:7).
   The truth continues on, *"If we confess our sins, He is faithful and just to forgive us our sins, and to*

cleanse us from all unrighteousness" (I John 1:9).

It is in that order: confession, forgiveness and cleansing.

Jesus said, REPENTANCE and REMISSION of sins is to be preached. It is in that order. There is no forgiveness without repentance. God has forgiveness available for all mankind--but on His terms--repentance, both from root sin and fruit thereof (Luke 24:47).

You have been in the high position and authority of an elder. "To whom much is given, the more will be required." Greater light, greater responsibility, greater judgment. That is why you are being dealt with "not as any other sinner."

"Against an elder receive not an accusation, but in the mouth of two or three witnesses . . . those elders that sin REBUKE BEFORE ALL that others may fear" (I Timothy 5:17-20). This is the biblical discipline for an elder!

7. You may believe the "discipline" you are under is legalistic, hard, etc. It is not.

"Marriage is honorable in all, and the bed undefiled, but whoremongers and adulterers, GOD WILL JUDGE" (Hebrews 13:4).

Note the list of those who find their place in the lake of fire, if unrepentant, in Revelations 21:8 and 22:14,15.

The one who commits adultery lacks understanding, moral principle and prudence. He destroys his own life. He is not innocent. This is *"a wound, dishonour and reproach that shall not be wiped away"* (Proverbs 6:24-35).

In your case, you have so far experienced only that part of Divine punishment which is self-inflicted. The "discipline" you are under is nothing compared to full Divine discipline from God.

It can be easy for you, as so many have done, to be under discipline and disfellowshipped in your home church, and then run off to another church for "fellowship." It could not be done in Corinth! But this is the poblem today of a divided church!

8. No one at this church ever told you that "counseling is for the birds, anyway." Counseling can be a trap if people want only to counsel, and not take action to amend their lives. Obviously we are not against counseling because we developed a counseling course and a teaching series on counseling. But if it is counseling only for the sake of talk without action, and degenerates into a "guilt-and-blame-game," then it is a snare and a trap, and I refuse to support it.

You talk about suicide, which is self-murder, which would send you to hell. Where does love for your wife and children fit into such selfish statements?

FINALLY, you ask what we expect you to do for restoration to the house of the Lord.
1. Experience the reality of genuine repentance, root and fruit. Seek for Holy Spirit conviction, from the pattern of II Samuel 11-12 and Psalm 51.
2. Bring forth fruit of repentence (as spelled out in the lesson on basic principles of the New Testament Church, from a teaching series which you know so well).
3. Experience deep humility of the heart, and shame for the evils of the past--not just acting as if nothing happened.
4. Refer to the church's handbook for elders, regarding our policy for discipline of ministry in relation to morals.
5. It will be necessary to come to the elders with genuine repentance.
6. It will be necessary for a true, honest statement to be made to the church body in order to be restored to fellowship as a member, and this only upon a period of probation.
7. A period of probation will be required. Though I cannot tell you exactly how long this will be, because it depends on the rate of your own spiritual rehabilitation, these periods are usually 6 to 12 months. It takes years to build up confidence and trust. It can be destroyed overnight, but it cannot be restored overnight. It will take TIME for this to be restored.
8. Seek the Lord, with your wife, to restore and rebuild the broken walls of your marriage relationship, and each of the other areas that need to be worked upon.

Our prayer is that you will know deep Holy Spirit conviction and repentance, and come into cleansing, forgiveness and restoration to fellowship, and the rebuilding of your marriage and home.

In Christ Jesus,
In Behalf of the Eldership,

Your Pastor

Conclusion

God's leaders must use discipline wisely and firmly to help the Church grow "in the midst of a crooked and perverse generation." Otherwise, the Church will lose her ability to act as salt and light for a fallen world. We can all thank God that He has given us clear instruction in the Bible on how to deal with sinning Church members and leaders.

As God restores New Testament leadership, which the Church so desperately needs, we must keep our hearts open and changeable. God will have to change our thinking as well as our hearts as He brings His people back to scriptural patterns and priorities. Today, God is telling His leaders to allow His Spirit to prepare their inner attitudes and motivations and thoughts for a great moving of His Spirit in the future. Through His own tests and trials, God will prepare the vessels that He desires to use in specific functions. He will require His leaders to obey the Word, and be living examples of it, rather than just studying or hearing it.

Remember that the issue in preparing Church leadership is not the ability of the leaders--but the ability of the One who prepares them. If you are called by God to a governmental ministry, you can have confidence in the outcome of the process. Avoid digressions. Cooperate with the dealings of God and the anointing of the Holy Spirit. If you do these things, you will experience the full release of your gifts and ministry, and you will help bring other believers into the same release.

The goal of anointed servanthood, of preparing the Bride for her wedding day, lies before us. Let all of God's people cooperate with Him as He continues the making of a leader in each one of us.

BIBLIOGRAPHY

Brown, Colin (ed.) **The New International Dictionary of New Testament Theology** (Grand Rapids: Zondervan) 1986.

Douglas, J.D. (ed.) **The New Bible Dictionary** (Wheaton: Tyndale House) 1982.

Freeman, James **Manners and Customs of the Bible** (South Plainfield: Bridge Publishing) 1985.

Kittel, Gerhard (ed.) **Theological Dictionary of the New Testament** (Grand Rapids: Eerdmans) 1985.

Lindsay, T.M. **The Church and the Ministry in the Early Centuries** (London: Hodder-Stroughton) 1903.

Orr, James (ed.) **The International Standard Bible Encyclopedia** (Grand Rapids: Eerdmans) 1944.

Pick, Aaron **Dictionary of Old Testament Words for English Readers** (Grand Rapids: Kregel) 1979.

Strong, James **Strong's Exhaustive Concordance** (Nashville: Thomas Nelson Publishers) 1984.

Thayer, Joseph Henry **The New Greek-English Lexicon of the New Testament** (Grand Rapids: Baker Book House) 1977.

The Compact Edition of the Oxford English Dictionary (Oxford University Press) 1971.

Unger, Merrill **Unger's Bible Dictionary** (Chicago: Moody Press) 1979.

Webster's New Twentieth Century Dictionary of the English Language (Collins World) 1978.

Whiston, William **Complete Works of Josephus** (Grand Rapids: Baker Book House).

Wigram, George V. **Englishman's Greek Concordance of the New Testament** (Grand Rapids: Baker Book House) 1984.

Wigram, George V. **Englishman's Hebrew and Chaldee Concordance of the Old Testament** (Mott Media) 1982.

SUGGESTED READING LIST

Adams, Jay E. **Shepherding God's Flock, No. 1** (Baker Book House).

Adams, Jay E. **Shepherding God's Flock, No. 2** (Baker Book House).

Bonhoeffer, Dietrich **The Cost of Discipleship** (Macmillan).

Bridges, Charles **The Christian Ministry** (The Banner of Truth Trust).

Chambers, Oswald **Spiritual Leadership** (Moody).

Coleman, Robert E. **The Master Plan of Evangelism** (Revell).

Eims, Leroy **The Lost Art of Disciple Making** (Zondervan).

Engstrom, Ted W. **The Making of a Christian Leader** (Zondervan).

Gangel, Kenneth O. **So You Want to Be a Leader?** (Christian Publications).

Gangel, Kenneth O. **Competent to Lead** (Moody).

Getz, Gene A. **The Measure of a Man** (Regal).

Getz, Gene A. **Abraham: Trials and Triumphs** (Regal).

Getz, Gene A. **Moses** (Regal).

Keller, Phillip **A Shepherd Looks at Psalm 23** (Zondervan).

Redpath, Alan **Victorious Christian Service** (Revell).

Robertson, A.T. **Making Good in the Ministry — A Sketch of John Mark** (Baker Book House).

Swindoll, Charles R. **Hand Me Another Brick** (Nelson).

Turnbull, Ralph G. **A Minister's Obstacles** (Baker).

Other Resources Available by Frank Damazio:

Timothy Training Program
Teacher Manual
Student Manual

Lay Pastor Training Program
Teacher Manual
Student Manual

BOOKS

The Power of Spiritual Alignment
The Making of a Vision
The Gate Church
Crossing Rivers Taking Cities
From Barrenness to Fruitfulness
Seasons of Intercession
The Making of a Leader
Effective Keys to Successful Leadership
Seasons of Revival
The Vanguard Leader
Developing the Prophetic Ministry

SEMINARS & COURSES

mpowering Your Preaching
Audio Album
Seminar Syllabus

Foundation Truth Series
Teacher Syllabus
Student Syllabus
Audio Album

Maximizing Your Vision Potential
Audio Album
Video Series
Seminar Syllabus

Maximizing Your Warfare Potential
Audio Album
Seminar Syllabus

Maximizing Your Leadership Potential
Audio Album
Video Series
Seminar Syllabus

Harvesting Church
Audio Album
Seminar Syllabus

The Prophetic Church
Audio Album
Seminar Syllabus

CITYBIBLE
PUBLISHING

9200 NE Fremont
Portland, Oregon 97220
503-253-9020 / 1-800-777-6057
www.citybiblepublishing.com